Warmest
regards with
something to remember
der Vaterland by

J DEL

Germany Transformed

Germany Transformed

Political Culture and the New Politics

Kendall L. Baker
Russell J. Dalton
Kai Hildebrandt

HARVARD UNIVERSITY PRESS

Cambridge, Massachusetts, and London, England   1981

Library of Congress Cataloging in Publication Data

Baker, Kendall L
  Germany transformed.

  Includes bibliographical references and index.
  1. Elections—Germany, West. 2. Voting—
Germany, West. 3. Germany, West—Politics and
government. I. Dalton, Russell J., joint author.
II. Hildebrandt, Kai, joint author. III. Title.
JN3971.A956B34   324.943.087   80-18244
ISBN 0-674-35315-3

To Kraig and Kris Baker

To Robert and Alfreda Dalton

To Martha and Werner Hildebrandt
    and Susan Wendt-Hildebrandt

Preface

DURING THE WRITING of this book we have been fortunate in receiving help from many people both in Germany and in North America. Perhaps the most important contribution consists of the election studies on which this book is based. Over a period of nearly a quarter of a century a growing community of German scholars has collected surveys which today provide a rich and detailed source of data on the beliefs, attitudes, interests, and behavior of the German electorate.

This impressive array of survey data remained underutilized until in 1973 the Inter-university Consortium for Political and Social Research (ICPSR) in Ann Arbor, the Zentralarchiv fuer empirische Sozialforschung (ZA) in Cologne, and the Zentrum fuer Umfragen, Methoden und Analysen (ZUMA) in Mannheim decided to cooperate to make these data available to the international scientific community. The credit for launching this joint project must go to Richard Hofferbert, Max Kaase, Hans D. Klingemann, and Erwin Scheuch.

In 1974 Russell Dalton went to Cologne as the ICPSR participant in the archival project. In Ann Arbor Kai Hildebrandt translated the German questionnaires and provided technical advice to the project. Kendall Baker, who spent the same year in Cologne on an Alexander von Humboldt fellowship, collaborated on the archival project. We were fascinated by the opportunities offered by these surveys for the study of political change in Germany, and what was originally intended as a much smaller project grew into this book.

At the Zentralarchiv Maria Wieken-Mayser and Erwin Rose handled the international project and the complexities of the data with equal skill. We appreciate not only their contribution to the archival project and to a memorable year in Cologne but also their stimulating and continued interest in this book. We would also like to acknowledge the institutional support of the Zentralarchiv under Hagen Stegemann, as well as the support of Ekkehard Mochmann and other colleagues at the ZA.

In Ann Arbor the staff of the ICPSR provided parallel support for the archival work. We appreciate especially Carolyn Geda's professional skills and personal friendship.

From the beginning of our work on this book, the Institute for Social Research at the University of Michigan provided a very supportive environment, and we would like to thank Warren Miller and Raburn Howland for both tangible and intangible aid. In addition, the University of Wyoming, the Florida State University, and the University of Windsor facilitated the completion of this work.

During the development from early convention papers and chapter drafts to the final manuscript we received encouragement, advice, criticism, and help from many colleagues, some of whom read the entire manuscript or parts of it. We would like to thank Samuel Barnes, Paul Beck, Karl Cerny, Harold Clarke, Philip Converse, David Conradt, Alfred Diamant, Lewis Edinger, Barbara Farah, Scott Flanagan, Kenyon Griffin, Kent Jennings, Max Kaase, Hans Klingemann, Larry LeDuc, Michael Lewis-Beck, Helmut Norpoth, Franz Urban Pappi, Bradley Richardson, W. Phillips Shively, Burkhard Struempel, Oliver Walter, and Rudolf Wildenmann. We owe special debts to Ronald Inglehart for his help throughout this research and to William Domke for his interest and special assistance.

Aida Donald of Harvard University Press also deserves a special note of thanks. Her early interest, astute counsel, and editorial judgment helped us to complete the manuscript and left it much improved. We are also grateful to Dorothy Whitney for her careful and patient editing of the final manuscript.

We would also like to thank Debbie Eddy, Joyce Habowsky, Garland Montalvo, and Irene Paraschak for helping type various chapter drafts, and we are especially grateful to Karen Lyverse, Mary Flom, Eric Hall, John Polisini, and Kraig Baker at Wyoming for their patient and skillful typing, retyping, copying, verifying, and so on. Without them deadlines would not have been met and references would not be as accurate.

This book thus reflects the efforts of many individuals. To disentangle the genesis of ideas and their evolution is nearly impossible. In drafting the text, however, a division of effort emerged. Kendall Baker took primary responsibility for the introduction and chapters 1, 3, and 5; in addition, he was responsible for the final editing and preparation of the manuscript for publication. Russell Dalton concentrated on chapters 2, 6, 7, 9, 10, 11, and the appendixes. Kai Hildebrandt focused on chapters 4, 8, and 12. Although each of us brought different skills to this endeavor, every chapter reflects our joint efforts as we circulated multiple drafts and revisions to arrive at the final text. Thus, we shared equally in the conceptual, theoretical, and intellectual work of this study.

Foreword

by Max Kaase

SEVERAL YEARS AGO Peter H. Merkl noted in the *American Political Science Review* that German political science could be broadly categorized into the following three "schools": the empirical-analytical school, the critical-dialectic school, and the normative-institutional school. The validity of this distinction may be questioned by many observers of the contemporary academic scene. If, however, it is accepted and the development of the three schools is analyzed, then, contrary to the situation in the United States, it is the analytical-empirical orientation in political science that—except for an initial boost in the early sixties—has least succeeded in attracting young political scientists to its ranks. Thus, it is not surprising that regular empirical research has been conducted in only a few subfields of political science; among those, electoral sociology is probably the most highly developed.

There are many reasons for the prominence of electoral research in Germany, some systematic and some coincidental. Systematically, voting behavior is a highly institutionalized type of behavior and therefore lends itself particularly well to the application of quantitative research and analysis techniques. Furthermore, elections in Western democracies are of superseding practical and symbolic relevance, especially in a country like Germany, which after World War II had to establish itself as a reliable democracy. Additionally, because of its institutionalization, voting behavior can be studied cross-nationally more easily than almost any other kind of political behavior. On the coincidental side, it was particularly those German scholars interested in political sociology who joined the informal network of professional and personal relations existing among social scientists in the United States and many other countries, thus enabling them to become di-

rectly involved in the exchange of ideas, concepts, and research results.

Nevertheless, the lack of an adequate research infrastructure in
Germany severely limited opportunities to set up continuous, well-
integrated research programs that could tackle problems on any but a
day-to-day basis. Consequently, although there was plenty of empirical
research on elections in the sixties, this research could not sufficiently
cope with the need for clear theoretical foci and the establishment of
timeseries data bases. As a result, books or articles based on that
research typically covered only well-defined problem areas and rarely
attempted to extend the time perspective in order to allow a more
dynamic, developmental approach.

Fortunately, the cosmopolitan orientation of those international
scholars involved in electoral research, plus the creation of data-
archive networks (plus a variety of other supporting factors), succeeded in stimulating the conceptualization and completion of a project
designed to make available for the international community of social
scientists a set of German election studies for secondary analysis
covering (at present) the time span from 1953 through 1976: the German Electoral Data project (GED). This book by Baker, Dalton, and
Hildebrandt is the first major product that fully utilizes the GED
database.

This book is unique in many ways. At its core, it is based on the
secondary analysis of data whose lack of strict longitudinal comparability must have consistently stimulated the sociological imagination of
the authors. Since they were successful in coping with this challenge,
the book takes full advantage of the opportunity to watch a political
system grow from a feeble political order, whose institutional structure
was largely superimposed on the non-democratic attitudes of its
population, to a well-established, stable democracy of the Western
type. Furthermore, the particular professional and life-history mix of
the authors guarantees that full justice is done to the historical,
sociopolitical specialities of the German development while at the
same time never losing track of a more general theoretical perspective
and the relevance of the results with regard to the systematic *comparative* study of politics.

Particularly outside of Germany, perceptions of the German political culture are still greatly influenced by the Almond-Verba analysis in
The Civic Culture (1963). In this analysis, Germany appears as an
output-oriented polity in which subject (that is, passive) orientations
toward politics dominate. Based on these analyses, Almond and Verba
expressed considerable skepticism regarding the stability of the democratic regime under economic and political strain. Applying conceptual

tools derived from David Easton and others, Baker, Dalton, and Hildebrandt are able to show that a considerable amount of diffuse support for the regime has by now accumulated, making Germany—since diffuse support has rather been decreasing in the United States, Britain, and other countries—one of the most stable Western democracies. Furthermore, certainly in part through processes of educational upgrading and the increasing impact of television, political involvement has also been continuously rising in Germany, transforming it into a thoroughly politicized and participation-oriented country.

Surely the *Wirtschaftswunder* (''economic miracle'') was decisive in establishing the foundation on which German democracy is now resting. However, in accordance with more general theories of value change, the authors argue and are able to demonstrate that economic and safety priorities are declining in importance and are being supplemented by postmaterialist issues like the quest for more participation at work and in politics and more authenticity in personal relationships. These changes in value priorities are not only reflected in the changing political agenda in Germany—as elsewhere in Western democracies—but also in strains on the established party system, since these potential sources of new cleavages are no longer adequately mirrored in a party system that is still tailored to the ''classic'' class and religious cleavages of the early twentieth century.

As the authors aptly point out, the relative stability of the German party system also reflects a conscious effort on the part of the political elites—especially the SPD and FDP leadership—to broaden the appeal (and image) of their parties. As ties between the social structure and the party system become weaker, the need arises for a concept that independently captures the psychological affiliation to political parties that citizens have to develop as a steering mechanism for the input and processing of political information. In the American context this intervening variable—party identification—has played a major analytical role, as represented, for instance, in the concept of a ''normal vote.'' Efforts to use party identification in *cross-national research* have not fared too well in the past. After discussing various efforts to apply the party identification concept in German electoral research, the authors develop a new measure of partisanship based on an eleven-point sympathy rating scale of the major political parties. The particular advantage of this measure lies in its over-time comparability, which not only permits a strict longitudinal analysis of the changes in levels and direction of partisanship but also the development of a causal model for the explanation of voting behavior between 1961 and 1976.

It may well be that the part of the book that deals with the changing social and political basis of partisanship and the vote will trigger a heated debate, for theoretical as well as for methodological reasons. Such a discussion should be most welcome, however, since this book represents the first effort to look systematically at the factors shaping the electoral process in Germany *over time on an empirical basis*. The book thus sets standards against which conclusions from previous electoral research on Germany will have to measure up. Students of German politics, it is hoped, will take up this challenge. Since all of the data sets on which the analyses rest are in excellent condition and freely available to interested scholars, truly cumulative work could emerge.

Undoubtedly, *Germany Transformed* is an excellent portrait of German electoral politics over the last thirty years. Focusing on the electoral process has permitted the authors to deal with a clearly identified set of concepts; an additional advantage is the contribution to a better understanding of elections in comparative perspective. Needless to say, there are other aspects of German mass politics that cannot be equally well covered by concentrating on voting behavior, in particular the emergence of uninstitutionalized, direct-action politics, which has become so visible in the form of *Bürgerinitiativen* ("citizen initiatives"). As single-issue movements, which at present are mostly concerned with environmental problems, they are ready to enter the electoral arena in the future as a political party (*Die Grünen*) and may, in this capacity, have a disproportionately strong impact on the electoral fortunes of the established parties, especially the SPD. But beyond their participation in elections, citizen initiatives and other forms of uninstitutionalized political action also pose a hefty (and probably healthy) challenge to traditional, encrusted politics in Western democracies that may, in middle-range perspective, thoroughly change the institutional makeup of democratic polities.

It remains to be seen what the nature of interchange between institutionalized and uninstitutionalized political participation is going to be in Germany and in other democratic political systems. This book may even help to better assess the nature of this complex process; that it is a significant contribution to the understanding of how electoral politics in Germany works and how a successful transition from a totalitarian to a democratic political order could be achieved is beyond question.

Contents

TABLES

FIGURES

Introduction

CHANGE IS A THEME of substantial interest to students of politics and it is especially important in the study of Western democratic societies.[1] At first the Industrial Revolution, the enfranchisement of the mass public, and the institutionalization of democratic systems shaped events. And now, Western societies are said to be on the threshold of a postindustrial era, in which the issues and the style of industrial politics will become less relevant.[2] Political change, then, is a continuing reality, but the nature of the change needs close scrutiny.

At the present time, advanced industrial societies are being transformed by increases in affluence, greater educational opportunities, mass communications, and fast transportation. In addition, geographic, social, and structural mobility have increased and this, in turn, has weakened the primary-group ties of the family, the church, and the community.[3] Citizens have also been enticed away from personal networks for political information and the interpretation of political events, and a traditional political style based on primary networks has become less relevant.

Indeed, politics itself has become more complex in the current era. No longer are the issues simple and clear-cut, and the electorate is increasingly confronted with sophisticated and often highly technical debates over complex issues. Today voters must decide on issues such as energy alternatives, economic planning, defense capabilities, and social engineering. Moreover, the pace of social and technological change often exceeds the public's ability to assimilate such changes.[4] Hence, keeping up with the flow of political information and orienting oneself to the complexities of politics have become more and more demanding tasks for the average citizen.

It is the cumulative impact of these social and political changes that

1

has produced a fundamental transformation in the nature of Western politics. For example, the electorate's involvement in politics has increased as rising educational levels have improved the public's conceptual abilities and cognitive skills and as the growth of the mass media has increased the amount of political information available.[5] Thus, the political skills and resources of the mass public have undergone dramatic changes, and the democratization of politics has been a major result. The social bases of partisan conflict have also shifted. The preindustrial cleavages of national, linguistic, regional, and religious conflicts were gradually superseded by class antagonisms.[6] Competition for support of the proletariat and bourgeoisie provided the framework for entire party systems. The political agenda reflected these controversies as economic issues predominated.

Recently, however, the unprecedentedly high level of affluence among Western societies has changed the perception of politics (and economics) as an intense class struggle; and, as social and economic cleavages have lost clarity or salience, the relevance and determining force of social characteristics as cues for political behavior have declined.[7] In addition, economic development has restructured the occupational force to include a large service and government sector that does not fit within the traditional bourgeois-proletariat alignment.

The affluence of Western democracies and the changing social norms have also served to redefine the areas of political discussion and debate.[8] The approaching resolution of material and security issues will result in the addition of new issues to the political agenda. Increasingly, politics will be concerned with questions of life-styles and the *quality* of life, rather than the *quantity* of economic rewards.

The long-term nature of these political changes poses a problem for empirical research on mass political behavior. Survey methodology for studying mass politics is a relatively modern invention. In the brief timespan for which scientifically collected survey data have been available, the short-term factors of specific choices and elite actions might easily obfuscate the longer-term trends. The timespan between a single pair of elections, or even a decade of surveying, is normally too brief to permit us confidently to examine the impact of these changes in Western mass publics. Thus, empirical research is handicapped in testing and studying these phenomena by the very nature of the hypothesized changes.

For several reasons, the Federal Republic of Germany provides an ideal laboratory in which to examine these phenomena. Society, economics, and politics have changed in West Germany at a dramatic rate over the past three decades because of specifically German conditions: the disruptive interlude of the Third Reich, wartime destruction, the reintroduction of democracy, and the Economic Miracle (*Wirtschaftswunder*). Historical conditions in Germany, therefore, have accelerated the normal process of change—and survey data are available for this period. Thus, the Federal Republic offers a fascinating, and unique, setting in which to examine many of these long-term theories and hypotheses of political change.

This book, consequently, attempts to combine two foci to advantage. First, it is a study of the development of the political attitudes, values, and behaviors of the West German electorate. Several chapters will stress topics that have traditionally intrigued observers of German politics, such as the question of the democratic nature of the postwar polity and the problems resulting from the division of the German nation. These trends inevitably reflect the specific conditions of modern Germany and its history. But they may also highlight more general processes of change among Western societies. Thus, the second purpose of this book is to investigate the development of a modern democratic electorate by using Germany as a test case.[9]

The German Historical Experience

Germany was a feudal society until almost the middle of the nineteenth century.[10] Only after the Industrial Revolution had run its course in most of the rest of northwestern Europe did it spread to Germany. This delay in industrialization retarded the development of many factors normally identified with a modern society: urbanization, literacy, extensive communication and transportation networks, and an industrial infrastructure.

More important, however, German industrialization followed a course quite different from that of the rest of Europe. It was managed and stimulated by the state, a state led by elite groups whose legitimacy and values derived from feudal Germany. This preindustrial elite continued to rule in accordance with its feudal Weltanschauung, and it refused to be integrated into the new social structure resulting from the Industrial Revolution.

This pattern of industrialization resulted in a continuation of traditional authority patterns and traditional values at all levels of society. Following the Prussian model, the military service, the civil service, the school, and the family were all based on the principles of discipline, obedience, and submission to constituted authority. At the same time, commitment to religious values remained strong, as did local and regional identifications.

The control of economic and political development by the landed aristocracy delayed the appearance of an influential middle class. In the rest of Europe the middle class, holding a crucial position in the capitalist system, played a major role in the advancement of social thought. Without either substantial economic or political influence the German middle class could not exert this influence. The middle class was therefore not able to act as a force for modernization, setting new value standards and changing traditional social relations. Politically, the weaknesses of the middle class slowed the development of liberal democracy. In the revolutionary fervor that swept Europe in 1848–49, scholars and intellectuals representing the middle class met in Frankfurt and drafted a democratic constitution, modeled on those of the United States and France; but the Prussian Kaiser refused to join with them and the effort to establish a constitutional regime failed.

In addition to producing only a small, ineffectual middle class, the particular pattern of industrialization in Germany perpetuated the intense class cleavages that had existed for some time. In a society where mobility was limited and the distinctions between the privileged and nonprivileged were sharp, the new bourgeois-proletariat cleavage refocused old social tensions and provided a strong basis for political division.

Another basis of political cleavage in Germany was religion. The population was divided between a Protestant majority and a Catholic minority, and religious conflict had been virulent in Germany since the Reformation. Indeed, from the Peace of Augsburg (1555) to the Treaty of Westphalia (1648), Germans had often battled along religious lines. And because traditional religious commitments were not moderated by the industrialization process, the religious cleavage continued to be important.

Germany also lagged behind the rest of northwestern Europe in developing a national identity. Before the Napoleonic consolidation at the beginning of the nineteenth century, over 1500 separate and sovereign political entities had existed in the territory that later became modern Germany. Thus loyalties were confined to local units, inhibiting the development of national unity and national identification. Even after Germany became a united nation in 1871, national and regional forces were often in a state of tension.

As it entered the twentieth century, therefore, Germany was a country in which politics and the general operation of the political system were heavily influenced by class, religious, and cultural cleavages. The bourgeoisie competed with the proletariat; Catholics were deeply suspicious of Protestants; liberals battled conservatives over the proper form of political organization; and members of the traditional social structure resisted assimilation into the new social structure spawned by the Industrial Revolution. According to Ralf Dahrendorf, what emerged from the Industrial Revolution in Germany was an "industrial feudal society."[11] Modernization and democratization were still to come.

When modernization finally came to Germany, it was impelled by external events. Social and political change occurred suddenly and disruptively. World War I removed many of the traditional bases of society; but the Weimar Republic, suffering from the stigma of having lost the war, was largely ineffective in its attempts to modernize and democratize traditional values, social norms, and political styles to fit the altered political and economic structures. Large portions of society remained unchanged, and the traditional elites continued to wield influence in the bureaucracy, the judiciary, the military, and the schools and universities—all of which became bulwarks against the new tides.

The major breakdown of old values and social cleavages came during the Third Reich. Since Hitler's goal was the total control of German society, he sought to destroy traditional allegiances and identifications and replace them with social ties and organizations controlled by the National Socialists. The federal structure of the Wilhelmine and Weimar regimes was abandoned in favor of a unitary organization of political authority. National organizations and ministries were established to propagate the Nazi ideology and to control education, youth, and workers. A new "religion" based on obedience to the Führer was created, transcending traditional religions. The traditional rule of aristocratic elites was undermined by Hitler's appointment of his lieutenants to positions of leadership. Although the Nazi "atomization of the individual" and "coordination" of society did not entirely destroy the traditional German way of life, it did contribute to a loosening of the bonds that had determined political and social relations for centuries.

This process was intensified by the destruction and dislocation caused by World War II and by the subsequent policies of the Western occupation forces. The ranks of the traditional ruling class had already been severely decimated by the war and by the purge that followed the abortive attempt on Hitler's life in July 1944. After 1945, the denazification program pursued by the Allied authorities tarnished the reputations of many of the remaining members of the aristocracy. The division of Germany helped to reduce the traditional conflict over religion because the Federal Republic was almost evenly divided between Protestants and Catholics. The military governors dissolved Prussia and redrew the regional boundaries on the basis of administrative convenience rather than historical traditions. And finally, the massive migration of Germans from former Reich territories in the East served to further reduce regional divisions within the Western zone. In a very real sense, therefore, the modernization of Germany began in 1945.

The Postwar Federal Republic

From the beginning, there was broad support for a democratic German polity among postwar elites. After the establishment of the Federal Republic in 1949 this consensus endorsed the basic principles of the new regime, although sharp differences existed between the parties over the policies of the new government. Initially, small extremist groups of both the right and the left sought to transform the West German state into the image either of the previous Third Reich or of the emerging East German regime, but popular support for these groups was limited; they garnered a total of only 7.5 percent of the valid votes in the first Bundestag election in 1949 and failed even to gain entry to subsequent parliaments. Perhaps still more decisive, especially in contrast with the experience of Weimar, was the unanimous rejection of both the left and right opposition to democracy by the vast majority of political elites. The Communist Party was eventually outlawed as unconstitutional in 1956, and the public was then presented with unanimous leadership supportive of and committed to the democratic ideals of the new state.[12]

Beyond their agreement on the democratic forms of the new Federal Republic, some elements of the political leadership followed policy courses quite different from those of previous regimes. The creation of the Christian Democratic Union (CDU) represented a break with the historical tradition of German political parties. Instead of an ideological, special-interest party, it was a pragmatic *Volkspartei* ("catchall party") whose most important unifying principle was that Germany should be reconstructed on Christian foundations, without an exclusively Catholic or Protestant orientation. Its founders were a heterogeneous group of Catholics and Protestants, businessmen and trade unionists, conservatives and liberals. The party wanted to appeal to all segments of society in order to gain governmental power, rather than to represent the interests of well-defined minorities in the political world. Thus, the CDU by its very existence cut across some of the old cleavage-based divisions of German politics.

The CDU and its Bavarian sister party, the Christian Social Union (CSU), surprised many analysts by narrowly winning control of the government (in a coalition with several minor parties) in the first federal election in 1949. Once in power, the CDU/CSU-led government launched dramatic new policies. The minister of economics, Ludwig

Erhard, continued to promote a free market economy, which led to the dramatic success of the Economic Miracle. The Christian Democrats also attempted to attract the support of the working class through a series of highly visible economic programs, including government-subsidized savings plans and the denationalization of industries accompanied by public sales of stock to workers. In the international arena, Konrad Adenauer pursued a policy of integration into the Western Alliance in order to lessen Europe's historic fears of German nationalism and to secure West Germany from attack by the Soviet Union.

While the CDU/CSU pursued policies aimed at weakening the cleavage bases of German politics, the actions of the Social Democratic Party (SPD) probably tended to accentuate these same divisions. Standing in opposition to the CDU/CSU, the Social Democrats launched unending attacks on Adenauer's domestic and foreign policy. They insisted that German industry be nationalized, and espoused Marxist doctrines emphasizing class divisions. Furthermore, the SPD opposed Adenauer's policy of integrating the Federal Republic into Western Europe and the North Atlantic Alliance, placing instead a high priority on the reunification of the two German states—if that should be necessary under the provisions of neutrality. But the SPD's persistent attacks upon the popular Adenauer and his policies ran counter to public sentiments, and the party's electoral support was confined mainly to its traditional ideological stronghold, the working class.

In the 1953 and 1957 elections the SPD made only modest gains at the polls, while the CDU/CSU made much more impressive gains by pulling in voters from the disappearing minor parties. In 1957 the CDU actually received an absolute majority, something no other party in German history had been able to achieve. The worsening electoral prospects for the SPD subsequently generated internal pressures for a transformation of the party in order to appeal more effectively to the German electorate as a whole. These pressures culminated in the development of a new party program at the Bad Godesberg conference in 1959. There the SPD abandoned its traditional role as the ideological voice of the working-class movement and began to transform itself into a Volkspartei. The Social Democrats dropped their anticlericalism and their commitment to the nationalization of industry; they accepted the necessity and value of German rearmament, free enterprise, and the protection of private property; they endorsed NATO, the developing European Community, and the integration of Germany into the Western Alliance.[13]

With the *Godesberger Programm* the SPD accepted the principles and direction of postwar German domestic and foreign policy as shaped by the two bourgeois parties, the CDU/CSU and the Free

Democratic party (FDP). By this time, too, the smaller radical parties of the left and right had all but disappeared. At last, the political animosities and divisions that derived from different ideologies and different attitudes about the proper regime form and appropriate social goals were replaced by a broad political consensus among virtually all German elites.[14]

Doubts remained, however, about the sincerity of the SPD's new image. These began to be resolved in 1966 when the CDU/CSU, faced with the defection of its coalition partner, the FDP, turned to the SPD, and together the two large parties formed a Grand Coalition government. Although conceived almost entirely at the elite level by party strategists, the creation of the Grand Coalition had substantial influence on mass politics. It was widely believed to have contributed to the legitimization of the SPD by finally convincing voters that the Social Democrats were capable of responsible government. And the sight of the two major parties sharing control of the government led to a further weakening of the cleavages between political camps, thus completing the integration of SPD partisans into what had been called by critics the *CDU Staat*.

After three years of coalition government, the election of 1969 marked another major turning point in the politics of the Federal Republic. In the campaign the SPD emphasized social progress, the need for new goals to follow postwar reconstruction, and the "New Politics" issues typical of advanced industrialism. Its campaign slogan summarized this position: "We Create the Modern Germany." In the election the party won enough votes to form a coalition government with the FDP; for the first time government control passed from one of the two major parties to the other (*Machtwechsel*), putting the CDU/CSU into opposition.[15]

The SPD-FDP government pursued progressive policies that accentuated the pace of social change. Social welfare policies were liberalized and a high priority was placed on educational reform. Government leaders expressed support for such New Politics issues as abortion on demand, easier divorce rules, increased citizen participation, and quality-of-life questions like pollution. Equally important, foreign policy underwent a fundamental change. In contrast to the hostility and tensions that had characterized the German stance toward the Soviet Union and Eastern Europe in the 1950s and early 1960s, the government led by Willy Brandt followed a new policy of détente and reconciliation with the East (*Ostpolitik*). Thus, another source of political tension and conflict was removed and the earlier conflictual approach was replaced by a cooperative approach to problem-solving—even though the Ostpolitik was soon to become the source, or perhaps the vehicle, for renewed domestic tensions.

Yet, as old cleavages were being de-emphasized, new issues were bringing new polarizations to the political elites. It was probably not accidental that the major New Politics initiatives of the SPD-FDP government—increased democratization, domestic reforms, and Ostpolitik—became hotly contested issues between government and opposition. But observers were surprised how quickly the pragmatic consensus of the middle and late 1960s collapsed. The CDU/CSU even attempted to oust Brandt through the constitutional means of a "constructive vote of no confidence." Although the attempt failed, the Bundestag was deadlocked and the SPD-FDP coalition had to call for new federal elections in the fall of 1972.

The 1972 election probably marked a temporary high in New Politics interest as both large parties bowed to the theme of progress in their campaign rhetoric. The government coalition focused its campaign on achievements and goals and was returned to power with a comfortable majority.

In subsequent years both public interest in and elite support of the New Politics probably lessened. The oil embargo and the ensuing recession not only limited the further development of social programs by the SPD but rekindled economic worries among the German public. Symbolically, the replacement of Willy Brandt by the more pragmatic Helmut Schmidt also slackened the pace of change. Finally, in the 1976 election the CDU/CSU directly challenged the SPD themes of progress and change in an attempt to capitalize upon the resurgent fears of economic uncertainty and radical terrorism, prompting even the SPD to give greater attention to traditional economic and security issues. Still, the basic commitment of the SPD-FDP government to social reform and progressive legislation remained; and the CDU/CSU, under the new leadership of Franz Josef Strauss, attempted to become the focus of conservative forces.

Sources of Change

In just three decades the Federal Republic has experienced a massive transformation of political and social norms and values: from a traditional social order and a war-ravaged economy to a progressive advanced industrial society; from a country plagued by severe conflicts and cleavages to a highly stable, integrated society in which the democratic political system constructed after World War II seems to enjoy substantial legitimacy. Thus the Federal Republic exemplifies—possibly accentuates—the general development of modern Western democracies. The nature of its development, however, provides an opportunity to observe the corollaries of this transition: the growth of political interest and public involvement, changes in the bases of partisan voting, changes in the political agenda, and the development of special and general system support.

How has West Germany accomplished this dramatic transformation in the postwar period? Although several explanations have been suggested, those most commonly accepted emphasize three factors: the impact of economic development; generational change; and the actions of political elites.

Economic Development   The dramatic economic improvement made since World War II is undoubtedly one of the factors contributing to the Federal Republic's accelerated political development. By 1950 industrial production had exceeded its 1936 value, and by 1961 it had increased by an additional 162 percent.[16] At the beginning of the 1980s, Germany's industrial production far exceeds that of any of its European neighbors, placing the German economy in the forefront of advanced industrialism. The gains in individual and social affluence during the past three decades have also been impressive: in 1950 the average German worker earned 250 DM per month, but by 1978 his earnings had risen to about 2250 DM per month.[17] Along with affluence have come increases in education, the use of the mass media, and other elements of an advanced industrial society. In nearly all sectors Germany's economic recovery has been so phenomenal that it has earned the label of Economic Miracle (*Wirtschaftswunder*).

The effects of rapidly increasing affluence have been reinforced by a gradual change in the occupational structure of the Federal Republic. In 1950, 22 percent of the population was employed in agriculture and 33 percent in the service sector; in 1978 these proportions were 5.8 and 48.7 percent respectively.[18] The most notable aspect of this changing labor force has been its effect upon the composition of the middle class. Traditionally the middle class has comprised the self-employed (*Selbständige*) and professionals (*freie Berufe*). The shift in employment toward the government and service sector has given rise to a new middle-class grouping of salaried white-collar employees (*Angestellte*) and civil servants (*Beamte*). Between 1950 and 1978 the number of individuals in the "new" or "modern" middle class more than doubled, leaving the traditional old middle class to account for only 29 percent of the middle-class total.[19]

Several analysts have focused on the new middle class as a defining characteristic of advanced industrial societies.[20] This group constitutes the "technological elite" whose skills and background make them well-suited for the complexities of modern life. In general, its members display a greater openness to new societal developments and thus a greater receptivity to the issues of the New Politics. The new middle class, on balance, is better educated and has more leisure time than other occupational strata; its members, therefore, have greater conceptual ability, better contextual knowledge, and more opportunity and inclination to become involved in politics. ،

The new middle class is also important because it lacks a previous assignment in the class conflict between the working class and old middle class. The separation of management from capital (a development Marx did not foresee) has created a new social stratum that differs from the old middle class because it does not own capital, but that also differs from the blue-collar workers of the traditional proletariat because of its life-style. As a result, the loyalties of the new middle class are divided between these two other social strata. Its members lack clear political and voting cues and consequently cross class lines and split their votes between the parties of the left and the right.

The Economic Miracle has had other effects on German society and politics. The spread of affluence and the dramatic growth of the mass media have increased the amount of political information available to the electorate. The expansion of educational opportunities has gradually increased the political sophistication of the public. Greater leisure time has increased the opportunities to participate in politics. Thus, the economic development of postwar Germany has contributed to a dramatic rise in the political awareness and involvement of the German electorate.

As affluence and economic security have become widespread, questions of economic distribution have become less crucial to political decisions. With the size of the pie rapidly expanding, voters have become less competitive over economic issues, and economic cleavages in politics have weakened.

Finally, the emergence of advanced industrialism has brought changes in the political agenda. Political concerns have broadened beyond economic questions to a group of issues that collectively reflect New Politics or advanced industrial interests.[21] For example, terms such as *Bildungsnotstand* ("educational crisis") and *Qualität des Lebens* ("quality of life") have only recently entered the German political vocabulary, while issues like environmental protection, divorce reform, abortion, and *Mitbestimmung* ("codetermination") have increased in salience.

Considered as a whole, economic change has played a major part in Germany's transition from a ruined, defeated nation to an advanced industrial society. This book explores the extent to which economic and occupational trends have strengthened support for democratic norms, increased political involvement, changed the language and content of the political agenda, and weakened class cleavages.

Generational Change   The second important factor in the postwar sociopolitical development of Germany is the succession of political generations. Long ago, Auguste Comte observed that "the pressure of one generation upon the other was the most important phenomenon of social life."[22] More recently, Karl Mannheim has discussed the role that generations play in the evolution of society. He places emphasis on "generational units"—aggregations of individuals who experience during their formative years a common environment that has similar and lasting effects on all or most of them.[23]

The subject of generational change is unusually relevant to the study of West Germany's postwar development because the discontinuities of recent history have produced vastly different life experiences for succeeding generations. German cohorts socialized before World War II lived through long periods of economic hardship and felt the destructive consequences of the war. Younger Germans, by contrast, have grown up during a period of rapid social change, economic advancement, and greater international stability. The Federal Republic and Weimar generations were raised in democratic political settings, while the Third Reich and Wilhelmine generations lived under autocratic regimes. And finally, the weakening of traditional social cleavages has led to great differences between the formative experiences of the younger and older cohorts.

If, as socialization research has shown, early life experiences are particularly important in the development of basic attitudes toward politics and the political system, an understanding of generational units may be essential in explaining changes in mass politics.[24] For example, the older generations' early exposure to the symbols of the Third Reich or of the Weimar Republic could have influenced their evaluations of the Federal Republic and their perceptions of citizen responsibilities and participation in that democratic regime. But younger Germans, reared in the material and personal security of the postwar years, may have developed value priorities very different from the concerns of their elders. Similarly, as a consequence of the affluence and social change of the postwar period, the attention these younger generations pay to traditional socioeconomic cleavages has probably lessened, and individual attitudinal forces have replaced social and cultural forces as determinants of political behavior. The development of party identification in Germany has even been shown to have a distinctive generational component.[25]

Because generations differ in their political beliefs and behaviors, generational succession may serve as an important agent of social change at the aggregate level. Old cohorts gradually leave the electorate and are replaced by new, young cohorts with presumably different views. This steady progress of population turnover can in a relatively brief span of time induce fundamental social change. As an illustration, in 1953 only 12.2 percent of the electorate had reached adolescence under the political system of the Federal Republic, while approximately 44.9 percent had been socialized under the Wilhelmine Empire. By 1976, however, the Wilhelmine cohort accounted for only 6.9 percent of the electorate, and the postwar generation constituted a clear majority (52.1 percent) of the adult population.

In order to explore the impact of generational change, generational units have to be defined. This defining process raises two problems.

First, at what age can one presume respondents will be maximally influenced by the events and forces occurring in their environment? The literature provides a number of suggestions,[26] but since this book is concerned with a wide range of political orientations, a cutting point early in the suggested timespan was selected. Specifically, the age of fifteen was chosen as the point of maximal environmental impact in Germany.

Second, how can historical periods be delineated that distinguish among generational units having common and unique formative experiences? Several factors should be considered: economic conditions, political environment, the international situation, and domestic order. All of these factors seemed to converge in the German setting when generations were defined in terms of the political regime of their early socialization, whether it was the Wilhelmine Empire, the Weimar Republic, the Third Reich, or the Federal Republic. The last regime was subdivided in order to distinguish between those whose formative experience fell partly into the chaos of the immediate postwar years and those who grew up in relative security and affluence. The specific definiton of each of these historical periods is as follows:

Wilhelmine	1918 and before
Weimar	1919–1932
Third Reich	1933–1945
Early Federal Republic	1946–1955
Late Federal Republic	1956 and later

Political Elites   The last of the three major factors contributing to the dramatic social and political changes Germany has experienced over the past thirty years is the action taken by political elites.[27] Whether elites have simply reacted to public moods or have actually influenced mass opinion, decisions taken by the leadership of the major parties have eased the acceptance of a democratic polity, accelerated the decline of a cleavage-based political system, and hastened the transition toward an advanced industrial society.

Should elite actions be viewed as effects or as causes of changing mass behavior? Clearly, both possibilities exist.

Initially, elites are often stimulated by their perception of the climate of opinion that allows for, or demands, their action. The Godesberg Program, for example, resulted from a decision by SPD elites to provide a new political program that would increase support from an electorate that had refused to accept the party's traditional appeal. Similarly, SPD strategist Herbert Wehner argued for a conscious policy of *Umarmung* ("embracement") with the CDU/CSU in order to increase public confidence in the SPD, and this ultimately resulted in the Grand Coalition. Other actions, like the *Machtwechsel* in 1969, followed more directly from popular actions, that is, from an election outcome.

But even as they respond, perhaps only partially, to emerging political trends, elites at the same time contribute independently to these processes of change. As parties shift their attention to new political issues in anticipation of political gains, the increased attention devoted to these issues adds to their impact. Similarly, attention given to new political issues weakens the relevance of traditional social cleavages and traditional issues as guides for voting behavior. Thus, the actions of political elites have facilitated, and indeed encouraged, political change in the Federal Republic.

Although much of the direct empirical evidence presented in this book focuses on the mass public, opinion change does not occur in a vacuum. Opinion trends are the results of complex interactions between political elites and the mass public. Moreover, these changes are often stimulated by events or processes lying outside the mass-elite dyad. Hence all of these forces must be examined in order to understand the nature of the change that has occurred in postwar Germany.

The Empirical Evidence

The dynamic aspects of the questions raised in this book called for a longitudinal research design. Fortunately, a database is available that is ideally suited to these needs and is unique in its historical breadth and richness of content. In 1973 an archival project involving three organizations—the Inter-university Consortium for Political and Social Research (ICPSR; Ann Arbor, Michigan), the Zentralarchiv für empirische Sozialforschung (ZA; Cologne), and the Zentrum für Umfragen, Methoden, and Analysen (ZUMA; Mannheim)—was launched to process a series of German political and election surveys covering the period from 1953 to 1976. This collection consists of ten separate national cross-section and panel surveys, conducted by major academic figures in German social research. These data are available to the international research community through either the ICPSR in Ann Arbor or the Zentralarchiv in Cologne. Technical information on these surveys is given in appendix A.

In terms of the principal interest of this book, namely, the transition of the German polity in the postwar period, this database has been invaluable. Since it was possible to draw from a rich storehouse of surveys collected over a 23-year timespan, measurements of public attitudes and behaviors could be made at several timepoints during the postwar development of the Federal Republic. Each later survey provided fresh data to broaden the understanding of German political behavior and verify trends and patterns observed for earlier years and under different political conditions. For example, surveys conducted in 1961 during one of the "hottest" points of the Cold War and in 1972 as the Ostpolitik reached fruition have been analyzed. Other studies have been used to compare mass responses before and after major elite-instigated events like the Bad Godesberg program and the Grand Coalition. Thus, because the environment of each survey is unique, we have a series of "natural experiments" that permit us to examine how opinions and behaviors have changed with objective conditions.

While secondary analysis such as this has the advantage of ready and often rich data resources, it also has potential dangers.[28] The secondary analyst, for example, has no control over the content of previously collected data. Although this problem was minimized by the high calibre of the database, it did impinge on the research in two ways.

First, the data are uneven in the attention given to particular topics. On the one hand, the pre-1969 surveys include surprisingly few questions concerning system support and political participation. On the other hand, nearly all of the studies contain a vast array of comparable questions assessing partisanship, issue orientations, and voting behavior. Consequently, the analyses in this book inevitably vary in detail and longitudinal coverage.

Second, the wording of questions is not entirely consistent. Since 1961, when the surveys began to be collected by alumni of the Cologne school,[29] standard question formats have been generally used. But intentional as well as inadvertent changes in question wording occur, and a question is occasionally omitted from a timepoint. Such inconsistencies are the curse of longitudinal analysis. Sometimes the construction and validation of comparable items by recoding, collapsing, and restructuring variables involved considerable strain. Most of this work will remain unknown to the reader, and the validation of scales and the collection of "side information" cannot be fully documented. In general, reliable and valid measures were developed, but at times less than ideal solutions had to be accepted. Thus, our relationship to the data as secondary analysts means that we have had to accept a *rich* but *preselected* store of empirical evidence on German political behavior.

Plan of the Book

This book attempts to provide a broad overview of the changes in the German electorate over the last thirty years. The analyses focus on Germany's path from an authoritarian to a democratic political system, including the transformation of a disengaged public to an involved electorate; from a war-ravaged and security-conscious society toward advanced industrialism; and from a system where political behavior was based on traditional social cleavages to one in which behavior is shaped by attitudinal orientations more directly linked to the political sphere. These three themes are dealt with in the first three parts of the book.

The Changing Political Culture   German history makes it especially important to determine the extent to which the current patterns of democratic government have a potential for survival. The experiences of the Weimar Republic first sensitized analysts to the frailties of democracy in Germany. This concern was reinforced by the early postwar surveys, which suggested that Germans had neither developed a deep commitment to the democratic forms of the Federal Republic nor adopted appropriate roles as citizens participating in a democracy. The landmark work of Almond and Verba, *The Civic Culture,* which described Germans as detached and nonparticipating subjects, perpetuated this characterization.[30]

Part One of this book addresses that characterization directly. The long-term growth of support for the political system and of democratic norms among the German public is treated in chapter 1. Chapter 2 traces the dramatic growth of *active* political involvement between 1953 and 1972, evaluating the relative importance of socioeconomic development, generational change, and increasingly democratic civic attitudes as possible causes of intensified political involvement. The final chapter examines a more *passive* form of political involvement—the intake of political information.

The Changing Political Agenda   Part Two traces changes in the economic and political environment over the past three decades and their impact on political attitudes and behavior. The first chapter describes the rapid growth of the West German economy after the war, showing that economic perceptions have become less important in cuing political behavior as the Economic Miracle has lessened economic hardship. Chapter 5 examines an equally important environmental factor—foreign policy. It describes the transition from a Cold War period of conflict and international tensions to a more cooperative period of East-West exchange beginning in the late 1960s. The last chapter in this part attempts to integrate the environmental changes described in the two preceding chapters into a broader perspective of political change. Present-day Germans are less concerned with the economic and security issues of the past and are paying more attention to the New Politics issues of life-style, freedom of expression, and the quality of life.

Changing Partisan Politics   In Part Three the impact of the changing political environment on partisan politics is examined. Chapter 7, which investigates the role of social characteristics as guides for German voting behavior, concludes that voting is less and less influenced by the traditional social cleavages of German society and that parties and the electorate are using other bases of political orientation. The eighth chapter suggests that partisanship is becoming increasingly important in providing cues for political behavior. Partisan attachments are shown to influence voting behavior and the level of campaign involvement. Most significantly, partisanship organizes and constrains perceptions and evaluations of candidates and issues, as well as vote change—and this constraint is increasing over time. The chapter also analyzes changes in the distribution and strength of partisanship in light of the discontinuities of Germany's political experience. Chapter 9 focuses more directly on the impact of party policies on the electorate's images of the Social Democrats and the Christian Democrats. It examines the images of the parties in terms of their abstract abilities to govern, their linkages to traditional social cleavages, and their competency in dealing with a range of Old Politics and New Politics issues. Integrating the previous three chapters, the causal modeling of chapter 10 demonstrates the changing impact of social characteristics, partisanship, and issue images on German voting behavior. It suggests that a process of gradual partisan conversion may be accompanying Germany's transition toward advanced industrialism.

Epilogue   One criticism of survey analysis is that it is ex post facto research. Survey researchers are accused of finding explanations for past events rather than predicting forthcoming events, just as the financial analyst can explain any turn in the stock market—after the fact.

Most of the ideas and theories presented in this book were first committed to paper in 1975. Subsequently the 1976 federal election results seemed to mark the reversal of many of the causal trends that had been presented. The OPEC oil embargo and the ensuing recession had slowed the hitherto rapid growth of the German economy. An increase in radical terrorist activities had raised concerns about the stability of German democracy. Furthermore, the Christian Democrats had attempted to capitalize on these reversals and recreate the public mood of the 1950s, seeking to recapture old antagonisms and appeal to traditional cleavage-based concerns. As a result, the SPD lost support at the polls for the first time since 1953. Many analysts thus saw the 1976 election as a regression to the traditional political issues and cleavages of an earlier period.

The first chapter in Part Four treats the 1976 election as a "natural experiment" to test the validity of prior theorizing. The format of the chapter reflects the organization of the rest of the book. First, the environmental changes that occurred between 1972 and 1976 are discussed. This is done in order to anticipate the political changes that should have resulted. Next, the impact of these forces on orientations toward politics, the political system, and the political agenda are examined. Finally, the chapter considers whether partisan politics has been fundamentally changed by the reversals in economic trends and the altered strategies of party leaders.

Theory testing puts one in a vulnerable position. Slight revisions had to be made in some earlier conclusions as a result of the 1976 findings, because the altered conditions drew new responses from the mass public and elite actors. Yet, the responses to a particular election take on a different image when viewed in the context of long-term trends. Thus the 1976 election substantiates the essential arguments of the book with respect to the slow but fundamental trends of system commitment, participation, value changes, and partisan behavior. It is still true, however, as the SPD learned with the end of the "comrade trend" in 1976, that one of the most persistent facts of postwar German politics is that even long-term trends can be reversed. In the final chapter of the book we take up some of the issues that may affect these trends in the future, not only in West Germany but in other advanced industrial societies.

Part One

The Changing Political Culture

1

Legitimizing a System

Orientations TOWARD POLITICS and the operation of the political system are among the most fundamental of political attitudes. In Germany, these attitudes have special salience and relevance because the legacy of Germany's turbulent history has often raised severe questions about the viability of the democratic system of the Federal Republic. Within a brief thirty-year period, three German regimes failed because they were not equal to the demands they faced: the Wilhelmine Empire collapsed in the catastrophe of World War I; during the Weimar Republic between a third and a half of the population refused even to accept the legitimacy of the new government; and during the Third Reich, Hitler led Germany into another disastrous world war and suppressed citizen participation in politics.

Immediately after World War II, Allied occupation forces, and later the German government in Bonn, undertook a massive program to reeducate the German public.[1] Nearly everyone was in agreement that the society inherited from the Third Reich had to be remade. This reeducation program included an active denazification effort to remove former Third Reich supporters from positions of power in the public and private sectors, and to punish war criminals. It used the mass media, the school, and public forums to conduct a major campaign of political education in democratic principles, emphasizing particularly the education of the young. Antidemocratic and extremist groups were prohibited, and all political activity was channeled into efforts to legitimize the new political system of the Federal Republic.

Beginning in 1945, public opinion surveys were conducted on a regular basis to assess the progress of these reeducation programs.[2] The conclusions of these studies were not very optimistic. During the early 1950s researchers found lingering support for the principles and institutions of earlier German regimes, including the Third Reich.

21

Moreover, there was no conclusive evidence that democratic political norms had firmly taken root. In 1963, the major academic treatise on the subject, Gabriel Almond and Sidney Verba's *The Civic Culture*, concluded that democratic attitudes were still in short supply after more than a decade of experience with the Federal Republic.[3] In a later study Steven Warnecke pointed to the "continued existence of attitudes among substantial segments of the electorate which prevent a sense of responsibility for politics and political efficacy from developing, impede the legitimation of the role of public opinion, prevent the individual from seeing society as an emanation from himself and others, and impede the voter from perceiving government as the executive committee of society."[4] Similarly, in the early 1970s Kurt Sontheimer still concluded that "democratic consciousness" in Germany "is a collection of attitudes and behaviors which is not strong enough to stand the test of any serious crises of the system."[5]

According to a number of commentators, therefore, West Germany lacks a political culture congruent with the existing political structure. Political culture refers, essentially, to the orientations that members of a society have about politics and the political system.[6] It encompasses everything from beliefs about the legitimacy of the system itself to beliefs about the adequacy and appropriateness of political input structures, governmental policies, and the role provided for the individual in the political process. Thus, the implication of the characterizations of these commentators is that the kinds of orientations necessary for a political system to persist in the face of stress are either weak or altogether missing in West Germany.

But is the contemporary German political culture really incongruent with the existing political structure? For several reasons this description may no longer apply to the Federal Republic. Over half of the members of today's electorate were socialized exclusively during the postwar period. Hence, many of the effects of the Third Reich that were salient in the immediate postwar period may have lessened.

Part One of this book will reassess the validity of previous descriptions of contemporary German political culture. Where change is occurring, the source of the change will be investigated. Are political beliefs still unsupportive of a democratic system? Do Germans remain political spectators and subjects rather than participants in the political system? Or has the German electorate become politically aware and involved?

Support for the Political System

Political systems must retain the support of their citizens if they are to remain viable. Yet, since all governments fail on occasion to meet public expectations, it is essential that short-term failures to satisfy public demands not be directly related to evaluations of the political system as a whole. In other words, a system requires a reservoir of popular support independent of immediate policy outputs if it is to weather periods of disaffection and dissatisfaction.

Almond and Verba conceptualized such generalized political support as a positive feeling toward the political system, or "system affect."[7] They believed that in times of stress an effective feeling toward the political system would act to limit expressions of discontent. For them the basic indicator of these feelings was the number of people who spontaneously mentioned the political system in an open-ended question assessing pride in German society. Although this question undoubtedly taps a dimension of political orientations related to support, it also presents problems. David Conradt notes that system affect implies the development of a psychological commitment or emotional tie to the political system that is not essential for citizen support of the system.[8] In addition, expressions of national pride might easily reflect policy outputs and might not be an independent measure of support.

The concept of "diffuse support" developed by David Easton appears to be a more helpful indicator of the basic and essential elements of system support.[9] According to Easton, diffuse support is a state of mind—a deep-seated set of attitudes including attachment to democracy, belief in the legitimacy of the political system, and attachment to its symbols—rather than an emotive expression of feelings. Support can be directed toward any one of three political objects: the political community, the regime, or the government.[10] For our analysis this is an important distinction because support for the regime—that is, constitutional principles—has been a major point of contention in discussions of postwar German politics. Easton's concept is also more helpful because it is perhaps easier to measure. As Conradt notes: "Unlike Almond and Verba's 'system affect,' diffuse support can be measured by means other than feeling questions, i.e. citizen support for key system values . . . a consensus on the validity of system structures . . . identification with system leadership."[11]

Although early analyses of German politics questioned whether the Federal Republic held the enduring support of the majority of its citizens, analyses of longitudinal data collected by the Allensbach Institute since the early 1950s present a more positive picture.[12] Some of the most relevant of these data are reproduced in figure 1.1. One set of trends indicates declining support for the symbols and personalities of previous regimes. For example, favorable images of Bismarck as the man who had "done the most for Germany" dropped from 35 percent in 1951 to 18 percent in 1964; the already low evaluations of Hitler also dropped from 10 to 3 percent over the same timespan. Support for restoration of the monarchy followed a similar decline from about a third of the electorate in 1951 to a tenth by 1965. Positive evaluations of National Socialism (not included in the figure) show an even more precipitous decline in the decade following the formation of the Federal Republic.

As ties to earlier regimes have weakened, the bonds to the new

Figure 1.1. Growth of system support, 1951–1965. Source: Elisabeth Noelle and Erich Peter Neumann, eds., *Jahrbücher der öffentlichen Meinung* (Allensbach: Institut für Demoskopie, 1951–1974).

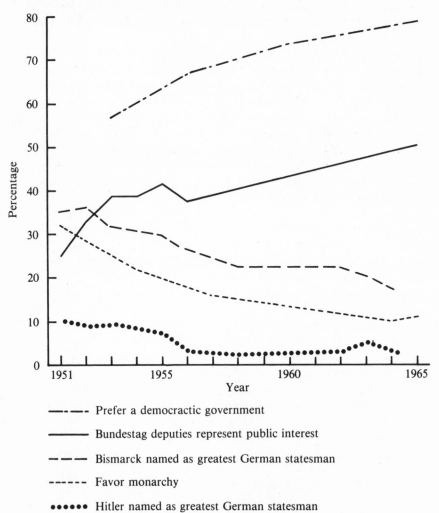

—·—· Prefer a democractic government

——— Bundestag deputies represent public interest

— — — Bismarck named as greatest German statesman

------ Favor monarchy

•••••• Hitler named as greatest German statesman

institutions and figures of the Federal Republic have grown stronger. For instance, the number of citizens who believed that Bundestag deputies represented the public interest doubled between 1951 and 1964. And, while just over half of the electorate favored a democratic form of government in 1953, over three-quarters preferred a democratic regime by 1965. These same basic trends are replicated by a multitude of other support measures. In fact, by the mid-sixties, political support was apparently so widespread that the Allenbach Institute discontinued annual monitorings of these basic indicators.

The postwar history of the Federal Republic suggests a similar conclusion about the growth of popular support for the current regime. Despite initial concerns to the contrary, the German political system has functioned as a model of political stability since its formation in 1949. Crises did occur when Adenauer decided to rearm the Federal Republic and attempted to increase the powers of the presidency, and when Franz Josef Strauss ordered the raid on the offices of *Der Spiegel* in October 1962. However, crises such as these were normally resolved without resort to nondemocratic rhetoric and actions (by either elites or masses) and without serious challenge to the basic principles of the Federal Republic. Domestic politics, therefore, has been marked by tranquillity and integration during most of the postwar period. This is partially reflected in the gradual decline of special interest and extremist political parties, and in the evolution of the present "two and a half" party system during the first decade of the Federal Republic.[13]

But it was not simply the absence of domestic disturbances that contributed to the image of the Federal Republic as a stable and well-supported political system. This image also derived from the enormous economic growth West Germany experienced after 1949. Increases in real wages and in purchases of consumer products were substantial, as were increases in trade volume, foreign exchange reserves, and gross national product. Moreover, unemployment was virtually nonexistent.[14] In short, the economic health of the Federal Republic stood in marked contrast to the economic crises that had undermined the Weimar Republic.

Overall, then, there is mounting evidence of a significant increase in support for the new democratic system of the Federal Republic. Two questions from surveys conducted in 1969 and 1972 suggest how widespread this support has become. One question is directed toward measuring "diffuse support" for the regime and reads as follows:

> What would you generally say about democracy in the Federal Republic of Germany, that is, about our political parties and our entire political system? Are you very satisfied, somewhat satisfied, or not satisfied with it?

Because of its very general nature, this question seems to include many of the specific institutions and symbols of the political system that were measured by the Allensbach Institute. The second question focuses on support for the current authorities and is closer to Easton's other concept, "specific support." It reads:

Are you more satisfied or more dissatisfied with what the SPD/ FDP [1969: SPD/CDU] government in Bonn has accomplished so far? Please tell me with the aid of this scale . . .

System support is a difficult concept to measure and we cannot be sure that these questions sufficiently capture all of its dimensions. Moreover, because feelings of satisfaction are evaluative judgments, it is likely that these indicators also reflect system performance. Even with these caveats in mind, however, it is surprising to see how overwhelmingly satisfied the electorate is with both the regime and the authorities (table 1.1). There was widespread satisfaction with German democracy in 1972; indeed, only 5 percent of the population voiced any discontent with the political regime. Individuals were somewhat less

Table 1.1. Political satisfaction with authorities and regime, 1969 and 1972.

	Authorities	
Satisfaction	Aug. 1969	Sept. 1972
Satisfied	84%	72%
Undecided	6	9
Not satisfied	11	19
Total	101[a]	100
(N)	(1833)	(2003)

	Regime[b]
Satisfaction	Oct. 1972
Very Satisfied	22%
Somewhat satisfied	73
Not satisfied	5
Total	100
(N)	(1506)

Source: Unless otherwise indicated, this and all the other tables in the book were derived from the database described in appendix A; dates identify specific studies.

a. Column does not total 100% because of rounding.

b. This question was not asked in 1969.

satisfied with the performance of the government in both 1969 and 1972; and there was a slight decline in this support between the two timepoints, reflecting in part the passage of power from the Grand Coalition to an SPD-FDP government. Nevertheless, support for the government was not confined to those who voted the coalitions into office, since at least 72 percent of the electorate were satisfied with the government's accomplishments at each timepoint.[15]

Although the significance of these findings should not be exaggerated, their implications are of major importance. The longitudinal trends and contemporary opinion measures suggest that support for the democratic political system has now permeated the contemporary political culture of the Federal Republic. This conclusion should not be surprising in view of the effort expended in this direction, but it does imply a revision of the conclusions of previous research. It still cannot be said with certainty what might happen if the legitimacy of the Federal Republic were severely threatened. But neither can confident predictions be made about the other nations of Europe.[16] What can be said is that support for the regime and the authorities has become so widespread that the political system should be able to survive substantially greater pressure than it could a decade or two ago.

The Growth of Civic Attitudes

In addition to generalized support for the political system, a democratic polity requires active involvement and the acceptance of the responsibilities of citizenship by its members. Such beliefs are part of an underlying attitudinal dimension that includes such concepts as citizen duty, political efficacy, system responsiveness, and political attentiveness. These concepts have been discussed at length by several authors.[17] Almond and Verba, for example, posit that strong affective attitudes toward elections and the democratic process and toward the individual's role in that process are important prerequisites for a functioning democratic regime.[18] Moreover, Norman Nie, G. Bingham Powell, and Kenneth Prewitt argue that these attitudes are crucial intervening variables in the development of political participation, an activity often regarded as a defining characteristic of democracy.[19]

Although there are several distinct components of civic attitudes. only one of the most central, namely, the feeling of political efficacy, will be examined here. Political efficacy taps an individual's belief that ordinary people have some influence and control over what the government does. It does not refer to actual attempts at influencing government but rather to the feeling that one can have some impact if one wants to. To many commentators, this kind of feeling is extremely important in a democracy; as Almond and Verba note, the democratic citizen "is not the active citizen; he is the potentially active citizen."[20] Strong feelings of political efficacy, therefore, indicate more than mere support for a political system; they also suggest that the norms and behaviors expected of a citizen in a democracy have been learned and internalized. In addition, as George Balch points out, political efficacy is a part of the larger cluster of civic attitudes: "the citizen who has a high sense of political efficacy is . . . politically active, supportive, informed, interested, loyal, satisfied and public regarding."[21] Hence, our findings in regard to political efficacy may be generalized to a larger set of beliefs for which longitudinal data are not available.

Several of the questions that have been repeatedly used to measure political efficacy were included in the 1959 Almond and Verba survey and in subsequent studies of German political culture. These questions measure feelings of efficacy as disagreement with the following propositions:

People like me don't have any say about what the government does.
Voting is the only way that people like me can have any say about how the government runs things.
Sometimes politics and government seem so complicated that a person like me really can't understand what's going on.
I don't think public officials care much what people like me think.

By following these questions over time a reasonable indication of how this civic attitude has changed as support for the democratic system has increased can be provided.

Figure 1.2 presents the four efficacy items according to the proportion of the sample answering in an efficacious manner. Although feelings of political efficacy are not as widespread as political support (compare table 1.1), these levels may be partially explained by the fact that efficacy is measured by a negative answer; the well-known "yes-saying" effect, therefore, will depress the number of efficacious responses.[22] In other words, these indicators are probably conservative estimates of the number of Germans who feel efficacious. Nevertheless, political efficacy was alarmingly low in 1959; indeed, only about a quarter of the population felt they had a say in what the government did and little more than a tenth saw means other than voting for influencing politics. Undoubtedly, earlier timepoints would uncover even lower levels of political efficacy.

By the 1969 election, however, political efficacy as measured by these two items had increased substantially, and during the brief period between 1969 and 1972 a further gradual increase occurred in relation

Figure 1.2. Growth of political efficacy, 1959–1972. Disagreement with efficacy items indicates efficaciousness. Sources: For 1959, Almond and Verba, *The Civic Culture;* for 1969 and 1972, see database described in appendix A (dates identify specific studies). Sources for all subsequent figures, unless otherwise indicated, can be found in appendix A.

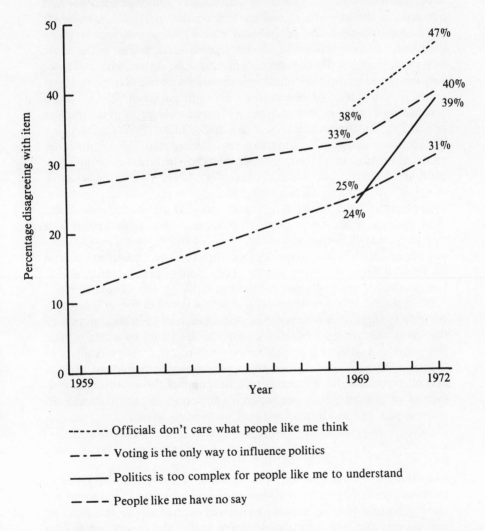

------- Officials don't care what people like me think

— · — · Voting is the only way to influence politics

———— Politics is too complex for people like me to understand

— — — People like me have no say

to all four items. Although not accepted by all Germans, the belief that the individual can exercise some control and influence over what the government does has become much more commonplace.[23] Moreover, approximately 40 percent of the respondents in the 1972 survey thought that politics is understandable and that the average person can have some say in politics. Less than a third, however, saw opportunities to exert political influence other than by voting at that timepoint. This is somewhat surprising in view of the dramatic rise in participation in citizen initiatives and unconventional forms of political behavior that occurred in the late sixties and early seventies in West Germany.[24]

Although these levels of political efficacy may not appear to be very high, the German public has internalized civic norms to the same degree as many other Western democratic societies. For example, surveys conducted in 1973 in the nine nations of the European Communities found that 44 percent of the Germans believed they could bring about change in their nation, compared to 41 percent for the rest of Europe.[25] Moreover, levels of political efficacy in West Germany have become comparable to those in the United States.[26] Significantly more Americans than Germans feel that they have a say about what government does, but Germans are more likely than Americans to disagree with the proposition that politics is too complicated for them to understand. Further, similar proportions of Germans and Americans think that there are other forms of participation besides voting, and that public officials care about the views of the common people. Adjusting for the different social compositions of the United States and the Federal Republic, especially the level of education, would probably increase the relative standing of the Germans on all of these items.[27]

In summary, these findings suggest that it is easier for an individual to voice support for a new political system than to learn and internalize the norms and behavioral expectations of a citizen in a democratic polity. Indeed, although system support has reached near unanimity in West Germany, there is still room for improvement in political efficacy and other civic attitudes. As is true for support, however, civic attitudes have grown steadily in the postwar period and have become an integral part of the German political culture.

Sources of Support for the Political System and Its Norms

Judgments about the significance of these changes in the German political culture depend largely on how one evaluates the nature of the new attitudes. Is system support deeply engrained in the political culture, or is it readily susceptible to reversal? Does the system indeed rest upon a stronger foundation today than it did twenty-five years ago? Other researchers have provided more detailed analyses of the growth of political support than those presented here, but the crucial question about the bases of support remains largely unanswered.

Many commentators feel that support for the democratic forms of the Federal Republic is overly dependent on the continuing success of the Economic Miracle.[28] These analysts believe that Germans continue to accept the new political forms only because of the economic benefits they have produced. This argument was partially confirmed when Almond and Verba found that only 7 percent of the West German population spontaneously mentioned the German political system as a source of national pride in 1959; in contrast, 33 percent named the economic system. Further evidence was provided by the dramatic, if short-lived, electoral success of the right wing National Democratic Party (NPD) in the mid-sixties when the Federal Republic was experiencing its first serious economic downturn since 1949. Many observers still fear that if put to the test, particularly in an economic crisis, support for the West German political system might collapse. There is a feeling that Germans maintain specific, output-dependent support for the system, but not diffuse support. These fears have consequently led to the question, "Is Bonn Simply Weimar (*Ist Bonn doch Weimar*)?"[29]

Longitudinal studies of German polling data, however, suggest a significantly different explanation of the growth of system support. According to G. R. Boynton and Gerhard Loewenberg, as well as Conradt, the performance of the political and economic system was an important factor in the growth of system support in the first fifteen years following the war.[30] For example, they find that in the first decade of the new Republic support for the chancellor's policies was an important predictor of support for the various institutions and symbols of the Federal Republic. However, they also find that the importance of performance as a source of system support began to decline by the late 1950s. Although these authors' indicators of system performance are less than ideal, their data still argue convincingly that early specific support has largely been replaced by a reservoir of diffuse support.

Performance, however, is only one explanation for the long-term growth of supportive attitudes and political efficacy. Another important source could be the changing character of postwar German society. One of the hallmarks of this development has been the transformation of the German social structure. As noted in the introduction, income has risen markedly, and in spite of the rigid educational system the number of students admitted to universities has increased. These developments are important because several types of civic attitudes, including political efficacy, are more common among the educated and those with higher incomes. Income and education help furnish the sorts of skills and resources necessary for political commitment, as well as the self-confidence and the access to the political system that nourish a sense of political efficacy.[31]

Not only may political efficacy be stronger among the educated and those with higher incomes, but such individuals may also show greater support for the democratic political regime. Seymour Martin Lipset has pointed to the phenomenon of "upper class liberalism": individuals at higher points in the social hierarchy are more likely to support democratic regimes.[32] Other commentators have noted that the "rewards and payoffs" and "indulgences" received from the political system are greater for members of society with higher status than for those with lower status; such individuals are, therefore, more likely to support the system.[33]

Finally, a person's age, or perhaps more appropriately in the German context, the generation to which a person belongs, may be related to support and political efficacy. Nearly half of the respondents in the 1972 survey were socialized after the fall of the Third Reich. Hence, their memories of the past as well as their formative experiences are dramatically different from those of older generations. In the schools and through the media they have learned of the excesses of authoritarian rule, and the political experience they have accumulated has been almost exclusively with a democratic polity. The expectation that younger Germans are more supportive of the existing regime and more politically efficacious is buttressed by a number of youth studies conducted since the mid-sixties. Max Kaase, for example, found both support for democracy and political efficacy stronger among students than among adults in a 1968 study.[34] In a 1967 investigation of Cologne adolescents, Kendall Baker found pride in the existing system and political efficacy stronger than that reported in the Almond and Verba study.[35] Finally, M. Kent Jennings recently reported that young people are more positively oriented to change and diversity than are adults.[36]

We have grouped these explanatory factors under two conceptual headings: evaluations of system performance, and background characteristics.[37] To determine whether the first of these, system performance, is crucial for political support, we have selected questions from the 1972 study that tap performance evaluations in three areas. One focuses on the economic achievements of the Federal Republic; a second assesses personal economic satisfaction. Both of these indicators serve as tests of past economic explanations of political support in Germany. A third question focuses on satisfaction with *Ostpolitik*, the major issue of foreign policy performance debated during the 1972 campaign.

These political performance measures reflect the conjoint influence of two processes. First, they tap satisfaction with government policy and achievements. Second, they reflect evaluations of the party in control of the government. Hence, supporters of the incumbent party should be more satisfied that "their" party is in power, regardless of the actual accomplishments of the government. To control for this purely partisan effect, we have included a measure of partisanship in the analyses that enables us to separate the purely partisan component of political support from performance evaluations.[38]

To examine the impact of the second factor, background characteristics, on these political orientations, three common demographic questions have been included in the analysis. As noted in the introduction, age is conceptualized as an indicator of historical experience to determine whether the failures of Weimar or the Third Reich can still be seen in contemporary political attitudes. Education functions as a measure of the cognitive skills and contextual knowledge of the citizen; it has been measured on a four-point scale, corresponding to the four major steps in the German school system.[39] Income quartiles have been used to approximate the social status of each respondent.

All of these predictors were combined in multiple regression analyses to separately predict authority satisfaction, regime satisfaction, and political efficacy.[40] The causal weights of each predictor are presented in table 1.2.[41] Clearly, the two sets of predictors have quite different impacts on the three different types of political orientations. Performance measures are related most strongly to satisfaction with political authorities, and they have significantly less impact on political efficacy. The reverse is the case for the background variables: although they

Table 1.2. Regression analyses of political orientations, 1972.[a]

Predictor	Authority satisfaction	Regime satisfaction	Political efficacy
Performance evaluations			
Federal Republic's economic situation	0.18	0.13	−0.02
Personal economic situation	.01	.11	.05
Ostpolitik	.30	.11	.02
Partisanship	.44	.08	.12
Background			
Education	−.06	−.02	.25
Generation	−.02	.00	−.13
Income	.04	.06	−.07
R^b	.75	.31	.40

a. Numerical entries are standardized regression coefficients (betaweights).
b. Multiple correlation coefficient.

predict feelings of political efficacy quite well, they have practically no effect on satisfaction with the regime or the authorities.

To be more specific, the indicators of contemporary economic conditions in the Federal Republic have a strong and direct impact on satisfaction with the political authorities. These evaluations are derived more from perceptions of the economic situation in the country as a whole (0.18) than from the respondent's own economic situation (0.01). Satisfaction with *Ostpolitik* has an even stronger impact on authority evaluations, reflecting the centrality of this issue to the 1972 election campaign.[42]

In addition to indicating the effects of economic and foreign policy performance on evaluations of the political authorities, these analyses also suggest that satisfaction with the government has a strong partisan component. In the bivariate relationship between these two variables, over 98 percent of the strong SPD supporters are satisfied with the government, while only 38 percent of the strong partisans of the CDU/CSU opposition express satisfaction.

Conversely, the three social background variables have hardly any effect on satisfaction with the government in power. Support for present authorities is quite evenly distributed among the various age cohorts, education groups, and income quartiles.

Many of these same causal patterns are replicated in predicting satisfaction with the regime, presumably a more diffuse support measure. The causal effects, however, are more muted. Support for the regime is not totally independent of governmental performance, although the relationships with economic and foreign policy outputs are attenuated. Similarly, while partisanship has a strong impact on satisfaction with the authorities (0.44), it has very little influence on regime satisfaction (0.08). An even more direct assessment of the importance of government performance to regime support can be obtained by directly correlating authority and regime satisfaction. The bivariate relationship between these two items is only modest ($r = 0.25$). And when we add authority satisfaction to the other predictors of regime support, its independent impact in regression analyses is relatively minor (0.10). Thus, regime satisfaction is largely independent of evaluations of political authorities.

Since comparable data from earlier timepoints are lacking, the argument that the importance of performance for system support has decreased over time cannot be evaluated. It is clear, however, that the impact of performance evaluations drops off dramatically as we move from a measure of specific support to items closer to Easton's concept of diffuse support. Moreover, using a question focusing on "satisfaction" probably maximizes the possible influence of performance on political support.

Regime support also shows only minor correlations with the three social background variables. Neither the upper-class liberalism hypothesis nor the proposition that higher-status individuals will more closely identify with the regime is supported by these data. Perhaps most surprising, young Germans do not support the system any more than older Germans do. Among the youngest cohort, 94 percent are satisfied with the democratic system of the Federal Republic, while an equivalent 87 percent of the Wilhelmine generation are satisfied. But this does not mean that social characteristics (and the causal influences they represent) are irrelevant to the investigation of system support. Indeed, earlier research has shown strong correlations between these variables and support for the German political system and its values. Rather, these findings suggest that support for the political system has become so pervasive in the German political culture that it is now relatively independent of specific social and political factors; that is, support is increasingly of the diffuse rather than the specific variety.[43]

In contrast, the overriding determinants of political efficacy are the social background variables. Education is strongly related to feelings that one can influence the government, suggesting that the cognitive skills and political resources represented by this indicator—not government performance—have been crucial to the growth of civic norms.[44] Perhaps even more important is the sizable generational variation in political efficacy. Germans who have grown up in the postwar Federal Republic are substantially more confident that they can influence the political process than are older individuals. These generational findings are consistent with the youth studies already mentioned.[45]

Performance evaluations, on the other hand, have little direct influence on feelings of political efficacy. The multiple regression analyses find an insignificant relationship between economic and foreign policy output and efficacy. Similarly, SPD partisans are only slightly more efficacious than CDU/CSU supporters. Indeed, combining all four performance measures (including partisanship) explains only 3 percent of the variance in this civic norm.

Nevertheless, system performance cannot be completely dismissed as an explanation of the over-time increase in political efficacy. Increases in education and income, and generational turnover, though important, are not of sufficient magnitude to account for all of the long-term growth.[46] As the data show, efficacy is not strongly related to system output, but feelings of efficacy should be sensitive to the policy process, that is, to how outputs are determined. As Germans have become familiar with the democratic process of the Federal Republic, they have come to believe that they can affect political decision-making, and, in this way, system "performance" may have contributed to the growth of civic norms in Germany.

It is somewhat risky to extrapolate from static correlations in a single survey to a dynamic theory of attitude change. Nevertheless, the implications of these findings suggest that the long-term increase in political efficacy, and presumably other related civic norms, is attributable to three factors. First, there has been a steady increase in the political skills and resources of the German electorate during the postwar period. Second, older Germans who were socialized under previous authoritarian regimes or the chaotic Weimar democracy have gradually been replaced by younger cohorts socialized into the norms and institutions of the Federal Republic. Third, the democratic processes of the Federal Republic have themselves contributed to the feeling of political efficacy in the German citizen.

Conclusion

Throughout the postwar period commentators have questioned whether the German political culture contained beliefs and attitudes congruent with a democratic political system. On the basis of the data reviewed and analyzed in this chapter, it seems appropriate to conclude that such questioning is not nearly as justified today as it may have been in the past. Equally important, the three political orientations examined seem to be the product of rather distinct causal processes.

Satisfaction with the government appears closely associated with evaluations of system performance and attachment to the incumbent party. This, of course, is what should be expected for any polity.

Satisfaction with the regime is also tied to system performance, but the link is less substantial. Moreover, the correlation between support and performance may be due more to the measure of diffuse support used in this analysis than to any lingering output orientation on the part of the German public. Taken together, these data suggest that the distinction between specific and diffuse support is a meaningful one to the German public, a distinction that is crucial to determining the significance of past research on political support in Germany. Furthermore, a large majority of Germans have apparently developed these feelings of diffuse support for the regime of the Federal Republic.

Finally, feelings of political efficacy reflect yet another causal process. It is those individuals who have more education, higher incomes, and postwar formative experiences, not those satisfied with government outputs, that manifest the strongest sense of political efficacy. This differentiation helps explain the dynamics of political efficacy and perhaps why civic norms are less common in Germany than support for the system. Continuing positive system performance does not seem to constitute a "shortcut" to the development of political efficacy as it may for system support. Rather, political efficacy seems to result in Germany—as perhaps elsewhere—from long-term social and political processes, such as expanding educational opportunities, the emergence of new generations with different formative experiences, and the successful and open operation of the democratic system.

2

The Involved Electorate

IN ADDITION TO BASIC ORIENTATIONS toward the political process and the political system as a whole, the political culture of a society embraces the nature and extent of citizen involvement in politics. There are many forms political participation can take, but some mass input into the political system is generally viewed as essential for democracy to be viable and meaningful. As Verba and Nie point out, "If democracy is interpreted as rule by the people, then the question of who participates in political decisions becomes the question of the nature of democracy in a society."[1] If political involvement is absent, then most analysts would argue that democracy is weak, because it is through discussion, popular interest, and involvement in politics that societal goals should be set and implemented in a democracy.

Citizen involvement in German politics has generally been characterized as limited. The German political culture was described as "detached" and "passive"; Germans were considered not as "participants" in the political system, but as "subjects" following the rules of elite decision-makers.[2] Certainly the history of Germany has not been conducive to developing widespread involvement in politics. Not only have three regimes failed since the turn of the century, but supporters of the previous regime have often suffered after the establishment of each new political order. The treatment of the political opposition following the National Socialists' rise to power as well as the denazification program after World War II probably convinced many citizens that political participation was a questionable, if not risky, pursuit.

Nevertheless, it is appropriate to reconsider the nonparticipatory characterization of the German electorate. The substantial change in German orientations toward the political system (already documented) may have carried over to active involvement in politics. Similarly, past performance of the democratic regime, the rise in affluence, increased levels of education, and generational change may have increased political participation.

The Growth of Political Involvement

Measuring citizen involvement in politics is a complex task. Citizens can become involved in several aspects of politics, including voting, working in a campaign, or joining with others to influence politics.[3] Each of these forms of involvement may reflect different aspects of the political culture and the political system, and may therefore yield different images of the German citizen.

Voting turnout, for example, has been exceptionally high since the formation of the Federal Republic. However, voting alone constitutes a minimal amount of political input, and turnout rates are largely dependent on institutional factors rather than underlying citizen interest and cultural orientations toward participation in general.[4] Thus, turnout rates cannot be considered a sufficient measure of whether the German political culture actually emphasizes participation. Similarly, campaign and group-related activities are highly dependent on institutional settings, and vary as much as a consequence of party strategies and elite mobilization as from individual attitudes.[5]

Therefore, as an indicator of citizen interest and involvement in politics, we selected a question measuring the frequency of informal political discussion. In democracies, political discussion is not constrained by the institutional setting and it is only slightly limited or stimulated by the structure of the system, interest groups, or political parties.[6] Thus, the frequency of political discussion should depend almost exclusively on the individual, on his or her beliefs and attitudes as shaped by the political culture.[7]

Each of the studies conducted between 1953 and 1972 includes a question on the frequency of political discussion. Although the phrasing of this question changes somewhat over time, there is sufficient continuity to allow for longitudinal comparisons.[8] The distribution of political discussion over two decades is presented in table 2.1.

Clearly, the frequency of political discussion shows a marked increase over time. In 1953, political discussion was dismally low: over 60 percent of the electorate admitted to rarely or never discussing politics. This must have partially reflected the impact of recent events—the authoritarian regime of the Third Reich, the defeat of World War II, and the depoliticizing environment brought on by the occupation and denazification programs. Almond and Verba's com-

Table 2.1. Frequency of political discussion, 1953–1972.[a]

Frequency	July 1953	June 1959	July 1961	Oct. 1965	Sept. 1969	Dec. 1972
Daily	8.6%	10.7%	10.3%	9.8%	37.1%	50.2%
Occasionally	28.5	49.8	50.7	65.7	39.5	34.3
Never	62.9	39.4	38.9	24.5	23.4	15.5
Sample mean	1.47	1.71	1.70	1.85	2.10	2.34
(N)	(3236)	(941)	(1362)	(1278)	(1141)	(1190)

a. Mean scores are based on the following coding: (1) never discuss politics, (2) discuss politics occasionally, and (3) discuss politics daily. See appendix B for a detailed discussion of the construction of this index.

ments on the late fifties apply even more to the immediate postwar era: "If ordinary men and women are to participate in a democratic political process, they must have the feeling that it is safe to do so, that they do not assume great risks when they express political opinions, and that they can be relatively free about whom they talk to."[9] This supportive, democratic environment was not fully apparent in 1953, nor even in 1959, as these authors point out. By 1959, however, the German electorate was much more likely to discuss politics. The number of uninvolved citizens declined to just under 40 percent. Further evidence of this trend was the gradual increase in political discussion through the 1965 election.

During the 1969 election there was another sharp increase in political involvement. This election, which was characterized by high levels of citizen participation, saw the emergence of voter initiative groups (*Wählerinitiativen*).[10] Over a third of the electorate claimed to discuss politics daily during the 1969 campaign. At the time of the 1972 election, citizen involvement rose to an even higher plateau.[11] Voting turnout in 1972 was the highest in the history of the Federal Republic, and American-style electioneering tactics proliferated.[12] To culminate this trend of increasing politicization, the 1973 European Community study found German levels of political discussion to be the highest in the European Community.[13]

Evidence of increased involvement in politics is also available from other sources. Elisabeth Noelle-Neumann has documented a substantial increase in political interest for the period between 1952 and 1973.[14] Similarly, the recent increase in citizen initiatives, beginning with the voter initiatives of 1969, contradicts previous stereotypes of German avoidance of group-related political activity.

Thus, evidence from several sources indicates the advent of a

Figure 2.1. Participation in politics, 1972.

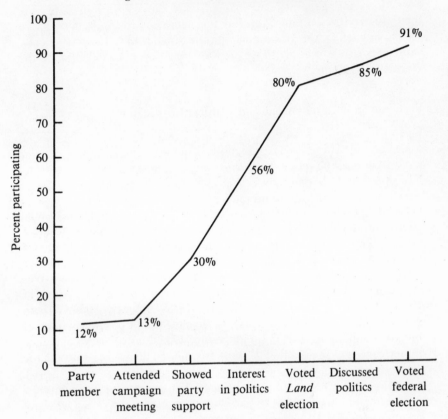

more active and involved German electorate. Indeed, by 1972 the German public was clearly involved in a full range of participatory activities (figure 2.1). The overwhelming majority of the electorate voted in federal and state (*Land*) elections, and discussed politics. General interest in politics was also high. Even in the more demanding forms of campaign activity—showing party support and attending meetings—sizable minorities said they were politically active.

If the data covered a shorter timespan and political involvement had increased over only a few elections, the increase might be attributed to the unique stimuli of each election. The sustained and broad growth of political involvement, however, argues that long-term processes underlie the aggregate pattern of change. Several factors—the performance of the democratic regime, the rise in affluence, increased levels of education, and generational change—may have contributed to this increase in participation. Therefore it is necessary to assess the relative weight of each factor, beginning with the broader theories of politicization, and to emphasize those factors that apply specifically to the German condition.

Socioeconomic Development and Political Involvement

One of the verities of political behavior is that citizens of higher social and economic status participate more in politics. Higher-status citizens have the time, the money, the knowledge, and the ability to be effective in politics. So common is this notion that Verba and Nie refer to social status as the "standard model" of political participation.[15] Similarly, in their cross-national analysis of political participation, Nie, Powell, and Prewitt suggest that economic development can be expected to increase the political involvement of the citizenry.[16] In addition, higher income increases the intake of political information as access to the mass media grows (home television, newspapers, magazines).[17]

The dramatic rise in income resulting from the *Wirtschaftswunder* ("Economic Miracle") may thus have contributed to greater political involvement in postwar Germany. Further, the economic-development literature stresses the spread of educational opportunities as an even more significant influence on politicization.[18] The level of education is an indirect measure of the political knowledge and political sophistication of the electorate. Evidence consistently shows that the cognitive abilities represented by education are very much a factor in determining whether or not an individual discusses politics.[19] Although changes in the structure of German education and the extension of educational opportunities have not been as dramatic as the increases in affluence, educational levels have gradually improved during the postwar period. In 1953, 14 percent of the German citizenry had received at least a tenth-grade diploma; by 1972, that proportion had increased by half. This extension of education may also have contributed to the long-term increase in German political participation.

Both income and education are clearly related to political discussion (table 2.2).[20] In 1953, for example, very few in the lowest income quartile discussed politics (mean = 1.29); in contrast, political discussion was substantially more commonplace among the top income quartile (mean = 1.61). In a general sense, high levels of education and income have apparently provided the skills and resources that stimulate interest and involvement in politics. Moreover, as overall income

Table 2.2. Political discussion and social status, 1953–1972.[a]

	July 1953	June 1959	Sept. 1961	Oct. 1965	Sept. 1969	Dec. 1972
Income quartiles						
Lowest	1.29	1.57	1.47	1.61	1.77	1.93
Second	1.41	1.72	1.65	1.84	2.12	2.24
Third	1.58	1.79	1.79	1.93	2.17	2.49
Highest	1.61	1.88	1.88	2.02	2.33	2.57
Eta	0.19	0.16	0.21	0.27	0.27	0.30
(N)	(3054)	(799)	(1290)	(1139)	(1122)	(1151)
Education						
Primary	1.36	1.55	1.53	1.63	1.78	2.07
Primary or technical	1.60	1.81	1.82	1.91	2.21	2.42
Secondary	1.67	1.97	1.90	2.09	2.44	2.64
Abitur	1.93	2.34	2.13	2.23	2.75	2.65
Eta	0.24	0.30	0.27	0.33	0.36	0.28
(N)	(3223)	(928)	(1406)	(1278)	(1142)	(1185)

a. Numerical entries are mean scores on the political discussion index.

levels have risen, political discussion has also increased *within* each income quartile. The *lowest* income group in 1972 was generally more affluent than the *highest* quartile in 1953; consequently, the lowest income group in 1972 discussed politics more often than the highest income group in 1953. Educational categories show a similar increase over time, perhaps also due to rising income levels within each educational stratum.

Although these analyses provide an overview of the simple relationships between social-status measures and political discussion, they give no indication of the total impact of social status. Items like education and income complement each other in capturing a diffuse concept like social status. Obviously these measures are closely related, but it can also be argued that each maintains an independent influence on political discussion. Therefore, these measures have been combined for a more powerful and refined analysis of the importance of the socioeconomic model.

Our approach to this problem is based on the use of Multiple Classification Analysis (MCA). MCA is designed for research using categoric (nominal-level) independent variables that are intercorrelated.[21] It is analogous to the statistical model of dummy variable regression. For each predictor, the simple correlation with the dependent variable

Table 2.3. Multiple Classification Analysis of political discussion and social status, 1953–1972.[a]

Social status	July 1953	June 1959	Sept. 1961	Oct. 1965	Sept. 1969	Dec. 1972
Education	0.21	0.29	0.24	0.27	0.28	0.20
Income	.15	.10	.13	.13	.15	.20
Occupation	.04	—	.11	.08	.13	.08
Multiple R	.28	.30	.32	.36	.41	.35
(N)	(3225)	(941)	(1406)	(1296)	(1142)	(1190)

a. Numerical entries are MCA beta coefficients, which measure the independent correlation of each predictor with the dependent variable. For the 1959 study, occupation of head of household was not available.

(eta coefficient) and a measure of correlation *controlling for* the remaining predictors (beta coefficient) are obtained. The combined effect of all predictors jointly considered is represented as a Multiple Correlation Coefficient (R).

Table 2.3 presents the independent effects (beta) of each social-status measure on political discussion, while controlling for the remaining predictors. In addition to education and income, occupation has been included to develop the strongest possible measure of the effects of the socioeconomic model.[22] Clearly, the most powerful predictor is the individual's educational achievement. The higher the level of education, the greater the frequency of political discussion. This remains true even after the effects of income and occupation have been removed. The independent effect of education, moreover, generally appears to be increasing over time, with the exception of the 1972 timepoint.[23] Income is weaker than education in its independent effects, although its causal impact appears to be fairly constant across time. Occupation exerts the least influence on the frequency of political discussion (even if measured by the simple eta correlation). Occupation primarily reflects a middle class–working class differential, which appears to have been moderated by the strong mobilizing influence of labor unions among German workers.[24]

The socioeconomic model apparently has considerable validity in explaining the growth of German involvement in politics. The predictive power of all three social-status measures is substantial, and it seems to be generally increasing over time. Still, this model does not provide a full explanation. For example, income has been presented as the driving force of the socioeconomic model, and as a factor that has experienced a long-term growth as dramatic as political involvement.

Yet, in the cross-sectional analysis, income bears only a modest relationship to the frequency of political discussion. Other factors must be considered.

Generational Change

The turbulence of Germany's political history has often focused research on generations as a source of political change. The succession of political regimes—Wilhelmine, Weimar Republic, Third Reich, and the Federal Republic—has produced within the span of half a century vastly different life experiences for succeeding generations. In a general sense, there seems little doubt that such historical and environmental forces constitute important socialization factors. A number of authors have taken this view in connection with a wide range of political attitudes and behaviors.[25] The differences arise, however, when one asks what form generational change should take. Two different models of generational change—early learning and accumulated learning— might help to explain the long-term growth of political involvement, and both appear viable in the German context.

The early learning model stresses the importance of formative experiences during childhood and early adolescence. As David Easton and Jack Dennis and others argue, early life socialization is particularly important in the development of basic attitudes toward politics and the political system—including orientations toward political involvement.[26] The socialization of democratic participatory norms may be especially important in relation to political discussion, an active form of political involvement.

The early learning model suggests that cohorts retain the mark of their early formative experiences throughout their life span. Citizens raised during the autocratic regimes of the Wilhelmine Empire and the Third Reich should display a hesitancy to become involved in politics. The democratic interlude of the Weimar Republic might result in a slightly stronger commitment to participatory norms and behavior by this cohort, and might consequently lead to higher levels of political involvement. Finally, the youngest generations socialized in the postwar era should be most receptive to the democratic environment of the Federal Republic and thus be most active in politics.

In recent years, questions have been raised about the pervasiveness of the early learning model. One commentator, for example, suggests that it is not altogether clear when "*meaningful* attitudes take shape."[27] Others demonstrate that a good deal of political learning occurs during adolescence and postadolescence, particularly in the areas of political interest and "in the differential salience of political systems, in the relative emphasis on various citizenship norms, and in overall political trust."[28] In short, the focus on early childhood as the critical period in the socialization process has been moderated in recent years by a more differentiated view suggesting that learning accumulates through the life cycle to form and reform certain political attitudes and behaviors.[29]

Several studies of political participation in stable democracies have already applied this accumulation model to explain life-cycle differences in political involvement.[30] In a stable democratic system (such as the United States), experience in a democratic participatory role steadily accumulates through life, and political involvement consequently increases with age before dropping off after retirement.

In the German context, however, there are marked differences in the types of political learning accumulated over the life span of different generations. The accumulation model suggests that a generation's level of political involvement reflects the sum total of its life experiences, and thus it leads to expectations differing from the "normal" age curve in stable democracies. For example, the German postwar generation should be most politically involved since it has only experienced the democratic environment of the Federal Republic. The Third Reich generation should be a bit more hesitant to discuss politics because it has also experienced the autocratic Nazi regime and the trauma of World War II. The Weimar generation should be even more removed from politics because in addition to the Third Reich experience it has witnessed the fragmentation and default of democracy in the 1930s. And finally, the Wilhelmine generation has experienced all of this as well as the destruction of World War I and the collapse of the Kaiserreich; hence, it should be most distant from politics.

There are thus basic differences between the two models in the causal processes they hypothesize and in the way they order generations in expected political involvement. Yet both suggest similar consequences for the nature of political change in the postwar period. Both models predict that the youngest cohort will have the highest level of political involvement. Population turnover can therefore be expected to gradually raise levels of political participation as younger, more involved citizens replace the older, more detached, more passive cohorts. Similarly, both models suggest that the introduction (or reintroduction) of a democratic system in 1949 and subsequent exposure to it will have a far greater impact on younger generations, either because their early learning occurs in this environment or because they are accumulating only supportive democratic experiences. Older cohorts, according to both models, will be less affected by the ways and norms of the new system, because their customs and habits have been "set"

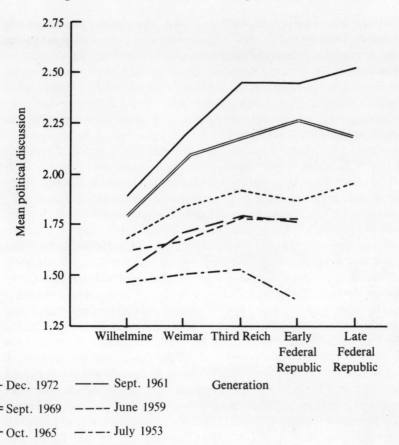

Figure 2.2. Political discussion and generations, 1953–1972.

Mean political discussion

2.75

2.50

2.25

2.00

1.75

1.50

1.25

Wilhelmine Weimar Third Reich Early Federal Republic Late Federal Republic

Generation

——— Dec. 1972 — — Sept. 1961

═══ Sept. 1969 – – – – June 1959

----------- Oct. 1965 – - – - July 1953

by their early childhood learning in one model, or by a large store of already accumulated experience in the other model.

In analyzing the change in attitudes toward political discussion across time, we have defined five generations in terms of the political regime during individuals' early formative years: Wilhelmine, Weimar, Third Reich, early Federal Republic, and late Federal Republic.[31]

The political-discussion mean score for each generation at each timepoint is presented in figure 2.2. The several cross-sectional generation curves present a fascinating pattern. To describe the 1953 relationship either in terms of the early learning or accumulated learning model may be neither warranted nor accurate, for the principal characteristic of these data is the generally flat nature of the curve. The most important thing about this timepoint—the generally limited political involvement of *all* generations in 1953—has little to do with either model.

By the next timepoints, 1959 and 1961, the pattern has noticeably changed. The age curve now begins to give evidence of generational differences. The youngest generation, reared in the democratic environment of the Federal Republic, displays the highest level of political discussion. In contrast, older generations show successively lower levels of political involvement. These generational differences intensify in subsequent years, and by 1972 a very wide gap separates the youngest and oldest generations. A full 61 percent of the late Federal Republic generation are discussing politics daily, while only 27 percent of the Wilhelmine cohort are equally involved in politics.

It appears from these age curves that early learning is *not* of primary importance in determining levels of political involvement. The distinction between democratic and autocratic formative environments is not evident. On the contrary, the Weimar generation is consistently less involved than the Third Reich cohort, even though the former was raised in a more democratic setting and the latter in an autocratic one.

Instead, these data suggest that accumulation of learning throughout the life cycle is the important factor in determining German political involvement. Older cohorts have accumulated experiences that should make them hesitant to become actively involved in public affairs. The older the cohort, the more often its members have experienced the suppression of political dissent and the failure of political regimes. It would be difficult to argue within the early learning framework, for example, that the political environment of the Third Reich was more supportive of open political participation than was the environment of the Weimar Republic. Yet the Third Reich generation is consistently more likely to discuss politics than the Weimar cohort. This generational pattern probably results because the Weimar generation was more strongly dissuaded from becoming involved in politics by experiencing *both* the Nazi regime and the traumatizing political events leading up to it. This accumulation of depoliticizing generational experiences generally leads to a monotonic decline in political involvement from the youngest to the oldest cohorts. Consequently, the age curve in Germany is dramatically different from that in other Western countries where involvement increases with age.

Germany is unique in the degree of historical and political change experienced since the turn of the century, and this may explain why early learning patterns do not persist. But, as noted earlier, the causal processes hypothesized by the cumulative learning model are also consistent with the considerable research done on age and participation in stable democratic systems.[32]

It is clear, too, from figure 2.2 that all cohorts exhibit rising levels of political involvement over time—perhaps reflecting the spread of par-

Table 2.4. Growth of political discussion by generation, 1953–1972.

Generation	Absolute difference, 1953–1972	Per decade[a] increase
Wilhelmine Empire	0.42	0.22
Weimar Republic	.68	.36
Third Reich	.92	.46
Early Federal Republic	1.07	.54
Late Federal Republic[b]	.57	.81

a. Per-decade change is calculated by regressing the mean score of a generation at each timepoint on the year of the study.

b. Data based on the 1965–1972 time period.

ticipatory norms, experience in the democratic citizen role, or economic advances. However, cohorts do not share equally in the increase. Table 2.4 documents this finding more directly. When the rate of political-discussion increase was calculated for each generation, the per-annum growth rates were found to be several times larger for the postwar generations than for the oldest cohort.[33] Over a decade, the mean political-discussion score for the early Federal Republic cohort averaged a 0.54 increase, while the score for the Wilhelmine cohort increased by only 0.22.

This pattern of generational change is also consistent with the accumulation model. This model predicts that the Federal Republic generations participate more because they have accumulated only consistent democratic experiences, and that, in contrast, older cohorts must overcome the inertia of several years of nondemocratic experiences in order to embrace open democratic participation. Thus, although all cohorts have experienced the Federal Republic's democratic environment, these experiences have made a greater impact upon the young. The long-term growth of political involvement for all cohorts again argues that political learning is an ongoing process, even if its rate depends on prior experiences.

The possible spuriousness of these generational patterns should also be considered. Political involvement is strongly related to social status, and increases in social status have been most concentrated among the postwar cohorts. Affluence, for example, has increased most rapidly among the young.[34] The extension of education has obviously centered among younger generations. Therefore, might not these generational findings on political involvement be merely reflections of increasing social-status differences between the young and the old?

Figure 2.3. Political discussion and generations, 1953–1972 (adjusted and raw scores).

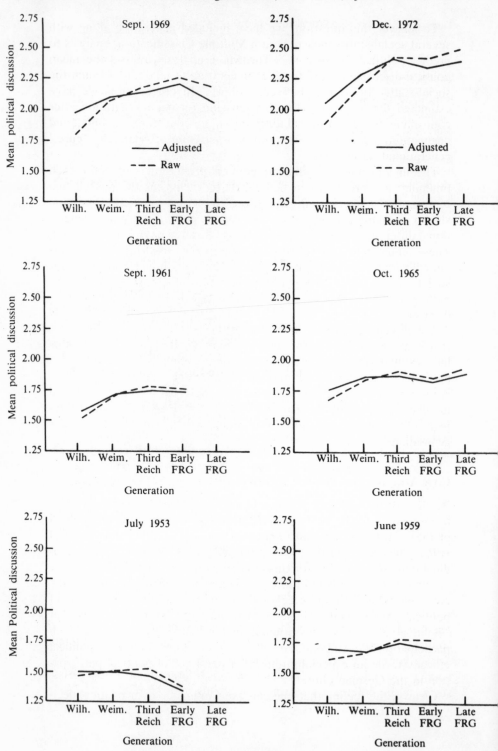

To answer this question, we have included generation along with several social-status measures in a Multiple Classification Analysis to predict political discussion.[35] The MCA analysis adjusts the mean political-discussion score for each generation to take into account the social-status differences between cohorts. In other words we have estimated the level of political discussion for each generation after controlling for generational differences in education, income, and occupation. What remains should be a measure of relatively "pure" generational differences.

The unadjusted and adjusted political-discussion scores for each timepoint are presented in figure 2.3. In each year the dashed line represents the unadjusted generational pattern in political discussion shown in figure 2.2. The solid line represents the remaining generational differences after the effects of social status have been removed. These adjustments for social-status differences tend to lessen generational variation in political discussion. But even though controlling for social status weakens the generational pattern, the basic outline of the pattern remains—the young still maintain higher levels of political discussion.

A new generation has developed in the postwar years in Germany that is more involved in the democratic political system. In part, this has resulted from the accumulation of experience in the role of a participatory citizen, but it may also involve the inculcation of democratic norms of participation. Thus, one source of increasing political involvement must be the growing size of the young participatory segment of the electorate and the acceptance of their example by older generations.

Civic Attitudes and Political Involvement

Because of its turbulent political history, a good deal of attention has been devoted to the study of civic attitudes in Germany. Although all of these attitudes have an impact on political involvement, political efficacy has received the most emphasis in past research, and longitudinal data are available for this concept. Feelings of political efficacy are an essential element of citizens' beliefs in their role as democratic participants, and they are generally found to lead to higher levels of political involvement. Giuseppe DiPalma, for example, notes that "political efficacy is the orientation most strongly correlated with participation."[36] And Nie, Powell, and Prewitt find feelings of political efficacy to be an especially important predictor of political participation in the German context.[37]

Clearly, the feeling that one can exert influence over political decision-making should increase attempts to do so. Furthermore, Chapter 1 documented a long-term increase in feelings of political efficacy by the German electorate. Consequently, the spread of this civic attitude may constitute another source of the observed long-term growth of political involvement.

This hypothesis can be tested more directly since several of the studies contain a measure tapping feelings of political efficacy. While the specific wording of the question changes somewhat between surveys, it retains sufficient comparability to justify longitudinal analyses of the impact of this attitude on political discussion.[38] In every survey, there is a modest correlation between political efficacy and political discussion (1953, 0.35; 1959, 0.29; 1965, 0.22; 1972, 0.22). However, the relationship between the feeling that one can influence politics and the actual discussion of political matters has been decreasing over time. Apparently, when political efficacy was a rare commodity in 1953, it had a large impact on political participation, but as feelings of efficacy have spread and begun to permeate the political culture their causal significance has weakened.

A Model of Political Involvement

Three factors that seem to have contributed to the long-term growth of German involvement in politics have been separately considered: social status, generational change, and civic attitudes.[39] Obviously, all three factors are interrelated.

Higher-status individuals participate more than others, partially because they possess the skills and resources that facilitate involvement; but higher-status individuals also participate more because they feel they can effectively influence the government through their participation. Nie and his colleagues see participatory norms as an important intervening link between social status and participation. They argue that "political life styles of citizens will not be markedly changed until extensive industrialization alters the status structure of society and thereby increases the overall level of political information, attentiveness, efficacy and so forth."[40]

Similarly, the discussion of generational patterns of participation has touched on the importance of civic attitudes. The historical and political experiences of generations are, in part, significant to the study of political involvement because of the values and attitudes formed as a result of these experiences. Successful democratic participation should reinforce participatory attitudes, while political experiences in autocratic systems should retard the formation of such values.

Because of the interrelatedness of these three factors—social sta-

Figure 2.4. Causal model of political involvement.

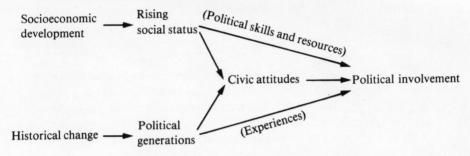

tus, generations, and civic attitudes—they should be examined as part of a common causal framework (figure 2.4). Social status and generation are social characteristics that capture the effect of long-term aggregate developments; hence, they are placed near the beginning of the causal chain. On the other hand, political efficacy partially intervenes between these social characteristics and participation.

One causal process begins with socioeconomic development acting as the agent of change, increasing the average social status of the population. The arrows in figure 2.4 indicate that this change in social status is *directly* related to political involvement because of the conceptual skills and information resources that social status represents—qualities useful in dealing with the complexities of politics. In addition, because social status is strongly related to feelings of political efficacy, it can also exert a significant *indirect* impact on political discussion through its influence on political efficacy.

A second causal process represents historical factors. The frequent change in German regimes since the turn of the century has resulted in the formation of distinct political generations. For each generation, its unique combination of experiences with democratic or autocratic authorities *directly* affects participation levels by accumulating personal experience in the role of participant or subject, by witnessing how political dissent is treated, or by similar learning. These life experiences also influence the formation of civic attitudes, and thus may have an additional *indirect* influence on political discussion through their effect on feelings of political efficacy.

The results of applying this hypothesized model to the data are presented in figure 2.5.[41] The values in the figure are standardized path coefficients, which measure the strength of each causal link.[42] As neither the 1961 nor the 1969 survey contains a measure of civic attitudes, these timepoints have been excluded from the analysis.

Figure 2.5. Causal analyses of political discussion, 1953–1972. Figure entries are partial standardized regression coefficients (betaweights).

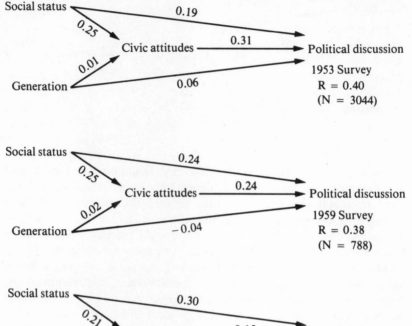

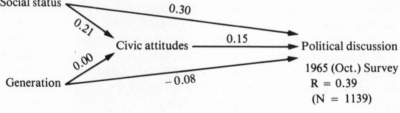

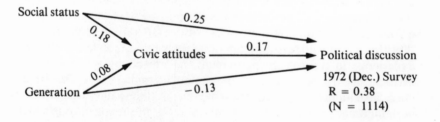

The pattern of the path coefficients generally resembles the simple relationships between political discussion and each predictor. Over time, social status has been generally increasing as a determinant of political discussion. However, it is now clear that it is the skills and resources component of this measure (direct link) that has been changing. This path increases from 0.19 in 1953 to 0.30 in the 1965 survey, and then dips slightly in 1972.[43] The indirect influence of social status through civic attitudes is substantial, but the causal importance of this indirect path has apparently been declining slightly over time.[44]

Even after controlling for the direct effects of social status and generation, civic attitudes remain a significant determinant of political involvement. Individuals who feel that they *can* influence the political process are more likely to participate. However, the independent impact of such attitudes has been decreasing over time. In the 1953 portion of the figure, the relationship between civic attitudes and political discussion is the strongest predictor, with a robust path coefficient of 0.31. By 1972, this path has declined to 0.17, well below the direct effect of social status. As the postwar regime has become accepted and legitimized, appropriate civic attitudes have gained wider support. Perhaps these attitudes now permeate the political culture to such an extent that they no longer differentiate political discussion. Another factor behind the declining importance of civic attitudes may be the increasing complexity of contemporary German politics. There is obviously a gap between feeling that one can influence the government and actually attempting to become involved. Even those who feel that they can affect political decision-making may now be more hesitant to invest the time and energy necessary to become politically active. This interpretation is especially convincing because the figure shows that the skills and resources that enable the individual to cope with the growing complexity of politics have been increasing in causal importance at the same time that the causal impact of civic attitudes has been decreasing. Whatever the interpretation, the gap between civic attitudes and actual behavior clearly widened between 1953 and 1972.

Finally, generational patterns present a surprising picture. The unique experiences of German generations and the impact these experiences are having on political involvement have been emphasized. Yet, after controls for social status have been added to the analysis, only weak differences remain in civic attitudes across generations. The path between generations and civic attitudes is always less than 0.10.[45] This means, for example, that members of the Wilhelmine or Third Reich cohorts are almost as likely as postwar Germans of the same social status to feel that they can influence politics. Only in 1972 are the young significantly more likely to feel efficacious. Thus, the significant independent generational differences in political efficacy presented in the last chapter appear to be a relatively recent phenomenon rather than an enduring trait of generational experience.

The absence of generational differences in political efficacy is all the more puzzling when these findings are juxtaposed with generational differences in actual political involvement. In 1953, after controlling for social-status differences and political norms, older voters are slightly more likely to discuss politics than are younger citizens. Apparently, the young reacted more strongly to the depoliticizing environment of the immediate postwar period. But as the new regime became accepted, the postwar cohorts became receptive to the new democratic politics of the Federal Republic. From 1959 on, the direct link between generation and political discussion increases in importance. In 1972, the direct path between generation and political discussion is a moderate -0.13. This again argues that generational differences in political discussion reflect the accumulation of learning through the life cycle (rather than the distinct experiences of early learning), because these relationships strengthen as the experience of participating in a democratic setting accumulates.

Conclusion

This chapter has documented the development of political involvement in postwar Germany. Political discussion has increased dramatically over the past several decades as well as political interest and other forms of conventional and unconventional political participation.[46] The stereotypic view of the German citizen as a detached and uninvolved "subject" no longer applies. Equally important are the determinants of increasing political involvement. Members of the postwar generation are more politicized than older cohorts—the reverse of the age pattern normally found in stable democratic systems. Feelings of political efficacy are also an important determinant of involvement, but this component is decreasing in importance.

Most interesting are the findings in regard to social status. In a complex and quickly changing society, possession of the skills and resources needed to grapple with the world of politics is a necessary prerequisite to involvement in politics. The volume of information made available by the mass media can seem like a cacophony to those lacking the conceptual abilities and the structure of a belief system to process this information.[47] Today's issues of debate often touch complex technical subjects, or at least are wrapped in technical jargon. Consequently, political involvement in contemporary Germany, as elsewhere, is more and more dependent on the skills and resources represented by higher social status—education in particular. Although participation levels are also increasing among lower-status groups, participation has grown more rapidly among higher-status individuals. The result has been an ever widening *participation gap* between social strata.

If political participation influences the outputs of a democratic system, as democratic theorists postulate, then this trend is not a welcome one.[48] Politics may leave behind some segments of society as debate moves on to new and complex topics. A widening participation gap may contribute to an even greater elite bias in representation. Yet the emergence of a participation gap is apparently not limited to the Federal Republic. Verba and Nie present similar evidence of increasing status differences in participation in American politics.[49] In other analyses, Max Kaase and Alan Marsh find a comparable phenomenon in other Western industrial societies.[50] DiPalma's review of the evidence similarly leads him to conclude that the nature of modern politics "requires participants to possess unprecedented expertise."[51]

A word of caution and optimism should be added. Over the past thirty years the Federal Republic has not only been developing a democracy but also reconstructing its economy and moving toward a postindustrial society. Alvin Toffler could not have found a more appropriate example of fast-paced social change that strains the social and political system.[52] The trends in political involvement are undoubtedly exaggerated by these dramatic changes in German society. Moreover, these sources of change may be receding. The war is now more than thirty years in the past, and over half the population has been raised under the regime of the Federal Republic. The Wirtschaftswunder has given way to steady, but less miraculous, economic growth rates. Therefore, the steep increase in the level of political discussion should begin to level off. Political participation may continue to grow, but not at the rate of past growth; and future growth is more likely to take place in forms other than political discussion.[53]

After the past decades of dramatic expansion in participation, the electorate and the political system may begin to adapt themselves to the new environment, and this will affect the sources of participation. Social-status differences in involvement may begin to narrow as actors in the political system make efforts to involve lower-status citizens and as these citizens accommodate themselves to the dramatic changes that have taken place. The process of population turnover can be expected to promote further increases in participation levels as older cohorts are gradually replaced by the more activist postwar generation. In time, the normal relationship between life cycle and participation should emerge within the postwar generation—that is, the youngest age group should be least interested in politics, and involvement should increase through the life cycle. This life-cycle pattern would tend to level off future growth in political participation.

3

Sources of Political Information

GERMAN ORIENTATIONS TOWARD POLITICS include not only the active forms of political involvement—political discussion and voting—but the more passive form of seeking out information on politics. As a result of the changes of the past few decades, the traditional description of the German citizen as inefficacious and non-participatory is no longer appropriate. But has change also occurred in that other aspect of contemporary political culture, the use of political information sources?

In contrast to its other more negative images, *The Civic Culture* described the German public as well informed about politics.[1] Germans were better able to identify party leaders and ministries than the other nationalities in the study, and they were more likely to follow politics than any citizenry except the Americans. Yet Almond and Verba criticized even these political orientations as reflecting a passive, "subject" orientation to politics. Germans, they argued, followed politics in the mass media, but they were reluctant to engage in interpersonal discussions of politics.

Passive information-seeking, which is exemplified by newspaper and magazine reading, provides the citizen with information about politics and exposes him to new political ideas and values. Indeed, in postwar Germany this has been an important part of the reeducation process. Yet, unless citizens are willing to actively discuss and examine new political ideas and values, the significance of political information is likely to be limited and the psychological commitment to new attitudes may be tenuous. If, on the other hand, political information is gained through an active process of information-seeking (such as through discussions of politics with others), the knowledge gained may have substantially greater meaning. It is a familiar experience to find that one does not understand an idea until one is able to explain it to others. Communication research has shown that the internalization of political ideas generally requires the reinforcement provided by interpersonal political discussions. And if individuals discuss political ideas with others, especially friends and people interested in politics, they are more likely to obtain the broad information base that is necessary for the collective decisions a democracy requires. Thus it can be argued that in a democratic political culture it is not sufficient merely to be informed about politics: the intake of information should occur, at least partially, through active information-seeking processes.[2]

In this chapter, changes in active and passive information-seeking that have occurred in postwar Germany will be examined. If it can be demonstrated that West Germans are increasingly seeking information about politics—especially in the active mode—additional evidence will be available to dispute the traditional characterization of Germans as quiescent citizens or "subjects."

Information Sources in the Federal Republic, 1961-1969

Mass communication research normally identifies two sources of political information: mass media and interpersonal interaction. The media, because they provide a good deal of news about public affairs and require limited individual effort, are generally assumed to be the principal sources of political information. Voting studies conducted in the United States and abroad over the past thirty years have repeatedly demonstrated that heavy media users have more extensive and accurate information about the personalities and issues in a political campaign than do light users.[3]

Some commentators, however, are not convinced that the mass media are as effective as agents of information transmission as has been assumed. John Robinson, for example, after detailing the limited knowledge many Americans have of the most rudimentary aspects of the political process, concludes that "researchers [have] compiled a dismal scorecard on the effectiveness of the media in conveying news information."[4] Moreover, P. J. Tichenor and his colleagues argue that the mass media may have increased rather than decreased the knowledge gap, a finding similar to the one mentioned earlier in connection with the effects of social status on German politicization.[5]

At the same time, those who are suspicious of the media's information-transmission abilities admit that their conclusions are based on data measuring only the public's "book" knowledge of politics. They concede that the media provide important information about public events and policy as well as information useful for solving the problems of everyday life.[6] Moveover, there is some evidence that media users pick up a good deal of information inadvertently; a substantial amount of incidental learning seems to occur as a consequence of media exposure.[7]

The other important source of political information is interpersonal interactions. According to Robinson, there is "ample evidence of interpersonal conversation being a more powerful transmission mechanism than the media."[8] Walter Weiss points out that well over half the respondents in various studies reported learning about Kennedy's assassination and Roosevelt's death through personal communication.[9] In a recent series of experimental studies, Steven Chaffee and his associates have found that while media may be important sources of information for news items, personal sources are important in relation to what are sometimes called consumer topics.[10] The reasons for the importance of interpersonal sources in information diffusion have been succinctly summarized by Maxwell McCombs: "Unlike mass communication, interpersonal communication enjoys a high level of feedback. Political messages flowing in interpersonal channels can quickly be adjusted to each recipient and often enjoy the bonus of group endorsement."[11]

The use of both interpersonal and media sources of political information in the Federal Republic fits the expectations of past research quite well. This is apparent from table 3.1, where the responses to the following question, asked in 1961, 1965, and 1969, are reported:

Table 3.1. Average use of six sources of information, 1961–1969.[a]

Source	July 1961	Oct. 1965	Sept. 1969	Per annum change, 1961–1969[b]
Interpersonal				
Friends	1.51	1.71	1.77	0.033
Family	1.45	1.48	1.73	.035
People interested in politics	1.49	1.59	1.63	.018
Media				
Radio	2.22	1.97	2.00	−.028
Television	1.68	2.15	2.65	.121
Newspapers	2.43	2.36	2.49	.008

a. Numerical entries are mean scores based on the following coding: (1) little or nothing, (2) something, (3) a lot, (4) very much.

b. Calculated by regressing the mean score at each timepoint on the year of the survey.

> I am now going to mention some ways in which one can obtain
> information about politics. How much would you say you per-
> sonally learn about politics from . . .[12]

Although all sources are used at each timepoint, the mass media
definitely predominate. For example, although almost 50 percent of the
respondents in the 1961 survey indicated that they used newspapers
"very much" or "a lot" to learn about politics, only 16 percent
obtained political information from their friends that frequently. The
difference in the use of these two sources narrows somewhat by 1969,
but it remains substantial.

Not only, however, have West Germans been making extensive use
of the mass media to obtain political information in the postwar period;
there has also been an important change in the most heavily used
medium.[13] More and more, Germans have come to rely on television.
In 1961 newspapers were the most important source of political information (mean usage = 2.43); their usage remained at a high level
through 1969 (mean usage = 2.49), but by that timepoint they had been
replaced by television as the principal source of political information.[14]
This tremendous growth in the use of television is not surprising in
view of the increasing number of German homes that have television
sets and the ease with which political information can be obtained from
that source. Between 1961 and 1970, the number of radios in Germany
increased from 15.9 million to 19.4 million, but the number of television
sets increased much faster, from 4.6 million to 15.9 million.[15] Moreover, by 1972, 96 percent of all German homes contained at least one
television set.[16]

Germans, then, make heavy use of the mass media to learn about
politics. They also use interpersonal sources, however, and the use of
these sources increased quite rapidly during the decade of the 1960s.
For example, although almost 65 percent indicated that they obtained
"little" or "no" information from their friends in 1961, only 43 percent
gave one of these answers in 1969; and the use of the other two
interpersonal sources increased significantly during that time period as
well.

This finding is important. The quiescent-citizen model of contemporary Germans is clearly no longer appropriate. The per-annum change
coefficients in the last column of table 3.1 indicate that the active mode
of interpersonal information-seeking has increased more rapidly than
the use of all the media sources except television. Moreover, interpersonal information-seeking is definitely not confined to the family, for
Germans are using such sources as friends, acquaintances, and political activists more and more each year.

But these data have implications beyond those related to the political image of contemporary West Germans. In particular, they have implications for the political socialization process in the Federal Republic. Studies have demonstrated that Germans apparently regard television news broadcasts as quite authoritative;[17] and other evidence suggests that the images presented on television can have a considerable impact on the reactions of individuals to such things as war, violence, and political candidates.[18] Hence, the increasing use of television as a source of political information may be quite important. A similar argument can be made about the increasing use of interpersonal sources. It can be hypothesized that people who rely on other individuals for political information get not only factual materials from such interaction but also reinforcement for the belief that political activity is expected, proper, and safe. And there seems little doubt that the development of such attitudes will be important in the future evolution of German democracy.

The separate impacts of these sources of information are likely to be enhanced, however, if the two basic types, media and interpersonal interactions, are used together. Weiss makes this point well when he suggests that the "linking of the media to personal channels multiplies considerably their potential significance."[19] Chaffee suggests the reasons for this increased significance when he notes that "we should expect a constant interplay between these kinds of sources, which could have mutually reinforcing functions."[20] The media, for example, provide information for interpersonal political discussions,[21] and interpersonal discussions provide the motivation to obtain political facts from the media. Perhaps more important, the impact of media messages is likely to be substantially greater if they are subsequently discussed in the interpersonal environment, for as a consequence of this interaction they may be internalized as operative norms and attitudes. Although an individual is unlikely to become active in politics as a consequence of media information about the nature of the political environment and the citizen's obligation, such behavior may be quite likely if the cognitive cues are discussed and reinforced in an interpersonal environment. Conversely, it is possible that political activity would be substantially lower if individuals sought political information only from their personal environment and ignored media messages about politics and about the obligations of citizenship. In short, the two sources can act in a reinforcing and complementary fashion, and individuals who use both sources are likely to differ politically from those who rely exclusively on one or the other.

To determine whether a pattern underlay the use of information sources, principal components analyses were conducted (table 3.2).

Table 3.2. Principal components analysis of sources of information, 1961–1969.

Source	July 1961 I	July 1961 II	Oct. 1965 I	Oct. 1965 II	Sept. 1969 I	Sept. 1969 II
Interpersonal						
Friends	0.71	−0.44	0.72	−0.40	0.72	−0.43
Family	.64	−.50	.55	−.39	.62	−.31
People interested in politics	.72	−.27	.71	−.37	.70	−.46
Media						
Radio	.64	.49	.57	.46	.58	.40
Television	.53	.40	.48	.33	.67	.46
Newspapers	.72	.43	.66	.52	.71	.40
Eigenvalue	2.64	1.11	2.30	1.04	2.67	1.02
Percent variance explained	44.0	18.5	38.3	17.3	44.6	17.0

These analyses clearly identified the same two basic dimensions at each timepoint. The second dimension distinguishes between information sources: at each timepoint, the media questions load at one end of the continuum, while the interpersonal sources load at the other end. But, from the first dimension, it is clear that all six sources are positively related; users of one information source are likely to consult other sources.

Hence, the use of media and of interpersonal sources of political information does not appear to be mutually exclusive in the German context. Given the socialization implications of an interaction between the use of the two types of sources, this is an important finding. In addition, the principal components analysis confirms and expands on the patterns already observed. Television, for example, had become the dominant component of the media dimension by 1969, echoing the movement away from radio as the prime electronic source of political information. And just as the character of the media dimension changed between 1961 and 1969, so did the interpersonal dimension. In 1961, family and friends were the principal components of this dimension, but by 1969 the family had been displaced by other people interested in politics.

Thus, a gradual transformation in the personal sources from which Germans obtain information about politics seems to have occurred. Instead of being confined to family and friends, information-seeking increasingly involves friends and political activists. Since politics is, by definition, likely to be salient for "people interested in politics," this change in interpersonal information-seeking habits suggests that Germans are more and more exposed to diverse political views, often strongly held.[22] In short, the kind of information-seeking model postulated for a democratic society at the beginning of the chapter seems to be emerging in the Federal Republic.

But to what extent does information-seeking vary with background? This is an important question, since it has already been shown that individuals with better educations, higher incomes, and new middle-class occupations are most likely to exhibit attitudes and behaviors compatible with a democratic political system.

Patterns of information-seeking are often assumed to vary with social status. For example, higher-status individuals—whether measured by income, occupation, or education—are more likely to have the funds necessary to buy television sets and subscribe to newspapers and magazines. More important, such individuals are likely to be expected to be informed about politics; to have the cognitive abilities, motivation, and leisure time to listen to political broadcasts and read political commentaries; and to move in social circles in which politics is a frequent topic of discussion.[23]

In the German context, generational differences may also be important in understanding patterns of information seeking. Since members of the postwar generations have not had the kinds of negative experiences with interpersonal interaction outside the family that some members of earlier generations have had, they should be less reluctant to talk to others in order to find out about politics. In addition, because of the greater mobility of postwar Germans, the traditional notion that social interaction should be confined to the family and a very few close friends has declined in the postwar period. And because of the absence of long-term accumulated experiences, it is likely that this erosion has been greater among the young than among the old. In contrast, generational differences in the use of media sources may be much smaller because of the increasing availability and accessibility of printed and electronic media.

The data in table 3.3 show that the use of both sources of political information is related to social status. Moreover, the relationship is quite uniform: at each timepoint, higher-status individuals are more frequent users of both types of information sources. To be more specific, while the average media-use score was 2.08 for the workers in 1961, it was 2.32 for the new middle class; for those with only a *Volksschule* education, the mean was 1.91 at this timepoint, while for those with an *Abitur* education or better, it was 2.40. Moreover, the differences between the groups are generally increasing. In 1961, the eta coefficient summarizing the relationship between education and the use of interpersonal sources of information was 0.19; by 1969, it had increased to 0.29. As in the case of political involvement, therefore,

Table 3.3. Sources of information and background characteristics, 1961–1969.[a]

Source	July 1961	Oct. 1965	Sept. 1969
Interpersonal[b]			
Occupation	0.12	0.14	0.18
Education	.19	.23	.29
Generation	.13	.15	.18
Media[b]			
Occupation	.17	.16	.19
Education	.22	.23	.25
Generation	.12	.06	.09

a. Numerical entries are eta coefficients.

b. For this analysis, the interpersonal and media sources were combined into simple additive indexes.

there is evidence of a widening gap in the use of information sources on the part of individuals representing different segments of the stratification system.

A similar interpretation seems appropriate with reference to the relationship between generation and the use of interpersonal sources of information. Here, too, the eta coefficients indicate increasing differentiation among the groups across time. Moreover, the principal users of these sources in 1965 and 1969 are the members of the postwar generations. With reference to media, however, the differences between the generations have declined since 1961. As already indicated, this is probably a reflection of the increasing accessibility of various media to all segments of the German population.

In sum, precisely the same socioeconomic and demographic groups that were found to be most likely to exhibit attitudes compatible with a democratic political system are the ones that most actively seek political information from multiple media and interpersonal sources. Again, therefore, there is evidence that the development of some democratic norms and behaviors is facilitated by certain kinds of environmental influences. At the same time, however, there is evidence that the participation gap discussed with some concern in chapter 2 applies to information-seeking as well as political discussion.

The Consequences of Information-Seeking: Politicization

It was stated at the beginning of this chapter that if information-seeking in the Federal Republic included extensive use of nonfamily interpersonal sources and the mass media, we would have additional evidence of the growth of attitudes and behaviors compatible with the operation of a democratic political system. Such sources have in fact become increasingly important in the political information-seeking process in the past decade or so, and therefore the information-seeking habits of postwar Germans, like their political efficacy and involvement, do suggest the growth of a political culture congruent with the existing political structure. But beyond that general conclusion, what have been the consequences of these patterns of information-seeking for political involvement?

It has long been argued that individuals who are knowledgeable about politics are more likely to participate than those who are not.[24] Presumably, such individuals have a better appreciation of the stakes in an election campaign and are therefore likely to engage in various forms of political participation, including voting, talking to others about politics, and working for a candidate. Studies have repeatedly demonstrated that frequent use of information sources is associated with greater knowledge about politics. In West Germany, too, that has been the case. In 1969, for example, heavy users of both types of sources were substantially more likely to know both the function and number of the votes an individual casts in national elections. But can it also be said that heavy users of information sources are more involved in politics?

To test this hypothesis we examined the relationship between the use of information sources and political discussion. The relevant zero-order correlations are presented in table 3.4 along with the regression coefficients. Since both kinds of sources are rather strongly related to political involvement at each timepoint, there is little doubt that heavy users of information sources are more involved in politics than light users.

Table 3.4. Sources of information and political discussion, 1961–1969.[a]

	July 1961		Oct. 1965		Sept. 1969	
Source	r	b	r	b	r	b
Interpersonal[b]	0.52	0.50	0.49	0.40	0.50	0.40
Media[b]	.35	.15	.36	.17	.41	.22
Multiple R		.57		.53		.54

a. Cell entries are Pearson correlation coefficients (r) or unstandardized regression coefficients (b).

b. For this analysis, the interpersonal and media sources were combined into simple additive indexes.

What is interesting about these data, however, is the growth in the impact of media on politicization between 1961 and 1969 (0.35 to 0.41). Since the simple correlation between television and politicization increases from 0.20 to 0.38 during the timeperiod, this is probably a reflection of the infusion of television into German politics. To further examine this hypothesis multiple regression analyses of the relationship between media use and political discussion were conducted for each timepoint. The results indicate that while the regression coefficient for television increased monotonically from 0.02 to 0.13 during this timeperiod, the corresponding coefficient for radio remained essentially unchanged and the coefficient for newspapers increased only slightly.

To those who emphasize the importance of television in contemporary politics, these findings would not be surprising. Through television, one can presumably experience the excitement and controversy of politics directly. One can know what is happening in government and politics immediately and make judgments about personalities and issues on the basis of one's own observations rather than someone else's interpretation. Although the "reality" of television is undoubtedly somewhat biased, the visual images it provides probably can promote the kinds of conditions that lead to political involvement.[25]

Yet, the regression analysis in table 3.4 reveals something else about the relationship between sources of information and political discussion: the impact of interpersonal sources on political involvement is significantly greater than the impact of media sources. At each timepoint, interpersonal sources are better predictors than media sources by a substantial margin. This finding tends to confirm a hypothesis mentioned earlier, namely, that individuals who use interpersonal sources probably obtain not only political information from such interaction but also reinforcement for the notion that political involvement is expected, proper, and safe. The present data indicate that greater use of interpersonal sources is indeed related to involvement in politics. A positive relationship, of course, also exists between use of media sources and politicization, but it is not nearly so strong, probably because of the absence of reinforcement mechanisms in media usage. Hence, although the infusion of television into politics has undoubtedly had some impact on the political involvement of German citizens, it is clear from these data that it is not a substitute for personal interaction in the growth of politicization.

It could be argued, of course, that these are spurious findings. In other words, since the measure of politicization used in this analysis taps essentially *interpersonal* politicization, one would expect a stronger relationship between interpersonal sources and politicization than between the media and political activity. At least at one timepoint, 1969, this objection can be tested empirically because the election study for that year contained a second measure of politicization, interest in politics.[26] The multiple correlation coefficient for the relationship between interpersonal sources and political interest at this timepoint is 0.76; for media, it is 0.41. In other words, use of interpersonal sources is a substantially better predictor of political interest than media use. Hence, the conclusion that the use of interpersonal sources to learn about politics has a greater impact on the development of political involvement in Germany than the use of media sources is not entirely dependent on the variables used in the analysis.

Conclusion

The data reported in this chapter indicate that all sources of information except radio are increasingly utilized to learn about politics in the Federal Republic. In addition, the interpersonal information-seeking environment increasingly consists of friends and political activists, and the use of the two basic types of sources is not mutually exclusive. This latter finding has important implications for the socialization process in the Federal Republic. Finally, the same population subgroups that are most likely to be efficacious and involved in politics are generally the ones most likely to make the greatest use of all information sources.

In one sense, the analysis in this chapter confirms and expands the conclusions about German democracy reached earlier. Yet it has also shown that the level of information and the nature by which it is received have important consequences for political behavior. Although its emergence in the postwar period has been consequential, television is not a substitute for interpersonal interaction in the development of political attitudes. Interpersonal sources of political information seem to be more important for the development of democratic political involvement than mass media.

Part One of this book has examined the West German political culture. Our own analyses and those of others have shown that support for the institutions of the contemporary regime has grown substantially in the postwar period. Indeed, in 1972, only about 5 percent of the population voiced any serious dissatisfaction with German democracy. More important, perhaps, system support seems to be increasingly of the diffuse rather than the specific variety. No longer do Germans support the current system exclusively because of the economic gratification it provides.

Support for the norms of the current regime also seems to have increased significantly in the postwar period. Feelings of political efficacy were almost as common in Germany in 1972 as they were in the United States, and active and passive involvement in the political process has increased substantially since 1949. It seems fair to conclude, therefore, that the traditional characterization of the average German citizen as quiescent and uninvolved is no longer appropriate.

In addition to documenting the growth of the German political culture in the postwar period, Part One has explored the dynamics and sources of this growth. The expansion of education, the growth of the new middle class of salaried white-collar workers and officials, and the unprecedented economic growth of the postwar period have been critically important in the development of active and passive political involvement and political efficacy. In each instance, the educated members of the new middle class have seemed to exhibit the attitudes most compatible with a democratic political system. The importance of generational change to the general transformation of the German political culture in the postwar period has also been emphasized. Because of the absence of long-term accumulated experience with autocratic regimes, young Germans have apparently inculcated the norms and values of a democratic society more effectively than older Germans. Finally, the impact of performance on the postwar transformation of the German political culture has been evaluated, and the complex interactions between background characteristics, political norms, and information-seeking in the development of political involvement have been explored.

All of the evidence suggests that a viable democratic political culture has developed in the Federal Republic during the postwar period. Because diffuse support for the system and its norms is quite pervasive, it is increasingly inappropriate to argue that the German political culture is incongruent with the existing political structure. This, of course, does not mean that the current system is impenetrable and that it could not collapse if subjected to substantial pressure. It does mean that the present system rests on a stronger foundation than its predecessors did and that it will more strongly resist any threat to its existence. The nature of the causal forces uncovered by this analysis make this generalization particularly sound. Population replacement will mean that more and more of the participants in the political process in the future will be educated members of the new middle class socialized almost exclusively in the postwar period. Although such individuals are less likely to challenge the basic legitimacy of the system, they are likely to demand that it live up to its ideals. Consequently, it is probable that the substance of German politics will be quite different in the future.

Part Two

The Changing Political Agenda

4

Politics and the Economic Environment

THE NEW POLITICAL CONDITIONS introduced by the restoration of democratic government in the Federal Republic in 1949 have brought about long-term changes in German views and approaches to politics, particularly with respect to the individual's role in political life. Sustained increases have occurred in politicization, feelings of political efficacy, and support for the postwar political system; and the nature of the electorate has changed dramatically.

Part Two of this book turns to other factors that have exerted a different but perhaps no less fundamental impact upon politics and individual political attitudes. By altering the environment in which politics occurs, these ongoing trends have changed the perceptions of both the elite and the mass concerning the most desirable domestic and foreign policies.

The first chapter in this sequence focuses on the domestic arena, specifically on the political effects of the Economic Miracle (*Wirtschaftswunder*) and the widespread and unprecedented affluence it has created. The second deals with the evolution of German foreign policy and the change from Cold War and confrontation to détente, cooperation, and *Ostpolitik*. The final chapter of Part Two suggests a common way of looking at all of these changes and attempts to derive some expectations about future developments in German politics.

Economics and Politics

That economics influences politics is a major tenet of political lore, ranging all the way from the iron-clad economic determinism of Marxist thought to the widely held belief that a government's popularity and electoral fortunes are closely tied to the performance of the economy.

73

Elites attempt to manipulate the economy or the election timing so that elections occur when unemployment or inflation rates are low. Consumers, workers, or employers who are satisfied with their economic situation are expected to support the government. Conversely, disappointed economic expectations, poverty, or scarcity of work or resources may be expected to erode the public's trust in the present incumbents or even the system of government, and these conditions could eventually lead to active opposition to the system.

Germany's history dramatically exemplifies the connection between economics and politics. The political instability of the Weimar Republic resulted partially from the weaknesses of its economic system. For example, Weimar's general economic recovery after World War I lagged several years behind that of other European countries and the United States; inflation was rampant in the 1920s, with prices increasing at the phenomenal rate of over 26 billion percent between January and November 1923.[1] And the final collapse of the Republic has been linked to the severe effects on Germany of the Great Depression of the early 1930s. Conversely, the initial popular approval of the Nazi regime was due to its success, albeit by questionable means, in dealing with economic catastrophe.[2]

Increasing affluence in the postwar period has contributed to the growth of political involvement. In addition, prosperity has probably lessened economic dissatisfaction and produced support for those political forces that are credited with the improvements in economic conditions. Both the electoral victories of the CDU/CSU and the initial stability and success of the Federal Republic itself have been attributed to the Economic Miracle.[3]

The content of a country's political agenda, too, reflects the nature of its economic environment. At the height of a depression, the call for more jobs tends to dominate political discussions. In more prosperous times price stability may become a major concern for the middle class, while the labor unions demand higher wages or increased participation in industrial decisions.

Finally, long periods of continued economic expansion and well-being may result in weakening the causal relationship between economics and politics. In most Western democracies economic divisions underlie long-term party alignments. Rich and poor, professionals and workers, the industrial sector and the agricultural sector tend to vote differently. The prosperity and economic security of the Wirtschaftswunder may have weakened this basic relationship between economic factors and political cleavages. Future relapses into economic crises will surely resurrect bread-and-butter demands for jobs, unemployment benefits, and price stability. Such demands may, however, have a weaker impact upon political behavior if they come after prolonged periods of prosperity.

The Economic Miracle

Germany presented a gloomy picture in 1945. The Allies occupied and ruled the entire German territory, and the economy had ground to a halt. Much of the country's productive capacity either had been destroyed, was idle, or was being dismantled by the victors. Estimates suggest that industrial production in 1946 was nearly 67 percent below the 1936 level, and that national income reached only 40 percent of its prewar level. The transportation system had broken down: railways and waterways had been blocked by Allied bombs or by the retreating German troops. Almost 50 percent of prewar housing units had been destroyed or damaged, and the number of homeless was swelled by the several million refugees and expellees from the eastern territories. Agricultural production, especially in the more industrialized western occupation zones, could not feed this large population. It is estimated that even with the help of American food donations the average daily food intake over the years 1945 to 1947 was only 1300 calories per person. Not until December 1947 did the American military command conclude that the German people had sufficient food.[4]

If the present looked bleak in 1945, Germany's economic future did not look much brighter. The Allies' initial postwar construction plan, the Morgenthau Plan, envisioned turning Germany—highly industrialized and technologically advanced (though then partially destroyed)—into an almost entirely agrarian society. Germany was to be denied the means of waging another war.[5] Although this plan was not fully carried out, its rationale guided Allied (especially American) occupation policy for some time. It justified the dismantling of industrial plants in Germany and their reassembly in Allied countries, as well as the destruction of German industrial capacity. The harshest provisions of the Allied plans were soon softened, but German economic recovery proceeded only gradually. From its 1946 level of 33 percent of prewar output, industrial production grew to only 47 percent of the prewar level by 1948, fully three years after the end of the war.[6]

Even while the restrictive policies were still in effect, the emerging cold war between the former Allies altered the Western design for Germany's future. Germany was to be included in the program of American aid to Europe—the Marshall Plan, or European Recovery Program. At the same time, the day-to-day administration of German affairs, including economic policy, was put increasingly into German hands. Following the early establishment of local and regional

(*Länder*) governmental units, the British and American occupation areas were combined to form the *Bizone* in 1946. In 1947 the French Zone was added, and the first German national administrative unit, called the Economic Council, was established in Frankfurt. It included many of the future leaders of the Federal Republic and developed some of the eventual party coalitions of the Bundestag. In the economic realm, the Economic Council took the early decisions that led Germany toward rapid recovery.

However, the Germans were no more united in deciding just how to engineer recovery than the Allies had been about German reconstruction. On one side of the debate stood those who wanted to harness economic power groups because they remembered the role that many large industrialists and landowners had played in Hitler's rise to power. The Social Democratic Party had, of course, always advocated public ownership of key industries, especially those controlled by monopolies. Beginning in 1946, the SPD's programs called for large-scale nationalization and for politically controlled economic planning by workers and consumers.[7] In areas where the SPD controlled political power, it attempted to realize these aims. For example, the Hessian state constitution provided for the possibility of nationalization, and in North Rhine–Westphalia nationalization legislation was actually enacted. Both provisions were struck down, however, at the insistence of the American High Command.

On the other side of this debate stood large parts of the CDU/CSU and the Free Democrats. Initially, some forces in the CDU/CSU wanted to bridge Christian and Socialist values. Thus, the first national CDU party program concluded that the "capitalist economic order had failed in Germany" and called for limited nationalization.[8] But other ideological elements quickly gained control of the party, advocating a more moderate stance toward the capitalist system. Under the directorship of Ludwig Erhard, CDU/CSU and FDP members of the Economic Council advocated policies leading to a "Social Market Economy" (*Soziale Marktwirtschaft*). Following "neo-liberal" economic theories, this economic model was based on a free enterprise system that left as much room as possible for competition and private initiative. The role of the state was limited to stabilizing the economy as a whole, to ensuring competitive markets, and, if necessary, to providing for those too weak or too handicapped to succeed in the open market. To achieve the Social Market Economy, first priorities were to be given to the establishment of a sound currency as the base of the free market and to the loosening or abolition of such postwar constraints as rationing, price and wage controls, and high rates of taxation.

The Currency Reform of June 1948 was the first step in defining the future course of the economy, and along with the American Marshall Plan aid it is usually credited with stimulating the Economic Miracle.[9] By establishing a new currency, abolishing many of the price controls, and later lifting the wage restraints, Erhard restored public trust in the *Deutsche Mark* (DM). Entrepreneurial initiative was encouraged through tax and other incentives that freed the available skills and resources. Display windows were filled almost overnight. The economy quickly began to grow within a basically capitalistic framework. Using official figures, Werner Kaltefleiter has reported that "from July to December, 1948, the industrial production index climbed at *monthly rates* which later were achieved only in full years."[10] Although unemployment and inflation rose to higher levels in the next two years, the Economic Council and later the federal government with its minister of economics, Ludwig Erhard, were steadfast in their support of the free market principle. By 1950, helped along by the worldwide Korean War boom, the German Economic Miracle was well under way.[11]

The Result of the Economic Miracle: Affluence

In order to document the Economic Miracle's effect on the affluence of German society we have assembled several different economic indicators. Gross National Product (GNP) is probably the most basic of these, measuring the total annual value of all goods and services produced by the society. The growth of GNP was quite rapid and almost uninterrupted from 1947 to 1972. GNP increased by 67 percent between 1947 and 1952, and by 1950 its value of 143.6 billion DM reached the prewar level of 1936 (figure 4.1).[12] In the 1950s the average annual growth rate of 6.2 percent lay considerably above those of most other Western industrial nations (figure 4.2). In the 1960s the growth rate slowed, largely because of the slight recession of 1966–1968. But this slowdown was only temporary, and the overall growth rate for the sixties averaged 4.0 percent—still high by Western standards. By 1972 the total GNP reached 564 billion DM (figure 4.1). Thus, from its initially weak position the Federal Republic has developed into one of the strongest economies in the world.[13]

Similarly, per capita Gross National Product has also registered impressive and almost constant gains during the postwar period (figure 4.3). In constant 1962 prices, average wealth per capita has nearly tripled from 3061 DM in 1950 to 9146 DM in 1972. Initially, in 1950, per capita GNP in the United States was over twice as high as in West Germany (2.13:1); by 1972 the German economic output per capita had almost closed the gap (1.17:1). In Europe only Sweden and Switzerland

Figure 4.1. German GNP, 1950–1972. Source: Statistisches Bundesamt, *Bevöl-kerung und Wirtschaft, 1872–1972.*

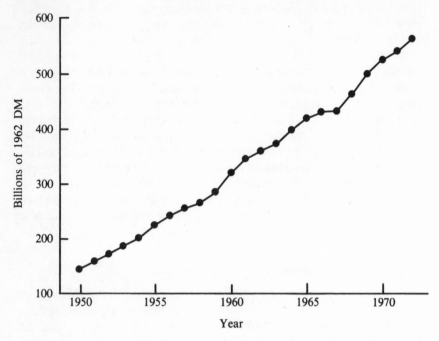

have maintained higher GNP per capita rates than the Federal Republic.[14]

The aggregate economic recovery expressed in GNP translates into immense increases in the standard of living enjoyed by large portions of the German population. Incomes have risen continually and dramatically. Gross hourly wages for industrial workers increased almost 500 percent between 1950 and 1972. If the net monthly incomes of all employed persons are considered, economic growth has boosted wages and salaries from almost 250 DM (about US $60) to almost 1400 DM (over US $400) during the same time span. Even adjusting for inflation, wages in 1972 were still about three and a half times as high as 1950 wages.[15]

Of course, a large portion of the increased incomes was spent on consumer goods, especially in the 1950s. Observers at the time talked about "consumption sprees" of food, clothing, and travel as the Germans released pent-up material demands. Goods that once had been luxuries for the upper social strata became widely affordable. In 1955, only 5 percent of working-class households owned a refrigerator, but in

Figure 4.2. GNP growth rates, 1950–1972. Source: Statistisches Bundesamt, *Bevölkerung und Wirtschaft, 1872–1972.*

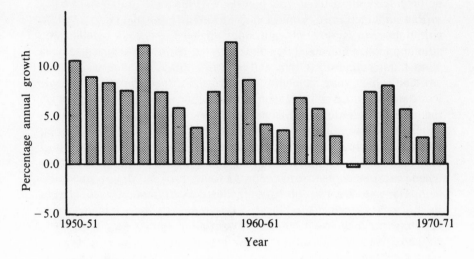

Figure 4.3. GNP per capita, 1950–1972. Source: Statistisches Bundesamt, *Bevölkerung und Wirtschaft, 1872–1972.*

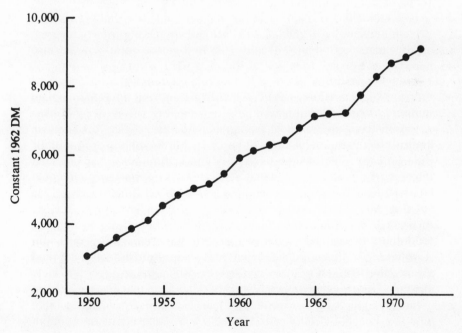

1972 virtually all of them did.[16] Television ownership has become almost universal, with 96 percent of working-class homes owning a set in 1972, compared to just 50 percent in 1964. But perhaps the most visible and important symbol of widespread affluence has been the automobile. In 1950 there were only 500,000 passenger cars for about 50 million West Germans. By 1972, the number of cars had increased almost thirty times, to 14.8 million. In addition, car ownership has become widespread, almost without regard to social class: in 1964 less than one-third of working-class households owned a car; by 1972 the proportion had more than doubled, although it was still lower than for middle-class households. Similar trends exist for other consumer goods; the gap between workers and the middle class has narrowed as many of the former luxury goods, though not all of them, have become widely affordable.[17]

As Germans have become able to afford more consumer goods, they have also had more leisure time to enjoy them. The average work week for industrial laborers, for example, shrank from 48.6 hours in 1955 to 42.8 hours in 1972. In addition, most labor contracts now provide for at least three and often four weeks of paid vacation a year, and even working-class families have the time and resources to spend weekends and vacations away from home.[18] Thus, although work obviously remains a central life concern, it fills less of the German's day both in terms of hours spent on the job and as a focus of attention.[19]

Although the Economic Miracle is most evident in the affluence of private consumption, advances in the infrastructure are also impressive. The first task after the war was to repair war damages, but efforts soon went beyond that. An early priority was the construction of housing. Through tax incentives to builders, sizable direct state investments, and state-supported saving, the number of housing units—10.3 million in 1950—had increased 60 percent by 1960; and by 1970 it had grown by 100 percent to 20.8 million units.[20] At the same time, rent controls on government-subsidized housing kept rents affordable, especially for those who had lost their possessions during the war or in the flight from the East. In the sixties, with the immediate housing shortage resolved, new construction upgraded the quality of available housing. Moreover, and partly to keep pace with the rise in private car ownership, the government embarked upon a large-scale program of road construction and improvements. Most dramatically, the web of *Autobahnen* ("freeways") doubled in size between 1950 and 1972. And the rail and communication systems, both state-run industries, were expanded and modernized.[21]

Increasingly, however, observers have described Germany, in Galbraith's terms, as a modern society where "private affluence" coexists with "public poverty." Although the level of education has increased in the postwar era, the gains have been small compared with those in other West European countries. Similarly, the availability of public health insurance cannot compensate for the shortcomings of the German medical system.[22] Yet even such criticisms may well document the success of the economic miracle: they bewail shortcomings that can draw attention only after the more immediate economic-subsistence problems have been solved.

The empirical evidence suggests that not all groups have profited equally from the Economic Miracle. Determining how severe the economic inequality is, and whether equality has improved or deteriorated under the Economic Miracle, depends on what statistical definitions and economic measures are employed. As an example, German income distribution, as summarized by GINI Indexes, has remained in the 1970s (as it was in the 1950s) one of the less equitable in Western Europe.[23] At the same time, income differences have narrowed slightly over this timespan, whereas the trend in many other Western industrial countries has been in the opposite direction.[24] Yet income inequality during this period translates into even sharper inequalities of wealth, savings, or property. For instance, while working-class households increased their net worth by an average of 1,600 DM between 1950 and 1959, white-collar employee and civil servant households gained 6,000 DM and the self-employed gained about 13,000 DM. And the ownership of productive capacities—that is, machines, plants, land, or stocks—was even more skewed.[25]

The Social Democrats pointed to such figures, especially in the 1950s, as the inevitable results of a capitalist society.[26] The CDU/CSU and FDP, on the other hand, sought to broaden and reinforce popular attachments to the Social Market Economy, especially among blue-collar and lower white-collar workers, by encouraging them to accumulate property. Tax incentives for saving and for the construction or acquisition of single-family housing were enacted for this purpose early in the 1950s. Later, several government-owned companies, among them Volkswagen, were "reprivatized" when low-income earners were allowed to buy stock in them at very advantageous prices.

Apparently such measures have been ineffective in offsetting the inequalities in wealth. However, another (perhaps the main) objective of these measures, namely, to increase support for the economic system, has clearly been achieved. Yet it is questionable whether the almost unanimous acceptance of the Social Market Economy and its free enterprise principles is due primarily to the accumulation of property by the lower classes. More likely, this acceptance has resulted from the rising standard of living brought about by the expanding size of the pie rather than by its distribution.

In any case, the widespread support for the existing economic system eventually persuaded the SPD to give up its principled opposition to the modified free enterprise system that had evolved in Germany. The SPD's stand through the 1950s had provided the CDU/CSU with campaign ammunition, without offering equivalent gains for the SPD among any but a few die-hard Marxist followers. Thus, when the SPD revised its party program in 1959 at the Bad Godesberg conference, it embraced the principles that had led to the Wirtschaftswunder and sharply reduced the traditional calls for economic planning: "As much freedom [of individual economic decision-making] as possible, as much planning as necessary."[27] With this conversion of the SPD, virtually all elements of the political elite as well as the mass public agreed on the basic form of the economy.[28]

The picture painted so far shows increasing collective and individual prosperity, even if that prosperity has not been uniformly distributed. Generous supplies of consumer and even luxury goods have become available, and less working time has been necessary to obtain them. With these quantitative gains have come qualitative changes that are likely to be as important socially and politically as the arrival of affluence. One change has involved a restructuring of the economy and of the labor force. Especially in the 1950s, the number of people employed in the agricultural sector declined rapidly; conversely, employment in industry and in the tertiary sector (the service industries and trade) increased (table 4.1).[29] The shrinking role of agricultural production has meant that over the past three decades two out of three persons employed in the primary sector have left farm work. In contrast,

Table 4.1. Percentage of labor force employed in three economic sectors, 1950, 1960, 1972.[a]

Sector	1950	1960	1972
Agricultural (primary)	22.2%	13.3%	8.2%
Industrial (secondary)	44.7	48.4	48.6
Service and trade (tertiary)	33.1	38.3	43.2
Total	100.0	100.0	100.0

Sources: For 1950 and 1960, Statistisches Bundesamt. *Bevölkerung und Wirtschaft 1872–1972;* for 1972, Statistisches Bundesamt, *Statistisches Jahrbuch, 1973.*
a. Excluding the state sector.

employment in the industrial sector has remained fairly stable (between 44.7 percent in 1950 and 48.6 percent in 1972), and the proportion of the labor force in the service sector has grown sharply from 31.1 percent in 1950 to 43.2 percent in 1972. As the vestiges of agricultural society have faded and the service sector has expanded, Germany has come to the threshold of a postindustrial society.

Just as the changing sizes of the economic sectors may indicate progress toward a postindustrial state, so too may the distribution of occupation types. The traditional European middle class or "old" middle class comprises farmers and the self-employed. When agriculture and the entrepreneurial sector decline, so should the size of the groups working in these areas. On the other hand, white-collar employees (primarily in state employment, the service sector, and large corporations) constitute a "new" middle class. These groups of civil servants (*Beamte*) and nonmanual salaried employees (*Angestellte*) are a major component of a postindustrial society. As figure 4.4 indicates, the new middle class almost doubled in size between 1950 and 1972. The expansion of this class occurred chiefly at the expense of the old middle class (self-employed) and the farmers, but even working-class occupations declined slightly from 51.0 to 46.2 percent during this period. These social-structural changes, and in particular the rise of the new middle class, are an exceedingly important aspect of the relationship between economics and politics.

First, discussions of post-industrial societies focus particularly upon this group. The new middle class embodies the skills and resources of the new society and appears most likely to gain power in it.[30] This group is relatively well educated, and it has more leisure time and, because its expansion is recent, is younger than other population groups. Thus the members of this stratum are open to the new economic ideas and values that may accompany the postindustrial revolution.[31]

Second, a unique combination of the type of work done by the new middle class and the nature of its relationship to its employer sets this class apart from the two traditional social classes, the bourgeoisie and the proletariat. New-middle-class members are employees, just like the working class; yet they do white-collar work in professional and managerial positions, like the entrepreneurs and self-employed professionals of the old middle class. In addition, upwardly mobile offspring of the working class have moved primarily into new-middle-class jobs, rather than into the old middle class.[32] Because of this unclear or dual status, the standing of the new middle class in the traditional, economically based, political-cleavage system is ambiguous. It is symptomatic that the longest debate in the struggle for a new codetermination law

Figure 4.4. Distribution of occupation types, 1950–1972. Sources: For 1950 and 1960, Statistisches Bundesamt, *Bevölkerung und Wirtschaft, 1872–1972;* for 1970, Statistisches Bundesamt, *Statistisches Jahrbuch, 1973.*

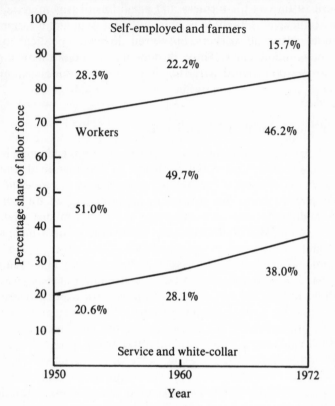

(*Mitbestimmungsgesetz*) in the early seventies occurred over the question of whether the votes of high managerial employees of business enterprises should be counted among the workers and other employees or among the owners. The social cues for the proper electoral choices of the new middle class are similarly nebulous or contradictory. The new middle class has in fact shifted its political position in the electoral arena and thus has been crucial in facilitating changes in the party system and in the very nature of German politics.

Third, the members of the new middle class enjoy a high degree of economic security, deriving from their occupational positions as white-collar employees and particularly as civil servants. Although this is obviously true of German civil servants with their strong tenure rights, it is almost equally true of the salaried employees of large enterprises. During economic crises blue-collar workers tend to be the first to lose their jobs. Similarly, economic crises and structural changes can present serious threats for farmers and small businessmen. As a result, economic survival is likely to remain in the foreground for farmers, the old middle class, and workers, but to recede behind political concerns for the new middle class. Thus, throughout this book the new middle class will be considered a leading force in the process of political change.

Fruits of the Economic Miracle: Security

Although Germans may be experiencing an unprecedented level of affluence, a second independent theme to consider in defining the economic environment is the stability and security of economic gains. Basic economic concerns are not necessarily allayed by increasing affluence: the more one owns the more one stands to lose. Therefore, the effect of the Wirtschaftswunder on economic security must also be examined.

Several factors contribute to the economic security of a country and its people. For example, the changing distribution of jobs away from agriculture toward the tertiary sector increases the job security of the population. The basic conditions for actual and perceived security, however, are generally considered to be full employment and price stability. Traditional economic theory often holds these two goals to be mutually exclusive, with one being achievable only at the expense of the other.[33] The German recovery appears miraculous in this respect as well. The population shifts during the war, the low level of industrial production, and particularly the vast influx of refugees from East Germany and Eastern Europe after the war resulted in a large pool of unemployed or underemployed Germans. But the remarkable economic growth of the 1950s created an ever increasing number of jobs. The expansion of the economy cut unemployment almost in half between 1950 and 1955, from 11 percent to 5.6 percent.[34] It has been argued that the relatively rapid integration of all parts of the population, including potentially discontented and restless groups like the refugees, was a crucial factor in integrating them politically into the new system. This is borne out by ecological analyses suggesting that the Bund der Heimatvertriebenen und Entrechteten (BHE; "Federation of Expellees and Dispossessed Persons") attracted greatest support in areas where unemployment was highest among the refugees.[35]

By the fourth Bundestagswahl ("federal election") in 1961, the unemployment rate had dropped below 1 percent, where it remained throughout the 1960s except for the 1966–67 recession period. Even during 1967, the worst year, there were fewer than 500,000 unemployed (2.1 percent). Unfilled jobs outnumbered the job-seekers by ratios of up to five to one, and these figures still underestimate how far the need of the continuously expanding economy exceeded the available work force. Not only were refugees absorbed and women increasingly mobilized into the work force, but after 1960 more and more *Gastarbeiter* ("guest workers") had to be recruited, until by 1972 over 2.3 million (or almost 11 percent of the work force) were foreign workers.

The guest workers freed the Germans from doing many of the least desirable menial or hard manual jobs; at the same time they provided a safety valve that could protect the German work force from the effects of business cycles and the instability of a free market economy. For example, in both the 1966–67 recession and the post-1972 slump foreign workers were laid off first; as the unemployment rate climbed, the number of *Gastarbeiter* fell.[36] The consequences for the laid-off foreign workers as well as for their home economies were undoubtedly traumatic; but for German workers this meant that jobs were more secure. The cushion of guest workers also helped keep the West German unemployment rate considerably below that of other industrialized countries in the wake of the oil crisis.

For much of the postwar era, therefore, unemployment was not a threat to the Germans' economic security. Even during the economic recessions the proportion of job-seekers remained below the normal rates of other industrial nations.[37] Unemployment may have been a latent though rarely a crucial or pressing concern for the German public and German politicians. The threat of inflation was a more constant worry. The currency reform of 1948 ended several years of perpetual currency uncertainty. In the following three years, the suddenly released demand for all types of goods drove prices up; but when the first run of catch-up consumption had abated, governmental policies encouraging saving, capital accumulation, and high rates of reinvestment began to take hold. Although the inflation rate was still 7 percent in 1951, it was never more than 3 percent a year in the following decade. The average inflation rate of 1.25 percent between 1952 and 1960 was much lower than that of other Western industrial nations during the same period. And even though the rate more than doubled to 2.7 percent for the 1960s, German prices remained comparatively stable.

By international standards, then, West Germany appeared to have tamed the twin threats of unemployment and inflation. This feat is the more remarkable because both Keynesian economic theory and the experience of most industrial nations suggest that price stability can only be achieved at the cost of high unemployment, and full employment only at the expense of steeply rising prices. Economists plot this inverse relationship by means of the Phillips curve, and its logic (that governments through economic policy can strive to maximize either full employment or price stability) seems to be intuitive to party strategists as well as ordinary voters.[38] Generally, conservative parties, which often cater to middle-class voters, seek above all to avoid inflation; in contrast, leftist parties, supported by the working class, stress the need for job security over price stability.[39] Yet, the long period during which the Christian Democrats appeared to have a virtual monopoly on governmental power was characterized not by high unemployment but by both low inflation and low unemployment.

The levels of unemployment and inflation for each of the twenty-one years between 1951 and 1972 are shown in figure 4.5. Except for 1951, perhaps the last of the early postwar years, the points coincide quite well with the expectations of a Phillips curve. Even under the conditions of the rest of the 1950s (low unemployment *and* low inflation) a trade-off between unemployment and inflation generally existed. The German data thus fit the international pattern, although the absolute levels of both unemployment and inflation are lower than in nearly all of the other advanced industrialized nations.[40] Assuming that a country's Phillips curve describes the acceptable levels of inflation and unemployment, West German elites faced a more restrictive range of policy options than other countries. Because of historical experience Germans will not tolerate either unemployment or inflation. And even if the CDU/CSU governments could not take full credit for the "low" Phillips curve, their successful avoidance of the twin economic evils surely contributed to the electorate's continued support of the party that brought "Peace, Freedom, Affluence" (the CDU's campaign slogan in 1965).

In fact, the simultaneous achievement of security from the threats of inflation and unemployment during the 1950s resulted as much from the rapid pace of economic recovery as from conscious governmental policies. Until the mid-1960s, the CDU-led governments were very conservative (or "noninterventionist") in their economic policies. They kept government spending below tax incomes during the fat years and saved the resulting surplus to balance the budget during the intermittent lean years. Such cautious fiscal policies were well suited to curb inflation, but they would not stimulate the economy sufficiently to avoid layoffs in times of recession. Happily for the CDU/CSU and the German economy, until 1965, economic "hard times" manifested themselves merely in slowdowns of economic growth, which still fell

Figure 4.5. Inflation and unemployment (Phillips curve), 1951–1972. Source: Statistisches Bundesamt, *Bevölkerung und Wirtschaft, 1872–1972.*

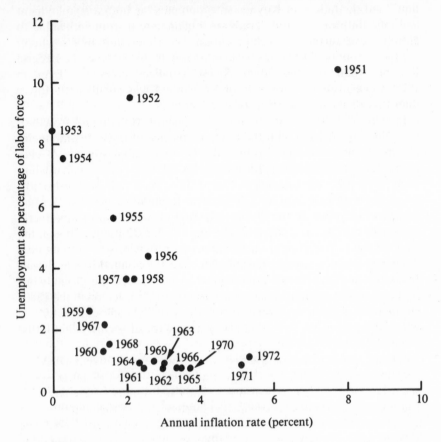

no lower than 3.5 percent per annum (see figure 4.2). The general expansion of the West German economy continued unabated and kept employment high.

Unemployment and especially inflation have climbed somewhat since 1965 (figure 4.5). The Grand Coalition government of the CDU/CSU and the SPD overcame the recession of 1966–67, but this success was only temporary. For a short period from 1968 to 1970 the SPD and later the SPD/FDP coalition basked in the effective policies of Economics Minister Karl Schiller, who had stimulated the economy through government spending.[41] At the same time he managed to restrain labor and business from making inflationary demands on the reviving economy by bringing them together in a "Concerted Action," essentially a voluntary wage-and-price-control council. But the Federal Republic soon was caught up in the global developments that brought "stagflation" and the failure of Keynesian economics, as both unemployment and inflation rates soared. Traditional economic instruments failed to entirely reverse these developments in West Germany as elsewhere; yet the economic difficulties were relatively less serious in the Federal Republic than in other advanced industrialized countries. Even in 1972, Germany's inflation rate of 5.5 percent was significantly lower than that of most other European economies.

In spite of these recent setbacks, the general strength and growth of the economy coupled with the relative absence of inflation and unemployment have combined to give the German public a sense of economic security. Moreover, for those who still face economic hardship, such as the old, the unemployed, and the sick, a tight-webbed net of social security is available. The Federal Republic is the first German regime to incorporate the characterization of *Sozialstaat* (imperfectly translated as "social welfare state") into its constitution, although the idea that the state should make extensive provisions to help its economically weaker citizens far antedates the Economic Miracle. It was Bismarck, a conservative politician, who introduced the groundwork of the present German social security network.[42] Ever since the 1880s Germany has been an exception to the usually clear-cut picture in which conservatives fight every advance in social security that leftist forces attempt to secure.

Indeed, government and opposition, the conservative CDU/CSU and the socialist SPD, have competed in extending the net of social security. At first the needs of war victims and refugees were stressed. But as the economy picked up, the parties turned their attention to more general provisions. Continuous public concern over old age security led to the extension of the old-age pension system to middle-level salaried employees, farmers, craftsmen, and other self-employed. By the mid-1960s, 94 percent of all working Germans were entitled to old age pensions and were insured against injury and death; and 90 percent were part of the public health insurance.[43] In addition, in 1957 pensions were tied to the income levels of the active work force, so that benefits for the elderly could be better protected against inflation. Not surprisingly, such a large commitment to social welfare has resulted in a relatively high tax ratio. In 1971 the German tax effort (taxes compared to GNP) was almost 34.5: about the same as in France and Great Britain, and almost exactly halfway between the considerably higher efforts of the Scandinavian countries or the Low Countries and the much lower level of taxation in the United States.[44]

In sum, the magnitude and speed of the Economic Miracle have had important effects in those areas where economics is linked to politics. In the postwar period Germany has been blessed with the rare combination of high employment and low inflation. In addition, the already well-developed system of social security has been extended and improved. Thus, the sources of economic worries have diminished, even if they have not completely disappeared.

Perceptions of Affluence

Economic factors do not lead directly to political consequences; they need to be perceived as politically relevant and subject to political decisions before they can have an impact upon the actions of political elites or the mass public. For example, the German recovery was termed miraculous because the effects of World War II receded so quickly. But "objective" realities are not always instantly perceived by the public. As late as 1952 an absolute majority of Germans still felt that they were worse off than before the war (figure 4.6), even though

Figure 4.6. Comparisons of prewar and postwar living standards, 1950–1964. Source: Kaltefleiter, *Wirtschaft,* table V.

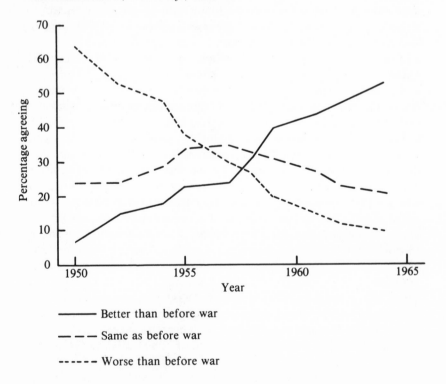

GNP per capita had exceeded prewar levels in 1951. Not until 1958 did a plurality feel better off than during the 1930s, and only in 1964 did an absolute majority share that feeling.

The considerable lag in acknowledging the Federal Republic's economic achievements may have been due to several factors: the long-term effects of the war, the immediate postwar confusion, high unemployment and inflation rates persisting into the early fifties, or perhaps a basic attitude of pessimism, springing from German history in the twentieth century.[45] In his sweeping work on the relation between politics and economics in Germany, Werner Kaltefleiter suggests that the speed of the recovery raised expectations faster than even an Economic Miracle could fulfill them.[46] Another interpretation is that it is difficult to make objective comparisons between the present situation and one that prevailed twenty or more years earlier, especially when young people have not directly experienced that earlier period. Indeed, when the point of comparison is shifted to a more precise and uniform referent, namely, the immediately preceding year, then the rapid success of the Economic Miracle is reflected in public perceptions (figure 4.7). In 1951, the still unsettled economic and political climate was mirrored in the view of 56 percent of the population, who thought that the economic situation had deteriorated during the past year. As the economic policies of the German government and the worldwide economic stimulus of the Korean War resulted in dramatic gains in production and equivalent drops in unemployment, the proportion of "pessimists" plummeted to 19 percent (1953). Since then, reports of negative economic change have hovered at or below that level, but the economic recovery has not greatly increased the proportion of Germans who feel that the economic situation has continued to improve. Instead, an increasingly large group of Germans perceive a stable economic situation.

This apparent stability in perceptions reflects the economic success in a more subtle way. During the 1950s, many Germans expected and demanded economic growth and improvements. When asked in 1957 whether they would be content if their situation remained unchanged over the next five or ten years, roughly equal groups responded positively and negatively. After seven more years of increasing affluence and well-being, over two-thirds expressed satisfaction with no further personal economic advances, while only about one-quarter were dissatisfied.[47] Theoretically, one could argue that the Germans curtailed their expectations to fit reality. In view of the impressive economic gains, however, it seems much more plausible that the prosperous reality had caught up with more slowly rising expectations, at least for two-thirds of the population.[48]

These developments can be summarized in dramatic fashion by

Figure 4.7. Short-term comparisons of economic well-being, 1951–1972. Source: Kmieciak, *Wertwandel,* table VI-3.

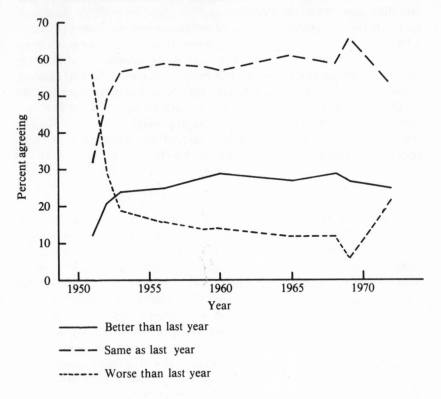

——— Better than last year

— — — Same as last year

------- Worse than last year

Table 4.2. Perceptions of Germany's best period, 1951–1970.[a]

Period	1951	1959	1963	1970
The present	2%	42%	62%	81%
World War II	—	—	1	—
1933–1939 (Third Reich)	42	18	10	5
1919–1933 (Weimar Republic)	7	4	5	2
Before 1914 (Wilhelmine Reich)	45	28	16	5

Source: Elisabeth Noelle and Erich Peter Neumann, eds., *Jahrbuch der Öffentlichen Meinung 1968–1973* (Allensbach: Verlag für Demoskopie, 1973).

a. Responses to the question, "When were things best for Germany during this century?" The percentages do not total 100 because "Don't know" responses are not shown.

analyzing the responses to a question asking "when things were best for Germany" (table 4.2). (It should be kept in mind, of course, that considerations other than economics influence the public's choice of such a period.) In October 1951, only 2 percent chose "the present," while nearly 90 percent placed Germany's golden years either before World War I or between 1933 and 1939. In contrast, by 1970 an overwhelming 81 percent preferred present conditions in the Federal Republic, and only 12 percent longed for any period in the past. It took some time for the changed realities of a recovered Germany and of the Economic Miracle to be perceived by the public, but these figures suggest that Germans are at last aware of and satisfied with their economic conditions, and with life in general.[49]

Effects of the Economic Miracle: The Political Agenda

How have the dramatic economic changes of the last three decades affected politics in the Federal Republic? Germans, not unexpectedly, have felt the effects of the Economic Miracle and have become quite satisfied with their situations; furthermore, this satisfaction, spilling over into noneconomic realms, has speeded up the initial acceptance of the new political regime of the Federal Republic. In addition, prosperity should have changed the public perception of what politics is all about. To the extent that politics deals with the issues people face individually or collectively, changing objective conditions should leave their imprint upon the political agenda. Naturally, many issues have vied for public attention: domestic and international problems, economic and nonmaterial issues. Only issues from the domestic realm will be considered at this point.[50]

Since 1951, the Allensbach Institute has regularly asked Germans, "Which, in your opinion, is the most important question we in West Germany should occupy ourselves with at present?" The responses give a good indication of the urgency accorded to economic questions by the German mass public. The proportions of respondents that listed economic problems as the most pressing ones between 1951 and 1976 are plotted in figure 4.8.[51]

Economic issues were of outstanding importance in the very early fifties, when nearly half the respondents spontaneously named such concerns. As recovery took hold, the urgency of economics dropped to about one-third of the 1951 level toward the end of the decade. Until the mid-sixties this level fluctuated between 14 and 27 percent, with, on average, just over 20 percent of the Germans worrying most about prices, wages, currency problems, or pensions. For much of this time no other domestic issues were mentioned often enough to warrant

Figure 4.8. Urgency of economic concerns, 1951–1972. Source: Elisabeth Noelle and Erich Peter Neumann, eds., *Jahrbücher der öffentlichen Meinung* (Allensbach: Institut für Demoskopie, 1951–1974).

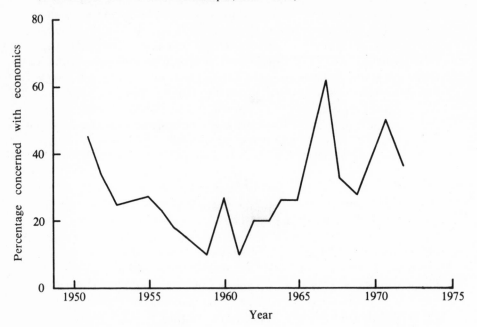

inclusion as separate coding categories by the polling agency.[52] During the sixties public attention began to shift to noneconomic issues such as education, pollution, social tasks, crime control, or domestic reforms. Even then, however, other issues rarely reached the level of economic concerns; obviously, general social issues seldom have the immediacy of threatened jobs or steeply rising grocery bills.

This immediacy was shown in the rapidity with which economic concerns became the most important problem during economic downturns, and then in their equally rapid decline as soon as the economy recovered. Thus, during the recession of 1966–67, economic concerns more than doubled from 27 to 62 percent; but they plummeted again to 30 percent, less than two years later. The largest components of the category "economic problems" were unemployment and inflation worries, both of which were extraordinarily sensitive to economic fluctuations, showing jumps of 20 to 30 percent in a single year.[53]

The responses to the Allensbach surveys are reactions to short-term forces rather than long-term trends. This is not surprising. Contemporary events, including the ups and downs of short- and medium-term

business cycles, are dramatic and attract public attention, while gradual trends, such as the long-term growth of postwar prosperity, take
place almost unnoticed.

Affluence and Partisan Evaluations

Public perceptions of the most important problems aid in defining the
political agenda. For example, if the majority of the public responds to
a sharp rise in the jobless rate with concern about reducing unemployment, politicians and parties will have to pay more attention to this
issue.

But this does not mean that a majority of Germans base their individual political decisions mainly on economic motivations. Considerations other than the public's perception of the country's "most important problem at this time" influence actual political behavior. In democratic political systems, perhaps the most important form of political
behavior is the electoral choice between competing political parties.
For that reason, empirical research on the nexus between economics
and politics has focused on voting and elections.

An important question in this area deals with the extent to which
political cleavages are based on economically defined social groups.
Class voting is one of the relatively stable aspects of political behavior
because the consequences of economic growth, industrialization, and
prosperity are reflected only gradually in the changing class composition of society or in increased social mobility. Such changes are usually
glacierlike: under normal conditions motion is barely perceptible over
short timespans, and it is not easily halted or reversed.

In contrast, the ups and downs of economic cycles, good times and
bad times, alternate quite rapidly. If voters "vote their pocketbooks"
by rewarding governments for a boom or turning them out if inflation or
unemployment soars, then the political effects of such economic forces
should quickly be felt. It is these short-term economic effects that are
of interest here.

Almost all survey-based studies agree that a relationship exists between perceptions of economic conditions and voting behavior: economic optimists are more likely to support the incumbent party, while
pessimists desire change and vote for the opposition. These correlations, however, cannot be taken as evidence of the economic determination of political behavior. More detailed analyses suggest that the
actual causal relationship is not a one-way street. Of course, some
voters do support the incumbent party because they are satisfied with
the government's economic record or expect the government to do
well in the future. But for others the causal flow runs in the opposite

direction, and long-term partisan predispositions color perceptions of the economy. These voters are optimistic about the economy when their party is in office and pessimistic when their party is in opposition.[54]

The most dramatic evidence of the partisan nature of economic attitudes comes from polls conducted during the 1965–1969 period. Before 1966, SPD voters were much more pessimistic about the economy than Christian Democrats, but with the SPD's entry into the Grand Coalition, these differences all but disappeared until 1969. As a result of the election the SPD gained the chancellor's office, and the CDU/CSU had to exchange their cabinet seats for the opposition benches. In a strikingly parallel movement, Christian Democratic voters changed their optimistic views of the economy and began to see the situation in a much more pessimistic light than did SPD supporters. These changes were far greater than can be explained by the slight shift in partisan strengths. Rather, SPD voters apparently saw a brighter economic future under their own party's leadership, while CDU supporters lost confidence with their party's fall from power.[55] Perceptions of the economy changed in response to altered political constellations, not political allegiances in response to economic events. Moreover, this pattern has been found in survey data from several other national settings.[56]

Yet, the debate over the primacy of partisan or economic factors should probably not be couched in either-or terms; instead it should be seen as a question of degree. Under what conditions are economic perceptions the more powerful force? Conversely, when will partisan affiliations prevail?

Dieter Roth finds that among the minority of citizens who are directly affected by economic hardships (for example, the unemployed) economic considerations play a dominant, independent role in deciding the vote.[57] In contrast, economic conditions do not merit so much attention among the better-off majority, who are not so directly affected. The economic views of these individuals echo their partisan orientations and thus cannot be said to independently affect their political choices. Roth (for 1972 and 1976), and Helmut Jung and Hartmut Garding (using data from 1971 through 1976) all present evidence that party affiliations have a far larger effect than economic conditions in contemporary Germany.[58] Jung estimates that economic motivations for vote switching can be ruled out for 80 percent of the electorate; this group either changed votes for demonstrably noneconomic reasons or did not change political positions at all. Thus an economic model remains possible for only 20 percent of the electorate at most. Using different approaches, Roth arrives at very similar findings for the 1972 and 1976 elections. His early analyses argue that the logical prerequisites of rational economic voting—realistic perceptions of economic conditions, clear evaluations of the parties' economic positions, or at least their economic competence, and the belief that politics affects individual economic well-being—are evident in the responses of very few voters. Like Jung and Garding, Roth concludes that economic perceptions appear to be prestructured more often by political factors, such as long-standing party affiliations.

These results suggest that national economic conditions have fewer direct consequences for politics than is often assumed, albeit no less important ones. Recessions may stimulate opposition to incumbent governments as many people are directly touched by the loss of a job or of income or by high inflation rates. In contrast, protracted "good times," instead of translating into government support, may merely reduce the amount of criticism based on economic criteria.[59] Then voters may evaluate the government on other, noneconomic grounds that do not guarantee positive judgments. Even if achieved, economic success may not buy support for the incumbents.[60] These conclusions stand in dramatic contrast to the expectations, common in the fifties and early sixties, that modern governments could sustain strong popular support by applying the logic and instruments of Keynesian economics to steer their societies safely between the twin dangers of inflation and unemployment.[61]

The series of surveys upon which this book is largely based might appear to constitute an ideal setting for analyzing economic effects over time, but a closer look reveals that not many questions were asked in the same form at multiple timepoints, and thus comparisons are questionable. However, these data do confirm the discovery of Angus Campbell and his colleagues that there are at least two distinct dimensions of economic evaluation: the personal and the national.[62] While perceptions of personal fortunes are closely related to demographic variables (income, occupation, education) and only loosely connected with partisan political attitudes, the reverse is true for perceptions of national economic conditions.[63] It is important, too, to distinguish among evaluations of past, present, and future economic conditions. When all these factors are considered, the surveys yield few indicators with enough timepoints to justify a display of trends for individual items.[64]

None of the individual trends, if taken alone, appears very convincing; however, when they are viewed together, a general pattern can be detected. For voters who report stable voting preferences in successive elections, the relationship between economic evaluations and party preference becomes stronger in the later surveys, while for the much smaller group of voters who report switching parties the correlation between economics and partisanship becomes weaker over time.

In order to solve this puzzle, it should be recalled that as affluence spreads and economic worries subside, a growing number of voters apparently base their economic evaluations on partisan attitudes. Therefore, the increasing association between party choice and economic evaluations among stable voters is probably due to the fact that partisan attitudes determine economic perceptions. Such a conclusion is reinforced by the finding that among voters who switch parties between elections the relationship between economics and voting is declining. The members of that group are more likely to base their political choices on economic conditions, and yet in their case the association between the (new) party choice and economic perceptions declines over time. These results suggest that economics has receded as a factor for changing political allegiances among this group as well.

This survey evidence is merely suggestive; a more precise determination of the linkage between party support and economics requires the development of a dynamic model that goes beyond static survey data. In the absence of good panel studies this is only possible through the use of macro-level timeseries data. The macro approach does not predict individual party preferences but attempts to explain trends and variations in partisan support from such economic-performance data as inflation or unemployment rates, changes in national income, and perceptions of economic conditions.

At first glance, the findings of macro-level studies appear to flatly contradict the results based on survey data. For example, in his path-breaking study of U.S. congressional elections, G. H. Kramer maintains that voting shifts are at least partially decided by the ups and downs of the economy and by what voters expect of the future.[65] Similarly, several European researchers have attempted to relate trends in party support to various economic indicators. Although the precise form of the economic relationship is the subject of much debate, most of these researchers agree that economics has a significant impact on the popularity of governments or parties.[66]

The most impressive evidence of the economics-politics link comes from studies of Great Britain and Germany. David Butler and Donald Stokes for Great Britain and Gebhard Kirchgässner for the Federal Republic convincingly show that monthly party (or government) popularity series can be quite successfully predicted from perceptions of economic conditions.[67] Butler and Stokes' economic measure is the public's perception of the parties' economic competence, while Kirchgässner uses evaluations of the general economic situation. These analyses confirm at least one survey finding, that the national economic situation is much more relevant for political behavior than is an individual's own financial condition.

At the same time, Butler and Stokes as well as Kirchgässner directly face the contention of survey researchers that economic perceptions are little more than reflections of the public's partisan predispositions. Kirchgässner rejects this argument after explicitly testing it with alternative formulations of his model in which he reverses the temporal sequence of the competing concepts of partisanship and economic perceptions. Similarly, Butler and Stokes argue that if party bias were responsible for the parallel movement of voting intentions and approval of the parties' handling of the economy, the same pattern should be evident with respect to the parties' handling of other issues, such as foreign policy and housing. But they find very little agreement between voting choices and any issue other than economics.

Thus, there are apparently sharp contradictions between the conclusions gained from survey research and timeseries analyses. Survey researchers—like Garding, Jung, and Roth—reach negative conclusions about the effect of economics upon German partisan preferences in the seventies, while Kirchgässner, a timeseries analyst, arrives at the opposite result for the same time period.

It appears, however, that these contradictory findings are largely an artifact of methodology and not a real contradiction. Survey researchers are primarily concerned with the behavior of the total electorate. Their micro-level studies indicate that most voters either have stable partisan preferences or change their preferences for noneconomic reasons. Hence, economics can explain at best the behavior of only a small part of the electorate, those who actually change their vote. In contrast, a timeseries analyst like Kirchgässner focuses only on the behavior of this small group, because *changes* in economic indicators are correlated with changes in voting (or polling) results.[68] Since these vote changers determine the results, timeseries analysts are bound to find a clear link between economics and politics. Survey researchers, too, find that economic factors have a significant, though perhaps a declining, impact among this same minority of switchers. Hence, both survey researchers and timeseries analysts agree that economic forces and perceptions can have a strong enough impact to change the political decisions of concerned minorities in the population. And if these minorities are large and pivotal enough, economics may well determine the outcome of elections.

This discussion of economics and partisanship has clarified the nature of the linkage between the two areas, but the primary research

question still remains: has the Economic Miracle loosened the traditionally strong ties between economics and voting in Germany since
World War II? Although none of the studies just discussed deals with
the possibility of long-term change in this relationship,[69] their findings
imply that the impact of economics should have declined since the
immediate postwar years. To examine the linkage between party support and economics requires the specification of time periods and
independent and dependent variables.

First, the postwar era can be divided into four politically defined
time segments. The earliest one begins in 1951, after the immediate
effects of the war had been overcome, and covers the remainder of the
decade. It was a time of rapid economic growth for which an economic
explanation of German politics is generally used. This first period ends
with the programmatic SPD party congress at Bad Godesberg, which
marked the party's decision to accept the principles of the free market
economy upon which the Economic Miracle was founded. In order to
allow a few months for the Bad Godesberg program to "take effect,"
January 1960 was chosen as the start of the second period.[70] From that
point on, all major political parties accepted the economic system in
principle, and debate centered on the fine points rather than on the
basic direction of economic policy. This timespan ends with the beginning of the Grand Coalition, which coincided with the recession of
1966–67. The third period covers the tenure of the Grand Coalition,
including the recession and recovery. And finally, the fourth period
begins with the replacement of the Grand Coalition by the Brandt-
Scheel government after the election of 1969. (Although this is secondary to the analysis here, it will be useful to see whether the partisan
repolarization after the Grand Coalition can be detected in these data.)

Second, the model must specify the influence of economics upon
politics. A complete model would include perceptions of economic
conditions; but since perceptual data are not available for most of the
postwar years, economic predictors should be selected that are known
to be salient to the mass public. Inflation and unemployment, perhaps
the most crucial economic features to Germans, certainly belong at the
head of the list.[71] Other public demands include economic growth and
increasing real income, but these measures indicate "good times,"
while prior research suggests that "bad times" tend to stimulate stronger popular reactions. The sudden steep rises of concern with unemployment seem to indicate that the loss of or lack of a job may be the
most traumatic economic condition. Therefore, the level of joblessness
should be a good indicator of deep economic worries. However, when
the number of jobless drops sufficiently, unemployment may become

primarily an individualized (and thus a psychological) hardship, rather than a group (and thus a social and often political) problem. As a result, changes in the level of unemployment may become the more potent economic influence when there is almost full employment, as was the case during the 1960s. Similarly, it is not the absolute level of prices, but the rate of price increases (inflation) that affects people's sense of economic security. Thus the simple model used here contains only these "bad times" indicators: the rate of price increases, the rate of change in unemployment, and the level of unemployment.

Finally, the dependent variables are the percentages favoring CDU/CSU and SPD as measured in surveys conducted by the Allensbach Institute.[72] CDU and SPD popularity are analyzed separately in order to distinguish between incumbent and opposition effects. These relationships are estimated with G. E. P. Box and G. M. Jenkins' ARIMA timeseries model, which represents an advance over many previous timeseries analyses because the unique statistical problems of timeseries data are taken into account in the estimation procedures.[73]

The economic correlates of both CDU/CSU and SPD support are presented in table 4.3. These analyses provide dramatic evidence that the importance of economic factors has declined over time in response to the Wirtschaftswunder. In the 1950s over three-quarters of the variance in CDU/CSU support could be explained by the three economic indicators ($R^2 = 0.76$). In part, this confirms impressionistic evidence that the CDU/CSU's early electoral successes were closely tied to the Economic Miracle. From 1960 on, however, economic factors produced only a minor impact on evaluations of the incumbent party, even during the 1966–67 recession. The R^2 for the CDU/CSU reached only 0.18 in the 1960–1966 period, and dropped further to 0.14 during the Grand Coalition. Following the *Machtwechsel* ("change in power") in 1969, support for the newly incumbent SPD can be predicted by the economic variables at the same level ($R^2 = 0.15$).

Clearly, therefore, economic conditions now exert relatively little influence on party preferences. The review of earlier research suggests that this result is due to decreases in the number of voters who are intensely concerned with economic conditions. By focusing on marginal party change, the timeseries approach maximizes the apparent effect of economic factors; the actual impact of economics on the partisan attitudes of the total electorate is even weaker than table 4.3 implies.

Beyond the incumbent trend, the separate timeseries for the CDU/CSU and the SPD provide further insights into the workings of German politics. The CDU/CSU series, taken alone, shows nothing but support

Table 4.3. Impact of economic factors on party popularity, 1950–1972.[a]

Period	Constant	Percent unemployed	Change in unemployment	Rate of inflation (t−4)	R^2	DW	Rho
Predicting levels of CDU/CSU popularity							
1950–1959 (N = 111)	55.33[b]	−0.99[b]	0.68	−0.77[b]	0.76[c]	2.14	0.81
1960–1966 (N = 82)	46.86[b]	−1.43	−1.73[d]	.21	.18[c]	1.96	.28
1967–1969 (N = 35)	40.2[b]	.82	−.15	.34	.14[c]	1.99	.13
1970–1972 (N = 39)	44.84[b]	−.86	−1.12	.48	.07	1.74	.51
Predicting levels of SPD popularity							
1950–1959	40.0[b]	−0.28[d]	−1.53[d]	0.29	0.23	2.05	0.52, 0.29
1960–1966	45.55[b]	.34	2.77[b]	−.11[b]	.32	2.06	.58
1967–1969	46.3[b]	−.83	1.26[d]	.40	.36[c]	1.95	.42
1970–1972	51.15[b]	−1.91	4.05	−1.63	.15[c]	1.83	.42

a. For technical details, see note 73 to this chapter.
b. Significant t-values at $p < 0.01$.
c. Party in government.
d. Significant t-values at $p < 0.05$.

for our expectation of declining economic influences as the Multiple R^2 declines monotonically over time. And while the party's opposition role may help explain its low R^2 after 1969, its attacks on the Brandt/Scheel government for fiscal irresponsibility and economic incompetence surprisingly did not increase the saliency of economic factors in the public's evaluations of either party.

Support for the SPD, on the other hand, displays less of a longitudinal decline. Apparently in the earlier periods the opposition role of the SPD steadily attracted economically dissatisfied voters to the party, though never with the force of the CDU/CSU's appeal in the fifties. When the SPD assumed government control in 1969, its support did not become more dependent on economic conditions, although it might have been expected that the public would tie its evaluations of the party to the government's economic performance.

Additional insights into these different CDU/CSU and SPD trends can be gained by scrutinizing the separate coefficients of the three economic indicators. It is noteworthy, for example, that the unemployment level is an important variable only during the 1950s, and for both parties. Above all, this reflects the increasing support for both of the large parties as a result of the dramatic economic improvements of the early fifties, even if the CDU profited more strongly.

Since the 1960s, the *level* of unemployment has been exceedingly low in Germany. Yet, unemployment has remained a politically relevant variable, as the significant coefficients for the *change* in unemployment rates attest. But rather than reflecting actual individual suffering (a minor factor, because unemployment fluctuated around 1 percent), changes in the level of unemployment may signal economic conditions to the electorate as a whole. Moreover, since the fifties, rising unemployment has helped the SPD (both in opposition and in power), while higher inflation rates have usually hurt the party. In contrast, high inflation has led to gains for the CDU, while growing unemployment has lowered its popularity, again regardless of government or opposition status. However, few of the CDU's coefficients after 1960 are statistically significant.

These results should strengthen confidence in the analyses, since they fit the general interpretations of German politics rather well. For example, unemployment often hits hardest among the unskilled and skilled workers, who are likely to seek more favorable policies from the SPD (not from the CDU). Conversely, those who suffer relatively more from inflation (the middle class) have traditionally turned conservative in times of economic distress. If they had considered supporting the Social Democrats for noneconomic reasons, sharply rising prices would have turned them back once again to the CDU.

Conclusion

This chapter has presented extensive and varied evidence that objective economic and material conditions have improved at dramatic rates and to unprecedented levels as Germans have transformed their country in an Economic Miracle from the ravaged battleground of World War II to one of the most prosperous and economically most powerful nations in the world. Economic problems and worries, which had plagued Germans for so long and which had influenced politics to such an extent, have objectively receded. But would German perceptions and attitudes follow, and economic concerns and calculations lose their predominance in the public's views on social and political matters? The evidence suggests that the Wirtschaftswunder has indeed freed Germans from the economic stranglehold so that attentions could be turned toward new social and political tasks and goals.

At the same time, long-term economic changes have altered the structure of society, reducing the role of some groups and elevating the importance of others. The affected groups have different political characteristics, which gives political significance to the process of change. The most dramatic event has been the rise of the new middle class. To this group economics should be less crucial, not only in the sense of class struggle but also with respect to financial and security concerns.

Expectations that the overall effect of economics on German politics should have diminished as a consequence of all these changes have been tested in several different respects. The analyses have covered: perceptions of well-being and of economic improvement; the role of economic concerns on the public agenda; and, more directly, the impact of economic perceptions on voting choices and of economic conditions on partisan popularity. Even if none of these analyses has been fully convincing by itself, the variety of the evidence has strengthened the conclusion that traditional economic factors have indeed weakened their hold over politics in Germany since 1945.

5

Politics and the International Environment

IN MOST NATIONS foreign policy is remote to the citizenry, something that neither touches their lives nor interests them. In West Germany, however, because of its defeat in World War II and its location, geographically and symbolically, at the border between East and West, the nature of the international environment has been considerably more salient. During the Cold War the Federal Republic, especially Berlin, often found itself serving as the pressure point testing the resolve and might of the superpowers. Therefore, in defining the environment in which Germans work, live, and form their political attitudes, just as much importance must be attached to international affairs as has been given to economics in the domestic arena.

Foreign policy is an integral aspect of the changing German political system with which this book is concerned. Germany's postwar foreign policies and commitment to European integration and international cooperation have brought it a new international stature among its Western allies. In addition, the Federal Republic has progressed from a position of constant and intense conflict with the nations of Eastern Europe to a position of cooperation and conciliation with them.

This change, however, did not occur by chance. Throughout the postwar period, German elites have been keenly aware of the Federal Republic's vulnerable position between the superpowers, and different policies have been advocated and pursued by the two major parties to maximize Germany's security. Indeed, debates over foreign policy have been an integral part of the partisan conflict of the postwar period. Similarly, German elites have carefully monitored the changing relations between the East and the West as well as the changing values and attitudes of the German population, and they have adjusted existing policies and initiated new ones to accord with the times.

This chapter reviews the elite and mass behavior that has led to Germany's present relations with the East and the West. The emphasis is on the Federal Republic's relations with Eastern Europe, in part because these relations have experienced dramatic highs and lows in the postwar period, but more importantly because the changes in these relations, which must be regarded as one of the most significant achievements of the postwar period, have had important consequences for both the German population and the general international environment.

West Germany and the Eastern Bloc: An Overview

Determining the state of relations between nations is neither an easy nor a straightforward task because the public pronouncements of foreign policy elites may sometimes obscure the real state of governmental relations. Not all or even the most significant, decisions made in the inner sanctum of the Chancery or behind Kremlin walls become public knowledge, but the results of these decisions usually do. Moreover, in explaining the public's perceptions of foreign policy, several commentators have argued that public exchanges are the realpolitik and that policy opinions are formed by what citizens read and experience in the public domain, not by maneuverings behind the scenes that they never experience.[1]

Empirical evidence to define the foreign policy environment is available in several research projects that draw on this public record. Media reports of international interactions between nations have been coded on several dimensions, including the nature of the event, the initiator or actor nation, and the recipient or target nation. The events used here to describe West Germany's relations with the East between 1945 and 1972 have been extracted from two of these studies.[2]

International events normally involve either a conflictual or a cooperative exchange between nations. A conflictual exchange or act is a critical, threatening, or hostile interaction between actor and target nation, such as the filing of a diplomatic protest, the mobilization of troops, or actual armed aggression. Conversely, cooperative acts are complimentary, conciliatory, or peaceful exchanges between nations: for example, the signing of a treaty or a visit by a head of state. By computing the difference between the number of cooperative and the number of conflictual exchanges recorded in a series of three-month periods (or quarters), it is possible to produce a single empirical measure of the nature of Germany's foreign relations with the East.[3] A positive difference indicates a preponderance of cooperative events and a favorable international climate, while a negative value signifies a period of tension and hostility in the foreign policy environment.

Figure 5.1. Conflictual-cooperative nature of East-West interactions, 1945–1972.

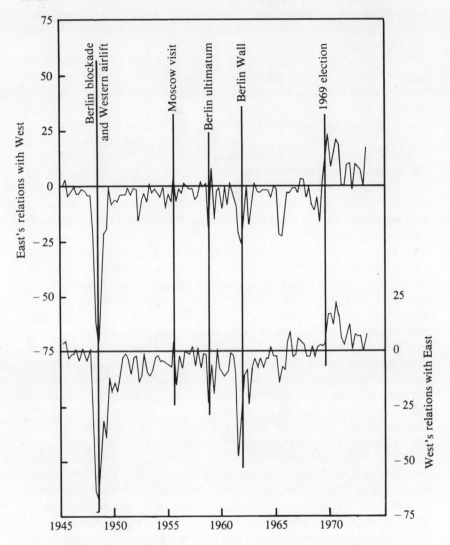

Figure 5.1 plots the relative conflictual-cooperative balance of the Federal Republic's foreign policy environment between 1945 and 1972. The top line in the graph plots events initiated by the Eastern bloc and directed toward the Federal Republic, and the bottom line records interactions in which the West, including the Federal Republic, was the initiator. For most of this timespan the two trendlines look much the

same. Seen from this long-term perspective, Germany's foreign policy has apparently passed through three distinct historical periods: the confrontation of the immediate postwar years, a transition period during the early sixties, and the fruition of *Ostpolitik* beginning in the mid-sixties.

The *confrontation period* of the early postwar years begins on a balanced note, with interactions at or near the neutral point (0) of an equal number of conflictual and cooperative events. In the years immediately following the war, East-West interactions dealt with global issues that seldom touched directly on the specific interests of the defeated Germany. With the onset of the Cold War, however, conflictual acts began to increase in relative frequency. The Berlin Blockade of 1948–49 and the Western airlift, which, in a sense, formalized the Cold War, were the first events to generate substantial conflict on both sides. The Western announcement of the Bonn Conventions in 1952—which laid the groundwork for the achievement of West German sovereignty and NATO membership in 1955—and the Soviet suppression of the workers' strike followed by the uprising in East Berlin and East Germany in June 1953 led to the next, much less intense, period of conflict. The only positive note sounded during this conflictual period was Chancellor Adenauer's 1955 visit to Moscow and the subsequent release of German POWs. But these effects were short-lived. The Berlin Ultimatum, announced by Khrushchev in 1958, initiated a three-year period of recurring conflict between the two blocs, which culminated in the building of the Berlin Wall in 1961. This ultimate expression of the Soviet policy of the two Germanys generated more conflict between the two sides than any other event in the postwar period except the Berlin Blockade.

With the construction of the Wall, however, the German government's intense adversary orientation toward the East came to an end. The Wall dramatized the failure of past policies and required acceptance of a new status quo, namely, the reality of a divided Germany and the long-term loss of the former German areas in the East. The next several years, therefore, marked a *period of transition* in Germany's relations with the East. Although the general nature of East-West interaction still tended to be conflictual, the head-to-head conflicts of the past were largely avoided. Berlin was no longer the pressure point of East-West competition. The attention of the superpowers turned to other areas, and policymakers within both the government and the opposition SPD considered alternatives to the past policies of confrontation.

With the beginning of the Grand Coalition and Willy Brandt's tenure as foreign minister at the end of 1966, German foreign policy took a new direction. Although the groundwork for an opening to the East had been laid earlier under Gerhard Schröder's direction, the *fruition of Ostpolitik* was only accomplished after the change in administrations. As the bottom curve in figure 5.1 indicates, Western-initiated actions slowly but clearly moved toward cooperative relations from 1966 on. For example, there are definite peaks in the curve in 1970 when negotiations with the Soviet Union and Poland on renunciation of force treaties were initiated, and in 1972 when those treaties, along with the *Grundvertrag* ("Basic Treaty") with East Germany, were ratified by the Bundestag.

The East, however, did not respond immediately to the Federal Republic's overtures. At all other times between 1945 and 1972 the two interaction profiles run remarkably parallel to each other. Only between 1967 and 1969 does the Eastern curve lag behind Western actions. Apparently, the leaders of Eastern Europe were either unsure about how to respond to the Western initiatives or regarded them as insufficient evidence of a basic change in policy. At any rate, the East's relations with West Germany remained essentially conflictual. Not until after the 1969 election, which brought the SPD/FDP coalition to power, did the Eastern bloc assume a more cooperative stance in its dealings with West Germany and Berlin.

These trendlines, which clarify German foreign policy by empirically defining historical periods, still tell little about how and why foreign policies were formulated and later changed. To answer these questions, it is necessary to trace the actions and motivations of government and political leaders in the foreign policy domain.

From Defeat to Integration into the Western Alliance

In 1945, Germany was exhausted, defeated, and occupied.[4] Sizable portions of the country were barely habitable; major cities, like Cologne, Frankfurt, and Munich, lay in ruins; many of the factories and much of the machinery that had been the source of Germany's enormous industrial capacity had been destroyed or severely damaged; and almost six million soldiers and civilians were dead. In addition, at the Potsdam Conference of July-August 1945, the victorious powers indicated that "German militarism and Nazism will be extirpated and the Allies will take in agreement together, now and in the future, the other measures necessary to assure that Germany will never again threaten her neighbors or the peace of the world."[5]

The Allies' goal, however, was not to destroy Germany, but to provide the opportunity for Germans to rebuild their country and their lives. Nevertheless, few Germans anticipated the creation of a new political system in the near future. In a survey conducted in September 1946, for example, 27 percent of the respondents in the American Zone and 55 percent of those in Berlin expected occupation to last ten years or more, and approximately 20 percent in both areas thought the Americans would remain for fifty years. By February 1947, these views had changed only slightly: 75 percent of the community leaders inter-viewed at this time indicated that occupation would continue for at least ten years, and 25 percent thought it would last twenty years or longer.[6]

At the same time, few in East or West Germany anticipated the disintegration of the wartime alliance between the Soviet Union, the United States, Great Britain, and France. This alliance had been held together by one goal: the desire to defeat Nazi Germany. Once that had been accomplished there was little to unite the Western and Eastern components of this marriage of convenience. That the alliance had to end became clear after the failure of the Four Powers to agree on policies in postwar Germany at the Moscow Conference in March-April 1947. Indeed, according to one commentator, the failure of the conference marked the beginning of the Cold War between the East and the West.[7] Soon the Soviets began to step up their campaign against the "capitalist and imperialist" West, and General Lucius Clay authorized an anti-Communist campaign in the German-language media in the American Zone.

The inflammatory rhetoric of the Cold War had begun. But it was not mere rhetoric. Both the East and the West committed themselves to conflict by engaging in hostile acts. In October 1947 the Cominform was established; in February 1948 Prague was lost to the Soviets; in March the Soviet representative to the Allied Control Council walked out; in April the Soviets began to obstruct U.S., French, and British access to Berlin; and in June 1948 the Berlin Blockade was initiated as a result of Soviet reactions to the currency reform proposals announced by the Economic Council and the Western occupying forces. All of these incidents indicated a breakdown in East-West cooperation, which was formalized by the establishment of NATO in April 1949.

The Cold War was on and the "German problem" was unresolved. What, therefore, was to be done? The West's answer to this question was to integrate the western zones of occupation into the Atlantic Alliance. Hence, only four years after the war, and to the surprise of many residents, a new West German political system was created. As Alfred Grosser has noted: "The Federal Republic was born in 1949 as a twin sister of the Atlantic Alliance. Their father was the Cold War."[8]

The Allied decision to tie the western zones of occupation to the

Atlantic Alliance was not dictated solely by a desire to secure West German resources for the fight against Communism. There were at least two other important motivations. First, there was the desire to protect future German democracy from the threat of Communism. Second, there was the wish "to alleviate, if not eliminate, the consequences of Germany's historical position as a *Land der Mitte* ('land of the middle.')"[9] In short, with Western protection, German democracy could flourish, and with the integration of the new Federal Republic into the Western Alliance, the "insecurities" that had involved Germany and Europe in two world wars in this century could be controlled.

The first chancellor of the Federal Republic, Konrad Adenauer, shared these Allied goals. In an early address before the newly created Bundestag, he made his views quite clear. "There is," he said, "only one path to freedom. It is the attempt to extend our liberties and prerogatives step by step and in harmony with the Allied High Commission."[10] Although his Catholic Rhineland background may have predisposed him to a Western alliance, Adenauer's decision to move in that direction was based primarily on his perception of the future evolution of world politics. He believed, first, that the final resolution of the German problem would be made in Washington and Moscow, and second, that in the struggle for power the West, because of its liberal democratic institutions and traditions, would inevitably become stronger. In the long run, therefore, the German problem would be settled on Western terms, and it was in Germany's best interests to pursue a strong relationship with the West.

Adenauer began the process of formally integrating the Federal Republic into the Western Alliance at the Petersburg Conference in late 1949. The agreements reached at this conference started West Germany on the road to recovery, equality, and political respectability by relaxing some of the restrictions the Allies had imposed on the German society and polity. In 1951 German foreign policy made further progress toward the goal of respectability and equality through the Western Alliance. The occupying powers agreed that Germany should have a foreign office—with Adenauer as the first foreign minister—and permitted the gradual establishment of diplomatic and consular relations between Germany and other members of the international community. By 1953 such relations had been established with forty countries.

In his negotiations with the Allies, Adenauer did not insist on absolute autonomy for the Federal Republic. He wanted Germany to be a respected and equal partner in a strong Western Alliance, and he realized that such a goal might not be compatible with absolute national sovereignty. He realized, further, that Germany's future influence in world politics would come through its association with other European nations rather than as an individual nation-state. Hence, he was quite willing to hand over some of the independence granted the Federal Republic by the Allied authorities to international organizations and institutions. Adenauer, for example, was an early advocate of European integration, arguing that "the age of the nation state belongs to the past, a past full of jealousy and steeped in blood."[11] Moreover, he firmly endorsed both the European Coal and Steel Community (ECSC) and the ill-fated proposal for the creation of a European army. Thus, Adenauer's willingness to relinquish national sovereignty in favor of international institutions had an almost paradoxical effect, for it hastened the establishment of a sovereign nation-state.[12]

The Federal Republic, then, was integrated into the Western Alliance. Within the government, however, there was a growing belief that Germany should also contribute to the strength of the alliance. When Adenauer first raised the issue of German rearmament in November 1949, it met with strong internal and external opposition. But in 1950, in reaction to the Korean War, the Americans suggested to the French and the British that Germany be permitted to reestablish its army within the confines of NATO. Since the memories of German aggression in World War II were still very fresh, this proposal came as a considerable shock. The reaction to the prospect of a rearmed Germany was often simply: "I don't know if they would frighten the Russians, but, by God, they'd frighten me."[13] In order to avoid the creation of a German national army, the French proposed the establishment of a European army in 1952. However, the treaty establishing the European Defense Community (EDC) was rejected by the French National Assembly in 1954.

Since Germany was to become a sovereign nation-state concomitant with the establishment of the EDC, the defeat of the treaty was a blow to the Federal Republic.[14] To deal with that problem, Anthony Eden, the British foreign minister, suggested that German armed forces be included in NATO. This proposal was accepted by the Allies and embodied in the Paris Agreements of October 1954. The latter were ratified by Germany in February 1955 and became effective on May 5. On this date, the Federal Republic became a sovereign nation-state, although the Allies retained the right to maintain troops on German soil.

In only six years, therefore, Adenauer had led Germany from a position of political dependency to one of equality and respectability within the Western Alliance. And public opinion in the Federal Republic seemed quite pleased with this outcome. In March 1953, for example, 83 percent of the respondents to a nationwide poll indicated that the Federal Republic should cooperate particularly closely with the United States; in contrast, only 18 percent felt that way about the Soviet Union. The German public also seemed to share Adenauer's distaste for the USSR; in 1952, for instance, 67 percent perceived the Soviet Union as a threat to West Germany.[15] Not only, however, did the German public endorse the general direction of Adenauer's foreign policy, they also supported him at the polls. In the 1953 election, Adenauer's CDU/CSU won over 45 percent of the popular vote, a gain of 14 percent over the proportion of the vote the party had received in 1949. Although the outcome of the election was certainly not due exclusively to the character of Adenauer's foreign policy, it did play a role.

Opposition to the Policy of Strength

Support for Adenauer's foreign policy was by no means universal. Elements within the CDU/CSU and the FDP (the principal coalition partner) opposed Adenauer's conception of Europe and his inflexibility toward the Soviet Union. But the staunchest opposition to Adenauer's pro-Western foreign policy came from the SPD. To the Socialists, reunification was the principal foreign policy objective, and they believed that rearmament and integration into the Western Alliance would inhibit the accomplishment of this goal. The Socialists, therefore, were the principal advocates of German national unity in the early postwar period. In this role, they accused Adenauer's government of inadequate response to Soviet proposals for reunification, bitterly opposed rearmament because it would make reunification essentially impossible, and objected to the ECSC because it would "impede German unification" and handicap Germany's economy.[16]

The Socialists' opposition to Adenauer's foreign policy was based on an approach fundamentally different from his. On the one hand, they favored reunification, perhaps in part because the traditional strongholds of SPD support were now located in East Germany. On the other hand, because of their anticlericalism and anticapitalism, they were not enthusiastic about the prospect of a Western Europe dominated by Catholics and conservatives. For a number of reasons, however, Socialist protests generally fell on deaf ears. First, most West Germans regarded the Soviet Union as a threat to the security of the Federal Republic and thus were unwilling to endorse any proposals that might result in closer ties between the two countries. In East Germany and in the reaction of the Soviet government to the uprising in Berlin in June 1953, they could see what life in a Communist system would be like—and they wanted no part of it. Second, the Germans felt that because a settlement negotiated with the Soviets would not be acceptable to the United States, it could result in a decline—and possibly an elimination—of the aid and support that had contributed so greatly to Germany's ongoing recovery. Third, reunification, no matter how important philosophically, was increasingly not worth the cost to many residents of the Federal Republic. Finally, the Socialists were advocating a nationalist policy at a time when many Germans were only too familiar with the consequences of such a policy. Hence, many were concerned with the identification and development of European rather than German interests.

Opposition to Adenauer's policy was not, of course, entirely internal. The Soviet Union also objected vehemently to the integration of the Federal Republic into the Western Alliance. And this opposition was crucial as far as the question of reunification was concerned. At no point—precisely as the SPD argued—was the Soviet Union willing to permit the unification of the two Germanys when one of them was closely allied with the West. Both Moscow and Washington apparently recognized that reunification under such circumstances would probably produce a pro-Western Germany, and, to Moscow, this would give the West an unacceptable advantage in the Cold War struggle. Hence, the Soviet Union called for a neutralized, united Germany throughout the period between 1949 and 1955 even though such a Germany was unacceptable to both the West and the Federal Republic.

Had Adenauer's perception of the future evolution of world politics been correct, the demands of the Soviet Union would have been unimportant in the settlement of the reunification question. In other words, if the West had become stronger in the Cold War competition with the Soviets, reunification might have been achieved on Western terms and Adenauer's decision to tie the Federal Republic to the West would have been correct and very beneficial. The West, however, did not become stronger as the Cold War progressed. By the mid 1950s the Soviets had acquired a nuclear capability and in 1957 the first Sputnik was launched. The West, therefore, could not impose its reunification terms on the Soviets.

But neither could the Soviets impose their terms on the West. Although the Soviet Union did not become progressively weaker as Adenauer had predicted, it was never strong enough to insist on neutralization as the essential condition for reunification. For example, the Soviets could stop neither the Paris Agreements of 1955 nor West German rearmament. This led to a fundamental revision in the policy of the Soviet Union toward Germany. Instead of promoting a neutralized united Germany, the Soviets began to insist on the recognition of postwar frontiers and the basic division of Germany. Clearly, this new policy implied the long-term existence of two separate polities, economies, and societies in the two parts of Germany. After 1955 the Soviet Union started to take steps to implement this development in East Germany.

The most visible sign of the new policy was, perhaps, the Berlin Ultimatum that Khrushchev sent to the West in November 1958. Essentially, Khrushchev called for the withdrawal of Western forces from Berlin and the transformation of the city into a demilitarized "free city." Through this ultimatum, the Soviets hoped to achieve de facto recognition of the East German regime and abrogation of Four Power responsibility for Berlin and German reunification. If implemented, the Soviet ultimatum would have required the West to negotiate directly with the GDR on such things as access routes and would have created a "third" German state with no ties to the West or the Federal Republic. Both of these possibilities were anathema to Adenauer, and consequently he counseled the West to resist. It was, however, becoming increasingly clear that the interests of the West were different from those of the Federal Republic. Hence, Great Britain and the United States were a good deal more willing to negotiate in this Berlin crisis than was the Federal Republic, and they did not tie their negotiations to the question of German reunification. Indeed, the last time the question of reunification was discussed by the superpowers was at the Geneva Conference of 1959, and essentially nothing was accomplished there.

Changes in the International and Domestic Environments

By the late 1950s, then, relations between the Federal Republic and the United States were deteriorating. They declined further after the death in 1959 of John Foster Dulles, whom Adenauer considered a like-minded, close personal friend, and the election in 1960 of John F. Kennedy. With Kennedy came a new American policy emphasizing détente and cooperation (insofar as possible) with the Soviet Union and recognizing that there was little room for maneuver in a nuclear world.

However, deteriorating relations with the United States and the emergence of détente were not the only occurrences of the late 1950s and early 1960s that profoundly affected West German foreign policy. Since de Gaulle was the only Western leader who supported Adenauer's plea that the West not yield to Soviet demands in 1958, a close relationship between these two leaders and their countries began to develop; and it culminated in the signing of the Franco-German Friendship Treaty in 1963. Therefore, at a time when German and American relations were deteriorating, Franco-German relations were improving. In the long run this was not an entirely beneficial development for the Federal Republic because Bonn increasingly got caught in the middle of the ongoing conflict between Paris and Washington. This, in turn, led to the development of the so-called Gaullist and Atlanticist factions within the CDU/CSU.[17] Indeed, in the early 1960s the CDU/CSU contained not only the principal advocates of the government's foreign policy but also its principal opponents.

An important change in the German public's view of the East-West struggle paralleled these changes in the international environment. By 1958, for example, only about half of the German population felt threatened by the Soviet Union and almost a third indicated that the Federal Republic should cooperate closely with the Soviet Union. In addition, by 1962, over a quarter of the German population believed that the Federal Republic should recognize the Oder-Neisse line as the boundary between Germany and Poland.[18]

Finally, and partly as a consequence of these changes in public opinion, the SPD's persistent and sometimes bitter opposition to the Western Alliance changed. In 1954, the SPD had reversed its position on the Coal and Steel Community and in 1958 it reluctantly accepted the Common Market. But the most important year from the point of view of the transformation of the SPD was 1959. In February, Carlo Schmid, Fritz Erler, and others journeyed to Moscow for talks with Khrushchev, and shortly thereafter the SPD issued its "Germany Plan," which represented a final effort to achieve reunification. This proposal recommended direct negotiations with the East German regime on the basis of equal representation. Although it, in effect, provided recognition for the GDR, little was gained from it, and the Socialists themselves quickly discarded it. Thus it became increasingly clear to the SPD leadership that the Soviet Union was uninterested in beginning negotiations for reunification, no matter what the terms. Later in 1959, the party adopted the Godesberg program, which transformed the SPD from a Marxist-reformist to a "people's party" intent on gaining governmental power. In this new program, the SPD dropped its opposition to rearmament and embraced European integration as well as the Western Alliance.[19] By the 1961 election, therefore, the SPD was essentially saying that it could do anything the CDU/CSU could do—only better.

However, at the very time that the SPD was embracing the Western Alliance, the United States was in the process of redefining its foreign policy goals. As already indicated, Kennedy was interested in reducing tensions between the superpowers. But the necessity of disengagement did not become clear until after the building of the Berlin Wall in 1961 and the Cuban missile crisis of 1962. Both of these incidents demonstrated the perils of confrontation politics and, as a consequence, the "fitful search for détente of the 1960's and 1970's" began in earnest.[20]

Because of its dependence on the Western Alliance, the Federal Republic was obligated to acquiesce in the new policy of cooperation between the superpowers. Its acquiescence, however, was reluctant at best, for détente had several potentially negative implications for West German foreign policy. For example, it constituted a severe blow to the policy of strength pursued by the Federal Republic since 1949. Official policies, like the Hallstein Doctrine and *Alleinvertretung*, made far less sense in an era of cooperation between East and West.[21] Insofar as détente threatened the policy of strength, it also threatened the unity of the CDU/CSU, for commitment to Adenauer's pro-Western foreign policy had been one of the most important factors holding the party together in the postwar era.

But there were other implications. If the goal of the superpowers was a relaxation of tensions, there was the possibility that the question of reunification might be solved bilaterally, at the expense of the Federal Republic. Another possibility was that the German problem would be ignored in the era of peaceful coexistence so that the superpowers could shore up the increasing fissures in their own alliance systems, and in that case the West might simply accept the status quo in Europe. Both of these alternatives were unacceptable to Bonn. Yet at the same time the German government realized that only through a relaxation of tensions would it be possible for one of the superpowers to permit reunification on its opponent's terms. Furthermore, the government recognized that if it were to pursue its reunification demands in an unyielding fashion, it might be without influence in the final settlement. Hence, Bonn accepted détente; but Chancellor Erhard pointed out in 1963 that "the German question is one of the principal causes of tensions in the world and one cannot hope to eradicate these tensions if the German question remains unsolved."[22]

Although détente was threatening to Bonn, it came at a time when there was increasing dissatisfaction in Germany with the government's foreign policy.[23] Although the 1950s had witnessed changes in Soviet leadership and there were indications of resistance to Soviet hegemony in East Germany, Hungary, and Poland, Adenauer remained thoroughly anti-Communist and deeply suspicious of any efforts to reduce tensions between East and West. This attitude was never more clearly manifested than in his reaction to the building of the Berlin Wall in 1961. He refused to visit the city immediately and "called the crisis a

Khrushchev trick to help the SPD." In contrast, the Socialists and Willy Brandt reacted to the Wall quickly and comprehensively—even though this event seemed to still all hopes for the achievement of the SPD's long-term goal of reunification. Brandt "called for all-party unity on this issue [and] addressed a personal letter to Kennedy requesting that something be done for the morale of Berlin."[24] Nevertheless, the CDU/CSU won the election. But Adenauer's reaction to the Berlin Wall as well as his involvement in the presidential succession crisis of 1959 severely damaged his position in German politics, though he gave little indication of this in the long and intense coalition negotiations that followed the election. The new government produced by these negotiations included the same principal parties, the CDU/CSU and the FDP, that had ruled prior to the election. Adenauer, however, had agreed to step down as chancellor before the expiration of the four-year term, and Heinrich von Brentano had resigned as foreign minister.

Beginnings of Ostpolitik and the Grand Coalition

The resignation of Brentano was of immense importance to German foreign policy. The new foreign minister, Gerhard Schröder, pursued a new foreign policy, known as the "policy of movement." The essence of this policy was to demonstrate Germany's genuine desire for a relaxation of East-West tensions by pursuing economic and cultural contacts with the East. Trade missions were established in Poland, Rumania, Hungary, and Bulgaria, and in 1966, three years after Adenauer had been replaced by Ludwig Erhard, Bonn issued a "Peace Note" that "cautiously endorsed a nuclear-free zone, non-aggression pacts, and the exchange of military observers with Warsaw Treaty members."[25]

Overall, however, Schröder's Ostpolitik met with limited success. This was true for at least two reasons. First, Schröder's policy of conciliation explicitly excluded the GDR and thus created the impression that the Federal Republic was trying to isolate the GDR and generate pressure from the other East European countries to persuade the Soviet Union to pursue a unification policy favorable to the Federal Republic. Schröder denied that this was a motivation of his policy, but his exclusion of the GDR was not lost on the Soviets, who concluded the Mutual Assistance Pact with the East Germans in 1964. Second, Schröder's Ostpolitik, while emphasizing Germany's good intentions, refused to brook any compromise on the important political issues of the Hallstein Doctrine and East European frontiers. The importance of these matters was clearly evident in the failure of Schröder's negotiations to establish trading links with Czechoslovakia.

Nevertheless, Schröder's overtures represented a recognition on the part of the West German government of a need for an Eastern as well as a Western policy. Hence, the Erhard administration marked the beginning of a new direction in West German relations with the East. And this new foreign policy enjoyed increasing support among the West German population. In 1967, 41 percent of a national sample felt the Federal Republic should cooperate closely with the Soviet Union, and the proportion of the population that felt threatened by the Soviet Union had declined to about 33 percent by April 1966. Opinion on recognition of the Oder-Neisse line was unchanged in February 1966; that is, only 27 percent continued to favor recognition.[26] However, by 1967 the majority of the West German population favored recognition of the Polish-German border, particularly if it would produce better relations with the East.[27]

In short, a growing consensus on the necessity of improved relations with the East seemed to be developing in the Federal Republic. This consensus represented the views of sizable segments of the public, the SPD, and the more liberal elements of the CDU/CSU-FDP governing coalition. Not surprisingly, therefore, calls for bolder initiatives were forthcoming. At its annual conference in June 1966, for example, the SPD concluded that the superpowers did not intend to pursue reunification because it was not in their best interests, and that the Federal Republic should therefore take a more active role. Consequently, the Socialists called for a revision of the Hallstein Doctrine as it applied to Eastern Europe, for the abrogation of the Munich Pact as a step toward normalizing relations with Czechoslovakia, and for the negotiation of a "compromise" on the Oder-Neisse line.[28]

Ludwig Erhard and Gerhard Schröder, however, were not to be the individuals to pursue these or any other new initiatives with the East. This task fell to Kurt Georg Kiesinger, Willy Brandt, and the Grand Coalition that took office in the fall of 1966. The new government made it quite clear that continued improvement in relations with the East would be an integral part of its foreign policy. At the very outset, for example, Kiesinger "called 'a German contribution to the maintenance of peace' the foremost aim of the foreign policy of his administration."[29] Thereby he committed the Federal Republic to détente and reversed the traditional German view that reunification was a prerequisite to normalization of relations between the East and the West. Instead, normalization of relations was a prerequisite to reunification. In addition, Chancellor Kiesinger indicated the new government's desire for improved relations with Poland. Finally, in his inaugural address before the Bundestag, Kiesinger emphasized the importance of Soviet-German rapprochement and the renunciation-of-force agreements suggested earlier by the Erhard administration.

Kiesinger even demonstrated some flexibility on the East German question by indicating a tentative willingness of the Federal Republic to pursue increased contacts and understandings with the GDR.

The new government began its Ostpolitik immediately, and in January 1967, in large part because of the earlier efforts of the Erhard administration, diplomatic relations with Rumania were established. This was followed by the opening of a trade mission in Prague in August 1967, and by the establishment of diplomatic relations with Yugoslavia in 1968. Shortly after taking office, therefore, the Kiesinger-Brandt coalition recognized two East European countries that also recognized the GDR. Since the Hallstein Doctrine clearly specified that West Germany would not enter into diplomatic relations with any country—save the Soviet Union—that recognized East Germany, these decisions made it clear that the new government did not entirely endorse this long-term component of German foreign policy. A cosmetic attempt was made to hide the dismantling of the doctrine by arguing that it did not apply to countries that, because of their domination by the Soviet Union, had no choice in the question of diplomatic recognition of East Germany. Nevertheless, the substance and implications of Germany's recognition policy had been significantly altered by the new government.

In Eastern Europe, however, there was increasing resistance to Bonn's Ostpolitik. Ironically, therefore, when the Federal Republic was dismantling its Hallstein Doctrine, the East Germans were constructing one of their own. The essence of this policy, first proposed by the East Germans in July 1966, was that "no socialist country should open diplomatic relations with the Federal Republic until Bonn was ready to recognize East Germany, to accept the existing borders in Europe, to renounce any nuclear role, and to recognize West Berlin as a separate political unit."[30] These conditions received general endorsement from the Warsaw Pact Foreign Ministers Conference in February 1967, and from the Conference on European Communist Parties in April 1967. Moreover, they were at least "partially accepted and formalized" in a series of bilateral pacts that the East Germans concluded with Poland, Czechoslovakia, Hungary, and Bulgaria in 1967.

Bonn, therefore, could not bring about a normalization of relations between the Federal Republic and Eastern Europe exclusively through economic contacts and diplomatic recognition. On the contrary, the important political questions involving territorial frontiers, the recognition of East Germany, and the status of Berlin would have to be faced and settled. The central importance of this fact was underscored by the Soviet invasion of Czechoslovakia in 1968. Clearly, the Soviets feared that liberalization in Czechoslovakia would undermine bloc solidarity in domestic and foreign policy. Equally clearly, Bonn's Ostpolitik was motivated, at least in part, by a desire to generate some liberalization in Eastern Europe in order to produce a climate more conducive to the eventual unification of Germany. Hence, the Soviets' decision to stop liberalization in Czechoslovakia "dealt . . . a decisive blow to . . . Bonn's Eastern policy."[31]

From the Czechoslovakian invasion, therefore, Bonn learned that it could pursue economic and diplomatic contacts with the East only so far. It also learned something Adenauer had pointed out long before, namely, that the keys to a relaxation of tensions in Europe were in Moscow. Courting Eastern Europe was fine, but ultimately Bonn would have to negotiate with the Soviets if it intended to achieve a normalization of relations in Europe. And this meant that Bonn would have to be prepared to deal with the unresolved questions stemming from World War II.

Fruition of Ostpolitik under Willy Brandt

The realization that a change in foreign policy was needed was not lost on the Brandt-Scheel government, which took office in 1969. Accordingly, the "new Brandt Government quickly began to signal its resolution to do what all previous Bonn governments had sought to resist: to accept the postwar status quo for what it was."[32] Within six weeks of taking office, the Brandt government had signed the Nuclear Non-Proliferation Treaty, thus removing a long-standing obstacle to improved relations with the Soviet Union. By the beginning of 1970, moreover, West Germany began negotiations on a renunciation-of-force agreement with the Soviets. In the same year, discussions were begun with Poland, and in the spring Brandt held his famous meetings with East German Premier Stoph in Erfurt and Kassel.

The stage, therefore, was set. The first success came in August 1970 in the form of the Renunciation of Force Agreement with the Soviet Union. In this treaty, the Federal Republic and the Soviet Union agreed to "maintain international peace and achieve détente [and] to further the normalization of the situation in Europe and the development of peaceful relations among all European states, and in so doing [to] proceed from the actual situation existing in the region." In addition, both nations renounced the use or the threat of the use of force and territorial claims. Bonn agreed, as well, to negotiate similar treaties with the GDR, Poland, and Czechoslovakia and "to treat East Germany as 'a second German state within German territory' on a basis of equality and non-discrimination, and no longer to claim the right to represent all Germans."[33]

Perhaps most important, Bonn specified—in part because of domestic political pressure—that the Renunciation of Force Agreement could not be ratified until a satisfactory settlement on Berlin was achieved by the Four Powers. Negotiations on the Four Power Agreement, therefore, began in earnest and were concluded in September 1971. In this settlement, the Four Powers agreed to "unimpeded" access to West Berlin, the maintenance and development of West Berlin's relations with the Federal Republic, the improvement of West Berliners' visitation rights in East Berlin and the GDR, and the international representation of West Berlin by the Federal Republic. According to the agreement, the details of traffic to and from Berlin as well as the visitation rights of West Berliners were to be resolved in intra-German negotiations. After considerable discussion—and some stalling on the part of the East Germans—these details were worked out in the fall of 1971.

With the agreement on Berlin signed and the intra-German negotiations successfully completed, Brandt could submit the Moscow and Warsaw treaties to parliament for ratification. Debate was intense and prolonged, and ratification was not a foregone conclusion. Both treaties clearly departed from the foreign policy the CDU/CSU had advocated and practiced during most of the postwar period, namely, unbending opposition to negotiations with the East on the outstanding issues of World War II. Both treaties, moreover, represented efforts to reduce tensions in Europe, a policy the CDU/CSU had always found difficult to accept. Hence, after the Berlin agreement, Rainer Barzel, the aspiring CDU leader, argued that the SPD had aided in the "permanent division of Germany" and had disregarded the rights and aspirations of Germans living behind the Wall. In the parliamentary debate on the Eastern treaties these and other arguments reappeared. In the Bundesrat's consideration of the treaties in February, for example, the CDU/CSU argued, among other things, that the Moscow Treaty might endanger self-determination and the prospects of reunification for Germany and hamper European integration.[34] The CDU/CSU majority in the Bundesrat agreed with these critiques and the treaties seemed in grave danger. Matters appeared to worsen when an SPD representative defected to the CDU, and an FDP deputy moved to independent status. Barzel then called for a constructive vote of no confidence (*konstruktives Misstrauensvotum*) to oust the Brandt government and prevent ratification of the treaties. By a two-vote margin, however, Brandt beat back Barzel's challenge, and a vote on the treaties seemed assured.

Since the CDU/CSU could not defeat the treaties by ousting Brandt, it had to decide how to vote. Public opinion was not very reassuring in relation to the CDU/CSU position. Increasingly, the population had shifted toward support of the government's Ostpolitik. By 1970, for example, most West Germans favored recognition of both the Oder-Neisse line and the GDR, and in late 1967 over half of the public admitted that they had become accustomed to the division of Germany.[35] Perhaps most important, however, a poll released shortly before the Bundestag vote in 1972 revealed that 52 percent favored quick ratification of the treaties and that the SPD would receive a plurality of the votes if a national election were held at that time.[36]

Clearly, German public opinion favored ratification of the treaties. The same could be said for the United States, since both documents accorded quite well with America's continuing emphasis on détente. Consequently, the CDU/CSU was in an untenable position, and in May the CDU Executive Committee agreed to endorse the treaties. On May 17, 1972, the ratification votes were taken and both treaties passed with an insignificant number of negative votes and a disproportionate number of abstentions. Finally, in December 1972 the Basic Treaty between the two Germanys, which provided for de facto, though not de jure, recognition of the GDR, was signed.

In three years, therefore, Brandt had engineered a series of negotiations and treaties that "amounted to a virtual settlement of World War II."[37] West Germany had accepted Poland's borders, recognized East Germany, and contributed to the resolution of the stalemate in Berlin. For all of this Brandt received the Nobel Peace Prize, while the two Germanys received admittance, on an equal basis, to the United Nations. A new era in West Germany's relations with Eastern Europe had begun.

Foreign Policy Dimensions and the Mass Public

In the history of postwar Germany, conflict and cooperation are the endpoints of a single dimension of foreign policy alternatives. During the postwar period, foreign policy apparently shifted from a more conflictual to a more cooperative stance. But are these two poles also present in the public's evaluations of foreign policy, as is suggested by the responses to the isolated survey items already presented?

Fortunately, the data needed to answer these questions are available in three studies. In 1961, 1969, and 1972 respondents were asked to evaluate the importance of several foreign policy issues. The list of issues changed between timepoints, reflecting changes in the international environment and the foreign policy agenda. Mirroring the constant elements in German foreign policy throughout this period, however, four general issues were examined in a similar fashion in each study: the importance of relations with the Soviet Union (or Eastern Europe) and with the United States (or the West), the threat of a military attack from the East (military security), and the question of German reunification. Other issues examined in the three studies included European unity, aid to developing nations, and the maintenance of good relations with China.

To determine the character of the public's perception of foreign policy, we performed principal component analyses at each timepoint with all of the available issues. Although the issues change to some extent with the changing foreign policy agenda, at each election the first two dimensions are very similar (table 5.1).[38] All of the responses to the foreign-policy-importance questions are positively correlated and load positively on the first dimension—a salience dimension—at each timepoint. The highest-loading issue on the first dimension at each timepoint is relations with the United States (or, in 1972, with the West), the cornerstone of the public's view of foreign policy. In general, the other high-loading issues are, not surprisingly, Soviet relations and the German question (reunification), the two other central issues of postwar foreign policy. By comparison, other issues—with a few exceptions—are less central to the Germans' foreign policy perceptions.

The second dimension in each of these analyses is more important to this chapter because it reflects the two poles in German postwar foreign policy. At each timepoint, foreign policy issues that are associated with cooperative activities in international politics, like the development of good relations with countries in all parts of the world—both East and West—and the integration of Europe, load at one end of the continuum. Conversely, issues that stress the conflictual aspects of Germany's external environment, like those dealing with national security and terrorist attacks, cluster at the other end of the dimension. Most important, this conflictual-cooperative dimension appears to cut across East-West lines, providing a broad theme underlying most aspects of German foreign policy. For example, the issue of relations with the USSR generally tends toward the cooperative pole, while security from Russian attack is a conflictual issue. Thus, attitudes toward the Soviet Union do not fall into a single mold; rather, the German public distinguishes between the cooperative and conflictual aspects of East-West relations. This general conclusion can be abstracted from all three surveys, including the 1961 study, which predates the opening to the East. Similarly, the German public does not perceive relations with the superpowers in bipolar terms: relations with the United States and relations with the Soviet Union are generally

Table 5.1. Principal components analysis of foreign policy issues, 1961, 1969, and 1972.

	1961			1969			1972	
Issues	I[a]	II[b]	Issues	I[a]	II[b]	Issues	I[a]	II[b]
Aid to developing nations	0.59	-0.52	USSR	0.78	-0.43	Eastern Europe	0.58	-0.63
Nuclear	.57	-.41	USA	.81	-.27	China	.70	-.34
European unity	.73	-.16	Reunification	.74	.17	West	.72	.08
USA	.82	.02	Attack	.67	.64	Military security	.62	.44
USSR	.70	.04				Foreign terrorists	.56	.49
Reunification	.63	.46						
Attack	.60	.52						
Eigenvalue	3.16	0.97		2.29	0.71		2.07	0.96
Percent variance explained	45.3	13.9		57.3	17.9		41.4	19.5
(N)	(1329)			(705)			(1714)	

a. First dimension: salience.
b. Second dimension: cooperative-conflictual relations.

perceived in similar terms by the public. Thus, the cooperative-conflictual dichotomy seems to characterize popular attitudes toward foreign policy just as it characterizes elite behavior and the actual interactions between West Germany and the East.

An understanding of these dimensions can be increased by identifying the positions of various social groups in this two-dimensional foreign policy space.[39] This can be accomplished by computing the group's mean score for the principal components scores. These mean scores define the coordinates of a group's location in the two-dimensional foreign policy space. The group's position is determined both by the average salience that foreign policy as a whole holds for the members of the group and by the relative conflictual or cooperative nature of their foreign policy interests.

Both of these dimensions are important in the determination of foreign policy. The conflictual-cooperative axis indicates the foreign policy alternatives a group is most interested in. Individuals located near the conflictual pole are predominantly concerned with issues such as national security, while those near the cooperative pole are oriented toward such cooperative themes as maintaining good relations with other countries. As a test of external validity, the component scores for the conflictual-cooperative dimension were correlated with independent measures of foreign policy attitudes. For 1969, for example, those in favor of recognition of the German Democratic Republic locate themselves at the cooperative pole (Pearson's $r = 0.12$). For 1972, a more comprehensive index makes it possible to measure attitudes toward the Ostpolitik of the SPD/FDP government. This index assesses support for the three main policy outcomes of Brandt's Ostpolitik: the Basic Treaty between the two Germanys, the treaty with Poland, and the treaty with the Soviet Union. Approval of these components of the opening to the East correlates at a satisfying 0.29 with the conflictual-cooperative dimension.

Quite apart from the attitude a group holds on foreign policy, higher mean scores on the salience dimension suggest that a group is more likely to be interested in the actual formulation of foreign policy. This notion of issue publics is particularly important in foreign policy because that policy area is often of marginal concern to the average voter. Consequently, the attentive publics tend to have an accentuated influence on foreign policy decisions.[40] To assess whether the salience scores measure the relative interest of German citizens in foreign policy, these scores were correlated with independent indexes of interest in foreign and domestic policy.[41] This analysis produced correlation coefficients (r) of 0.22 for 1961 and 0.18 for 1969.

Partisan Supporters

Insofar as foreign policy acts as a basis of party cleavages in Germany, supporters of the two major parties should align themselves in the two-dimensional foreign policy space very much as the party elites do. Figure 5.2 plots the distribution of party supporters in the foreign policy space, using a five-point partisanship index ranging from strong supporters of the CDU/CSU to strong supporters of the SPD, with

Figure 5.2. Placement of partisan groups in foreign policy space for 1961, 1969, and 1972. Partisan classification (number following label designates year of data): S-CDU = strong CDU/CSU; W-CDU = leaning toward CDU/CSU; Nonpart = nonpartisans; W-SPD = leaning toward SPD; S-SPD = strong SPD.

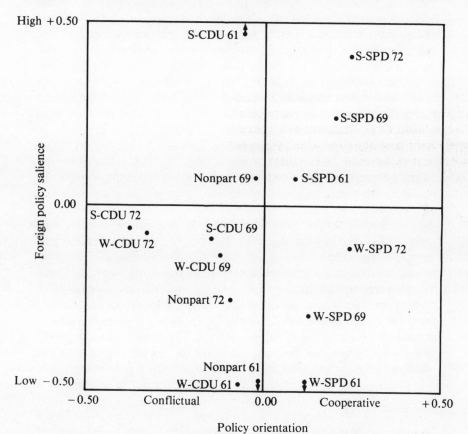

nonpartisans forming the midpoint.[42] The vertical dimension measures the overall salience of foreign policy, and the horizontal dimension determines whether a group is more interested in conflictual or in cooperative issues. Partisan groups are differentiated in the space by strength of partisanship and the year of the survey. Thus, the position of strong CDU/CSU supporters in 1961 is identified in figure 5.2 as S-CDU 61. The expected differences between supporters of the two major parties are strikingly confirmed by the data. Like the party elites, CDU/CSU supporters are found in the conflictual half of the space at each timepoint; in contrast, SPD partisans, like SPD elites, are located in the cooperative half.

These data also graphically highlight differences in the political significance of the foreign policy options of various partisan groups. Partisans are generally located in the total two-dimensional space in a V-shaped distribution. The mouth of the V-shape is formed by the strong supporters of both major parties. Strong partisans (of both the SPD and the CDU/CSU) have high scores on the salience dimension, and they are most polarized on the conflictual-cooperative dimension. Weaker partisans are less interested in foreign policy and also less polarized on the conflictual-cooperative dimension. And finally, for nonpartisans, who generally display the least interest in the ephemeral world of foreign policy, there is little difference between interest in conflictual and interest in cooperative issues.

In short, those partisan groups most interested in foreign policy also tend to be more polarized in their conflictual-cooperative issue interests. Moreover, to the extent that longitudinal comparisons are possible, these data suggest that the foreign policy cleavage between the parties has increased between 1961 and 1972. In 1961, supporters of the two major parties were not too divergent with respect to the conflictual-cooperative dimension. By 1969, the gap between the parties had widened considerably. And in 1972, after Brandt's initiation of an active Ostpolitik had stimulated strong opposition from the Christian Democrats, the distance between strong SPD and strong CDU/CSU supporters was quite substantial. Thus, although the major parties were agreed on the basic goals of German foreign policy—supporting the Western Alliance and restoring Germany's stature in the world—the differences between them on the appropriate policies to attain these goals increased from 1961 to 1972.

Education

To the average voter foreign policy is usually a remote and abstract area, and therefore the proportion of the population that is very much interested in foreign policy is relatively small. The educated members of a society, however, because of their background and the positions many of them hold, are likely to be substantially more attentive to foreign policy matters. But is the attentive public oriented more toward conflictual or cooperative issues?

Figure 5.3 shows that education is strongly related to the salience dimension. Respondents with a secondary education and those with an *Abitur* or higher are located high up on the salience dimension. Conversely, at all three timepoints those respondents with only a *Volks-schule* education display a decided disinterest in foreign policy issues.

Figure 5.3. Placement of educational groups in foreign policy space for 1961, 1969, and 1972. Type of education (number following label indicates year of data): Volks = only Volksschule; Volks+ = Volksschule and vocational training; Sec. Sch. = secondary school; Abitur = Abitur or higher.

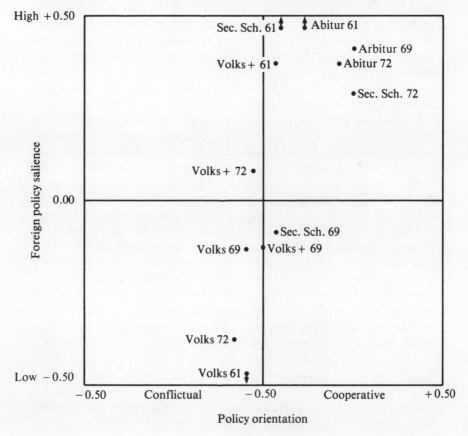

Educational differences on the conflictual-cooperative dimension are relatively minor. However, there is a slight tendency at every time-point for the highly educated (and politically involved) to be more interested in cooperative issues, while those with only a Volksschule education are more oriented to issues of international conflict and national security—and these differences appear to be widening over time.

The impact of education also carries over to other social-status indicators, such as social class. When social classes are positioned in the foreign policy space (not shown), only minor differences exist on the conflictual-cooperative dimension. All three social classes—middle class, workers, and farmers—are located near the midpoint of this dimension. This is not surprising, since the political relevance of social class derives from the opposing interests of the classes in economic affairs, not from foreign policy. However, social class does appear relevant to the level of interest in foreign policy, as indicated by the significant differences on the salience dimension. Farmers display a marked disinterest in foreign policy at all three timepoints; the middle class generally shows a high level of interest; and workers cluster around the midpoint of this dimension. The pattern of these class differences strongly suggests that they are due to the differing educational levels of these social strata, rather than to the influence of class per se.

Considering both foreign policy dimensions simultaneously, one can see how political elites may perceive support for cooperative foreign policy issues that is disproportionate to the actual distribution of opinions within the electorate. The political disinterest of workers, farmers, and the less educated implies low involvement in politics, and the impact of their conflictual concerns in setting Germany's foreign policy agenda is weakened proportionately. Conversely, the greater political involvement of the highly educated probably lends greater voice to their support for a more cooperative German foreign policy.

Generations

Since the turn of the century both Germany's position in the international sphere and its foreign policy goals have varied dramatically. The widely differing historical experiences resulting from these changes should have left different imprints on the foreign policy opinions of succeeding generations. For example, older Germans should be more oriented toward conflictual politics—concerned more with national defense and the threat of further war. Younger Germans, on the other hand, who have not directly experienced war, may show less concern for national security issues, and they may approach international relations with a more cooperative orientation.

Although foreign policy opinions are heavily influenced by short-term factors, figure 5.4 does uncover some residue of historical experience in the broad foreign policy orientations of German generations. And even though foreign affairs are not particularly salient to individuals raised after World War II, the orientations of these cohorts are generally cooperative. In contrast, older cohorts give greater attention to conflictual issues; moreover, these individuals are generally more interested in foreign policy than are members of the younger generations.

Figure 5.4. Placement of generations in foreign policy space for 1961, 1969, and 1972. Generation (number following label indicates year of data): LFRG = Late Federal Republic; EFRG = Early Federal Republic; Reich = Third Reich; Weim = Weimar; Wilh = Wilhelmine.

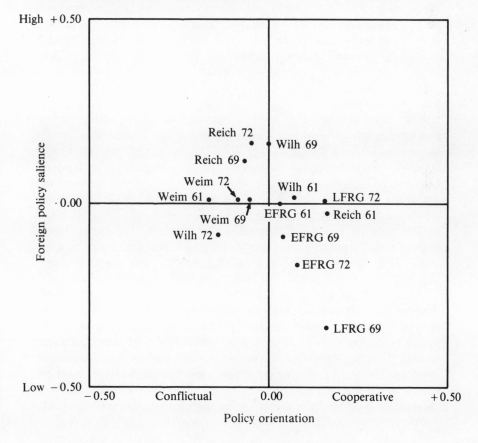

A detailed examination of this figure also suggests that polarization between the generations is apparently widening over time. The generational patterns for 1961 are not very distinct. However, in 1969 and even more obviously in 1972 a clear generational pattern can be abstracted from the data. For example, in 1972 those raised before World War I exhibit the greatest interest in conflictual issues (−0.13), while members of the youngest Federal Republic cohort turn their interest toward cooperative issues (+0.15). Indeed, other data from our studies, and the work of other researchers, consistently find that support for Brandt's Ostpolitik and for international organizations such as the European Communities is greatest among the postwar cohorts.[43]

Cohort differences on the salience dimension may therefore reflect life-cycle effects—the lower policy interest of the young—while variations on the conflictual-cooperative dimension may be attributable to differing generational experiences. Of course, the available data do not provide conclusive proof of these assumptions. If, however, conflictual-cooperative orientations do reflect generational differences that tend to endure through life, then these data suggest a slow but steady growth in the German public's interest in cooperative politics as the size of the postwar cohort continues to grow relative to the older, conflictually oriented generations.

Expellees

One of the few groups that should have a clear interest in German foreign policy, and specifically in conflictual issues, is the expellees. Expellees are inhabitants of former German territories in Eastern Europe who either fled westward when the German armies were driven out at the close of World War II, or who were expelled from those areas immediately after the war.[44] Their foreign policy opinions have undoubtedly been influenced by these experiences. First, the conditions of their expulsion were extremely harsh, often accompanied by loss of property and life. Second, when they arrived in West Germany they faced a difficult process of assimilation. Many came from a traditional, agricultural background and had distinctive accents that marked their heritage. Expellees often found themselves at the bottom of the economic ladder in the Federal Republic, competing for scarce economic resources in a war-devastated nation. Furthermore, Germans already living in the Federal Republic were frequently less than eager to accept the expellees. Consequently, their longing to return to their homes in the East was not merely prompted by the wish to return to their place of origin (*Heimat*) but also by economic and social considerations.

Figure 5.5. Placement of expellees and the general public in foreign policy space for 1961, 1969, and 1972. Expel = expellees; Public = general public.

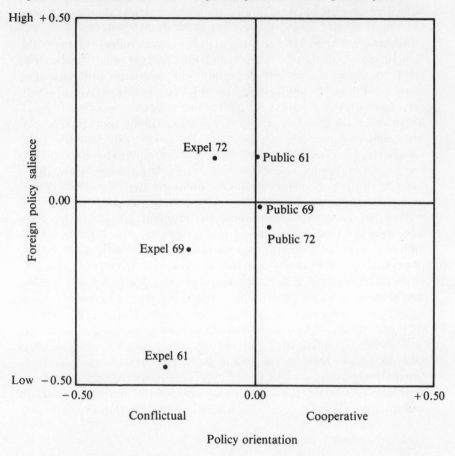

Unlike the rest of the population, the expellees have a personal stake in the results of Germany's policies toward its Eastern neighbors. Expellee groups were organized soon after the war to represent these interests, and they have remained very active, very vocal, and politically quite powerful advocates of a foreign policy aimed at the retrieval of the "lost" areas in the East. These organizations, or *Landsmannschaften,* have done their best to prevent the normalization of Germany's relations with Eastern Europe. They have been among the most intransigent opponents of the emerging new Ostpolitik, which they have perceived as the "surrender" of Germany's "legal rights" to the former German areas. Therefore, the expellees should be located on the conflictual side of the foreign policy space, and they should attach greater salience to foreign policy as a whole than the general public.

Figure 5.5 displays the position of expellees in contrast to that of the general public in the 1961, 1969, and 1972 foreign policy space. (For 1961, the figure shows only the location of supporters of the expellee party, Bund der Heimatvertriebenen und Entrechteten (BHE), which should represent a politically active and cohesive minority.)[45] In all three years, the expellee group is located toward the conflictual pole of the conflictual-cooperative dimension, but in 1961 especially the BHE supporters are oriented toward conflictual issues. Although it might be expected that the expellees' conflictual orientation would intensify as Brandt's more conciliatory Ostpolitik unfolded, the 1969 and 1972 data show very little movement along the conflictual-cooperative axis.

But the changing foreign policy environment seems to have been reflected in changes in foreign policy salience. In 1961, expellees attached very little importance to foreign policy as a whole—even though only the position of BHE supporters is measured. This low level of interest could have resulted from any one of several factors: the general agreement among the three major parties on policies compatible with the expellees' position, the expellees' increasing integration into West German society, or the generally low level of education and political sophistication among expellees. However, when the SPD proposed an opening to the East in the mid-sixties, the interest of the expellees intensified. And in 1972, when Ostpolitik was one of the central issues of the campaign, the interest of the expellees in foreign policy was substantially greater than that of the population as a whole.

Conclusion

Between 1949 and 1972, West German foreign policy manifested gradual—if at times grudging—change. During most of the Adenauer era, West Germany allied itself exclusively with the West. As long as it could be assumed that the West was committed to reunification on Western terms, Adenauer and the Federal Republic essentially ignored the East, and relations between West Germany and the Warsaw Pact nations were highly conflictual. During most of this period, popular sentiment strongly supported the government's policy, but by 1961 attitudes had begun to change, particularly among those groups for whom foreign policy issues were salient.

In addition, important changes in international and domestic German politics occurred at the start of the 1960s. The Cuban missile crisis and the construction of the Berlin Wall demonstrated the perils of confrontation politics; hence, the search for détente between the superpowers became a central component of the international agenda. In the Federal Republic, the SPD gave up its long-term opposition to Adenauer's foreign policy and the CDU replaced its hard-line foreign minister with Gerhard Schröder, who was interested in improving relations with the East. As a consequence of these domestic and international changes, a new policy toward the East—the policy of movement—was initiated. For the most part, however, this policy met with limited success because it did not face up to and accept the consequences of World War II. The Brandt-Scheel administration eliminated this barrier to improved relations almost immediately after taking office, and negotiations for a normalization of relations between West Germany and the Warsaw Pact began in earnest. Public support for the government's Ostpolitik had been growing throughout the 1960s and by 1972 it was substantial, a situation that seems to have been related to the increasing youth and education of the electorate.

What do the results of our analysis portend for the future? A straightforward interpolation of the survey data just examined suggests that over the long run the German public will be increasingly interested in foreign policy and will increasingly support or demand a cooperative foreign policy stance. There seems little doubt that the German mass public has profoundly altered its foreign policy preferences since 1949. Moreover, although the component scores used in the analysis of foreign policy space are normalized and thus do not completely warrant evaluations of the overall movement of mass attitudes, the fact cannot be ignored that two growing population groups, the young and the highly educated, stress a cooperative orientation to foreign policy.

Yet, the analysis also indicates that the foreign policy orientations of SPD and CDU partisans have become increasingly divergent during the time period covered by these data. For example, while the difference between the scores of strong CDU and SPD partisans on the conflict-cooperation dimension (in figure 5.2) is 0.14 in 1961, it grows to 0.70 by 1972.

In sum, it would probably be a mistake to argue that there is a lasting consensus on a cooperative foreign policy in Germany, even among those most interested in such questions. Conflictual orientations remain strong among certain groups, and since foreign policy attitudes are quite fluid, and, unlike some other orientations, are easily influenced by events, it is possible that the cooperative stance of 1972 will change in the future.

6

Old Politics and New Politics

THE DRAMATIC CHANGES that have occurred since World War II in economics, foreign policy, and other sociopolitical areas have had mutually reinforcing effects on German politics. Over the past three decades, the German public has moved from a time of uncertainty and insecurity—both economically and internationally—to a time of unprecedented affluence and international stability within Europe. Furthermore, these economic and foreign policy changes have been paralleled by changes in social domains.[1] Social relations, loosened by the turmoil of the war, have become less rigid, and geographic and social mobility has increased. The educational system, although it has retained its basic class structure, has become more permeable, and the content of class instruction is gradually being adapted to keep step with societal and political change. Affluence and the opening of borders within the European Communities have made travel to foreign countries almost commonplace, and a sense of European identity has become more widespread. Affluence has also increased the amount and richness of leisure time opportunities. The separate effects of these diverse trends may overlap to produce a single wave of social change, leading to an increasingly stable, secure, and progressive political environment.

Some of the important results these changes have had on the language and content of German politics have already been discussed, but their impact on the political attitudes of the German public still needs to be examined. How have political opinions, beliefs, and values shifted in response to these changes in the domestic and international situation?

The Changing Political Agenda

One immediate consequence of a change in the political environment is a change in the political agenda—in what people believe are the most important issues facing society.[2] Respondents to survey questions must examine the entire political landscape in order to choose the most pressing issues, and for this reason their responses provide a broad evaluation of the public's domestic and foreign policy interests and priorities.

Since 1951 the Allensbach Institute has been periodically monitoring public opinion on the most important questions facing West German society.[3] The open responses range over a multitude of issues between 1951 and 1972, but five major themes stand out: economic problems; reunification; Berlin problems; maintaining peace and furthering détente; and social policies.

In the immediate postwar years the devastation wrought by the war pushed economic problems to the fore (table 6.1). Even in 1951, a clear plurality (45 percent) mentioned wages, prices, unemployment, and other economic issues as the major problems facing the country. These concerns far outweighed interest in the Berlin question or the maintenance of peace; and social policies were mentioned by only an insignificant number of people. Thus, early descriptions of the Federal Republic as a system with primarily economic concerns (rather than political concerns) appear consistent with the content of the political agenda.

Increasing affluence in the later 1950s and early 1960s resulted in a gradual decline in the salience of economic issues. During most of this period only about a fifth of the public mentioned economic problems as the most important issue for Germany. As these concerns receded, others became salient to the public. The issue of German reunification, an "objective" concern since at least 1949, became more important in the minds of Germans. It was the most frequently mentioned issue between 1953 and 1965, partially reflecting the recurring debate on the subject among partisan elites; and it was only temporarily reduced in importance by the construction of the Wall in August 1961, the "hottest" period of the Berlin problem.[4] Concerns with national security and national identity, expressed in the themes of Berlin and reunification, were also evident in the increased interest in maintaining peace and furthering détente. This theme reached a temporary highpoint in salience following the building of the Wall.

The temporary impact of political events on the political agenda was also evident in the late 1960s. The recession of 1966–67 triggered a sharp rise in attention to economic problems as the most important issue facing Germany. In the 1967 survey a full 62 percent of the respondents mentioned economic worries, of which fear of unemployment was often uppermost. Yet, a year later the level of economic concern receded to 33 percent, only to rise again with the onset of economic difficulties in the early 1970s.

Table 6.1. Salience of selected themes of the German political agenda, 1951–1972.

Major themes	1951	1952	1953	1955	1956	1957	1959	1960
Economic problems	45%	33%	25%	28%	22%	18%	15%	27%
Berlin problems	—	—	—	—	—	—	16	6
Reunifi- cation	18	23	38	34	38	43	45	38
Peace, détente	20	24	12	16	13	17	16	16
Social policies and domestic issues	—	—	—	—	—	—	—	—

Source: Elisabeth Noelle-Neumann, ed., *Jahrbücher der Öffentlichen Meinung* (Allensbach: Institut für Demoskopie, 1951–1974).
a. Entries for these years are based on more than one survey.

In this same timespan reunification and, especially, Berlin ceased to occupy the attention of the German public. Berlin no longer served as a major pressure point in East-West confrontations, and reunification became a remote goal at best. Instead, the German public grew interested in another approach to foreign policy, *Ostpolitik,* which emphasized foreign policy problems as part of a more general quest for peace and for the development of better relations with Germany's Eastern neighbors. By the 1972 election, this "cooperative" approach was the primary foreign policy interest.

As both economic problems and international threats subsided in the late 1960s, the German public shifted its attention to a new set of domestic political issues.[5] Topics such as codetermination (*Mitbestimmung*) increased in salience, and the reform of the educational system became a major worry. In general, such "quality of life" concerns as environmental protection and better care for children and the aged drew new public interest. These issues had not been mentioned in the surveys of the 1950s, though they were then the topics of elite debate. But by the 1972 survey nearly a quarter of the population felt that these issues of social policy (*Sozialpolitik*) were the major questions facing the country. The new political environment of the 1972 election was reflected in two themes, Ostpolitik and Sozialpolitik,

Table 6.1. Continued

1961[a]	1962	1963	1964	1965	1966	1967	1968[a]	1969[a]	1970	1971	1972
14%	20%	20%	27%	27%	46%	62%	33%	29%	40%	49%	38%
21	23	11	7	4	2	1	2	2	1	2	1
27	30	31	41	47	29	18	21	21	12	2	1
21	26	15	11	10	12	8	20	18	19	18	28
4	—	8	5	6	4	3	11	11	15	22	24

which together outranked economic worries as the major concern of the German public.

Thus, the agenda of German politics changed in several ways between 1951 and 1972. Sudden crises (such as the Berlin Wall or the 1966-67 recession) have occasionally stimulated dramatic short-term shifts in the political agenda, but several longer-term trends can also be extracted from this series of opinion surveys. Economic issues have fluctuated in salience according to prevailing economic conditions; the general trend, however, has been a decline in the salience of economic problems, paralleling the dramatic success of the *Wirtschaftswunder*. As international relations have taken on a more cooperative tone, issues of national security and Cold War competition have also decreased in salience. In short, the citizenry has broadened its concerns beyond the traditional worries of economic and international security to include a group of new social issues. The nature and content of political debate in the early 1970s has therefore differed noticeably from the lines of discussion that typified the early 1950s. Admittedly, however, just as in the past the political agenda has reversed itself several times in reaction to events, this new agenda may also be susceptible to change.

The Old and New Politics

While the contemporary political agenda undoubtedly reflects the political and social environment of a nation, several analysts argue that environmental influences may also shape basic political values. Such values tend to be socialized early in life, and they may persist throughout life even if the environment subsequently changes. Thus the ebb and flow of the political agenda may leave a more telling, and permanent, mark on German public opinion.

Ronald Inglehart has accumulated extensive empirical evidence of a generational change in European political values reflecting the same environmental trends discussed here.[6] In addition, Inglehart develops a theoretical structure for explaining the process of value change and the likely distribution of value priorities within the general public. Drawing on the work of Abraham Maslow, he suggests that there is a hierarchical order to human goals. Man first seeks to fulfill subsistence needs: water, food, and shelter. When these basic needs are met, he continues the search until enough material goods are acquired to attain a comfortable margin of economic security. Having accomplished this, he may turn to higher-order postmaterialist needs, such as the need for belonging, self-esteem, participation, self-actualization, and the fulfillment of aesthetic and intellectual potential. Or, aptly put in the German vernacular, *Erst kommt das Fressen, dann kommt die Moral.*[7]

A basic assumption of this process of value change is that the childhood environment has a fundamental and enduring impact on value formation. Indeed, both Inglehart and Russell Dalton have independently presented evidence that indicates that such basic values tend to reflect the childhood environment in which these values are first socialized, and that these values tend to persist through the life cycle.[8]

For over two decades, Germany has shared with other European nations a relatively high level of individual and societal affluence, coupled with an absence of overt, external military conflict. The changes in these aspects of Germany's historical experience over the past few generations are probably the largest within Western Europe. Under these conditions, the "materialist" concerns—economic gains, domestic order, and social and military security—that have preoccupied prewar generations could diminish in urgency. Having grown up in an environment where materialist and security needs seemed assured, postwar generations may be shifting their primary attention toward postmaterialist concerns. Thus, the change in the stability and security of Germany's political environment may be leading to changes in political beliefs that are far more basic than the perceptions of the political agenda, changes that have far greater implications for the operation of the political system. But, what exactly is the nature of these two contrasting political value systems?

The economic conflict between the haves and have-nots, embodied in the traditional bourgeois-proletariat cleavage, exemplifies the essence of materialist values. Both sides in that struggle are driven by a desire for economic gain and security—whether they seek to safeguard it and defend it, or to acquire and increase it.

But the definition of this materialist orientation should be widened to include the need for noneconomic security—for example, the need to maintain a traditional social order and domestic tranquillity. Still more broadly, this cluster of values should encompass the preservation of national sovereignty based on international respect for German strength, as well as the reunification of the two Germanies.[9] Clearly, materialist values involve more than just economic concerns; they touch on life styles, traditional religious values, and foreign policy orientations. Thus, instead of calling such concerns materialist, it may be more accurate to refer to them as the concerns of the *Old Politics.*[10]

It is easier to identify issues typical of the Old Politics of industrial societies than to predict the postmaterialist, or *New Politics,* concerns that a postindustrial society might emphasize. Value changes occur in all affluent societies, albeit at different rates, but particular New Politics concerns may, to some extent, be country-specific. The New Politics may center on historicopolitical conditions, such as the ethnolinguistic conflicts of Belgium or the racial conflicts of the United States. Alternatively, it may respond to pressing social issues, such as the treatment of the *Gastarbeiter* ("guest worker"), or seek solutions to the problems of the working class through worker participation in industry (*Mitbestimmung*). Or again, it may develop around questions common to most highly industrialized societies, such as environmental pollution, the dangers of nuclear energy, the questions of women's equality and human rights, and the need for peaceful international coexistence and for helping the Third World.

In spite of this diversity, the value system of the New Politics emphasizes some common elements. Regardless of which particular *ends* are championed, the New Politics stresses the importance of open access to political *means* and resources. Freedom of speech for minorities, access to the decision-making machinery of the state, the ability to participate in politics, and, if necessary, to resort to demonstrations and other forms of elite-challenging political behavior are not only necessary instruments of the New Politics but are also ends in themselves.

Evidence that values are indeed changing among Western publics comes from several sources. Inglehart has analyzed a series of surveys beginning in 1970 that show sharp generational differences in the emphasis given to the Old Politics goals of economic and domestic security and to the New Politics objectives of participation and freedom of expression.[11] Arnold Heidenheimer and Donald Kommers document a long-term reversal between 1949 and 1970 in the public's priority for two freedoms—freedom from want and freedom of speech.[12] In addition, Noelle-Neumann interprets extensive over-time and age differences in attitudes toward work and leisure habits and social attitudes in a similar vein.[13] Briefly, an apparent shift in political values or goals has accompanied the dramatic material success of the Wirtschaftswunder and the growing stability of the international environment.

Identifying Old Politics and New Politics

Survey questions measuring issue salience provide an ideal opportunity to verify the existence of an Old Politics–New Politics value dimension in the German context and to define more precisely the issues falling within each grouping. In the 1961, 1969 and 1972 surveys, respondents rated the importance of a broad range of contemporary issues. By analyzing the interrelationships between interest in these issues it should be possible to determine if an Old Politics–New Politics value dimension actually does underlie German perceptions of the political agenda. Moreover, the data used here embrace a period of considerable fluidity in the political environment, predating the surge of interest in the New Politics that began in the late 1960s. Thus, the study of political values can be pushed back beyond the more recent timespan covered by Inglehart's data, and changes can be traced back more closely to their beginnings.

The analysis begins with the full set of issues available in each of the three studies. These sets mix long-term issues of German politics with "flash" issues of short duration. The pattern of the relationships between issue interests should identify which issues, if any, are seen as tapping the concerns of Old Politics and New Politics. The link between any specific issue and the underlying value dimension is, however, largely defined by the social and political context.[14] For example, support for education can tap a New Politics interest in self-improvement and intellectual enrichment, or it can reflect a materialist awareness that education is a ladder to economic success. Specific issues may also change over time in the strength and nature of their relationship to the value dimension. Thus, attention will focus on the broad patterns of the entire value dimension, because a changing political environment may manifest this dimension in different ways over time.

To identify these patterns in a systematic and parsimonious fashion, the data were subjected to a principal components analysis.[15] As table 6.2 shows, all of the issues load positively on the first dimension (I) of

Table 6.2. Principal components analysis of issue salience, 1961–1972.

	July 1961			Nov. 1969			Sept. 1972		
Issue	I[a]	II[b]	Issue	I[a]	II[b]	Issue	I[a]	II[b]	
				Old politics					
Price stability	0.40	0.69	Price stability	0.44	0.70	Law and order	0.38	0.61	
Old age	.43	.58	Old age	.46	.58	Price stability	.23	.55	
Economy	.41	.47	Reduced taxes	.47	.29	Old age	.41	.39	
Reduced taxes	.48	.42	Honesty	.62	.23	Terrorists	.48	.29	
Reunify Germany	.65	.13				Health	.49	.24	
National secur.	.59	.13				National secur.	.48	.21	
Honesty	.59	.05	National secur.	.60	.05	USA relations	.62	.02	
Short hours	.38	.02	Church tax	.33	.00	Housing	.52	.00	
Housing	.62	−0.06	Reunify	.67	.06	Agriculture	.54	.00	
						Tax redistrib.	.46	−0.03	
						Environment	.52	−.05	
				New politics					
USSR relations	.59	−.18	Education	.64	−0.14	China relations	.59	−.28	
Education	.65	−.25	USA relations	.70	−.21	East relations	.45	−.28	
USA relations	.73	−.26	USSR relations	.67	−.23	Education	.58	−.31	
Eur. unity	.66	−.27	Recognize GDR	.24	−.34	Abortion	.47	−.38	
Nuclear ques.	.43	−.42	Codetermin.	.51	−.36	Gastarbeiter	.45	−.44	
Underdeveloped	.52	−.51	Redefine states	.34	−.56				
Eigenvalue	4.67	1.96		3.72	1.64		3.86	1.64	
Total variance	31%	13%		29%	13%		24%	11%	
(N)	(1,299)			(689)			(1,577)		

a. General issue salience.

b. Old Politics–New Politics salience.

the principal components analysis, reflecting a general interest in political issues.[16] If an individual is interested in politics, he or she tends to be generally interested in all political issues, while the uninvolved citizen is often disinterested in all issues. Consequently, this first dimension measures general issue salience.

The second dimension (II) in table 6.2, however, delineates two distinct groups of issues at each timepoint. This implies that, after controlling for general issue salience, individuals tend to focus their interest on one of two distinct sets of issues.[17]

Beginning in 1961, a broad set of issues apparently taps a common Old Politics theme. Price stability and old age security have the highest loadings. They are joined by two other domestic issues, improving economic conditions and reducing taxes, which reflect a clear materialist emphasis on economic security, and by the foreign policy issue of national security.

Conversely, in the same year a second cluster of what are apparently New Politics issues loads at the opposite end of the second dimension. The two issues of support for education and for relations with the United States fall within this grouping. They are joined by several foreign policy items that emphasize a cooperative approach to international relations: improving relations with the USSR, strengthening European unity, aiding underdeveloped nations, and dealing with nuclear questions.

The previous chapter presented evidence that the electorate apparently can and does distinguish between the conflictual and cooperative aspects of foreign policy. The present data translate this conflictual-cooperative distinction into a broader conceptual perspective distinguishing the Old Politics from the New Politics.[18] Significantly, the issue of relations with the USSR clusters together with such New Politics issues as relations with the United States, European unity, and aid to underdeveloped nations. Conversely, security from Russian attack, a foreign policy item with an explicit national security theme, tends toward the Old Politics end of the continuum.

The 1961 pattern is generally repeated in the new set of issues in the 1969 survey.[19] Price stability and old age security again show the highest Old Politics loadings on the second dimension, but now they are joined by the issues of reducing taxes and honesty in public life (*Sauberkeit im öffentlichen Leben*).

The 1969 New Politics cluster again includes a mix of foreign and domestic issues. Better relations with the United States and the USSR cluster together as in 1961, implying that German interests in improving international relations are not directed solely at the West but include the East as well. In the domestic arena, support for education is joined by the issue of codetermination, whose goal (to increase employee participation in the general decision-making process of large firms) bears a direct relationship to other New Politics goals.[20]

By the 1972 election, the issues of the New Politics had been clearly defined in German politics. The change in government following the 1969 election brought the more progressive SPD/FDP coalition to power, and the Social Democrats implemented a broad set of domestic reforms in health, education, and social services. The new foreign policy of discussion and reconciliation with the nations of Eastern Europe (Ostpolitik) lessened international tensions and marked the beginning of a new cooperative era in German foreign policy. To symbolize his commitment to domestic reforms, the Social Democratic chancellor, Willy Brandt, said that he wanted to be a *Kanzler der inneren Reformen* ("chancellor of domestic reforms"), and it was for the success of his Ostpolitik that he received the Nobel Peace Prize in 1972. It can be hypothesized, therefore, that by the 1972 election the New Politics had established itself in the minds of the German public as a new dimension of political cleavage as well as a new element of the political agenda.

Thus it is not surprising that the clearest distinction between the issues of Old Politics and New Politics appears in 1972. Interest in the Old Politics issues of price stability and old age security are again prominent, tapping the economic concerns of materialists. At one end of the second dimension these issues are joined by two items reflecting the domestic security and national security aspects of the Old Politics: the problem of law and order and protection from attack by radical foreign terrorists.

The New Politics cluster in 1972 also represents a broad range of political concerns. The issue of support for education emerges with a strong loading on the second dimension along with two other domestic issues: equal rights for foreign workers (*Gastarbeiter*) and abortion on demand. And again, improvement in international relations is viewed as a New Politics theme, including good relations with the People's Republic of China and improved relations with Eastern Europe.

Four of the issues discussed above—price stability, old age security, support for education, and relations with the United States,—were included in comparable form in all three surveys.[21] Because subsequent analyses that attempt to maximize longitudinal comparability will focus on these core issues, a special effort should be made to verify that these four items alone are adequate measures of the Old Politics–New Politics dichotomy. The best evidence comes from table 6.2, which ties the four issues to the full agenda of German politics. These analyses consistently indicate that the issues separate into Old Politics and New Politics clusters. Interest in price stability and old age security results in one set of issues. Conversely, interest and support for education tends to accompany interest in good relations with the United States.

To further substantiate these results a separate series of principal components analyses were run on the four core issues (table 6.3). The first dimension again represents general interest or salience. The second dimension sorts the four issues into the same two groups as before: Old Politics concerns and New Politics concerns. The issues of price stability and old age security load positively on the second dimension. The materialist emphasis of these issues on economic security clearly fits a model of political conflict along Old Politics lines. Conversely, support for education and relations with the United States seem to reflect a common interest in New Politics questions. While education can be seen as a means toward economic advantage, the political discussion of the 1960s stressed other aspects of this issue. Improving educational facilities includes a concern for cultural and intellectual enrichment, which is at the heart of New Politics values. The drive for more equal distribution of educational opportunities, a more contemporary curriculum, and the growing student movement on German campuses in the late 1960s injected a strong New Politics component into the debate on the educational system.

The area of foreign policy can also entail two divergent value concerns. On the one hand, the division of Germany in the postwar period and the generally high level of East-West conflict have made national security especially salient. On the other hand, concern with the world outside Germany, especially when it involves an element of interna-

Table 6.3. Principal components analysis of issue salience, four core issues, 1961–1972.

Issues	July 1961		Nov. 1969		Sept. 1972	
	I[a]	II[b]	I[a]	II[b]	I[a]	II[b]
Price stability	0.69	0.53	0.74	0.47	0.48	0.61
Old age	.73	.46	.74	.47	.56	.50
USA relations	.64	−0.53	.59	−0.60	.70	−0.37
Education	.58	−.62	.64	−.53	.63	−.51
Eigenvalue	1.76	1.19	1.87	1.10	1.45	1.04
Total variance	44%	30	47	27	36	26

a. General issue salience.
b. Old Politics–New Politics salience.

tional cooperation as in the issue of European integration, is another aspect of the broadening world perspective of the New Politics.[22] Given this divergence, the designation of "relations with the United States" as an indicator of New Politics orientations may seem open to debate. For some Germans the issue of U.S. relations may connote ties to the NATO alliance and national security, while for others the New Politics element of international cooperation is more salient. Here, however, we believe it is justified to emphasize the latter element. The analysis presented in table 6.2, the prominence of Ostpolitik, and the general improvement of East-West relations all indicate that the issue of U.S. relations has a decreasing security and an increasing New Politics connotation in contemporary Germany.

Thus, the public's perception of both the four core issues and the full set of issues included in the three surveys appears to fit well into an Old Politics-New Politics perspective. All the surveys provide substantial evidence that such a framework organizes the public's interest in specific political issues. This is true even for the 1961 survey, which predates the increased visibility of New Politics themes in the late 1960s. The Old Politics–New Politics dimension is consistently the first basis of issue-differentiation to emerge from the principal components analyses, a fact that underscores the importance of this conceptual structure to German politics. Moreover, this classification of issues is fairly similar across major subgroups of the German population.[23] And finally, the broad classification of Old Politics and New Politics themes parallels the results of other analyses of German public opinion.[24]

A Measure of Issue Orientations

In order to further validate the distinction between Old Politics and New Politics and to examine the distribution of these issue orientations throughout the electorate, the next task is to construct a single measure of issue orientations. A broad index of interest in Old Politics versus New Politics issues should allow analysis and discussion of basic political beliefs, since short-term variations in the salience of specific issues will tend to balance out when multiple indicators are used.

Inglehart maintains that most people place a positive value on both material and postmaterial goals:

> It is not a question of valuing one thing positively and the other negatively . . . But in politics it is sometimes impossible to maximize one goal without detriment to the other. In such cases the relative *priority* among valued objectives becomes a vital consideration . . . it appears that although nearly everyone strongly favors freedom of speech (for example), there are striking differences in the priorities given to it by various social groups.[25]

Therefore, to assess value priorities Inglehart forces respondents to choose between alternatives by *ranking* four social goals.[26] Based on this classification, he finds that only about 10 percent of the German adult population can be considered "pure" postmaterialists, while nearly 50 percent are "pure" materialists.[27] This small proportion of postmaterialists, or New Politics citizens, should not seem surprising. The change from the Old to the New Politics should take several generations to complete, and viewed in historical perspective the conditions fostering the New Politics in Germany have only existed for a short time. But even if only a small proportion of the population supports the New Politics, its importance should not be discounted because the postmaterialists are disproportionately represented among political elites and among those actively involved in politics.[28] Moreover, postmaterialist concerns are increasingly affecting contemporary politics.

The issue-interest measures do not allow a ranking of issues in relation to one another. Indeed, the positive loadings for all issues on the first dimension of the principal components analyses in this study indicate that an individual's general level of issue salience affects all issue responses; that is, people who are interested in any issue are generally interested in all. But it is not the absolute level of value (or issue) importance that is crucial. Rather, it is the relative importance of Old Politics issues versus New Politics issues when a decision must be made. Therefore, to measure Old Politics–New Politics orientations with the issue-interest questions requires another approach.

One way to arrive at such an approach is to view Old Politics and New Politics orientations as two endpoints of a single continuum. The issue interests of any individual may span a considerable range along this continuum. However, the needs (or political issues relating to these needs) that lie closer to an individual's own value position will receive greater attention than the more distant needs. Someone near the New Politics end of the continuum will concentrate more on New Politics issues, while another person near the center of the continuum will be personally interested in a mix of Old Politics and New Politics themes. Therefore, studying the relative importance a respondent gives to a series of issues along the entire continuum should help in identifying his or her location.

There are several ways in which this model can be put to use. The simplest is to compare the average salience of Old Politics issues with that of New Politics issues.[29] The relative importance of these two domains would assign each individual a location on the Old Politics–New Politics continuum. These issues vary, however, in their relationship to the underlying value dimension. Therefore a more precise approach would weight issues by the strength of this relationship, giving an issue with either a clear Old Politics or a clear New Politics content greater weight in constructing the index than a less clearly defined issue.

The principal components analyses of issue salience suggest what these weights may be, and they also provide a method of use. For the second, or issue-differentiating, dimension, an index score for each individual can be computed that is a weighted sum of the salience ratings of all issues.[30] In summing issue salience ratings, Old Politics issues are given positive weights based on their second-dimension loading; New Politics issues are given negative weights as functions of their loadings. A score of zero on this index indicates that the relative importance of the two domains is equal to the average for the total sample.[31] A large positive score thus represents a higher-than-average priority for Old Politics issues, and large negative scores indicate a higher-than-average priority for New Politics issues.

To obtain an issue-orientations index of maximum temporal comparability, index scores were computed from the second dimension of the principal components solutions using only the four core issues shown in table 6.3. A second, broader issue-orientations index is based on responses to the full set of issues in each survey, as given in table 6.2. These two indexes can be used nearly interchangeably, because they are highly correlated in all three studies (1961, $r = 0.79$; 1969, $r = 0.71$; 1972, $r = 0.66$).

Because the index scores for each year are standardized around the population average, the absolute distribution of Old Politics and New Politics orientations within the population cannot be determined. However, the absolute issue salience indicates that the most salient issues of German politics appear to tap Old Politics concerns: price stability, old age security, and international security.[32] Issues with an apparent New Politics emphasis—such as support for education and cooperative foreign relations—appear less salient to the public. Thus, to the extent that comparisons are possible, the data support earlier evidence that contemporary Germany is still predominantly oriented toward materialist goals. Trend analyses suggest, however, that although the salience of Old Politics issues has been fairly constant until quite recently, New Politics issues seem to be attracting increasing attention.[33]

Both of the issue-orientation indexes can indicate whether a citizen places more emphasis on Old Politics or New Politics themes, relative to the rest of the population. The inclusion of a wide range of issues may make it possible to go beyond measuring simple issue salience to indirectly measuring more basic political attitudes or political values.

Single issues are easily influenced by short-term factors; but if orientations are measured across a wide range of issues, short-term effects may tend to cancel out, yielding an index of more basic attitudes. Although the issue indexes may still not be so robust and direct as Inglehart's instrument in indicating political values, they should tap the same basic concept and reflect the same causal forces.

Distribution of Issue Orientations

Although Old Politics–New Politics orientations are undoubtedly influenced by events occurring during an individual's adult life, research on political values consistently stresses the importance of experiences during the formative period of adolescence.[34] The environments in which individuals grow up are influenced by two different types of forces. One type acts upon entire generations, as these are conceptualized by Karl Mannheim.[35] Each cohort shares similar experiences of societal affluence or scarcity, of peace and order or war and chaos. The other type acts on individuals to produce variations in experience within generations. Unequal distribution of resources within society, for example, produces some variation in formative experiences among members of the same generation.

Prior research stresses generational differences in value priorities.[36] Postwar European cohorts have grown up during a period of unprecedented prosperity and the absence of war. As a consequence, security needs are being replaced by a concern for New Politics themes. In order to capture the effect of general social and economic conditions in this study, generational units have been defined according to the political regime under which an individual was socialized: Wilhelmine Empire, Weimar, Third Reich, early Federal Republic, or late Federal Republic.

The two Federal Republic generations should be the most oriented toward New Politics issues. Expectations for the relative ordering of the three earlier generations are more ambiguous. All of these experienced external or economic turmoil during or soon after their adolescence: World War I, the collapse of the Kaiserreich, the inflation and political disturbances of the early 1920s, the depression, World War II and its aftermath. Possibly the oldest (Wilhelmine) respondents grew up during the most peaceful times; but to the extent that childhood values are malleable by subsequent events, earlier generations may have been affected by World War I and the turmoil that followed it.

Mean scores on the orientations indexes for both the set of four core issues and the set of full issues show that the Federal Republic generations are almost always more interested in New Politics issues than are prior generations (table 6.4). In 1972, for example, the youngest cohort displays a clear orientation toward New Politics concerns on the full issue index (− 0.68), while at the other extreme the Wilhelmine generation displays a stronger than average interest in Old Politics issues (0.59). With only one exception, the core issue set in all three years shows pure monotonicity across generations. The ambiguous expectations for the older generations are confirmed in table 6.4 by the full issue index, which contains three different patterns for the three pre-World War II generations. All in all, however, the data appear clearly supportive of previous findings on Germany: younger cohorts socialized during the affluent postwar era display relatively greater attachment to New Politics issues, while the older cohorts reared in more troubled times show a correspondingly higher priority for Old Politics issues. In addition, the power of the generational classification to differentiate between issue orientations increases over time, whether measured by the range of mean-score differences or with the eta coefficient from an analysis of variance.

Table 6.4. Issue orientations by generation, 1961–1972.[a]

Generation	July 1961	Nov. 1969	Sept. 1972
	Core Issue Index		
Late FRG	—[b]	− 0.23	− 0.30
Early FRG	− 0.17	− .06	− .19
Third Reich	− .05	− .09	− .01
Weimar	.02	.15	.24
Wilhelmine	.21	.22	.28
Eta	.11	.13	.21
(N)	(1366)	(724)	(1853)
	Full Issue Index		
Late FRG	—[b]	− .42	− .68
Early FRG	− .15	− .06	− .32
Third Reich	.06	.02	.18
Weimar	.05	.23	.41
Wilhelmine	.00	.09	.59
Eta	.04	.12	.27
(N)	(1296)	(689)	(1557)

a. Numerical entries are the mean index score for each cohort. Negative values denote New Politics orientations; positive values denote Old Politics orientations.

b. There were no members of the late Federal Republic cohort in the 1961 study.

The second hypothesized source of value change, individual economic circumstances during adolescence, should ideally be measured by the parental social status when the respondent was a child. Respondents raised in prosperous homes should be more oriented toward the New Politics than individuals raised in conditions of hardship. But it is not easy to determine how economically secure individuals were during their formative years; for many respondents the relevant events had occurred thirty or forty years earlier. It is, however, relatively easy to obtain indicators of their present economic levels. Occupation provides one such possibility. Middle-class occupations are generally better paid than industrial workers, and most workers are better paid than farmers and farm laborers. In addition, the highly stratified and fairly rigid German social structure means that individuals who presently hold middle-class occupations were probably raised in middle-class families.[37] Therefore, occupation may serve as a rough indicator of the economic situation of one's family during adolescence as well as of one's present economic situation. Admittedly, however, this relationship is far from perfect.

But occupation, besides indicating present income levels, also differentiates between individuals in terms of economic security. This criterion distinguishes particularly between the old middle class, consisting of the self-employed and professionals, and the new middle class of civil servants and salaried white-collar workers.[38] Both the old and the new middle classes are well educated and relatively affluent. For a large portion of the old middle class, however, economic security is based on the ownership of capital, generally via small shops or craft trades. The losses this group suffered as a result of the inflation of the 1920s, wartime destruction, or postwar revaluation most likely impressed upon its members the importance of economic stability and preservation of property. The old middle class thus is particularly vulnerable; it has a personal stake in the preservation of stability and order. In contrast, the new middle class enjoys most of the benefits of high-status occupations and takes fewer risks. German civil servants are relatively well paid, cannot be laid off, and enjoy comfortable retirement benefits provided by the state. Similarly, salaried white-collar employees, especially in large firms, are buffered from economic shocks more than are members of the old middle class. Their affluence is not tied to the accumulation and preservation of their own capital, but to their ability to manage and use other people's capital. Moreover, their fortunes are less dependent on the success of any single firm, and in times of hardship their mobility provides further security. At the bottom of the economic scale, farming is the least secure of all occupations, with futures tied to the land and the whims of nature. The position of the working class is only marginally better; workers lack the affluence of the middle class, although today's social security programs provide some benefits.

The data show that these expectations are generally fulfilled (table 6.5). The new middle class is clearly the most interested in New Politics themes, usually followed by the old middle class. With one exception, the farmers turn out to be the most traditionally oriented group in terms of both the core issue index and the full issue index. Workers are generally more interested in Old Politics issues, with positive scores in five out of six instances. Thus, it appears that both the economic level and the security of an occupation are relevant factors in determining issue orientations.

This alignment of social groups marks an important departure from the traditional bourgeois-proletariat class alignment.[39] Instead of the old middle class and the working class being polarized in their interests, the two groups share very similar concerns on the Old Politics-New Politics dimension. Moreover, not only are they interested in the same issues, but they often share common policy positions on that dimension.[40] In contrast, the new middle class of the postindustrial

Table 6.5. Issue orientations by occupational class, 1961–1972.[a]

Class	July 1961	Nov. 1969	Sept. 1972
Core Issue Index			
New middle class	−0.35	−0.09	−0.21
Old middle class	−.09	−.07	−.05
Workers	0.09	0.06	0.16
Farmers	.37	.10	.08
Eta	.20	.07	.17
(N)	(1251)	(629)	(1663)
Full Issue Index			
New middle class	−.53	−.08	−.25
Old middle class	.13	.18	.02
Workers	.16	−.02	.18
Farmers	.30	.34	.21
Eta	.16	.07	.12
(N)	(1186)	(602)	(1420)

a. Numerical entries are the mean index score for each occupational group. Negative values denote New Politics orientations; positive values denote Old Politics orientations.

society does not fit the traditional class alignment. Rather than adopting a perspective that lies between the views of the old middle class and the workers, this group distinguishes itself from both of the traditional class strata by embracing the New Politics. (These data preview the analyses given in chapter 7, which examine the role of the new middle class in affecting the bourgeois-proletariat alignment of German politics.)[41]

Another potential determinant of political values is education. Obviously the two variables, generation and occupation, are related to education: the young are more likely to be highly educated than the old, and education is almost a prerequisite for many middle-class occupations. At the same time, however, education may provide an even more accurate indicator of the economic conditions of the respondent's adolescence than does either age or occupation. Educational level in a class-stratified educational system such as Germany's is a clear reflection of family resources during an individual's youth.[42] More tangentially, educational attainment taps the varying instructional content of the different types of German schools, which have been quite rigidly separated. The *Gymnasium* and the university, on the one hand, have traditionally stressed creative intellectual fulfillment (*Bildung*), whereas the "lower" types of schools, on the other hand, provide more specifically job-related skills (*Ausbildung*). In addition, the spirit of social and political protest so evident in the 1960s apparently appealed most to Gymnasium and university students.

Both kinds of education, however, result in the same expectations about the education distribution of issue orientations, and these expectations are confirmed by the data (table 6.6). Respondents with a Gymnasium or university education place considerably more emphasis on New Politics issues than do respondents with only primary school education. The relationship is perfectly monotonic in all three years. In addition, education appears to be a relatively strong determinant of issue orientations, as indicated by the wide range of mean score differences and by the high eta coefficients.

Although Inglehart presents similar evidence not only for Germany but for a large group of other nations, his postmaterialist theory has been criticized by several commentators. Alan Marsh, for example, suggests that in Great Britain the postmaterialist, New Politics phenomenon is the result of middle-class radicalism and the rise of a counterculture in the late 1960s.[43] And Paul Abramson uses American survey data to suggest that generational change has occurred only among the college-educated—again implying that the New Politics is a recent phenomenon, tied to the campus unrest of the 1960s.[44]

During the late 1960s, the German universities and their student

Table 6.6. Issue orientations by education, 1961–1972.[a]

Education	July 1961	Nov. 1969	Sept. 1972
	Core Issue Index		
Primary	0.19	0.12	0.23
Primary and technical	−0.07	−0.02	.06
Secondary	−.21	−.09	−0.38
Abitur	−.88	−.47	−.68
Eta	.20	.13	.27
(N)	(1369)	(724)	(1841)
	Full Issue Index		
Primary	.31	.06	.37
Primary and technical	−.12	.04	.12
Secondary	−.58	−.06	−.71
Abitur	−1.11	−.69	−.96
Eta	.18	.11	.27
(N)	(1299)	(689)	(1548)

a. Numerical entries are the mean index score for each educational group. Negative values denote New Politics orientations; positive values denote Old Politics orientations.

populations displayed the same kind of unrest as that seen in America and the rest of Europe.[45] The political values of the young and highly educated are indeed quite different from those of the rest of the population, as suggested by the educational and generational patterns presented here; but in order to prove the occurrence of long-term (not fleeting) value change, further evidence is required.

Critics of postmaterial value change point out that Inglehart's analyses were based primarily on a series of surveys begun as recently as 1970, well after the onset of the counterculture movement of the 1960s. Yet, similar generational and educational patterns appear not only in the 1969 and 1972 surveys but also in the 1961 study, which considerably predated the growth of the student counterculture movement. These criticisms can be tested more directly, however. If age-group differences reflect the changes in formative experiences at different points in German history, sizable age-group differences should exist within each level of education. In addition, the more educated should be more interested in the New Politics than the less educated at every age level, and not only among the younger counterculture generation.

Because a table showing the full breakdown of value orientations by

Table 6.7. Issue orientations by generation and education, 1961–1972.[a]

	Education[b]								
	July 1961			Nov. 1969			Sept. 1972		
Generation	Low	Medium	High	Low	Medium	High	Low	Medium	High
Late FRG[c]	—	—	—	−0.04	−0.24	−0.41	−0.03	−0.12	−0.84
Early FRG	−0.01	−0.11	−1.04	0.10	−.05	−.53	0.06	−.07	−.70
Third Reich	0.10	−.10	−0.48	−.12	0.02	−.47	.15	0.06	−.42
Weimar	.24	−.09	−.48	.16	.19	0.01	.34	.26	−.13
Wilhelmine	.35	0.09	−.24	.43	−.09	.28	.42	.29	−.25

a. Numerical entries are the mean score on the core issue orientations index. Negative values tend toward the New Politics pole; positive values tend toward the Old Politics pole.

b. Low: only Volksschule. Medium: Volksschule and technical training. High: some secondary school or more.

c. There were no members of the late FRG cohort in the 1961 study.

generation and education would be quite complex, these data are presented only for the core issue index; both issue indexes display the same pattern, however. It is clear from table 6.7 that both generational and educational effects exist independently in the data. In all three studies, the young are generally more interested in New Politics issues, even after controlling for education. In 1972, for example, among Germans with only a Volksschule education (low) the young are slightly more interested in New Politics issues (−0.03) than the average citizen (hypothetically 0.00), while interest in the Old Politics steadily increases among older Volksschule-educated citizens (for example, Wilhelmine = 0.42). Similarly, the higher educated are also more interested in New Politics issues, even after controlling for generation. The phenomenon under investigation thus appears to be more than counterculture rhetoric among only the young college generation who were stimulated by the turbulent environment of the late 1960s. Furthermore, similar patterns again appear in the 1961 study, carried out long before student unrest appeared on German campuses.

Overview of the Changing Political Agenda

The evidence in Part Two of this book has documented fundamental changes in the German political environment and in public opinion. The past three decades have brought an exceptional improvement in economic well-being and a restructuring of the occupational force. Foreign policy has manifested a steady withdrawal from the Cold War politics of confrontation between East and West. Cooperation and reconciliation have become the guidelines of German policy.

This chapter has uncovered consistent patterns of change in both the political agenda and the political values of the German public. To a large extent these patterns can be traced to the effects of the political environment on opinions and attitudes. The economic and international uncertainty of the immediate postwar period heightened concern for the Old Politics issues of economic growth, economic security, and national security. But as domestic and foreign policy conditions have improved, the contemporary agenda of politics has altered to include an additional set of issues: Sozialpolitik and Ostpolitik, or the New Politics. Quite apart from its short-term impact on the political agenda, the sociopolitical environment during adolescence also shapes basic political values. Individuals socialized in an environment of economic hardship or physical insecurity apparently develop an enduring concern with these themes. Conversely, an environment in which economic and physical security is assured allows other values to gain priority, values associated with the New Politics.

In sum, the sociopolitical environment influences public opinion at two different levels. Short-term changes in the environment may be expected to have a fairly direct impact on perceptions of the political agenda. Political values, on the other hand, reflect the enduring consequences of political experience that may have occurred twenty or thirty or more years ago.

The causal importance of early life experiences and the sharp historical contrasts in Germany's sociopolitical environment have consequently led to large generational differences in the political values and orientations of the German public relative to other Western industrial societies. Pre-World War II generations were invariably reared in periods of economic or social hardship, or at least of great uncertainty. The data analyzed here, along with evidence from other sources, show that prewar generations still attach high priority to the Old Politics goals of ensuring economic and physical security. In contrast, the exceptional affluence and international stability of the postwar period have led younger Germans socialized in this environment to develop an open interest in New Politics themes. These persisting effects of historical experience emerge quite clearly and consistently.

In addition, the environmental correlates of social class affect the formation of values within generational units. New Politics orientations are strongest among the new middle class, reflecting the affluence of their middle-class upbringing and the later-life influence of occupational role. The old middle class display less interest in the New Politics because, despite their middle-class upbringing, their occupations reinforce Old Politics concerns. Strong interest in Old Politics is found among the working class, a product of their less affluent childhood and current position in the socioeconomic structure.

Of course, the formation of value priorities is also influenced by other factors. An individual's position in the life cycle has some impact on his or her current values.[46] In addition, elite actions or events may hasten or retard the pace of change. And the equalization of economic opportunities, economic security, and educational opportunities will also affect the speed of this process. Yet, while the potential impact of these factors should not be underestimated, early life experiences exert the dominant influence on value formation.

Thus, the extension of New Politics value priorities should be seen as a long-term process. The present number of New Politics types in the German electorate is fairly limited, because most adult Germans were socialized in environments of some hardship or insecurity. But the process of population turnover can be expected to move the population gradually toward New Politics interests as older, more traditionally oriented generations are replaced by younger, differently oriented cohorts.

The conditions of economic growth and international stability that have nurtured New Politics values among younger Germans are not necessarily permanent. The apparent reversals in these trends will be discussed in chapter 11. But if values are formed early in life, the immediate impact of the changing environment should be restricted primarily to the young, whose values are in the process of being formed; the values of older cohorts should be less affected. Moreover, unless the reversals are severe enough to make the young adhere to Old Politics values as strongly as the very oldest German cohorts, the process of population turnover will still move the electorate toward the New Politics, though at a slower rate of change. And finally, even if the very youngest cohorts are less interested in the New Politics, there will be some time lag before they are old enough to have a significant impact on the composition of the electorate.[47]

As support for the New Politics gradually accumulates, it should begin to exert a multifaceted and more visible impact on German politics. The New Politics transition may, for example, produce a change in basic orientations toward politics and the political system, reflecting the new motivations of the electorate. The postmaterial, or New Politics, stress on participation in decision-making is likely to increase demands for greater citizen input. Inglehart foresees a postmaterial society of declining trust in government and the rise of "elite-challenging" modes of political participation.[48] And indeed, the renewed interest in codetermination and especially the continued and rapid growth of citizen initiatives tend to support this conclusion.

New Politics supporters also emphasize political goals that traditionally have not attracted much public attention and certainly have not been the major concern of political decision-makers. As the number of New Politics citizens increases, their concerns are likely to enlarge the scope of the political agenda. In 1961 when the SPD attempted to get public support with the campaign slogan "Blue Skies over the Ruhr," the appeal was premature and did not attract widespread interest. Recently, however, environmental concerns have become a very salient issue in German politics.[49] Moreover, as elites sense the changing public concerns, they can be expected to vie for the attention and support of this new issue public, thus further accelerating the process of transition.

To some extent this awareness has already manifested itself in the changing vocabulary of election campaigns. The CDU as the traditional government party had throughout the 1950s and early 1960s adopted very conservative slogans like *Keine Experimente* ("No Experiments," 1957) and *Sicherheit für Alle* ("Security for All," 1965). In its attempt to win the confidence of crucial groups in the electorate, the SPD almost mirrored these slogans with sayings such as *Sicher ist Sicher* ("Better Safe than Sorry," 1965). The changing climate of opinion in the later 1960s led the SPD to espouse a theme of "We Create the Modern Germany" in 1969. Even the CDU in its attempt to regain power in 1972 bowed to the apparent new trend (at least in vocabulary) by including the word "Progress" in its cleverly balanced slogan, "Progress Based on Stability."

Finally, several authors have suggested that the transition to the New Politics should parallel a decline in social-cleavage-based politics.[50] As new issues and values develop that bear little relation to the traditional economics and class structure of the Old Politics, the relevance and determining force of social characteristics as cues for partisan behavior should decline.

Part Three

Changing Partisan Politics

7

Transition in the Social Bases of German Partisanship

THE POSTWAR CHANGES in the German political culture and political agenda have led to equally important changes in German partisanship and partisan behavior. Part Three focuses on these changes. This chapter considers the most basic source of political orientations, social characteristics, in particular, class, religion, region, and rural-urban residence, and their impact on voting behavior. Chapter 8 reassesses an alternative source of political orientations—partisanship—whose relevance for explanations of German voting behavior has frequently been criticized. Emphasis is placed on the development of partisan loyalties and on the functions of partisanship in political activities other than voting. In chapter 9 we explore the role of partisan images in explaining political change in the Federal Republic. Altering a party's popular image often leads to fundamental changes in partisan loyalties, and both the SPD and CDU/CSU have consciously worked to redefine their image in the public mind. The last chapter in this part integrates all three of these concepts—social characteristics, partisanship, and party images—into a single model of voting choice, enabling us to assess both the relative influence of each factor on partisan behavior and their interrelationships.

Traditional Partisan Politics

Traditionally, Germany has been described as a country in which politics and the general operation of the political system are heavily influenced by socioeconomic, cultural, and demographic cleavages. Although by World War I Germany had generally completed the transition from a primarily agrarian society to an industrial power, traditional

163

values and patterns of social relations persisted. Ralf Dahrendorf has described the Wilhelmine Empire as an "industrial feudal society," and Lewis Edinger has suggested that Germany's transition from a preindustrial society to an advanced industrial society was still taking place during the Third Reich.[1] These traditional forms of social relations carried over, of course, to the political sphere.

The polarized, fragmented, multiparty system of the Wilhelmine Empire catered to those constituencies that were distinguished from one another by class and religion. This unique party system not only survived the fall of the empire at the end of World War I, but it actually seemed to become more polarized and fragmented in the turbulent environment of the Weimar Republic. The adoption of proportional representation and other constitutional provisions served to further splinter the party system because they tied each party to an even more narrowly defined constituency.

The social and demographic changes brought about by World War II and its aftermath, as well as the dramatically increasing rate of prosperity associated with the *Wirtschaftswunder*, accelerated the political development of Germany. Yet several commentators maintain that social structure is still important in partisan politics.[2] Paul Abramson even suggests that the importance of social class may be increasing.[3] Thus, in many ways, Germany appears to exemplify a European party system structured around the same social cleavages that were present at the turn of the century.[4]

There is also evidence, however, that the influence of social cleavages may be declining in importance. With the emergence of advanced industrialism the motivations of the citizenry have become much more complex and heterogeneous. A significant and growing portion of the population has developed interests in New Politics issues that cut across traditional class lines.[5] New groups have arisen that do not have a clear or predetermined place in the sociopolitical space; economic and cultural forces that have shaped past cleavages may be weakening; and increasing geographic, social, and occupational mobility may be further loosening traditional ties.

The decisions and actions taken by party elites in the postwar era suggest that they have been attempting to further the dissolution of traditional, cleavage-based alignments. The CDU/CSU was formed after the war explicitly to bridge the religious cleavage that had been so prominent in the empire and the Weimar Republic. The social welfare policies that CDU governments pursued in the 1950s were designed to attract workers to the party, thus extending its base beyond the middle class. For example, CDU governments instituted government-subsidized saving plans and arranged the sale of stock of the government-owned Volkswagen corporation to lower-income families. The success of these strategies made the CDU/CSU probably the first large catchall party (*Volkspartei*) in Central Europe and prompted the SPD to also take steps to alter its image.[6] Through actions such as the Bad Godesberg conference, the shifting foreign policy debate, and participation in the Grand Coalition in 1966–1969, the Social Democratic Party has attempted to shed the public image of a socialist working-class party and to also be seen as a broad Volkspartei. The SPD's policies of rapprochement with the Catholic church and the church's receptivity to these overtures also suggest a gradual secularization of the religious bases of political conflict.

A typology derived from S. M. Lipset and Stein Rokkan will be helpful in determining the degree to which social characteristics are changing as guides to political behavior.[7] Their conceptual structure provides a framework for monitoring the persistence, decline, or transformation of essential sociopolitical forces. Four dimensions of partisan differentiation are examined here: social status, religion, region, and rural or urban residence. Although the meaning or definition of each of these conceptual dimensions may reflect idiosyncracies of the German political system and therefore may not be identical to those found in other European party systems, the dimensions do capture the essence of cleavage-based voting and thus link these findings to a broader body of empirical research.

Social Status and Partisan Behavior

Social-status politics appears to be deeply ingrained in the nature of German partisan behavior. Despite attempts by the two major parties to broaden their appeal, survey evidence continually shows that the Christian Democrats (CDU/CSU) draw disproportionate support from farmers and higher-status occupations and that a large portion of the electoral strength of the Social Democrats (SPD) comes from working-class voters.

Although voluminous research has been done on the politics of social class, most of the findings relate to its static properties and not to its dynamic aspects.[8] Class alignments are important. But has the nature and importance of these alignments changed over time? If so, for what reason? Moreover, how does a change in the class bases of voting allow German partisan behavior to respond to other factors?

One way to begin answering these questions on the degree to which social status guides political behavior is to measure the voting difference between social groups or classes. In order to do this, Robert Alford's index has been used.[9] This is simply the difference between the percentage of the working-class vote and the percentage of the middle-class vote for the SPD.[10] The occupation of the head of the household has been employed as the indicator of class position. Although the absolute level of SPD (or CDU/CSU) voting may change over time for all groups, the Alford index is sensitive only to relative levels between groups.

The percentages of working-class and middle-class votes for the SPD for the period between 1953 and 1972 are presented in figure 7.1, and the Alford class-voting index for federal elections during the same period is given in table 7.1.

The time series begins with a class-voting index of thirty points in the 1953 election. Probably because religion exists as a cross-cutting cleavage in German politics, this value is not as large as those generally found in Britain or Scandinavia. Nevertheless, it does support the

Figure 7.1. Class voting differences: Working and middle classes, 1953–1972.

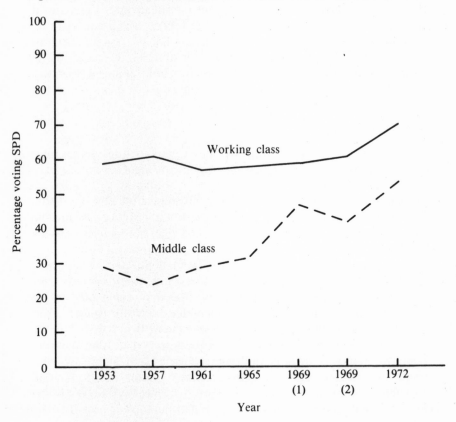

Table 7.1. Class voting index: working and middle class, 1953–1972.

Class	July 1953	June 1957	July 1961	Sept. 1965	Sept. 1969	Oct. 1969	Sept. 1972
Working-middle	30	37	28	26	12	19	17
(N)							
Working class	(394)	(549)	(505)	(501)	(385)	(234)	(669)
Middle class	(336)	(358)	(371)	(435)	(323)	(267)	(708)

historical emphasis on the class bases of German voting behavior. For two reasons class voting may have been weakened even more in the 1953 election. First, in 1953 the German party system was still somewhat fractionalized: six different parties won Bundestag representation. This fractionalization may partially explain why social classes were not more clearly aligned with the SPD or CDU/CSU. Second, foreign policy issues probably attenuated class voting. During the campaign Konrad Adenauer was forced to defend the controversial European Defense Community approved by the Bundestag in May; and the Russian suppression of the June 17 workers' uprising in Berlin partially overshadowed the election.[11]

Class voting increases significantly in the 1957 election (thirty-seven points).[12] Working-class support of the SPD rises slightly, but the sharp drop in middle-class support is even more noticeable. This election was the first in the postwar era not to be influenced by an immediate foreign policy crisis.[13] In addition, by 1957 the party system had become more stabilized; only four parties won Bundestag representation. The 1957 election, in fact, represents the high-water mark of postwar class voting in Germany.

But if the 1957 election result is an example of what could be expected in a strongly class-based system, it was not reassuring to the SPD. Between 1953 and 1957 the CDU/CSU had continued to absorb the support of the smaller parties at a faster rate than the SPD, and in 1957 it captured an absolute majority of the vote. Support for reformist elements within the SPD increased as a result of the disastrous 1957 election. Discussions and debate within the party culminated in the Bad Godesberg conference in 1959. Directed by Willy Brandt, Fritz Erler, and Herbert Wehner, moderates led the SPD to depart from its ideological traditions. The Godesberg program "discarded past demands for the socialization of basic industries and embraced 'free competition and free entrepreneurial initiative,' along with Keynesian economic policies. It abandoned the party's former opposition to German rearmament—atomic and conventional—and gave support to the new military establishment; it substituted a call for a harmonious 'partnership' between the SPD and the churches for previous attacks on 'clerical' influence in German politics."[14] In short, the moderate elements of the party sought to change the SPD's image from a socialist working-class party to that of a catchall party. These leaders felt that a moderation of SPD policies would broaden party support to include the elements of the middle class that the party needed in order to capture control of the government, without losing its traditional working-class base.

In 1961 class voting decreased sharply, by nine points. The differential in class support for the SPD was twenty-eight points, slightly lower than in 1953. Moreover, with the weakening of class voting the gap between the votes for the two major parties narrowed as the SPD picked up important new support from the middle class. This change in class voting may have reflected the SPD's changing image, but several other factors must also be considered.[15] Foreign policy was again a cross-cutting issue: Willy Brandt rallied opposition to the newly constructed Berlin Wall while Adenauer took a surprisingly moderate stance. Discussion of Adenauer's retirement also plagued the CDU during the campaign. But in the end the CDU/CSU maintained control of the government in coalition with the FDP.

The emphasis of the 1965 election was on domestic matters. The CDU/CSU stressed Ludwig Erhard's success in continuing the Wirtschaftswunder after he had assumed the chancellorship in 1963, and focused on the personalities of the candidates for that office in an extremely intense campaign. And yet, both social classes moved slightly toward the SPD in 1965 and class voting continued to decline (twenty-six points).

The following year the German economy drifted into a recession. Faced with difficult economic decisions and with opposition from the FDP to its proposed program, the CDU/CSU joined with the SPD to form the Grand Coalition in November 1966. Their joint economic efforts were generally successful, and by 1968 Germany was well along the road to economic recovery. Moreover, the SPD's first participation in the federal government and the party's success answered many questions about its integrity and its ability to govern (see chapter 9).

In 1969 the voters were faced with an unusual situation—an apparent lack of choice. The two major parties that had shared the government were competing for control, but in the eyes of the electorate the "era of good feelings" accompanying the Grand Coalition had undoubtedly blurred the distinction between the SPD and the CDU/CSU. Furthermore, until the election was over it was not clear whether the two major parties would continue the Grand Coalition. Prior to the election a majority of respondents (56 percent) felt that the coalition should continue. In this environment it is not surprising to find a dramatic shift in voting patterns. The pre-election survey shows that class voting decreased to less than half the pre-1969 level (twelve points). The SPD won sufficient support in the election to gain control of the government in a coalition with the Free Democrats, and for the first time in the history of the Federal Republic the CDU/CSU became the opposition party.

The dissolution of the Grand Coalition redrew the distinctions between the major parties. Class differences began to reemerge, increasing by seven points between the preelection and postelection surveys. Even with this increase, however, class voting was still below the pre-1969 level. Thus, the interpretation to be placed on the 1969 election is somewhat ambiguous. The preelection data suggest that the election was a critical point in a long-term process of change that was stimulated largely by short-term forces. But the postelection survey results suggest that the 1969 election marked the continuation of forces that had been gradually accumulating since the Godesberg program.[16]

The 1972 election provides some insights that help to interpret the 1969 results. The CDU/CSU emphasized economic issues during the 1972 campaign, and Karl Schiller, the SPD's former minister of economics, supported the CDU's claims that SPD policies were responsible for the recent slowdown of the economy. The fact that Schiller was widely viewed as personally responsible for the economic recovery in 1967–1969 made these criticisms all the more credible.[17] And yet, the pattern of class depolarization persists into the 1972 election with a class index still well below the pre-1969 level (seventeen points).[18]

It is clear, therefore, that although the Grand Coalition may have stimulated a short-term decline in class voting in 1969, the political alignment of that year was just one point in a long-term process of change that was evident again in the 1972 election. And SPD strategists certainly viewed the Grand Coalition as a part of their long-term plan to develop a new image for the party.

When other measures are examined, the same decline in social-status voting is generally apparent. For example, because educational opportunities have been extended only gradually in postwar Germany, education is still closely tied to the class structure. In 1972 over 33 percent of the middle class had completed at least a tenth-grade education (*Mittlere Reife*), while barely 3 percent of the working class had done so. Even among the youngest working-class cohort only 8 percent had reached that level. It is not surprising, therefore, that voting differences between educational strata show the same long-term trend as class voting (table 7.2). In 1953, 44 percent of the respondents with

Table 7.2. Educational level and SPD voting intentions, 1953–1972.[a]

	July 1953	June 1957	July 1961	Sept. 1965	Sept. 1969	Sept. 1972
Elementary school[b]	44%	48%	42%	45%	51%	60%
Secondary or more	19	23	29	38	49	51
Difference	25	25	13	7	2	9
(N)	(841)	(1033)	(1077)	(1086)	(889)	(1600)

a. Cell entries indicate the percentage of the major two-party vote intention given to the SPD.
b. Volksschule and some vocational training.

an elementary education (*Volksschule*) gave their vote to the SPD as against 19 percent of the voters with a secondary education or better. This difference declined dramatically over time until by 1969 only two percentage points separated the two educational strata. The 1972 election shows a slight increase in group differences, but the long-term pattern is very similar to that for class voting.

A better sense of the total impact of social-status influences can be obtained by combining several measures—class, education, and income—to predict voting choice. All three of these measures are highly related, and combining them should make a significant contribution to capturing the diffuse concept of social status. For each election between 1953 and 1972 these three measures were used in separate Multiple Classification Analyses (MCA) to predict voting preferences.[19] The combined effects of all three predictors are represented as the multiple correlation coefficient (R) at the bottom of table 7.3. These data show a long-term decline in voting based on social status in

Table 7.3. Social status and SPD voting intentions, 1953–1972.[a]

Measure	July 1953	June 1957	July 1961	Sept. 1965	Sept. 1969	Sept. 1972
Occupation	0.34	0.35	0.33	0.34	0.27	0.25
Education	.12	.07	.05	.08	.05	.06
Income	.11	.09	.07	.07	.09	.06
R	.39	.40	.33	.33	.26	.26
(N)	(841)	(1039)	(1077)	(1086)	(889)	(1608)

a. Cell entries are MCA beta coefficients, which represent the independent nonlinear correlation of each predictor with two-party vote intention.

postwar Germany. The multiple R for these three predictors declines from 0.39 in 1953 to 0.26 in both the 1969 and 1972 elections. The decline appears more gradual than that for class or education because the influences of all three social-status measures are combined.

The MCA beta coefficient for each predictor, given in table 7.3, is a measure of the unique effect of each social-status measure when controlling for the effects of the remaining predictors. The betas clearly show that class outweighs education or income in influencing partisan preferences. But all three of these predictors show a parallel decline in importance over time.

There are no inexorable trends governing election results; events or elite behavior may interrupt or reverse the patterns of change. But an attempt to identify the reasons for the trends can be made, and this may in turn suggest prospects for the future.

One explanation is suggested by the *embourgeoisement* theory of working-class voting.[20] The dramatically increasing rate of prosperity associated with the Wirtschaftswunder has been shown to produce an increasing overlap in the incomes and life-styles of people in middle-class and working-class occupations. As already mentioned, the CDU/CSU-led governments encouraged several programs to stimulate this process, including subsidized savings plans and the sale of Volkswagen and other state-owned corporation stock to low-income families. A narrowing of class voting differences may have accompanied this narrowing of objective class differences, if the affluent sector of the working class has assumed the values of its middle-class life-style.

Although this hypothesis seems plausible, there is little support for it in the data. The decline in class voting is not a result of the movement of the working class toward the conservative party. Over time, workers are actually voting somewhat more for the Social Democrats. Moreover, even within the working class voting differences are narrowing because of a general movement toward the SPD by all workers.[21] Rather, the middle-class movement toward the SPD is narrowing the gap between the classes. The process of change appears to be centered within the middle class, not within the working class.

An alternative explanation for the decline in class voting is the changing character of the middle class. The most notable aspect of this development is the rise of a so-called new middle class, consisting primarily of civil servants (*Beamte*) and salaried white-collar employees (*Angestellte*). This shift has been said to characterize the postindustrial society: a shift of manpower from industrial and agrarian occupations into the tertiary sector.[22] This change in occupations stimulates a change in outlook. While experience in the industrial sector leads individuals to emphasize efficient production and material achievement, those in the tertiary sector are less production-oriented and less concerned with material outputs. And it is within the tertiary sector that the new middle class is mostly concentrated.

During the postwar years the German new middle class has doubled in size, while farmers and the old middle class of professionals and self-employed have decreased substantially.[23] The crucial factor making the new middle class so important in the present context is its lack of a previous assignment within the traditional bourgeois-proletarian class structure. The separation of management from capital has created a social stratum that neither owns nor produces capital. Consequently, the new middle class finds itself with a position in the social structure and a life-style that places it between the working class and the old middle class.[24] As a result, its loyalties are divided between these other two social strata, and its votes are split between parties of the left and right. Thus, as the size of this group grows, its ambiguous voting behavior regarding social-status lines may lessen the overall importance of the class dimension of political cleavage.

This theory can be tested by recomputing the class voting indexes of the social strata to show the division of the middle class. If compositional factors are important, all three class voting indexes should be relatively stable over time, and the index comparing the old middle class and the working class should be generally higher than that comparing the new middle class and the working class. Thus class differences may be constant, but the redistribution of part of the electorate into two social strata that are less polarized vis-à-vis each other (that is, the new middle class and working class) may produce a total decline in social-status voting.

The percentages of the three social strata voting for the SPD are shown in figure 7.2. Differences between the old middle class and the working class produce a sizable index value within the 32- to 43-point range (see table 7.4). There is a slight decline after the 1969 election, but the total impression is one of high, and relatively constant, levels of class voting.[25] On the other hand, the voting behavior of the new middle class relative to the working class shows quite a different pattern. In 1957 only 26 percent of this stratum supported the SPD, producing a class voting index of thirty-five points. The movement of the combined middle class to the CDU/CSU in 1957 (see figure 7.1) can largely be traced to change by the new middle class. Following the Bad Godesberg conference in 1959 the SPD directed part of its attentions to winning the support of the new middle class. It appears that the SPD's policies were successful: by 1969 an absolute majority of that

Figure 7.2. Class voting differences: Working, old middle, and new middle classes, 1953–1972.

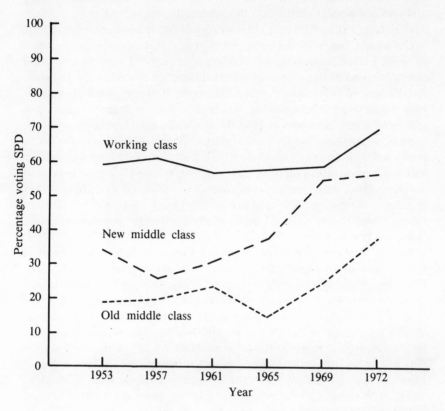

Table 7.4. Class voting indexes: working, old middle, and new middle classes, 1953–1972.

Class	July 1953	June 1957	July 1961	Sept. 1965	Sept. 1969	Sept. 1972
Working–old middle	40	41	33	43	34	32
Working–new middle	25	35	26	20	4	13
Old middle–new middle	15	6	6	23	30	19
(N)						
Working class	(394)	(549)	(505)	(501)	(385)	(669)
Old middle class	(120)	(107)	(103)	(115)	(80)	(167)
New middle class	(216)	(251)	(268)	(320)	(243)	(541)

class was voting for the Social Democrats, and in 1972 the party captured even more of its votes (57 percent).

As SPD support grew within the new middle class, the voting difference between that class and the working class steadily declined. Class voting decreased from the high of 1957 (thirty-five points) to an index of twenty in 1965, making the voting patterns of the new middle class closer to those of the working class (a difference of twenty points) than to those of the old middle class (a difference of twenty-three points). In 1969 the difference between the new middle class and the working class was only 4 percent, and in 1972 it was still only 13 percent.

Thus, the data in figure 7.2 and table 7.4 partially support the compositional hypothesis. The new middle class has shown substantially less class polarization than the old middle class, and the combined size of the two less polarized strata (new middle class and working class) is gradually increasing. But compositional change has been relatively slight: it is certainly not sufficient to fully explain the overall decline in class voting.[26]

Yet, to attribute even a portion of the total decline in social-status voting to compositional effects provides only a temporary answer. Changes in the quality and structure of German society are indeed occurring, and these changes are eroding the importance of social class as a basis of partisan differentiation. But, in large part, compositional change or change within the new middle class can appear important only insofar as it represents and stimulates a shift to political values that are independent of the social-status dimension. If the political values of the new middle class exactly mirrored those of the old middle class, then compositional change would not have any impact.

The lines along which these new political values may be developing, as well as the reasons behind the change, have been discussed in Part Two.[27] Economic factors have always been considered relevant to politics; and they have provided the basis for class conflict, that is, for pitting the haves against the have-nots. The unprecedented times of affluence and economic well-being associated with the Wirtschaftswunder may be satisfying basic economic needs, however, and nurturing feelings of economic security. Thus, for a portion of the German electorate the principal axis of partisan cleavage is shifting from economic issues to questions of life-style and the quality of life. Compositional change may be stimulating these New Politics values, but values—not mere compositional change—largely account for the decline in social-status voting.

The consequences of the rise of the new middle class are not restricted to that class alone. Political elites vying for the attention and support of the new middle class emphasize issues that are not within the realm of traditional cleavage politics—much as the SPD has done since inaugurating the Godesberg program. This, in turn, lessens the usefulness of traditional cleavage cues for the political orientation of other groups and further accelerates the process of change. Over-time trends toward the SPD within a class may thus reflect the electorate's awareness of changing party programs as the parties develop positions on these new issues. The new middle class, in short, is in the vanguard of the transition process, but the transition is not unique to this group.

Although a full discussion of the role of New Politics values in stimulating the decline in class voting is beyond the limits of the available data, these data do permit a partial test of the New Politics theory.

It is generally believed that basic value orientations are socialized early in life and maintained throughout the life cycle.[28] Therefore, if changing political values are critical in producing a decline in class voting, there should be a large generational component. Class voting should consistently be higher for the older, more materialist cohorts than for cohorts raised in the affluence of the postwar era. To test this hypothesis, five historically defined cohorts were tracked across the two-decade timespan of the data.[29] The proportions of middle-class (here, the whole class) and working-class voters within each cohort who supported the SPD at each election are shown in figures 7.3 through 7.7.

The generation that grew up during the Wilhelmine Empire was reared in a polarized environment in which a strong labor-union movement and the Social Democratic party provided an organizational focus for the class cleavage. Moreover, the socialist orientation of the SPD bore witness to Karl Marx's influence on German politics. When the Social Democrats moved away from doctrinaire Marxism, the founding of a vigorous Communist party served to keep the doctrine of class conflict alive up to the end of the Weimar Republic. Economic conditions during the first three decades of this century were also not conducive to erasing class differences. Moderate economic gains in the pre-World War I era were erased by the war and the postwar years. Consequently, figure 7.3 shows that the generally high level of class voting for the Wilhelmine generation in 1953 (38 points) continues relatively unchanged through 1972 (34 points).

The Weimar generation is in a similar position: it was socialized into politics in an environment of a party system highly fragmented by class and religion. The general postwar economic recovery of the 1920s was delayed in Germany as a result of domestic political instability and the continuing war reparations; and after economic conditions had begun to improve in the late 1920s, the depression hit Germany with particu-

Figure 7.3. Class voting differences: Wilhelmine generation.

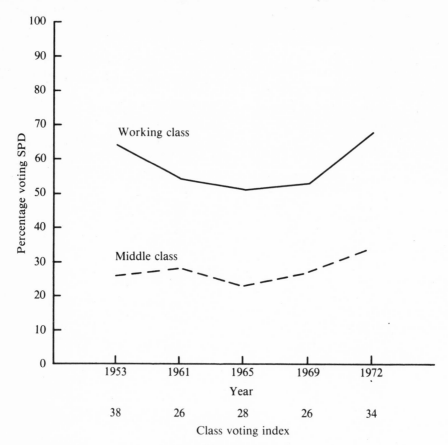

lar force. Consequently, the Weimar generation also displays a fairly high level of class voting, although it is lower than that for the Wilhelmine generation (figure 7.4). Moreover, the class voting index for the Weimar cohort remains fairly constant even beyond the depolarizing election of 1969. For both of these cohorts early life patterns of behavior have probably been carried through adult life. When materialist needs take priority and political parties are clearly linked in the voter's mind with fundamental social and economic cleavages, his or her social characteristics continue to be relevant in determining political predispositions.

Although the Third Reich generation also exhibits constant and

Figure 7.4. Class voting differences: Weimar generation.

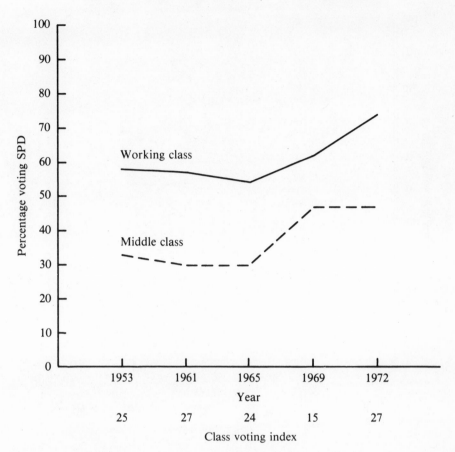

moderate levels of class voting similar to those of the Weimar generation, different processes have undoubtedly been at work with this
generation because it was not reared in a fragmented partisan environment (figure 7.5). But the class cues that existed in youth are nearly all
that this cohort retains to guide its present behavior. Moreover,
embryonic class differences were probably nurtured during its first
experiences with electoral politics under the Federal Republic, during
the most difficult period of economic reconstruction.

With the early Federal Republic (FRG) generation a change can be
detected in the class voting pattern (figure 7.6). Because the young are
more inclined toward New Politics values and less oriented toward the

Figure 7.5. Class voting differences: Third Reich generation.

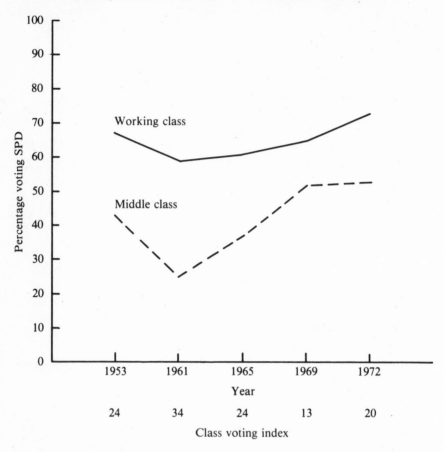

materialist concerns of their elders, the generations reared in the period of the Wirtschaftswunder would be expected to display less class voting than older cohorts. The early FRG generation begins with a moderate class voting index of twenty-five points in 1961, which drops steadily until it reaches fourteen points in the 1972 election. This decline is even more impressive when one considers that class voting normally increases through the life cycle as individuals accumulate class experiences and become more integrated into their class culture. The late FRG generation shows a still sharper drop in class voting; beginning with an index of eighteen points in 1965 this cohort drops to only a two-point difference in 1972 (figure 7.7). These declines in class voting among the young result largely from increased SPD voting by

Figure 7.6. Class voting differences: Early Federal Republic generation.

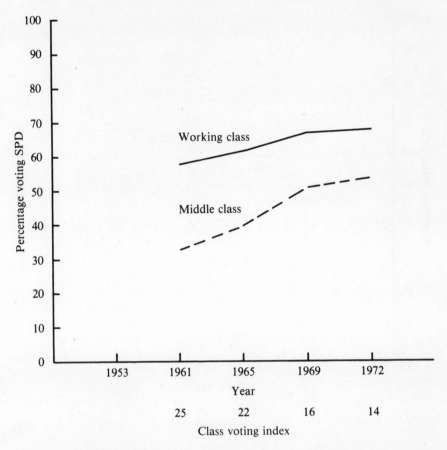

members of the middle class. More refined analyses show that the greatest change has come from members of the *new* middle class.[30] It is among the New Politics strongholds—the young and the new middle class—that the shift in class voting has been most noticeable.

In summary, strong and persisting relationships between class and vote are found among older generations that have experienced the uncertainties of world wars, the depression of the 1930s, or the hardships of a postwar recovery. But among postwar generations these relationships are weak and decreasing. A shifting economic and political environment appears to stimulate more change among the young because their values are more receptive to this new environment and because they are less locked in to long-standing patterns of behavior.

Figure 7.7. Class voting differences: Late Federal Republic generation.

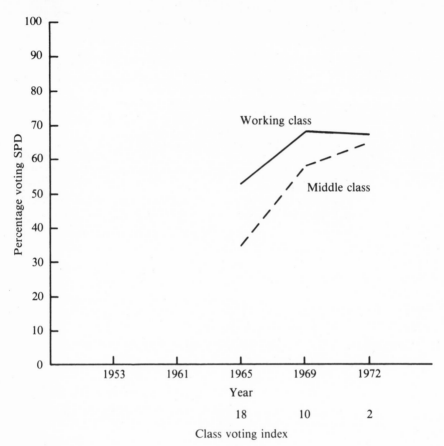

Religion and Partisan Behavior

Historically, religious conflict has been very intense in Germany. These conflicts took on more partisan overtones during the Wilhelmine Empire when Bismarck's policies of social discrimination against the Catholic church and its members (*Kulturkampf*) initially led to the formation of the *Zentrumspartei* representing the Catholic majority.[31] By mobilizing Catholics in defense of their interests the Zentrum became a major political force in both the Wilhelmine Empire and the Weimar Republic.

Religious conflicts carried over to the Federal Republic, although the situation had changed significantly. Catholics, who in 1937 had been a minority within Germany's borders, found themselves at parity with Protestants in the Federal Republic. The CDU/CSU, although it continued the traditions and appeals of the Zentrumspartei, also sought to reach beyond the Catholic sector and to become a broad-based religious party including both Catholics and Protestants. Its success in this attempt enabled it to control the government through the first two decades of the postwar period. Religious conflict was still intense in the early years of the Federal Republic, but it followed new lines. The traditional conflicts between Catholics and Protestants over church-state relations were replaced by differences between the religious and nonreligious sectors.[32] Hence the fiery rhetoric of the early electoral campaigns framed the contests as between Christian good (CDU/CSU) and Bolshevik evil (SPD).

Despite the historical importance of religion in German politics, both events and the behavior of elites convey the impression that religion is also declining as a basis of partisan differentiation. Beginning with its Godesberg program, the SPD has followed a conscious policy of modifying its antireligious public image. In the spring of 1965, a concordat between the SPD government in Lower Saxony and the Vatican guaranteeing the continued existence of state-supported religious elementary schools was viewed as an SPD concession to church interests. The visits of SPD leaders to the Vatican in the late 1960s were further attempts to achieve rapprochement with the Catholic church. Gradually the church has responded. The normalization of relations showed during the 1969 election when for the first time most Catholic bishops refrained from making public campaign statements to their parishioners in support of the CDU/CSU. As for the CDU/CSU, it continues to maintain its Christian image, though party elites have moderated their early religious campaign themes. In addition, there is convincing evidence of long-term decline in the associational and communal church involvement of both Catholics and Protestants.[33]

It was expected that the Social Democrats' policies of rapprochement with the Catholic church and the general secularization of society would produce a decline in religious polarization, but this has not occurred. Religious voting differences were measured by means of an index of religious voting similar to the Alford index of class voting. This index records the difference between the percentage of Protestants and the percentage of Catholics voting for the SPD. In 1953 the SPD was not very successful in appealing to either religious denomination (figure 7.8). Barely a majority of Protestants (51 percent) and less than a third of the Catholics supported the SPD in the election. The CDU/CSU's bi-religious image initially had a relatively strong attraction for both religious camps. Over time, however, the SPD's drawing

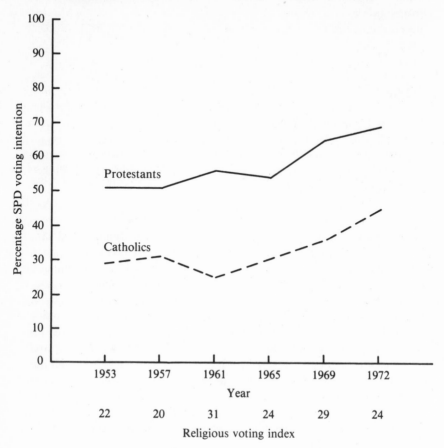

Figure 7.8. Religion and SPD voting intention, 1953–1972.

power has increased: in subsequent federal elections it received higher and higher proportions of the votes from both religious groups. Nevertheless, the gap between Protestant and Catholic support has not narrowed. From 1953 to 1972 the religious voting index hovers fairly constantly around the 25-point level. Whatever forces are drawing German citizens toward the Social Democrats are acting equally on Protestants and Catholics; religious affiliations are still as politically relevant in 1972 (index = 24) as they were in 1953 (index = 22).

A second aspect of religious voting is the strength of an individual's religious attachments. Church attendance is considered an important indicator of the associational aspect of religious attitudes, tapping both integration into the religious organizational structure and psychological

Table 7.5. Frequency of church attendance and SPD voting intentions, 1953–1972.[a]

Frequency	July 1953	June 1957	Sept. 1965	Sept. 1969	Sept. 1972
Never	63%	64%	64%	77%	74%
Occasionally	48	39	48	45	61
Frequently	17	19	17	32	28
Regression coefficient	0.23	0.23	0.23	0.22	0.22
(N)	(806)	(1035)	(1046)	(873)	(1514)

a. Cell entries indicate the percentage of the major two-party vote intention given to the SPD. Frequency of church attendance is not available for 1961. See note 34 to this chapter for the coding of church attendance in each survey.

identification with the religious subculture. The bi-denominational support of the CDU/CSU makes this an even more important measure in the German context. The data show that the SPD draws very heavy support from the nonreligious sector of the German population (table 7.5). Conversely, those who attend church frequently give only a minimal number of votes to the SPD. This relationship also remains remarkably constant over time. From 1953 until 1972 a fairly constant 45–47 percent difference in SPD voting separates those who attend church frequently from those who never attend church. Regressing the vote on frequency of attendance uncovers striking stability in the regression coefficients. (These coefficients are unstandardized measures.) Each group was voting more for the SPD in 1972 than in 1953, but the gap between the most frequent and the least frequent church attenders did not narrow.

The total pattern of religious influence can best be seen by combining denomination and frequency of church attendance into a single religiosity measure. A six-point religiosity scale was created by separately including three points of variation in frequency of church attendance (frequently, occasionally, never) for Catholics and for Protestants. Religiosity emerges as an extremely potent determinant of partisanship (figure 7.9). In 1953, for example, only 14 percent of those Catholics who frequently attended Mass voted SPD, while 65 percent of the Protestants who never attended services did so. The frequency of church attendance is less related to partisan behavior for Protestants than for Catholics. The regression of vote on frequency of Catholic church attendance yields a fairly stable regression coefficient of approximately 0.24 at each election (table 7.6). For Protestants the regression coefficient declines slightly from a highpoint of 0.18 in 1953 to around

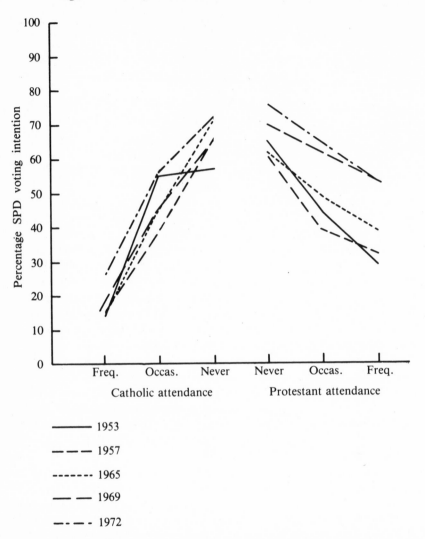

Figure 7.9. Religiosity and SPD voting intention, 1953–1972.

0.10 near the end of the timespan.[34] The overall pattern, however, is one of relative consistency in the nature of both relationships.

Explicitly religious issues apparently play a relatively minor role in the contemporary agenda of politics. Yet these several measures of religious influences appear to be surprisingly strong and persistent sources of partisan differentiation. Even when religious voting was studied from a generational perspective, little evidence of a decline in

Table 7.6. Regression coefficients: vote on frequency of church attendance, 1953–1972.

Year	Catholics	Protestants
1953	0.24	0.18
1957	.25	.16
1965	.28	.12
1969	.23	.07
1972	.23	.10

religious voting among younger cohorts was detected.[35] And still, the actions of SPD elites and the secularization of German society make these findings counterintuitive. Most observers of German politics believe that change in the religious bases of voting behavior is occurring.

In one sense these observers are correct. The focus so far has been on the degree to which religious cues guide partisan behavior, that is, the difference in voting patterns between religious groups, and not on the overall level of SPD or CDU/CSU voting. What has changed, however, is the level of SPD support. Because of the SPD's attempts to court the Catholic vote, attention has often focused on voting change only among the Catholic population. Indeed, even among strong Catholics 10 percent more are voting for the SPD than once did. But because precisely the same thing is happening among Protestants, the gap between Catholic and Protestant support of the SPD (and hence the explanatory power of religion) has remained constant. In short, the *level* of SPD support has increased among all religious sectors, but the *relationship* between religion and the voting decision has remained unchanged.

The decline in class voting has been tied in this study to Germany's transition toward postindustrial politics. The transition hypothesis is also compatible with the persistence of religious cleavages. Religion appears to reflect value orientations that parallel the Old Politics–New Politics value dimension. Ronald Inglehart has found that supporters of the New Politics are disproportionately Protestant and nonchurchgoers, but these groups already have SPD tendencies. Conversely, Catholics and churchgoers adhere to more traditional values and lifestyles, but they already support the CDU/CSU.[36]

Thus, the rise of postindustrial cleavages need not weaken the political impact of religious cleavages in the way that these same postindustrial cleavages contradict economic cleavages. The postindustrial transition might even strengthen the correlation between religion and voting as new sources of differentiation are added to the old. At the very least, the persistence of religious cleavages should not seem surprising.

Regional-Residential Differentiation

Regional variation has been another important theme in German partisan politics. While regional patterns in the Weimar Republic often reflected the spatial distribution of occupational or religious groups, other elements—regional history, elite behavior, and political subculture—also divided the support for political parties along regional lines.

Regional and local community ties were severely weakened by the policies of the Third Reich and by the wholesale population movements during and after World War II. Regional differences were further moderated after the war because the occupation forces consciously constructed artificial states (*Länder*), some of which had little continuity with traditional historical regions. The occupation forces also developed standard educational and communication systems within their occupation zones, which further moderated regional differences within the zones.

To tap the regional variation that still remains, the longitudinal voting patterns within all ten separate Länder must be considered. Aggregate electoral statistics are presented in addition to survey statistics in order to avoid the sampling variability of survey data for the smaller Länder. The Länder fall into apparently similar regional patterns, as table 7.7 suggests.

Bremen and Hamburg, for example, maintain their historical continuity as former Hansa city-states. Their largely Protestant and urban composition produces sizable SPD pluralities in most federal elections. On the other hand, the two northern states of Schleswig-Holstein and Lower Saxony are rural and heavily Protestant areas, sharing a common Prussian heritage. The citizens of both these Länder generally return CDU/CSU pluralities.

North Rhine–Westphalia might be considered not only a separate state but a separate region. This *Land,* artificially constructed after the war, divides its cultural traditions between the autonomous orientation of its Rhineland heritage and the Prussian orientation of Westphalia. It is the largest of the states, with over one-fourth of the Federal Republic's total population, and is heavily industrialized. The population is nearly evenly divided between Catholics and Protestants. Since 1957 North Rhine–Westphalia has shown a fairly steady trend toward the SPD, which in 1969 received its first plurality.

Rhineland–Palatinate and the Saarland represent the historical con-

Table 7.7. Vote by state (second vote) for the SPD, 1953–1972.[a]

State	1953	1957	1961	1965	1969	1972
Bremen	50.9%	55.0%	59.5%	56.2%	61.6%	66.3%
Hamburg	61.1	60.3	64.7	58.7	61.1	62.1
Schleswig-Holstein	36.0	39.0	46.5	44.5	48.4	53.6
Lower Saxony	46.0	45.6	49.8	46.4	49.2	53.0
North Rhine–Westphalia	39.4	38.1	43.9	47.4	51.7	55.1
Rhineland-Palatinate	34.3	36.1	40.6	42.6	45.6	49.5
Saarland	—[b]	31.4	40.6	45.9	46.3	52.5
Hesse	50.3	48.1	55.0	54.7	55.6	54.6
Bavaria	32.7	31.5	35.4	36.9	38.8	40.7
Baden-Württemberg	30.5	32.8	41.4	39.8	41.8	43.9
Sample eta	0.18	—[c]	0.11	0.12	0.18	0.15

Source: Karl Cerny, ed., *Germany at the Polls* (Washington, D.C.: American Enterprise Institute, 1979), pp. 230–231.

a. Entries show the percentage of the major two-party vote given to the SPD as recorded by the official election results.

b. Saarland was not formally part of the Federal Republic in 1953.

c. Region is not available in our version of the 1957 study.

tinuation of the Rhine province of the prewar era. The area is primarily Catholic and the CDU/CSU receives the support of the majority of both states.

Hesse, on the other hand, presents a very different pattern. This Land traces its history back to the Grand Duchy of Hesse. The population is primarily Protestant, and the state has a varied economic base. Because of its strong support for the SPD, in contrast to its conservative neighbors, it has been nicknamed "Red Hesse."

Finally, the two southernmost Länder of Bavaria and Baden-Württemberg form a single region. *Der Freistaat Bayern* has been the strongest of Germany's Länder in maintaining its regional identity. Bavaria traces its history back to the Kingdom of Bavaria, and it even maintained some degree of autonomy during the Third Reich. The area is heavily Catholic and agrarian in its orientation. The existence of the CSU (Christian Socialist Union), which was organized as a separate party representing the interests of Bavaria, underscores the state's political distinctiveness. By allying itself with the CDU in permanent political alliance, the CSU has maintained its interest and influence at the national level, and it appears as the sole Christian party on the Bavarian ballot. The CSU has consistently polled the majority of the votes in Bavaria since 1953. Baden-Württemberg, which combines the two prewar provinces of Baden and Württemberg, is fairly evenly balanced between Protestants and Catholics and is diversified economically. Historically this region has followed the Bavarian pattern, even while maintaining its independence. In terms of present voting patterns it parallels the Bavarian results, giving the majority of its votes to the CDU/CSU in every election since 1953.

There does not appear to be a clear trend of narrowing regional differences over time. Although each state is moving toward the SPD, each also retains some imprint of its cultural heritage. When the predictive power of the Länder is measured in each survey, the eta coefficients indicate that region has only a modest impact on vote, and there is no consistent pattern over time (see table 7.7).[37]

A second aspect of residential differentiation—rural-urban residence—is also worth considering. Although this dimension is often taken as a means of discriminating between rural and urban occupation groups, in theory it should also tap independent cultural forces. The isolation, homogeneity of opinion, and traditional values of rural society often pose a sharp contrast to the crowded, polycentrist, and modern perspectives of urban life.[38]

Although the population of the Federal Republic has grown dramatically during the past two decades, the rural population has steadily decreased in size. In 1953 over a third of the population lived in villages of less than 2,000 inhabitants, but by 1972 the size of this group had declined by about half. Moreover, transportation advances, the growth of the mass media, and the suburbanization of metropolitan areas have narrowed the distance and distinctiveness between city and country life. A long-term decline in partisan differentiation along the rural-urban dimension might therefore be expected.

The impact of rural-urban residence can be examined by classifying the size of the place of residence in terms of four broad categories (table 7.8). For all years there is a slight tendency for urban residents to vote for the SPD more than rural residents do. There does not, however, appear to be a decline in this difference over time. The regression of the vote on rural-urban residence yields a nearly constant slope of 0.07 in all elections. Therefore the gap between city and country voting has not narrowed despite considerable evidence favoring contrary expectations.

Building a Multivariate Model

Class and religion are generally seen not only as the major bases of party preferences in Europe but also as structuring the party systems themselves. It is unusual that these two lines of social cleavage should

Table 7.8. Town size and SPD voting intentions, 1953–1972.[a]

Population	July 1953	June 1957	July 1961	Sept. 1965	Sept. 1969	Sept. 1972
Under 2,000 (rural)	34%	35%	30%	29%	45%	45%
2,000–19,999	35	41	39	40	43	59
20,000–99,999	49	45	41	47	50	55
100,000 or more (urban)	53	52	50	55	66	69
Regression coefficient	0.07	0.05	0.06	0.08	0.08	0.07
(N)	(841)	(1039)	(1077)	(1068)	(889)	(1608)

a. Cell entries indicate the percentage of the major two-party vote intention given to the SPD.

exist simultaneously, as they do in Germany. Class is important, though not to the same degree as in Britain or Scandinavia. Religion, though also important, is probably less significant than in the Latin nations or The Netherlands. In part the impact of each dimension on German politics is moderated by the influence of the other.[39] The class vote splits on the basis of religion; religious camps divide along class lines. Yet both of these dimensions are crucial in German politics.

A simple cross-break of religious denomination by class provides an extremely potent predictor of voting patterns. The Protestant working class has been the bastion of SPD support, traditionally giving 70 percent of its two-party vote to the Social Democrats. At the other extreme, Catholic members of the middle class have voted 20 percent or less for the SPD prior to 1969, and 40 percent or less after 1969. The gap in SPD voting between these two most polarized strata is a very sizable 53 percent in 1953; by 1972 it is still a considerable 43 percent. SPD support from the two cross-pressured strata—Catholic workers and middle class Protestants—falls about equally between the two extremes. Generally these two groups vote about 20 percent more for the SPD than do the Catholic middle class, or conversely, 20 percent less for the SPD than the Protestant working class.

There are, of course, significant deviations from these broad trends, and more detailed studies of the interaction between class and religion are needed.[40] The behavior of the Catholic working class and Protestant middle class present ideal settings for studying the effects of cross-pressures on voting decisions. Similarly, the effect of increasing affluence on the working class can provide answers to theoretical and political questions of major importance. But such detailed analyses of population subgroups would detract from the broader historical perspectives of this volume. Moreover, in broad perspective these deviations are relatively slight in comparison with the basic effects of class and religion on voting behavior.[41]

The final stage of this analysis, therefore, is an additive multivariate model combining measures for each of the four social structural dimensions: religion, class, rural-urban residence, and region. To maximize longitudinal comparability, attention was limited to a subset of independent variables that appear in each survey in comparable form. The religious dimension was measured by religious denomination. The predictive power of the dimension would have been greatly enhanced if the frequency of church attendance had been included, but this measure was not available for all timepoints. Similarly, several measures of social status could have been incorporated into the model. But in the interest of comparability the occupation of the head of household was used, distinguishing between the old middle class, the new middle class, workers, and farmers. The rural-urban dimension was tapped by the four-point scale for the size of town. For region, the ten *Länder* were collapsed into four broad regions derived from the previous analyses.[42]

These measures were combined in separate Multiple Classification Analyses (MCA) to predict the vote for the major parties, SPD and CDU/CSU, at each election since 1953. Two basic questions require answers. First, what is the importance of each social structural dimension considered independently of the effects of the other dimensions, and how does this change over time? And second, to what extent do all four dimensions combine to predict voting behavior?

The MCA beta coefficients in table 7.9 show that the independent importance of the class dimension declines over time. Because this statistic is based on the entire occupational structure, including farm-

Table 7.9. Social structure and voting intentions, 1953–1972.[a]

Dimension	July 1953	June 1957	July 1961	Sept. 1965	Sept. 1969	Sept. 1972
Class	0.37	0.37	0.31	0.31	0.29	0.25
Religion	.26	.24	.34	.25	.25	.26
Town size (rural-urban)	.09	.07	.10	.16	.13	.13
Region	.07	—[b]	.13	.10	.08	.08
R	.46	.46	.46	.44	.41	.38
(N)	(841)	(1039)	(1077)	(1086)	(889)	(1608)

a. Cell entries are MCA beta coefficients, which represent the independent nonlinear correlation of each predictor with two-party vote intention.

b. Region is not available in our version of the 1957 study.

ers, the betas show a more gradual and constant decline than the Alford indices, which compare only two strata at a time. When controls for the effects of religion and the two dimensions of residential differentiation (rural-urban and region) are applied, the class beta declines fairly monotonically from 0.37 in 1953 to 0.25 in 1972. The findings in this chapter thus present a consistent pattern of the declining importance of social class, whether it is measured by a single variable or a composite index, or tested independently of other social structural dimensions.

The persisting importance of religion also mirrors the pattern found earlier with the index of religious voting. In 1953 the MCA beta for Catholic-Protestant differences is 0.26; by 1972 little has changed and the beta for that election is also 0.26. The intervening years give no hint of any long-term trend. In separate analyses the more sensitive religiosity measure, which combines denomination and frequency of church attendance, was examined. For the three timepoints where comparable indicators for each dimension are available, religiosity also displays great consistency (1953 = 0.36, 1965 = 0.37, 1972 = 0.37). Religious influences appear just as important in 1972 as they were in 1953 even when controlling for the remaining social structural dimensions.

Both of the dimensions of residential differentiation—the region of residence and rural-urban residence—also maintain a limited influence on partisan behavior over time. Both should reflect independent cultural forces; yet German research often considers them as surrogates for other dimensions. Region is linked to religion: Catholics to the South and West, Protestants to the North. Rural-urban residence is taken as a means of discriminating between rural and urban occupational groups. The beta coefficents from the MCA analyses control for these possibly spurious religious and social-status effects. Both residential dimensions maintain a fairly constant influence from 1953 to 1972 (table 7.9). The cultural influence of these dimensions is not diminishing, and it appears that the independent impact of the rural-urban dimension may even be increasing slightly.

The next question is whether the combined influence of social class, religion, rural-urban residence, and region as guides for partisan behavior has changed over time. The trends for the individual dimensions provide some clues to answering this question, but these individual trends are only suggestive of what the total pattern might look like.

Over the two decades from 1953 to 1972 there has been a general decline in the total explanatory power of the four sociostructural dimensions (table 7.9). Region as a dimension is not available in the 1957 study but if it were, 1957 would undoubtedly mark the highpoint in cleavage-based voting. The multiple R decreases from 0.46 in 1957 to 0.38 in 1972. The declining importance of class appears to be the major factor in accounting for the decline in the explanatory power of social characteristics as a whole. The multiple R for all four dimensions reflects a more general and gradual decline in predictive power than does the irregular decline for class.

A concluding word of caution is needed. These multiple Rs should not be considered as absolute measures of the importance of sociostructural factors. The total impact of the four dimensions depends on the subset of measures included in any single model. When the data permit a more extensive assemblage of sociostructural measures, a significantly stronger total predictive power for social characteristics can be obtained. For example, adding the frequency of church attendance, education, income, and union membership to the model increases the multiples Rs to 0.55 in 1953, 0.51 in 1965, and 0.45 in 1972. The subset of four longitudinal measures is broad enough, however, to permit a fairly confident assessment as to whether the combined influence of social characteristics has changed over time. Substantial and consistent evidence exists that a general decline has occurred.

Conclusion

The effect of sociostructural influences on individual partisan behavior has been a persisting concern of political scientists. The pioneering works of André Siegfried and Herbert Tingsten, among others, set the discipline on an early course of relating social characteristics to individual behavior. A quarter of a century later, Paul Lazarsfeld and his colleagues enshrined occupation, religion, and rural-urban residence as *the* predictors of party choice.[43] Moreover, S. M. Lipset and Stein Rokkan argue that since early in this century European party systems have frozen around these social cleavages.[44]

As the understanding of political behavior has grown, however, sociostructural variables have lost this preeminence and been incorporated into more elaborate and dynamic models of voting choice. Static social determinism has been replaced by the view that social structure is a prior force in initially shaping attitudes, a long-term source of political stability, and a structure for organizing and reducing political information. When political parties were clearly linked to fundamental social and economic cleavages, an elector's social characteristics were still seen as a potential cue in determining political dispositions.

The timeseries of German electoral surveys used in this study has made it possible to examine the social bases of German partisanship from a unique longitudinal perspective. Although the resulting picture is only a sketch, certain images have come through clearly.

A long-term decline in the determining force of social characteristics as a guide for political behavior has been found. This decline is most dramatic for measures of social status, but it also applies to the combined predictive power of all four sociostructural dimensions: social class, religion, region, and rural-urban residence. Religion, and to some extent region and rural-urban residence, show a persisting influence on partisan choice, in contrast to the marked decline in the importance of social class. On the whole, however, German partisanship reflects a social base less and less.

The longitudinal patterns of social status and religious voting present a surprising and fascinating contrast. What has led to this changing importance of social cleavages? Social characteristics remain viable for political matters only as long as the link of social cleavages with the parties and the link of the voter with social cleavages remain clear. But the fact is that both of these components are changing.[45]

The evidence on New Politics issue orientations presented in chapter 6 suggests that the citizen's link to the social structure—especially the economic aspect of social structure—is changing. Per-capita income is higher today than at any previous time in German history, and this affluence and stability present a sharp contrast for a society ravaged by two world wars, postwar reconstructions, and the inflation and depression of the Weimar Republic. In this new economic environment the young and economically secure segments of society are less concerned with the economic issues that are the driving mechanism of class-based politics. These groups are shifting their attention toward issues of life-styles and quality of life, New Politics issues that cut across traditional class lines. Such an ongoing process of value change helps to explain many of the patterns observed here. Increasing emphasis on New Politics issues by the electorate, for example, explains the general decline in class voting over time. And it is among the New Politics strongholds, the young and the new middle class, that the shift in class voting has been most dramatic. Religion, region, and rural-urban differences, on the other hand, reflect the cultural sources of voting differences. Therefore they generally retain their predictive ability as Germany moves toward a postindustrial age.[46]

8

Partisanship and
Political Behavior

IN MODERN MASS DEMOCRACIES political parties provide a crucial link between the individual citizen and the world of politics. As organizations, they furnish the means for contesting elections and for combining candidates and groups into a limited number of voting alternatives. They also allow the interested citizen to participate in politics beyond the voting act and beyond the limited duration of the election campaign.

Another aspect of parties is of interest to this study: namely, the party as a political object that serves to orient the citizen's thinking about politics. Voting choices are usually partisan; either candidates run under party labels, or citizens cast their ballots directly for a party as in the case of the list vote (*Zweitstimme*) in Germany. Issues and events are often presented to the public in partisan terms, as the parties take positions on the political questions of the day or react to actions of other actors in the polity.

To some extent German voting behavior can be accounted for without much recourse to partisan attitudes and perceptions.[1] Yet even if social class and religion have a strong direct impact upon individual voting choice, perceptions of parties must link the sociostructural and political subsystems. The ballot requires a decision for a party. Furthermore, parties help to reduce the complexity of politics. Political rhetoric, instead of referring to cleavages directly, uses party labels as a convenient shorthand to identify issues and personalities. Individuals, therefore, must know not only their group position, social class or religion, but also which party is most likely to represent the interests of their group. This fact has led Giovanni Sartori to insist, albeit in a slightly different context, that political parties and whole party systems will gradually acquire an independent effect upon poli-

194

tics, even if originally their role was entirely determined by the social structure.[3]

Partisan attitudes may become more directly important for another reason. Although the analysis in chapter 7 showed the still considerable weight of sociostructural variables for voting behavior, it also documented a gradual decline in their importance. Consequently one must ask what, if anything, is replacing the political cues previously furnished by an individual's social position or religious denomination. ⟨Apparently, affective ties to political parties—that is, partisanship—are rendering the parties increasingly important as political referents and as sources for political cues.⟩ The task of showing this is complicated methodologically because parties are highly visible political entities; therefore, they trigger responses to survey questions even if social class or religion, rather than the parties themselves, are the primary determinants of politics. For this reason particular attention must be paid to the construction of a partisanship measure, and the main focus must be placed on longitudinal change. The two crucial questions to be answered are, first, whether parties are important to the political belief systems of individuals, and, second, whether the nature of partisanship is changing in Germany.

Partisanship in Germany

American research has established the place of the construct of "party identification" in theories of electoral behavior. This variable has been examined for over twenty years, and its properties have been quite well documented. It is a very stable attitude that is often formed through the early-life learning of parental values. In the absence of clear and enduring class or religious voting, party identification takes on major importance as a determinant of voting choices and political behavior. In addition, it is of major heuristic value for the explanation of long-term political and electoral stability in the United States, and consequently it serves as a backdrop against which to specify the short-term forces that deviate from the observed long-term trends.[4]

Attempts to transplant this concept to the study of European political behavior have encountered several major difficulties. Apart from the significant problem of finding a functionally equivalent formulation of the party identification question, there are three types of findings that have been used to question the existence of party attachment and its conceptual utility in Europe.

First, party attachment and voting decision, though theoretically distinct, are actually intercorrelated at an embarrassingly high level. Either the two indicators used fail to differentiate properly between the two separate realities resulting in a measurement problem; or partisanship and the vote are in fact extremely closely related, so that there is little heuristic gain in including both concepts in analyses of voting behavior. Second, partisanship has not proved to be as stable as the concept implies or demands. These two facts together suggest that temporary voting defections seldom occur. Yet if voting defections tend to be permanent and to pull party identification with them in the same direction, then the homing function of partisanship is of little consequence. David Butler and Donald Stokes have found not only a higher incidence of concurrent change in partisanship and vote in Britain than in the United States, but even more distressing, they have found that the "theoretically impossible" combination of changing partisanship and stable voting occurs twice as frequently in Britain as in the United States.[5] And for the Netherlands, Jan Thomassen reports that this combination is actually more frequent than the opposite or "normal" case, where voting behavior changes but party identification remains stable. Third and finally, the extent of partisanship varies from country to country: in countries where fewer than 50 percent of the electorate identify with a party, the concept may not be very useful in explaining voting.[6]

In Germany, the concept of partisanship, and especially of party identification, has intrigued students of politics for some time. In the first application of the concept in Germany in 1965, Werner Zohlnhöfer found rates of partisanship very similar to those documented for the United States by Michigan's Center for Political Studies. Zohlnhöfer explained the differences he discovered—such as the lower frequency of partisanship and the greater incidence of refusals to answer this question among older respondents in Germany—in terms of the different historical experiences of the United States and Germany; in his view, the deviations actually strengthened comparability.[7] This early enthusiasm, however, quickly waned.

Using different measures of partisanship, both Max Kaase (1969) and Günther Radtke (1972) concluded from independent panel studies that party identification is much less stable in Germany than the data for the United States would imply.[8] Unfortunately, however, both Kaase and Radtke altered their questions slightly between their two timepoints. The result was that what appeared to be almost a 50 percent decrease in partisanship over the two-year period (from 54 percent to 29 percent identifiers) turned out to be entirely an artifact of the question wording when the two versions of the questions were tested together in a "split-half sample."[9] But even among those who were classified as partisan identifiers at both timepoints, only 65 percent maintained a constant partisanship over the two-year period.

Moreover, Kaase and Radtke found that, depending on the measure used, only from one-third to two-thirds of the German electorate could be classified as either strong or weak partisans. In 1972, however, using a different instrument, Manfred Berger discovered levels of partisanship similar to those cited by Zohlnhöfer. Over two-thirds of the electorate indicated a general leaning toward a party when the question phrasing included the possibility of voting for another party once in a while. Nevertheless, Berger remained skeptical about the long-term stability of partisanship.[10]

Perhaps of greater theoretical importance, in 1971 Uwe Schleth and Erich Weede argued on the basis of a causal analysis that party identification in Germany, rather than being causally prior to the vote as hypothesized by American research, may be only a correlate or even a consequence of actual vote and general partisan preference.[11]

In 1973, moreover, Franz Urban Pappi questioned the basic utility of the concept of party identification in a political system like the Federal Republic. He argued that when much of the change in vote divisions between elections represents a long-term trend toward one party (or when there is very little change), party identification does not have the heuristic value connected with the "normal vote" concept.[12] Further, partisanship is of doubtful value as an orientation device in the German parliamentary system, where the individual has but one vote to cast every four years at the national level. It is easy for a German to remember how to vote when he has only one voting decision to make. The American elector, on the other hand, "has to cope simultaneously with a vast collection of partisan candidates seeking a variety of offices at federal, state and local levels; it is small wonder that he becomes conscious of a generalized belief about his ties to a party."[13] In addition, partisanship as a homing device is more important when defection is easy. In the United States, defection in the vote for President requires a less painful decision if the rest of the ballot is still cast for one's party. Ticket-splitting (as partial defection) is likely to lead to less cognitive dissonance than casting one's *only* vote for the opposition. Even in the United States very few voters cast their congressional votes, let alone their entire ticket, against their party identification. If defection is a more momentous and painful decision for a German voter, vote changes are likely to remain permanent, so that the concept of temporary defection is much less useful. Permanent vote changes, however, cannot be explained by the concept of partisanship![14]

In 1972 W. Phillips Shively questioned the viability of German partisanship in a historical framework. Testing several implications of the party identification theory for voting patterns in the Weimar Republic, he detected high levels of aggregate voting stability in the Germany of the 1920s, but not stability of support for individual parties. Instead, there appeared to be several stable *blocs* of parties that were aligned with a few prominent social cleavages: the proletarian, Catholic, Protestant, and bourgeois blocs. Shively suggested that the class and religious cleavages defining these blocs—rather than party identification—provided the voters with sufficient guidance and information for political behavior. As a result voters, instead of identifying with individual parties, voted for the party or parties that were generally seen as furthering the interests of the voters' class or religion. As he put it: "If the social or economic conflicts in which a voter is involved are sufficiently clear; and if the position of parties or groups of parties with regard to these conflicts is sufficiently clear; then there is no need for the voter to develop lasting ties to any party, *per se,* and he will not do so."[15]

It should be noted that Shively discusses partisanship from a dynamic perspective. As long as the social positions of individuals provide cues for sufficient orientation in the political world, party identification is not necessary. "When clear social or economic position coincides with a clear choice of parties relative to that position, the voter is able to 'place' himself easily without going through the arduous and time-consuming job of developing a party identification."[16] Under such conditions both the voter's view of parties and his current ballot choice are functions of his sociostructural characteristics; responses to a partisanship measure, such as a survey question asking for the voter's party identification, simply reflect the translation of religious or economic ties into current party preference, rather than an independent attachment to a party. The term "social partisanship" is a convenient label for this type of indirect and instrumental relationship between the voter and a party.

It is evident that the concept of social partisanship is not completely adequate for Germany today. The power of social class to determine voting behavior has declined, and this decline has created a need for new cuing mechanisms to guide political behavior. Shively suggests that party identification could fill this role. In the United States party identification is useful for the voter partly because social cleavages do not offer clear, relevant, and viable cues for political behavior: the American parties are "catchall" parties, to use Otto Kirchheimer's term.[17]

As the Western European countries become more like the United States in this respect, party identification may become necessary and more common. The need for new sources of political cues will be more acutely felt by the younger cohorts, who are less influenced in their voting behavior by social status position than are older cohorts.[18] In addition, it has been shown, at least for the American case, that basic orientations such as partisanship are socialized early in the individual's life cycle and tend to remain stable. The later in life this identification with a party takes place, the more slowly it tends to grow.[19] The younger cohorts are thus not only more likely to need partisanship, but they will also be more open to developing such attachments. It is therefore not surprising that the most encouraging evidence on partisanship in Germany has come from studies that have focused on the young.[20] For example, Kendall Baker has found through a causal analysis of data from 1972 that the American model of partisanship fits considerably better among younger than among older cohorts. For the latter, socioeconomic variables have a direct impact upon voting behavior, while for the younger cohorts the effect of these variables is mediated by party identification. From indirect tests Baker was able to conclude that such differences are probably due to generational change rather than to life-cycle differences.[21]

This evidence suggests the development of a different type of partisanship, at least among the young. It is still related to "background" variables, but it mediates the impact of sociostructural factors and also has an independent impact on political behavior. Party choices are no longer completely determined by class or religion; instead, this type of partisanship entails a direct attitudinal attachment to a political party. Consequently, we will refer to it as "attitudinal partisanship."

German politics is characterized presently by a mix of the two types of partisanship. Some people behave like social partisans, others like attitudinal partisans. Contrasting Shively's deductions about partisanship during the Weimar Republic with the recent studies of the Federal Republic reveals that the incidence of attitudinal partisanship has probably been increasing. Thus, the questions about German partisanship should be posed somewhat differently from the way they have appeared in much of the literature: it is not as important to ask whether party identification in a narrowly defined sense exists as it is to ask whether attitudinal partisanship is increasing relative to social partisanship. In other words, is attitudinal partisanship becoming more important for analysis of political behavior in Germany, not only in voting but even more in shaping and organizing political attitudes and perceptions?[22] Before these dynamic and longitudinal questions can be approached, a measure of partisanship that covers as long a timespan as possible must be found.

A New Measure of Partisanship

German survey research has constantly reformulated the partisanship question, searching for the elusive concept of party identification. Consequently, the German election surveys contain several different and not comparable measures of partisanship. For example, between 1961 and 1972 the following survey questions were used:[23]

1961   Would you please tell me which party you like best? [If the respondent has a party preference:] Would you say you are a convinced supporter of the [party mentioned] or would you rather say you favor the [party mentioned] because it seems better suited to you given the present conditions?

1965,   [Following the question eliciting present vote intention or
1969   actual vote, voters were asked only the second part of the 1961 question; intensity of attachment was thus asked only for the party the respondent planned to vote for or voted for, making it impossible to operationalize defection from partisanship.]

1967   Generally speaking, do you think of yourself as a CDU/CSU supporter, an SPD supporter, FDP supporter, NPD supporter, a supporter of another party, or do you not feel particularly attached to a political party? [If the respondent is a supporter:] Are you a convinced supporter of the [party mentioned] or are you not particularly convinced?

1969   Generally speaking, do you consider yourself a supporter of a particular party, or do you not feel particularly attached to a political party? [If the respondent is a supporter:] Do you consider yourself a convinced supporter of the [party mentioned] or not?

1972   Many people in the Federal Republic lean toward a particular party for a long time, although they may occasionally vote for a different party. How about you: Do you in general lean toward a particular party? Which one? [If yes:] Taken altogether, how strongly or weakly do you lean toward this party: very strongly, fairly strongly, moderately, fairly weakly, or very weakly?

The search for party identification in Germany is most seriously hampered by the lack of a German equivalent of the American tendency to say, even without an interviewer's prompting: "I am a Democrat." In Germany only a formal, card-carrying member of the SPD would say, "Ich bin ein Sozialdemokrat." These linguistic differences certainly have political causes as well as political consequences. Erwin Scheuch observed in 1961 that in political discussions German citizens rarely refer to their own partisan preference; "instead, the independence of one's evaluations from the general orientation of a party is overemphasized." In fact, partisanship is used negatively: "to be called a partisan means largely not to have one's opinion taken seriously."[24] To examine partisanship in Germany, therefore, a relatively unobtrusive measure would be valuable. In addition, partisanship should be examined from a longitudinal perspective, and thus an indicator that is comparable for as many timepoints as possible is needed. Finally, the measure should obviously tap the theoretical concept: affective attachment to a party.

The measure that seems to satisfy these conditions best is based on the scalometer evaluations of the parties. Party scalometers were included in all election surveys conducted after 1961:

> I would be interested to know how you think right now about the following parties: CDU/CSU, SPD, FDP. We have here something like a thermometer. The higher you go up on the white squares, the more you like the particular party; the further you go down on the black squares, the more you reject the party.[25]

The analysis focuses on SPD and CDU/CSU partisans only.[26] If a respondent rated the SPD higher than any other party, he or she was coded an SPD partisan; CDU/CSU partisans had to have a higher score on the CDU scalometer than on the SPD or FDP measures.[27] Respondents who evaluated the CDU/CSU and the SPD at the same level, whether high or low, were termed nonpartisans. Each partisan group was differentiated according to how positively it evaluated the party. Respondents who gave their preferred party the highest possible score, +5, were called strong partisans; a score of +4 defined weak partisans. If partisans evaluated their party at +3 or below—but still above any other party—they were grouped together as partisan leaners.[28]

The final measure of partisan attitudes combined the separate SPD and CDU/CSU measures into a seven-point scale. This scale runs from strong and weak SPD partisans through Social Democratic leaners, nonpartisans, and CDU leaners to weak and strong Christian Democratic partisans.

Clearly the term partisanship is used fairly loosely here. It is not restricted to formal card-carrying party members, who account for only about 5 percent of the German electorate.[29] In fact, the partisanship measure merely requires the respondent to be willing and able to evaluate both parties and to prefer one party over the others. Partisanship, then, is on the surface a purely affective response to the stimuli "SPD" and "CDU/CSU." In this connection, therefore it is not proper to employ the common term "party identification," which means, in terms of both measurement and concept, self-identification with or psychological membership in a political party. The indicator of partisanship used in this study does not determine the individual's sense of identification with a party, at least not directly. Of course, the findings mentioned earlier suggest that many citizens may not have to use parties as primary political reference objects because their needs for political orientations are adequately served by sociostructural groups. Consequently, although a high CDU score on the measure used here may signify high affect for the CDU among such social partisans, they may not have used the party directly as the politically decisive reference group; rather, the church or the social class may have filled this role for them. Attitudinal partisans, on the other hand, use the party as both a direct or primary reference point and a source of political cues. Hence, attitudinal partisans probably will also have high affect for their own party. But for them the partisan measure not only will capture affect but will also behave like an identification indicator.

This indirect measure of partisanship is probably quite appropriate in Germany, where historical experience has made people reluctant to consciously accept or admit to a personal party attachment.[30] Parties may, in fact, play a more important role in the political thoughts and deeds of German citizens than the number of admitted party identifiers would imply. At least, more people behave like partisans than admit to partisanship. On the other hand, the indicator employed here probably contains a larger amount of short-term affect than a "true" measure of partisanship would; partisanship is, after all, conceptualized as a long-term attachment. As a result, this measure may be more unstable over time, reflecting the public's short-term reactions to political events and the roles of the parties in these events. Unfortunately, there are no long-term panel studies through which to test this assumption. The short-term stability of the measure, however, compares well with the more stringent indicator used by Manfred Berger in his 1972 analysis. Berger's seven-point identification question yields over-time correlations (tau_b) of 0.705 (three months) and 0.743 (one month), while our partisanship measure with correlations of 0.690 and 0.707 for the same timespans is only slightly less stable.[31]

Because the level of partisanship in Germany, as measured here, will not be explicitly compared with those found in other countries but will be employed in over-time comparisons within Germany, any imperfections in the instrument should be minimized.[32] It is an adequate measure for our purposes, although the problems with partisanship encountered by other scholars should caution the reader not to sanctify this particular indicator as the "true" partisanship.

The distribution of the partisanship measure from 1961 to 1972 is displayed in table 8.1. The long-term voting trend toward the SPD is reflected in several ways. The overall balance between CDU/CSU and SPD partisans shifts steadily from a CDU/CSU advantage of about 21 percent in 1961 to a CDU/CSU deficit of almost 17 percent in 1972. Strong partisans accentuate this trend, dropping from 24.7 percent to 9.2 percent for the CDU while increasing for the Social Democrats

Table 8.1. Distribution of partisanship, 1961–1972.[a]

Partisanship	July 1961	Sept. 1965	Sept. 1969	Nov. 1969	Sept. 1972
CDU/CSU					
Strong	24.7%	18.5%	21.3%	19.3%	9.2%
Weak	11.0	11.7	9.8	10.0	10.7
Leaning	17.4	20.0	10.6	13.8	16.2
Nonpartisans	14.7	13.0	16.9	11.0	10.9
SPD					
Leaning	11.4	12.2	7.0	10.8	17.0
Weak	8.1	8.1	11.4	14.2	16.3
Strong	12.8	16.4	22.9	20.9	19.7
Mean	3.52	3.78	4.04	4.10	4.43
(N)	(1341)	(1297)	(1027)	(683)	(1912)

a. Cell entries are the percentages of the sample that fall into each partisan group. In calculating the mean, partisanship was scored as follows: 1 = strong CDU/CSU; 2 = weak CDU/CSU; 3 = leaning CDU/CSU; 4 = nonpartisan; 5 = leaning SPD; 6 = weak SPD; 7 = strong SPD.

from 12.8 percent to 19.7 percent. The general shift is summarized by the mean values for the seven-point partisanship scale that are displayed at the bottom of the table. They move from a CDU advantage in 1961 (3.52, or 0.48 from the midpoint in the CDU direction) to a similar SPD advantage in 1972 (4.43, or 0.43 from the central point). This trend in partisanship reflects the vote changes over time. Since it has been argued that partisanship and voting behavior are conceptually quite close in Germany, this is not a surprising finding.

 Over time, the German electorate is moving toward attachment to one or the other of the parties: the proportion of nonpartisans, that is, respondents who do not distinguish between the parties in their evaluations, generally decreases over time from an already low 14.7 percent in 1961 to 10.9 percent in 1972.

It is apparent from table 8.1 that the 1969 election does not fit the overall trend. For example, the proportion of nonpartisans in the preelection survey of September 1969 is higher than at any other timepoint; at the same time the combined strong partisan groups (strong SPD plus strong CDU/CSU) are about 10 percent larger than in 1965. And the perceived polarization between the parties was particularly low in 1969 (see table 8.6).

One likely explanation for these findings is the "era of good feelings" that resulted from the Grand Coalition. Partisanship appears to be sensitive to this kind of short-term effect. The absence—or at least reduced level—of the usual mutual criticism and of partisan bantering between the two large parties could have reduced the voters' negative feelings for the opposition party and raised the affect for their own party. Within both partisan groups, therefore, the proportions of strong partisans increased.[33] At the same time, the cooperation of the two parties in the government made it apparently more difficult for casual observers of politics to distinguish between the parties either cognitively or affectively: the result was a slight increase in nonpartisans.

The postelection distribution for 1969 has been included in table 8.1 because it suggests that these "abnormalities" recede or disappear quickly. After the Grand Coalition was dissolved and the SPD and the FDP formed a coalition that pushed the CDU/CSU into opposition, the electorate immediately reacted. The proportion who did not see any difference between the parties dropped by a third (from 16.9 percent to 11 percent), and the polarization between the parties grew (see table 8.6). At the same time the number of strong partisans of both parties combined decreased by 4 percent, erasing almost half of the increase since 1965.

Clearly, partisanship reacts to some short-term forces in Germany more than, for example, in the United States. Nevertheless, over time the measure registers two important secular changes: a small reduction in the percentage of nonpartisans, and a steady shift in the partisan distribution toward the SPD. Neither of these trends is unexpected; rather, the results should be viewed as a first validation of the partisanship measure.[34]

Properties of Partisanship: Voting Behavior

The concept of party identification was first developed in the United States to capture stable attitudinal determinants of voting behavior.[35] In addition, the variable proved to be a powerful and heuristically useful concept for other aspects of political behavior and attitudes, including the organization of political perceptions and the reduction of the complexity of the political world. Still, it is most frequently used to explain and predict voting behavior. As a baseline, the German measure will be tested against several aspects of voting choice. A close association between partisanship and vote should be expected, because Germany's parliamentary system lessens the likelihood of vote defections. This relationship may not change over time even if the nature of partisanship undergoes the hypothesized transition from social to attitudinal partisanship: under the conditions mentioned—a clearly perceived connection between the social group and one political party—sociostructural cues will be as good and as strong a guide for voting as attitudinal partisanship could be.

Partisans at all levels of intensity tend to vote for their own party (table 8.2). In order to increase the variance on the dependent variable, "defection" (voting completely against one's party) and ticket splitting between the first (candidate) and second (party) vote have been combined. In all elections over 90 percent of the strong partisans of both parties cast both their votes for their own party. Partisan leaners defect at least twice as much as strong partisans in most cases, with the CDU proving an exception in 1969 and 1972. The increase in the number of Social Democrats after these SPD victories suggests that a bandwagon effect moved those CDU partisans, especially leaners who did not vote for their party, into the SPD partisan camp, thus artificially reducing the defection rate. (Postelection results are not shown.)[36]

The predictive power of partisanship for voting behavior drops monotonically from a high of 0.803 in 1961 to 0.775 in 1972 (Pearson r).[37] This is a very gradual change, but, if anything, it is a welcome one. The decline slightly disassociates the vote from partisanship, and reduces the likelihood that both variables measure the same thing. Such a development is consistent with increasing attitudinal partisanship, but it is not proof.

The concept of long-term partisan attachments requires that the more intense the partisanship the greater the stability in voting behavior over time. Strong partisans have a more basic commitment to their own party and view other parties as more distant psychologically.

Table 8.2. Vote defection by partisanship, 1961–1972.[a]

Partisanship	Nov. 1961	Nov. 1965	Oct. 1969	Dec. 1972
CDU/CSU				
Strong	8.3%	3.1%	9.7%	3.0%
Weak	16.7	11.4	15.0	8.2
Leaning	22.3	24.5	13.3	3.2
SPD				
Leaning	25.2	18.6	26.7	33.3
Weak	18.8	11.2	14.8	17.5
Strong	7.4	4.0	7.0	7.7

a. Cell entries are the percentages of first *and* second votes for SPD, CDU/CSU, or FDP that were cast contrary to the voter's partisanship; e.g., in 1961 8.3% of the strong CDU/CSU partisans cast either their first or their second vote, or both, for either the SPD or the FDP.

Among strong partisans, short-term vote defection or permanent changes in party affiliation can be brought about only by very strong political forces, while weaker partisans are more easily drawn away from their normal voting behavior.

No long-term panel studies are available from which to analyse interelection voting stability. Data can be used, however, from panels of preelection and postelection studies in 1969 and 1972 (figure 8.1). They show that strong partisans display a high level of congruence between vote intention (measured before the election) and actual vote (as reported after the election) in both elections. Conversely, those less strongly committed to a party display considerably less stability. Among voters with strong partisan attachments, campaigns apparently rarely alter the voting intention; instead, the campaign serves primarily as a stimulus to turnout. In contrast, voters with weaker party ties can evidently be persuaded to change their vote, and parties will direct their persuasion attempts largely at these potential "floating votes."

Figure 8.1. Over-time vote consistency: preelection and postelection surveys, 1969, 1972.

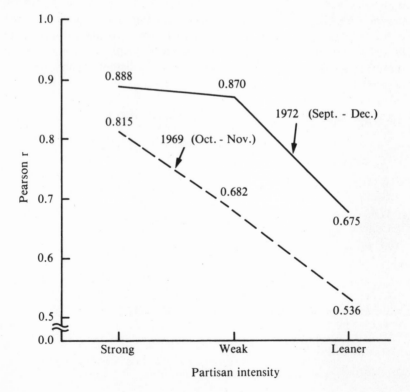

This finding leads one to expect that the intensity of party commitment will influence how far in advance of an election individuals decide how to vote. Strong partisans make up their minds much earlier than partisan leaners or nonpartisans. In fact, if the low tendency to defect among strong partisans reported in table 8.2 holds over time, many strong partisans could say that they have *always* voted for their own party.

Strong partisans are indeed more likely to report that they have "always voted this way" (table 8.3), but change is more frequent than implied by the data in table 8.2. And the increasing proportion (over time) of voters at each level of partisan strength who report always having voted for the same party is not surprising.[38] After all, the 1961 study was conducted soon after the stabilization of the present party system in the 1953 and 1957 federal elections. By 1972, voters had had another decade of electoral experience in a stable party system that should have increased their voting consistency; the data in table 8.3 indicate that this was clearly the case.

The small differences in voting consistency between CDU/CSU and SPD reflect their different party histories. The Christian Democratic Union's share of the valid votes grew between 1949 and 1957 from 31.0 percent to 50.2 percent, primarily because it profited from the disintegration of the small, mostly middle-class, regional or special-interest parties. By 1965 at least 70 percent of CDU partisans at each level reported always having voted for that party. The growth of the SPD, on the other hand, proceeded at a much slower, though steady, pace of about three additional percentage points per election: "Comrade

Table 8.3. Partisanship and vote regularity, 1961–1972.[a]

Partisanship	Sept. 1961	Sept. 1965	Nov. 1969	Oct. 1972
CDU/CSU				
Strong	71.0%	76.5%	81.0%	88.1%
Weak	51.0	70.4	70.0	86.6
Leaning	39.7	73.2	75.0	82.9
Nonpartisans	42.9	50.6	56.8	66.2
SPD				
Leaning	44.0	50.8	64.4	75.2
Weak	51.6	71.7	72.5	88.4
Strong	67.0	75.1	79.5	91.6

a. Cell entries are the percentages of each partisan group who report they "always voted this way" when asked about the time when they decided how to vote. The question was usually asked of persons indicating either a vote intention or a preference; in 1969 the question was asked in relation to the actual vote.

Trend" was seen as a welcome and dependable member of the party. The Social Democratic support, therefore, contains more recent converts, who only slowly have formed an attachment to their new party; they are likely to be leaners. Consequently, as table 8.3 shows, the SPD leaners right through the 1972 election report consistently less vote regularity than any CDU group.

Another indirect way to observe the degree of long-term voting stability uses direct personal accounts of past voting behavior. As is well known, recall questions usually underestimate change, as respondents seek to bring the recollections of past actions into line with their present behavior. It is quite possible that the impetus for such consistency is stronger for an individual when the attitude or behavior in question is more central or important to him. Strong partisans may therefore exaggerate the stability of their voting record more than do those with weaker attachments. If so, the data in table 8.3 could be read as evidence that strong partisans care more about being consistent over time in casting their votes, whether or not they actually behave accordingly. When present vote report is compared with past voting recall, 77.3 percent, averaged over four timepoints, of the strong partisans (CDU and SPD) and 69.5 percent of the weak partisans (CDU and SPD) report voting for their own party in two consecutive elections, but only 57.7 percent of the partisan leaners and 37.8 percent of the nonpartisans do so. The stability estimate using the recalled vote is considerably below that suggested by the proportion of respondents who "always voted for the same party" in table 8.3. Recall of actual voting behavior is apparently a "harder" measure than the question about the time of the voting decision. However, both measures—vote regularity and recall—suggest more voting volatility than the defection rates reported in table 8.2.

This evidence consistently supports two points. First, the intensity or strength of partisanship successfully differentiates levels of voting stability over time. Second, and not surprisingly, partisan attachments predict the direction of the vote very well, although enough defection exists in both a cross-sectional and a cross-temporal sense to indicate that the partisanship measure captures other factors besides short-term vote decisions.

Partisanship and Political Involvement

If partisanship was originally designed to explain the individual voting decision, it soon attained an independent status in explaining a wide variety of political behaviors subsumed under the heading of political involvement. At the individual level, the strength of partisan attachment has been shown in various national settings to be related to the propensity to vote, interest in politics and election campaigns, and participation in more "difficult" campaign activities such as contributing money or working for a candidate.[39] These characteristics in aggregate form explain the "surge and decline" in voter turnout and in the vote in presidential and midterm elections in the United States, and they may similarly account for differences among national, state, and local elections in Germany.[40]

Recent analyses have identified several dimensions of political involvement, which differ according to the extent to which they involve partisan activities. Strength of partisanship is more highly related to partisan activities like voter turnout and campaign acts than to the (individual) contacting of officials and community involvement or to elite-challenging forms of participation such as demonstrations.[41]

The most basic political activity in democracies is participation in elections. Analyses of turnout in Western Europe, however, suffer from a lack of variance, because approximately 80 percent of the eligible electorate vote. In addition, strong civic norms make voting a citizen's duty, so that serious *underreporting* of dereliction of this duty is to be expected. Between 1961 and 1972 actual turnout as reported in the official German election statistics averaged 88.1 percent; reported nonvoting in the surveys reached only 6.2 percent over the four elections. An additional 8 percent cannot, or more important, will not respond to the voting question. Table 8.4 combines the nonvoters with

Table 8.4. Partisanship and nonvoting or question refusals, 1961–1972.[a]

Partisanship	July 1961	Sept. 1965	Sept. 1969	Sept. 1972	Mean, four elections
CDU/CSU					
Strong	4.5%	8.3%	7.3%	15.4%	8.9%
Weak	15.1	13.2	11.0	12.8	13.0
Leaning	21.5	16.9	16.5	16.1	17.8
Nonpartisans	47.1	39.1	30.2	29.1	34.4
SPD					
Leaning	17.8	15.8	8.4	13.9	14.0
Weak	10.3	8.6	8.6	7.4	8.7
Strong	4.7	5.2	2.9	7.4	5.1
Full sample	17.3	15.0	11.8	13.6	14.4
(N)	(1332)	(1297)	(1024)	(1912)	

a. Cell entries are the percentages of each partisan group who did not report a vote intention; this includes respondents who did not intend to vote or who did not know or refused to say which party they intended to vote for.

those who refused to indicate the party for which they intended to vote.[42] The association between partisan strength and nonvoting responses is quite dramatic. Over the four elections, the mean percentage of nonvoting responses among strong partisans is 7.0 percent (SPD, 5.1 percent; CDU/CSU, 8.9 percent), but for nonpartisans it is 36.4 percent. Table 8.4 shows, however, that nonvoting responses for the full sample generally decline over time as more respondents become willing or able to indicate their voting choices; throughout, stronger partisans continue to vote more regularly than weaker partisans. There is, however, an increasing asymmetry between CDU/CSU and SPD supporters in the tendency to give noncommittal responses.

While voting is almost ubiquitous, more demanding activities in election campaigns are quite rare. Only recently has involvement in campaigns in Germany spread beyond the activist core of card-carrying party members. The writer Günther Grass began to drum up support for the Social Democrats in 1965; in 1969 he was joined by many others in "voter initiatives" (*Wählerinitiativen*). Composed mostly of nonparty members, such groups campaigned actively, mostly for the SPD in 1969 but for all parties after that. Prominent figures in television, the arts, labor, industry, and religion gave testimonials for one party or another in large advertisements paid for either by the parties or by the voter initiatives. Following these examples, even ordinary voters began to openly show their support for a party, by wearing tiny orange or blue lapel pins in 1969, and more visibly in 1972 (and more like American campaigns) with buttons or bumper stickers.

For more demanding forms of political activity a clear, positive relationship should exist between partisan intensity and the level of activity. Stronger partisans should be more active and open with support than people who are only weakly or not at all attached to a party. To assess this relationship four different campaign activities have been analyzed (table 8.5).[43] The data confirm the expectations: strong partisans are usually the most active or openly supportive group, while the nonpartisans are generally least involved. The intermediate partisan groups present a less clear picture, but they generally fall between the strong and the nonpartisan level.

In 1961 supporters of the Social Democrats and the Christian Democrats were about equally likely to attend political rallies. In subsequent years SPD partisans, especially the strongly committed, generally became much more involved than their CDU counterparts. By 1965, 23 percent of the strong Social Democrats, but only 14 percent of the strong CDU supporters, attended at least one rally. In 1972, SPD partisans, at each level, were about 7 percent more likely to "openly show support" than CDU partisans. The last column of table

Table 8.5. Partisanship and campaign activity, 1961–1972.[a]

Partisanship	Sept. 1961: saw a politician at rally	Nov. 1965: attended at least one rally	Dec. 1972: showed support for party	Dec. 1972: approved of showing support
CDU/CSU				
Strong	12%	14%	30%	31%
Weak	8	9	25	40
Leaning	10	11	20	26
Nonpartisans	5	8	9	36
SPD				
Leaning	9	14	28	49
Weak	13	12	32	62
Strong	16	23	37	65
Total sample	11	13	29	50
(N)	(1234)	(1175)	(1127)	(1107)

a. Cell entries are the percentage of each partisan group performing campaign activity.

8.5 suggests an attitudinal base for the differences in behavior. SPD partisans approve of open partisan activity much more than do CDU supporters: less than one-third of the CDU's but almost three-fifths of the SPD's partisans approve of openly showing support for a political party. Why is there this attitudinal difference between the two party groups?

In his analyses of the 1961 election, Erwin Scheuch noted that pro-SPD orientations were least encouraged in the family and most applauded by the voters' colleagues at work.[44] Conversely, CDU voters felt that their vote intentions were supported by their families but scorned at work. In short, only private environments seemed more supportive for CDU than for SPD partisans. Hence, CDU partisans would be hesitant to advertise their partisanship by, for example, attending political rallies. Seen in this light, the patterns in table 8.5 are not surprising.

It is remarkable, however, that this partisan imbalance occurred at a time (1961) when the majority political climate was favorable to the CDU/CSU and hostile to the SPD. The explanations that have been advanced for the greater openness and activity of SPD supporters in the early seventies are intuitively more obvious. In the general political climate of that time expressions of SPD support were perceived by the population as more legitimate than—or, at least, as preferable to—

CDU affiliation (see the last column of table 8.5). In a self-reinforcing feedback process, which Elisabeth Noelle-Neumann termed a "spiral of silence" (*Schweigespirale*), the favorable SPD climate was accurately perceived and led to overreporting of SPD voting intentions and vote recall; the interviewing process itself appeared to amplify this bias.[45] Conversely, the same process suppressed CDU affiliations, both in "real life" and as mirrored in survey responses. This changing balance of public opinion may not have replaced the underlying social distribution of partisan favors that Scheuch described, but perhaps it covered them temporarily. The two interpretations taken together may explain why the pro-SPD imbalance of table 8.5 increased during the 1960s and into the 1970s. Only by taking account of extraneous occurrences, however, can the dynamic process of the spiral of silence explain why the direction of the spiral might reverse eventually, or even oscillate repeatedly.

This interesting puzzle should not obscure the basic finding, namely, that the strength of partisan feelings is a powerful predictor for relatively simple as well as for more discriminating measures of partisan involvement in politics.[46] Such findings parallel those established for party identification in the United States, and they suggest that Germans at the higher levels of the partisanship indicator are increasingly involved with their party and more psychologically attached to it than those at the lower levels.

Party Polarization and Constraints among Political Beliefs

 One of the theoretically most important aspects of partisanship is its reference-group function as a force in shaping attitudes, that is, as a source of cues for opinions as well as behavior. This is particularly important in Germany, if attitudinal partisanship is gradually replacing other referents such as class and religion. Documenting the rise of attitudinal partisanship must be done indirectly because attitudinal partisans cannot be directly distinguished from social partisans. But if trends in the patterns of political belief or behaviors do indicate a more important role for partisanship as a focus for political perceptions, this finding would constitute crucial evidence in support of the thesis that partisan attitudes are indeed growing stronger.

One aspect of partisanship at the individual as well as the aggregate level is the perceived polarization between one's own party and the evaluation of other parties. Partisanship is not merely positive affect toward one's own party but identification with it; this, in turn, should stimulate evaluations of other political actors, such as other parties and their political leaders. For some voters, dislike of another party may establish or at least strengthen attachment to one's own party. Party evaluations, utilizing scalometer or "thermometer" scales, can be used directly to calculate these psychological distances between parties. The differences in the scalometer ratings can be interpreted as measuring the strength of affect for the in-group combined with the amount of hostility toward the out-group, for example, for one's own and the opposing party. Similarly, the distances may indicate the perceived differences in the issue positions of the various parties. The farther apart the respondents see the parties on one or more issues, the more their scalometer ratings of the parties may differ. However, evaluations of partisan political objects (like parties) are not always inversely related: if two objects are not connected in the respondent's belief system, there need not be any relationship between their evaluations, or both evaluations could be positive. Indeed, among nonpolitical respondents the judgments about leading candidates of opposing parties are often positively correlated!

Prior research has established that higher levels of partisan strength are associated with higher evaluations of one's own party and simultaneously, with lower regard for other parties.[47] The partisanship scale used here employs the scalometer evaluation of the respondent's preferred party to measure the strength of the attachment. This in itself does not mean that strong partisans must also perceive larger differences between the parties. For some respondents, response set, or intrasubjective forces, could be expected to increase all party evaluations.[48] But instead, table 8.6 confirms for almost all timepoints that the greater the strength of party attachment, the larger the per-

Table 8.6. Perceptions of party distances, by partisanship, 1961–1972.[a]

Partisanship	July 1961	Sept. 1965	Sept. 1969	Sept. 1972	Difference, 1961–1972
CDU/CSU					
Strong	5.30	5.45	3.50	5.85	+0.55
Weak	3.32	4.10	2.43	3.52	+.20
Leaning	2.95	3.03	2.12	3.30	+.35
SPD					
Leaning	2.34	2.81	2.91	3.44	+1.10
Weak	3.26	3.29	2.29	4.42	+1.16
Strong	4.46	5.55	3.28	6.79	+2.33
Full sample mean	3.28	3.62	2.42	4.09	+.81
Eta	0.608	0.607	0.523	0.621	

a. Cell entries indicate the average absolute difference in CDU/CSU and SPD scalometer ratings for each partisan group. By definition, nonpartisans evaluate both parties equally.

ceived distances between parties. The greatest polarization is perceived by the strong partisans, and the least by the partisan leaners. (Nonpartisans are defined as evaluating both parties equally.) Moreover, the strength of the relationship is remarkably stable over time, with etas (analysis of variance) between .523 in 1969 and 0.621 in 1972. Of course, a reverse flow of causality cannot be ruled out: the farther apart voters see the parties, for example in their issue positions, the better they may like the party closest to their own issue positions. But it is at least equally likely that closer party attachments will lead to greater differences in party evaluations.

These cross-sectional findings also buttress an over-time argument. If the polarization in the electorate's party perceptions increases over time, the source of such change could lie in increased attachments to parties, either as more citizens form such ties or as existing partisanship intensifies. Attitudinal partisans, for example, have a direct affective commitment to their party. The partisanship of social partisans, in contrast, only reflects that group's current collective judgment as to which party best represents its interests. Gradual over-time growth in party polarization could therefore result if attitudinal partisans became more numerous.

With the exception of the 1969 election, the perceived distance between the parties has consistently grown. For the whole sample it increases from 3.28 to 4.09—for strong Christian Democrats from 5.30 to 5.85, and for strong SPD supporters from 4.46 to 6.79. This means that in 1972 strong partisans of both parties gave the opposition a negative rating: Christian Democrats saw the SPD at −0.85, while Social Democrats rated the opposition at an even lower −1.79 (on a scale from −5 to +5).[49] This widening gap between the parties was disproportionately due to change in SPD perceptions. Comparing the endpoints of the series, 1961 and 1972, polarization increases between 0.2 and 0.6 points among different levels of CDU supporters, while the comparable rise for the SPD lies between 1.1 and 2.3 points. Unfortunately, data are not available to determine whether the overall trend toward polarization began in 1961, possibly reversing an earlier decline in hostility, or whether it merely continued an earlier development.

Increasing distances between the SPD and the CDU/CSU were not expected. After all, the history of the German party system at the elite level, at least until 1969, has been described as closing the large gap that separated the two major parties in the 1950s. Indeed, leftist critics in Germany, as in other Western political systems, have charged that these parties and their programs have become virtually indistinguishable.[50] When contrasted to these elite trends toward similarity, the partisan trends in table 8.6 are even more remarkable. Such changes in mass perceptions certainly cannot be explained as the product of parallel or prior changes at the elite level. Instead, the long-term trend fits the notion of gradual change in the nature of partisan attachments, although other explanations are no doubt possible.

The negative relationship between party evaluations is viewed here as a special instance of attitudinal consistency: political parties oppose each other, and consequently someone who highly values one party despises the other party or parties. And the more salient an attitude is, the more *constraint* or consistency is expected between it and related beliefs.[51]

Research on partisanship has established that the level of constraint between political beliefs rises as the subjective strength of party identification increases. This would be true for both types of partisanship, social and attitudinal, but the sources of constraint are not the same for both. For the social partisan, intensity of partisanship "refers to the motivational strength of the voter preference" and basically reflects the strength of the individual's cleavage ties.[52] As a result, beliefs of social partisans will be more constrained for objects related to the cleavage system and for voting choices. Their constraint should be lower for attitudes that are less closely related to the cleavage basis. For attitudinal partisans, on the other hand, the party itself establishes the frame of reference, and consequently all aspects of partisan politics should be tied together more evenly and more closely. These expectations can lead to inferences about the results of a change in the mix of attitudinal and social partisans in the population, even if individuals belonging to the two groups cannot be identified. If the proportion of attitudinal partisans in the population increases, constraint between belief elements should rise. Moreover, the range of constrained beliefs will expand to include perceptions and evaluations of political objects that have partisan connotations but are not directly related to traditional cleavage concerns.

To determine the level of constraint between belief elements, (average) intercorrelations (Pearson r) between items were used. This procedure taps what Philip Converse terms a static concept of constraint: it measures the degree to which political beliefs are related to each other, or how well one attitude can be predicted from knowledge of another.[53]

The first set of attitudes involves the evaluations of candidates for chancellor. Although in Germany the head of the ticket does not have the independent institutional status of an American presidential candidate, the candidates for chancellor are now prominently featured by the two large parties in their election campaigns. Therefore, the voters' perceptions of the two major party leaders should be influenced by partisanship. Not only will voters prefer the candidate of their own party, but the more they like him, the lower will they rate the other candidate. This expected relationship appears quite clearly in figure 8.2, where the signs of the correlations between the two candidate evaluations have been reversed for ease of display. At each election, the stronger an individual's attachment to the party, the greater the negative correlation between the two candidates, that is, the more his evaluations will be based on the candidate's party label.

This appears intuitively obvious; yet, a glance at the candidate correlations among partisan *leaners* uncovers, at least for the first two elections, only low negative correlation (around -0.2) between liking the SPD and CDU leaders. Moreover, at all the available time-points (the candidate evaluations were not included in the 1969 survey) *nonpartisans* actually show positive correlations between the evaluations of the two candidates: if they like the CDU candidate, they also rate his SPD opponent positively! These correlations among nonpartisans decrease only slightly from 0.27 in 1961 to 0.20 in 1972, and thus remain positive. Even in the face of perceived increasing polarization between the parties, which was displayed in table 8.6, nonpartisans still tend to like or dislike all political figures indiscriminately, or at least without much consideration for the party affiliation of the candidates. On the other hand, nonpartisans show a high consistency (between 0.6 and 0.8) of voting choice (vote stability) between elections; therefore their source of vote consistency apparently does not provide a guide for judging candidates.

While the correlations between candidate evaluations change only marginally for nonpartisans, the candidate evaluations are drawn closer into the party sphere among partisans. Figure 8.2 shows that for partisans the constraint among chancellor aspirants in 1961 was considerably below the level of constraint in other political domains (core issues, all issues, vote stability). But candidate constraint increased from -0.35 in that year to -0.65 in 1972 for strong partisans, and from -0.10 to -0.35 for leaners. These 1972 levels are similar to those for constraint between other political belief elements, such as voting stability or partisan issue perceptions.

Discussions of constraint among political belief elements are commonly based on the analysis of issue positions.[54] In his article on the nature of mass belief systems, Converse defines constraint between beliefs as "the success we would have in predicting, given initial knowledge that an individual holds a specified attitude, that he holds further ideas and attitudes."[55] Most American studies focus upon measures of issue positions in order to assess the extent to which common abstract dimensions underly responses of the mass electorate to political stimuli.[56] The German surveys are notably lacking in issue

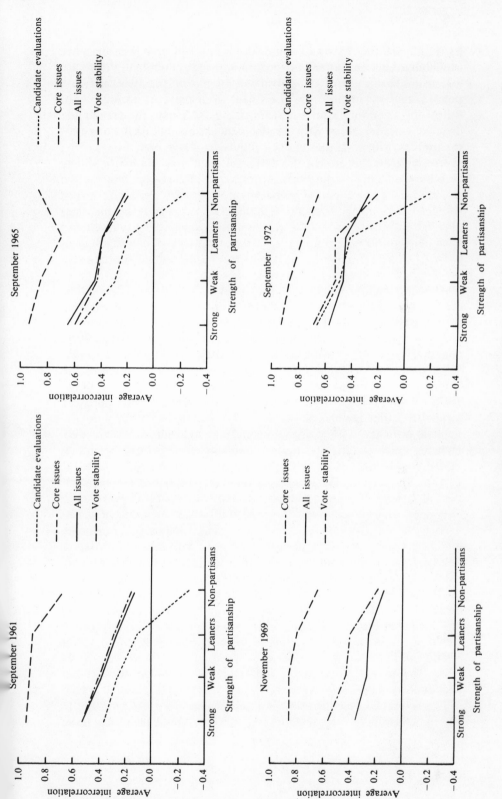

Figure 8.2. Partisan strength and attitudinal constraints, 1961–1972.

position questions. Only perceptions of partisan issue competency are available to serve as severe and meaningful tests of our hypothesis that increasing partisanship would result in increasing constraint between political belief elements. The use of these measures appears justified for two reasons. First, the American studies have uniformly noted that belief constraint grows with stronger partisanship: "political parties themselves, when sharply enough differentiated in policy terms, can serve as reference groups dramatizing 'what goes with what,' and thereby producing marked clusterings in an attentive mass public."[57] Second, since the function of parties is especially important in this respect, providing the party referent in the party competency questions may raise the overall level of constraint beyond what it would have been if position issues had been used. Still, the dynamic effect of *growing* constraint over time cannot be explained by the constant presence of the party referent in the questions.

At each election and for a changing set of issues respondents were asked whether they considered the SPD or the CDU/CSU more competent to deal with each issue.[58] Figure 8.2 presents average intercorrelations for the entire set of between eleven and sixteen issues available in each study. Four of these appeared in all surveys from 1961 to 1972: guaranteeing price stability, old age security, supporting and extending educational facilities, and assuring good relations with the United States. These are the four "core" issues for which mean intercorrelations are also shown. Clearly, the curves for the four core items and for the full set are very similar, even though the larger set includes items of only short-term interest—"flash issues," or issues that probably do not persist long enough to be integrated into the partisan framework. Both sets span a wide variety of more or less central concerns; some of these are closely connected with social cleavages while others cut across the traditional cleavage lines.

High intercorrelations between issue opinions indicate that respondents judge one party to be competent to deal with most or all issues. The party referent should cause strong attitudinal partisans, who are more responsive to this stimulus, to show higher constraint between the items than weaker partisans. In fact, averaged over all the election years 57.2 percent of the strong partisans judge their own party to be more capable on all four core issues, while only 42.5 percent of the weak partisans and 36.4 percent of the partisan leaners do so. This relationship remains fairly constant over time, as the similar slopes from 1961 to 1972 indicate. (Again, however, 1969 proves to be a slightly deviant timepoint.)

This is especially evident if the intercorrelations are rearranged as was done in figure 8.3 for the core issues. Most significantly, constraint

Figure 8.3. Issue constraint by partisan strength (four core issues), 1961–1972.

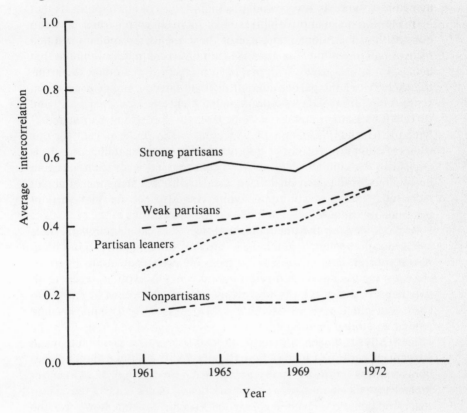

between the political objects has grown continuously since 1961. At each level of partisan strength the highest degree of consistency occurs in 1972. Thus, the average correlation between the core issues rises from 0.553 in 1961 to 0.680 in 1972 for strong partisans, while partisan leaners show an increase from 0.275 to 0.511.[59]

The results of the analyses of three domains—party distance (see table 8.6), candidate evaluation, and issue competency—are similar: they illuminate three aspects of the same general trend. Partisan political objects are increasingly viewed in a consistent manner. Even when the level of partisan commitment is held constant, the degree of constraint at each level of partisan strength still increases over time (see figure 8.3). In addition, the constraints operating upon perceptions of issue competency and candidate evaluations at each level of partisanship (but not for nonpartisans) are becoming more similar. This suggests that all of these partisan domains are becoming increasingly tied to the same source of constraint.[60]

In the domain of vote stability, by contrast, correlations between present vote intentions and recall of past voting decisions are much higher at all timepoints than in any other area (figure 8.2). But although these correlations might be expected to increase over time as the polarization between the parties sharpens, the opposite trend is discernible. Using only SPD-CDU two-party vote intentions and past vote, the correlations remain stable—0.94 to 0.92 for the strong partisans between 1961 and 1972—and they decrease from 0.89 to 0.75 for the leaners (compare also table 8.2). In part, this may reflect small increases in the number of actual vote changes, but it also suggests that during the decade partisanship, as measured here, became marginally more independent of voting behavior. The difference in the effects of partisanship can also be seen in the contrasting slopes of the curves for voting stability, on the one hand, and those for candidate evaluations and issue competency judgments, on the other (figure 8.2). Voting stability differs only slightly between levels of partisan strength—even among nonpartisans the correlations between the voting decisions at two consecutive elections are always above 0.60. But the attitude constraints in the other two domains are consistently and strongly related to strength of partisanship.

The analyses presented here do indeed support the position that the concept of partisanship may be only marginally useful in the explanation of voting behavior: many voters in Germany as well as in other West European countries receive adequate voting cues from sociostructural contexts. Even in relation to voting behavior, however, this rejection should not be absolute. Strength of partisanship has been shown to be clearly related to behavioral manifestations of the voter's commitment to his party, for example in the analyses of defection rates or of vote stability between preelection and postelection surveys. In addition, the hypothesis that sociostructural cues are declining in importance in relation to the voting act leads to the expectation that attitudinal partisanship will have increasing utility in the study of European voting behavior. The crucial role for attitudinal partisanship, however, lies in the extension of analyses of political behavior beyond the simple act of voting; for although voting constraint is stable or declining, the discriminatory power of partisanship increases for constraints relating to issues and candidate evaluations.

Whatever the mix of attitudinal and social partisans in the population, beliefs and perceptions of political objects are moving toward greater constraint. This increasing constraint appears to crystallize around partisan referents rather than around social structural groups, and leads to the conclusion that attitudinal partisanship is indeed spreading in Germany.

The Strength of Partisanship

One of the persistently replicated findings in party identification research, both in the United States and elsewhere, is the positive relationship between voter age and the strength of partisan attachments.[61] Age as such is not of interest, but it serves as an indicator of accumulated partisan experiences that cannot be more directly measured. Ever since the publication of *The American Voter* in 1960, researchers have questioned whether these experiences are related primarily to the life cycle or to generational change.[62] Recent cohort analyses by Converse find that in a stable democracy like the United States, the duration of partisan attachment is the "true" factor underlying the age-strength relationship, so that age approximates a life-cycle indicator. Even with the interjection of timeperiod effects in the late sixties, Converse confirms the importance of the social learning model that predicts the growing strength of partisan attachments as a function of more experience with electoral politics.[63]

The growth of partisan commitments with age presupposes the continuous existence of political parties and a democratic system. In Germany, however, neither the present parties nor the democratic rules of party competition have existed unchanged or uninterrupted during even the past sixty years. Consequently, studies of partisanship in Germany are divided in their expectations and their findings with regard to the age-strength relation. The repeated discontinuities of the party system and the active propagation of counter-ideologies make the smooth operation of a social learning model unlikely.[64] Yet, the existence of surprisingly stable voting blocs going back to the German empire before World War I make the long-term accumulation of electoral experiences more probable than a cursory glance at twentieth century German history would lead one to expect.[65]

We can bring our data to bear on these issues in several ways. The most straightforward one is to observe the distribution of partisan strength by cohorts over the timespan available. To measure the actual strength of partisanship, an indicator was constructed that runs from zero (nonpartisans) to three (strong SPD or CDU/CSU partisans).[66] The mean strength of partisanship in each election for the five broad historical generations is displayed in figure 8.4. At each timepoint there is a clear tendency for older cohorts to be stronger partisans. For example, in 1961 mean partisan strength reaches 1.73 among the early Federal Republic cohort (born between 1932 and 1940) and 1.90 among

Figure 8.4. Strength of partisanship at elections, 1961–1972. The figure plots the mean strength of partisanship for each generation at each timepoint.

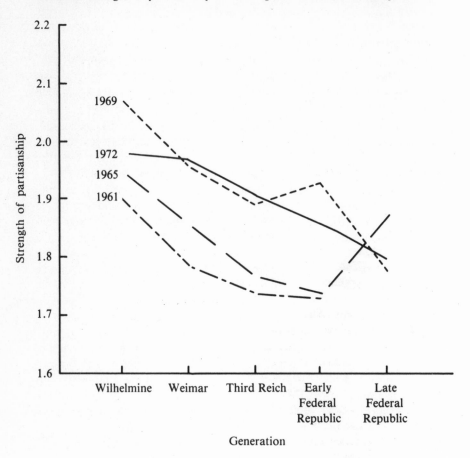

the oldest generation who were socialized during the Wilhelmine Empire. This confirms the results Helmut Norpoth and Franz Urban Pappi obtained with more finely broken cohorts.

While the age-strength relationship occurs at each timepoint, there is also an overall increase in partisan strength for most cohorts between 1961 and 1972. For example, the strength of partisanship among the two generations just cited grows to 1.86 for the younger and 1.98 for the older group after eleven more years of electoral experience. These increases are generally consistent with the learning model, but they probably exceed the growth predicted from a simple learning model. The mean partisan strength for the full sample rises from election to election, and younger generations exhibit stronger partisan values in 1972 than their elders did at the same age.

To some extent this pattern of growth may be due to the stabilization of the German party system between 1949 and 1961 as the major parties consolidated their strength by inheriting the voting support of the smaller parties. When the party system stabilizes and voters continue their experience with the same parties, party strength should grow steadily. The increase in partisanship, however, may also reflect the lagged effects of the learning model. Under the democratic forms of the Federal Republic, citizens should be socialized into relatively stronger partisanship than were citizens under previous authoritarian regimes. Consequently, as younger generations replace older cohorts, the strength of partisanship for the entire electorate should increase. All else being equal, the strength of German partisanship can be expected to grow over the next two decades through this process of generational replacement.

To fully understand the dynamics of the learning process in the context of systemic changes in Germany requires a more rigorous approach than mere visual inspection of figure 8.4. Converse has formalized a learning model of partisanship appropriate to this task in his article "Of Time and Partisan Stability." In a deceptively simple model, two factors are seen as primary influences on a cohort's level of partisan strength: the accumulated electoral experience of the cohort itself, and the "partisan push" received through socialization by the parental generation. Converse uses this model with considerable success to explain the strength of partisanship of cohorts he draws from Almond and Verba's *Civic Culture* study. The basic processes of Converse's cross-national analysis will be replicated here in modeling the German data, but this effort will deviate from Converse's work in several ways. Some variables will be measured in a slightly different manner, for reasons of convenience as well as data availability. In addition, the analysis will be limited to a single country, and this will have important theoretical and empirical implications.

Accumulated electoral experience is the social learning component of Converse's model. Continuing experience with political parties, and especially repeated support of the same party, should increase the strength of an individual's psychological commitment to that party. Since experience normally increases with age, age is often used as an indirect indicator of partisan experiences that are difficult to quantify precisely. But Converse stresses that the length of psychological attachment to a particular political party, not age itself, is the critical determining concept in the social learning model.

To approximate partisan experience, the total number of years an age group was exposed to the electoral process after becoming eligible to vote was estimated. Since exposure to politics is not, however, the same as participation, the political exposure measure was further adjusted to take into account the actual likelihood of electoral participation. The following factors were considered in this process. First, turnout has risen in each of the German regimes that has conducted elections: it was higher in Weimar than in the pre-World War I empire, and higher again during the Federal Republic. Second, because the young are less likely to vote, younger cohorts are estimated to accumulate electoral experience at a slower rate than older age groups. Third, survey findings indicate that the older people are, the more slowly they form new partisan attachments. Consequently, age groups whose first electoral experience was delayed beyond the normal age of enfranchisement were subject to a "resistance" factor when they did begin to participate. This resistance factor applies, first, to females who reached (male) voting age during the Wilhelmine Empire, and more important, to Germans who turned twenty-one when democratic procedures were suspended during the Third Reich. Following Converse's lead, the computed electoral experience of each cohort was adjusted to take all of these facts into account.[67] The resulting constructed variable, I_p, (accumulated electoral experience), reflects the social learning and experience a cohort has accumulated, and it should be positively related to the actual partisan strength of the cohort as measured in the surveys.

The calculated level of I_p that each birth year cohort reached in 1972 is plotted as the solid line in figure 8.5. The value of I_p is generally lower for the younger cohorts, since the young have accumulated less electoral experience, but this general trend is disrupted at two points. First, because the existence of the Third Reich delayed democratic participation until 1946, there is a corresponding dip in electoral experience for the 1911 to 1924 birth cohorts. Second, the very youngest cohorts accumulated electoral experience earlier because this age group reached voting age "prematurely" when eligibility was lowered to age eighteen for the 1972 election.

The second major component of the model, partisan push, captures the effects of parental socialization. A considerable body of data suggests that parents are the most successful transmitters of a sense of partisan loyalty for their offspring.[68] Individuals do not begin their electoral experience at the age of enfranchisement as completely blank slates. To some extent they have already received a partisan push from their parents.

The operationalization of this variable, I_f (impact of the father), is rather straightforward conceptually. According to Converse, the im-

Figure 8.5. Growth of partisanship in West Germany: Theoretical expectations of the model.

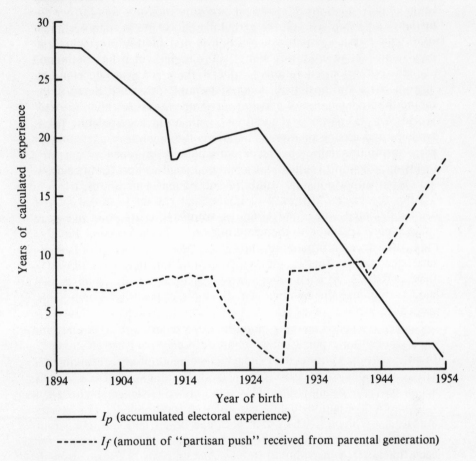

I_p (accumulated electoral experience)

I_f (amount of "partisan push" received from parental generation)

pact of the father is equal to the value of I_p (the electoral experience adjusted for late enfranchisement and turnout) that the parental cohort (assumed to have been born thirty years before the offspring) had attained when the offspring cohort was fifteen years old. These basic I_f values are adjusted to account for the more limited generational transfer that occurred during the suspension of electoral competition under the Third Reich.[69]

The curve for I_f is also plotted in figure 8.5. Except for the very slight incline as the disenfranchisement of women before 1919 loses its impact, the line is perfectly flat for all cohorts born before 1918. This constant value of I_f would hold true for any political system in which parental acquisition of partisanship had continued uninterrupted for the two previous generations. In such a country—the United States, for example—*all cohorts would receive an identical amount of parental partisan push*. Therefore, parental partisan push cannot explain cohort differences in partisan strength in a stable party system. I_f is only important in countries where suffrage has not been continuous over the two prior generations.[70] Indeed, there is a sharp decelerating drop in I_f for the post-1918 cohorts, because the Third Reich interrupted the transmission of partisanship from parents to children. After World War II, parental generations again begin accumulating partisanship, and among postwar generations the amount of accumulated partisanship transmitted by the parent gradually approaches "normal" levels once again. In future years parental push will probably begin to flatten out into a constant value for subsequent generations.

After the values of these two conceptual variables, I_p and I_f, had been calculated, the annual figures were aggregated for five-year cohorts corresponding to the age groups used in the surveys. Finally, the actual strength of partisanship (P_s in Converse's terms) was measured for each cohort in surveys from four timepoints: 1961, 1965, 1969, and 1972. At each timepoint two or three surveys were cumulated to increase the number of individuals in each age group. This procedure yielded forty-three cohorts as the basis for our analyses.[71]

Converse's social learning model places primary stress on electoral experience as an explanation of cohort differences in partisan strength. In large part the German data support such an emphasis, resulting in a satisfying 0.683 correlation between electoral experience (I_p) and actual partisan strength (P_s). This relationship is slightly higher than Converse's five-nation finding and than Norpoth's or Pappi's results for Germany alone.[72] The differences can be attributed to our larger database of four elections and to the use of pooled cohort estimates for each timepoint, which should stabilize the empirical partisan strength measurements.

In contrast to the high correlation between I_p and P_s, the simple relationship (r) between I_f and P_s is only 0.209, a nonsignificant value, with a sample of only forty-three. This finding confirms what a visual inspection of figure 8.5 already suggests: parental partisan push does not contain sufficient variation to make it a statistically important predictor.

Both I_p and I_f taken together explain slightly more total variance, with a multiple correlation of 0.721. In simple terms, over half of the variance in the strength of partisanship between German cohorts is explained by the two predictors. Moreover, these results do not derive from correlations of attitudes with attitudes; rather, partisan strength is explained with independent conceptual variables constructed from electoral statistics and turnout rates in German elections—a true cross-level analysis.

A final adjustment to this model was designed to further account for the effects of the Third Reich. It is likely that after twelve years of Nazi indoctrination the previous commitment of German citizens to democratic parties had waned. When democratic politics was reinstated after the war, some of the learning that had been accumulated before 1933 was forgotten. Consequently, a "forgetting function" was applied to both accumulated electoral experience (I_p) and parental push (I_f).[73] This final adjustment raised the multiple correlation with partisan strength to 0.741, and yielded the following equation predicting cohort partisanship (N = 43, R = 0.741, R^2 = 0.549).

$$P_s = 1.562 + 0.0128\ I_p + 0.0129\ I_f$$
$$(s_e:)\quad (0.056)\quad (0.0018)\quad (0.0049)$$

These analyses explain a considerable proportion of the observed variance in the partisanship of German cohorts, although their explanatory power is less than that of Converse's cross-national analyses. The learning part of the model, contained in accumulated electoral experience (I_p), actually performs as well as that in Converse's five-nation case. Thus, in Germany as in other democracies, the commitment to a party is strengthened by repeated electoral support of that party. But the addition of I_f, which produced a significant increase for Converse, does not substantially improve the explanatory power of our model.

In his independent replication of the Converse model, Pappi suggests that the low weight of I_f indicates that the "normal" parental socialization process has not worked in the German context.[74] This interpretation appears highly plausible in light of the discontinuities of Germany's political history and the obvious difficulty of transmitting democratic political values through the disruptive Third Reich period. However, these discontinuities have already been built into Converse's learning model, and in great detail. In addition, this interpretation of the findings overlooks the fact that in stable democracies there would be *absolutely no effect* from parental push (I_f) since its value would be a constant. In Converse's cross-national analysis I_f does not really measure the strength of the transmission process, but rather the variations in the aggregate level of partisanship among parental generations (and indirectly the duration of democracy in society).[75] The nonzero coefficient of I_f in our analysis shows that historical conditions such as the interruption of democracy by the Third Reich have indeed affected partisan strength in Germany. In fact, the impact of these historical conditions, which is accounted for in Converse's model, is confirmed by the German data.[76]

The ideal vehicle for studying the generational transmission of political values in a simultaneous survey of parents and children. In the absence of such surveys, recall data must be used to assess the socialization process. Although these data suffer from several methodological weaknesses, they can shed light on the topic.[77] The discontinuities of the German party system weakened the generational transfer of ties to specific parties. Even in 1972 only 48 percent of our sample could identify their parents' partisanship (table 8.7). Yet the instability of the parties does not mean that parental socialization was devoid of partisan content. Traces of parental impact emerged when the question was put more generally: 60 percent could recall the party for which their father usually voted; and fully 90 percent remembered the general political orientation, or *tendance*, of their father as either conservative, social democratic, liberal, or nationalist.

The different levels of recognition reinforce our earlier conclusions about long-term change in the bases of German partisanship. In the past, when party voting was heavily determined by social class and religion, without fixation on a particular party, commitment was to a bloc of parties—bourgeois, socialist, Christian—and indeed the data indicate that nearly everyone could recall his father's tendance. But because sociostructural orientations are only gradually being replaced by affective attachments to a specific party, responses to the more demanding questions about the parent's vote or partisan loyalties

Table 8.7. Proportion of samples recalling parents' political leanings.[a]

Generation	Knowledge of parents' partisanship (Dec. 1972)[b]	Knowledge of father's vote (Nov. 1969)	Knowledge of father's political orientation (Nov. 1969)
Full sample	48.3%	60.3%	89.7%
Early and late Federal Republic	56.2	61.0	88.3
Third Reich	—	60.7	88.8
Wilhelmine and Weimar	41.1	59.3	91.4

a. Cell entries are percentages of the sample (or generational subsample) that could recall the political orientations of their parents (column 1) or of their fathers (columns 2 and 3).

b. Question not asked of respondents born between 1915 and 1935.

showed a significantly less successful generational transfer of specific partisanship.

These conclusions about the changing content of the socialization process lead to several expectations for intergenerational differences with which we can test our hypotheses. For example, there would be only small differences between young and old in the ability to recall the general political orientations of the parents, since those orientations have been constant across generations. But the partisan socialization of the young should result in significantly larger generational differences in the ability to recall specific parental partisanship. The lower rows of table 8.7 confirm these expectations. Only 3 points separate the post-World War II cohorts from the prewar generations in ability to identify their father's tendance. By contrast, these two age groups differ by 15 percent in recalling parental partisanship—a difference five times greater.

The implications of these findings for the growth of German partisanship are similar to those that can be drawn from a cross-national study carried out by Philip Converse and George Dupeux.[78] They conclude that awareness of parental partisanship increases the likelihood that the offspring will develop their own partisan attachments. Our data indicate that this model fits Germany. Depending upon the definition of partisans (either excluding or including leaners), 68.7 percent (95.7 percent with leaners) of those who recall their parents' partisanship are partisans themselves, compared to 59.3 percent (89.7 percent with leaners) of those who do not. That these differences are not larger may be due to the "softness" of our partisanship measure, but similar results are found for all three measures of parental partisanship.

Although recall data are obviously fallible, these analyses provide "side information" to support the more rigorous social learning model proposed by Converse. Hence, the acquisition of partisanship in Germany generally follows the model Converse proposed to cover all democratic political systems. If partisanship levels among the present German population are lower than those in other countries, this could have resulted partly from the historical interruptions of the normal learning and transmission process and partly from the changing nature of partisan orientations.

Conclusion

With some exceptions, previous research has concluded that the level of affective party identification in West Germany is relatively low in comparison with that of other Western democracies. This finding alone would diminish the value of party identification as a factor in explaining political behavior in Germany, because it could not account for the voting choices of the large number of nonidentifiers.

This conclusion can be challenged in two ways. First, after the level of partisanship had been shown to be quite sensitive to instrument effects, experimentation with question wording yielded measures that captured over 70 percent of the identifiers. Similarly, the scalometer-based measure of partisanship used here succeeded in classifying the partisanship of most respondents without compromising the concept's ability to explain voting, participation rates, and perceptions of partisan polarization. Second, the analysis of partisanship has to take into account the effects of Germany's erratic democratic history. When this is done, as in Converse's learning model, it is clear that the level of German partisanship has been rising, and that it will continue to rise unless the democratic process and free elections are once again suspended. Hence, even if the conservative measurements of partisanship yield a relatively small number of partisans now, that number can be expected to increase in the future.

Another objection to the use of the concept of partisanship in Germany was that even higher proportions of partisans, however measured, would be relatively meaningless because the concept of party identification is much less useful for the understanding of voting behavior in Germany than in the United States, where the concept originated. This argument maintains that traditional social forces, like class or religion, provide sufficient cues to orient individuals in a political realm that deals largely with concerns related to those social cleavages. Under such conditions, partisanship could be only a secondary indirect expression of the more basic, underlying social positions, and hence it could possess only limited heuristic value.

Chapter 7 presented evidence of a steady decline since the early 1950s in the explanatory power of social factors, especially those that are class-related. In this chapter, longitudinal analyses have been used to discover whether partisanship might not gain in utility as the political cue-giving function of class and other social attributes weakened. These analyses have revealed that since 1961 partisanship has become a more and more potent force with respect to voting choice, defection rates, electoral stability, and campaign activities. Even more decisive is the finding that in public perceptions the parties have grown increasingly important as organizing foci for political attitudes on issues and candidates. Moreover, political issues, and to some extent candidates, are gradually becoming less related to the traditional social cleavages, a development that makes social factors an unlikely alternative source for increasing constraint among political belief elements.

Instead, this development can be interpreted as evidence of the growth of partisanship, for the direct attitudinal attachment to political parties can continue to provide cues for behavior in a political environment whose agenda is changing.

9

Partisan Images and Electoral Change

BOTH SOCIAL CHARACTERISTICS and partisanship by their very nature exert a conserving, stabilizing influence upon political behavior. Class interests have been a source of partisan division since the industrialization of Germany in the nineteenth century. Similarly, long-term affective attachments to a specific party have promoted political continuity in democratic systems.[1]

Yet considerable change in the importance of both these factors has been found during the past three decades. Short-term fluctuations in voting results from election to election are inevitable; the cumulative changes uncovered for these supposedly stable elements of political behavior, however, have been surprising. While the class alignment continuously and progressively weakened during the postwar years, there was a steady movement toward SPD partisanship between 1953 and 1972.

The outcome of a single election might easily be explained by the issues, personalities, and style of the campaign.[2] An exceptionally intense issue might produce a partisan shift that would persist over time, but the causal force of issues is normally of limited duration. The direction and magnitude of issue effects normally do not show much continuity, and certainly not enough to explain the steady changes in class voting and partisanship. Therefore these short-term factors alone cannot be expected to provide an adequate explanation of long-term electoral trends. Short-term forces must be integrated into a more basic and fundamental belief structure in order to have an enduring effect on the political landscape. According to other researchers, partisan images, the mental pictures the electorate has of what the parties are and what they stand for, are likely causes of change in electoral trends.

Donald Matthews and James Prothro, for example, demonstrate that party images played a crucial role in altering traditional voting patterns in the American South.[3] At a somewhat more theoretical level they argue that "while party image is not so deeply rooted or so stable as party identification, it is likely to be less ephemeral than voter attitudes toward the issues and candidates of specific campaigns."[4] They posit that party images carry over from election to election so that short-term factors may indirectly cumulate to produce the sorts of trends observed in this study.

Although partisan images are more durable than the issues of a single campaign, they remain in the realm of issues and provide a cognitive dimension of partisanship rather than resulting in an affective attachment to or identification with a party. Changes in party images, however, may well be the first step in a process leading to changes in affective partisanship. For example, Charles Sellers stresses the role of party images in the process of electoral change.[5] He argues that the critical issues stimulating an electoral realignment first alter the party images of large numbers of voters; then these new party images cause changes in party identification. In Germany party images gain further weight from the fact that both major parties, especially the SPD, have consciously introduced programs to change the image of the party in the voters' minds.

Partisan images have many facets. Some of the most general and salient involve abstract qualities and abilities. A party may be seen as capable of governing, or as unable, irresponsible, or unwilling to assume the mantle of leadership. A party may be considered dynamic and progressive or static and provincial. As David Butler and Donald Stokes note, these image qualities have more to do with the intrinsic values of a party than with policy programs and government outputs.[6]

Other partisan images are related to the interests the parties represent. The Christian Democrats are traditionally seen as the party of Catholics and the higher social strata. The SPD's links to the working class and secular interests are even more clearly perceived. The importance of such images in a political system based on social cleavages is obvious.[7] Hence, to what extent, it might be asked, has the change in class alignments in the postwar years been due to the public's perception that the Social Democrats are shedding their working-class orientation and developing a middle-class constituency?

Still other elements of the parties' images are more directly issue-oriented. Through programs and campaign announcements the electorate develops generalized beliefs about party positions on the issues. Although ordinarily unaware of the specific details of party programs, the voter still has a general feeling about which party can best deal with certain issues. Thus, feelings of issue competency serve to direct partisan behavior even if the strict requirements of "rational" issue voting are lacking.

The Qualities of Leadership

Certain abstract qualities, even more than party programs, are required for public support. Can a party be trusted to fulfill its campaign promises? Is it capable of running the government? Without such assurances campaign promises and party programs carry less weight. The SPD has grappled with these problems from the beginning of the postwar period. It has almost always been plagued by public doubts about its integrity and even its patriotism.[8]

The SPD's virulent opposition during the Wilhelmine Empire tainted the party from the beginning. The schisms and animosities of the Weimar Republic and its eventual collapse placed a further onus of irresponsibility upon the SPD. Although the party's opposition to the National Socialists during the Third Reich and its leadership immediately after the war may have partially rehabilitated its image, old doubts soon returned.[9]

As the Cold War emerged, the SPD's ideological proximity to Soviet communism was emphasized by the CDU/CSU, raising fears of what an SPD government might bring. In 1953 the CDU/CSU marched into electoral battle under the slogan, "All Marxist Roads Lead to Moscow—Vote CDU." And the Social Democrats' programs reinforced these fears. The majority of the electorate saw the SPD as opposed to the goals of German society. Indeed, during the early years of the Federal Republic the SPD challenged many of the principles of the CDU-led government, not just the policies to achieve these goals. For example, in the domestic field the SPD's socialist economic program would have dismantled the CDU/CSU's social market economy, a stand that was perceived as a threat to the *Wirtschaftswunder*. Similarly, Social Democratic foreign policy criticized Konrad Adenauer's policy of integrating Germany into the Western Alliance both economically and militarily, and placed a much higher value on German reunification. Because of its turbulent history, as Otto Kirchheimer notes, the SPD was unable to develop the image of a "loyal" opposition.[10] During the early years of the Federal Republic the party was not able to develop a popular consensus either on its ability to govern or on its loyalty to the nation as a whole.

Kurt Schumacher's initial policies of opposition for the SPD resulted in failure on nearly all fronts. Successive electoral defeats stimulated a strong movement within the party to end public doubts about its reliability and intentions. But the Social Democrats faced a major problem: in 1961 almost half of the population (47 percent) did not believe that the party was fit to govern. Far fewer (28 percent) raised that criticism against the CDU/CSU.

The Godesberg program was a step toward a new political style for the SPD. By minimizing their differences with the CDU/CSU in domestic and later in foreign policy, SPD strategists sought to lessen their radical image and increase their viability as an alternative government. In fact, the SPD moved toward a strategy of *Umarmung* ("embracement") vis-à-vis the CDU/CSU. In 1961 and more openly in 1965, Herbert Wehner suggested to CDU/CSU elites the possibility of a Grand Coalition between the two major parties. By responsibly sharing the reins of government the Social Democrats hoped to increase public confidence in them. Participation in the federal government, at nearly any cost, was given a high priority by many SPD leaders.

The SPD followed this strategy at both federal and *Land* levels, cooperating with the CDU/CSU in the Bundestag and often sharing power in Land governments. But the data show that in 1965 the Social Democrats' image still suffered in comparison with the Christian Democrats' (figure 9.1). On semantic differential scales the electorate expressed predominately positive views of both parties on the separate dimensions of reliability, responsibility, and trust.[11] Yet in 1965 the SPD received consistently lower evaluations on each dimension. For example, while 79 percent felt the CDU/CSU was to some extent reliable, only 62 percent felt the same about the SPD. (The mean score on the six-point scale shown in the figure was 4.4 for the CDU/CSU and 4.0 for the SPD.) The average 10 to 15 percent CDU advantage on these dimensions was obviously sufficient to ensure electoral victory for the Christian Democrats.

The SPD saw participation in the federal government as one way to banish all doubts. Its opportunity to complete this embracement strategy arose in November 1966. Faced with difficult economic and political decisions and opposition by the FDP to its budgetary policy, the CDU/CSU joined the SPD to form the Grand Coalition. From the SPD's standpoint its first participation in the federal government appeared a success, finally alleviating many questions about the party's integrity and ability to govern. Between 1965 and 1969 the SPD moved from a clear disadvantage to equality with the CDU/CSU on the dimensions of reliability, responsibility, and trust (figure 9.1).

The SPD not only improved its image of reliability and trust during the period of the Grand Coalition, but it also played an active role in resolving the nation's problems. Its minister of economics, Karl Schiller, was credited with Germany's recovery from the economic recession of 1967–1969. Willy Brandt was instrumental in laying the ground-

Figure 9.1. Reliability images of the parties, 1965, 1969. Entries are mean party scores on the semantic differential scales.

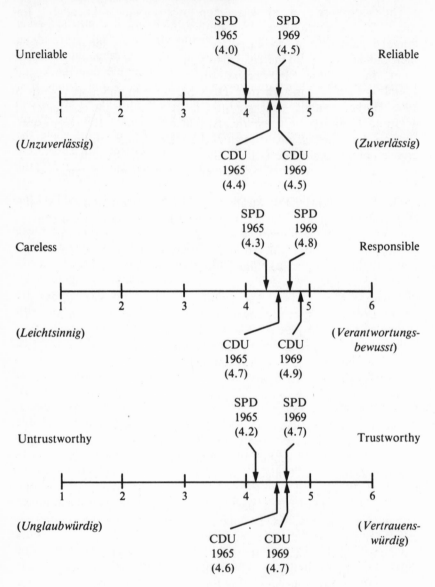

work for Bonn's new *Ostpolitik,* and Gustav Heinemann after a successful tenure as minister of justice assumed the office of federal President.

The ability to take the lead in problem-solving strengthened other aspects of the SPD's image. In 1965 the SPD and CDU were about equally rated in terms of their progressiveness, cosmopolitanism, and systematic planning (figure 9.2), but by the 1969 election the Social Democrats had a clear advantage on each of these dimensions. For example, the SPD and CDU/CSU were rated as equally progressive in 1965 (85 percent saw both parties as progressive), and four years later the SPD strengthened its progressive image (95 percent) while the CDU/CSU image actually deteriorated (77 percent). In short, the SPD's performance during the Grand Coalition gave the party the image of a dynamic, open, problem-solving organization. Not only could the SPD be trusted, the electorate believed, but it "could get the work done."

Additional data from the Konrad Adenauer Foundation allow these trends to be extended to 1972.[12] In that year the SPD chancellor-candidate, Willy Brandt, took a dramatic lead over the CDU/CSU candidate, Rainer Barzel, on the progressive dimension (figure 9.3). This is not surprising because during the preceding three years the Brandt-led government had experienced dramatic success with Ostpolitik, stable economic growth, and the enrichment of social programs. And Brandt himself had been awarded the Nobel Peace Prize for his efforts.

Equally important, these data give a better understanding of the nature of party images. Butler and Stokes note that the qualities of leadership are valence dimensions, that is, they are positively evaluated by nearly everyone.[13] After all, who would seek out an unreliable party, or one without goals? Although progressiveness is not necessarily a positive attribute, the German electorate saw itself in 1972 as fairly progressive, with a mean self-placement of 5.3 on a seven-point conservative-progressive scale. Moreover, most German voters saw the slightly more progressive Brandt (5.6) as closer to their own self-image on this dimension, while they perceived Barzel (4.4) as more conservative and farther from their own position.

These qualities of leadership are by no means permanent aspects of party images. They are flexible, reflecting party actions and recent events. This presumption underlies the SPD's efforts to remold its image over the past several decades. As a result this image has steadily improved, which must to some extent have contributed to the party's electoral gains.

Figure 9.2. Dynamic images of the parties, 1965, 1969. Entries are mean party scores on the semantic differential scales.

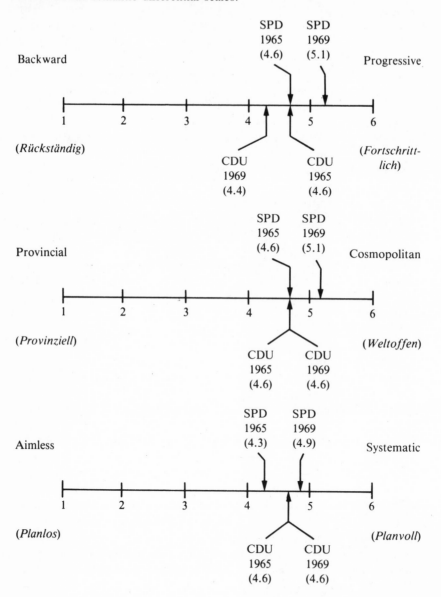

Figure 9.3. Images of the chancellor candidates and electorate, 1972. Entries are mean scores on the semantic differential scale. Source: Konrad-Adenauer-Stiftung, *1972 German Election Panel Study,* no. 7110 (Ann Arbor: ICPSR).

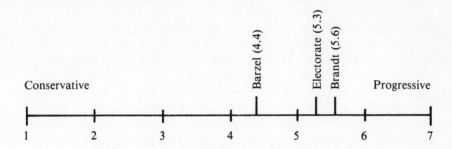

Both the SPD and the CDU/CSU are now legitimate contenders for government and are evaluated in terms of their programs. By projecting the qualities of leadership the SPD has not only legitimized its role as a loyal opposition but has also created the necessary base for building a majority coalition.

Social Groups and the Parties

Party images also serve to link the parties to the social structure. Most people see a party as representing distinct clienteles—class, religious, or regional. The social cues provided by these partisan images often serve as potent guides to behavior. Since the social bases of the parties are usually stable, the information costs of relying upon social cues are minimal. Electors who know which party generally represents their class or religious beliefs can easily (and efficiently) decide how to vote. A member of the working class who votes for a party of the working class is, in a very real sense, a rational voter.

W. Phillips Shively postulates that the importance of social cues rests upon two principles.[14] First, the issues of social conflict underlying social characteristics must be important to the electorate. Second, the positions of the parties on these conflicts must be sufficiently clear for the voters to link their own positions to the choice of a party. The steady decline in class voting suggests that one or both of these factors is changing.

Since Godesberg the Social Democrats have attempted to divorce themselves from their socialist, working-class image and to develop into a broader *Volkspartei* ("catchall party"). The decline in class voting and the increase in SPD support at the polls show that the SPD policy of blurring class cues in order to broaden its electoral support has apparently been successful.

Since 1957 data have been collected that allow an examination of popular perceptions of the social bases of the parties.[15] In these surveys respondents have been asked whether specific social groups generally leaned toward one or the other of the two major parties.

Perceptions of religious denominations did not change much between 1957 and 1969. In 1957 there was little ambiguity in linking Catholics to the Christian Democrats—83 percent identified the CDU/CSU leanings of most Catholics (table 9.1). Twelve years later a nearly equivalent 85 percent thought the same way. Data collected on Protestants between 1957 and 1961 (not shown in the table) also display little change in perceptions of their leanings.[16] This stability and clarity of religious cues may help to explain the persistence of religious differences in voting behavior observed during the postwar years.

Class images present a contrasting pattern. Images of class leanings have, if anything, become more clear-cut over time. In 1957, 75 percent of the electorate thought most workers tended to support the SPD. In

Table 9.1. Popular perceptions of partisan leanings of social groups, 1957–1969.

Social groups	July 1957[a]	July 1961	Oct. 1969
Perceived Catholic leanings			
SPD	1%	1%	1%
Both or other parties	16	9	14
CDU/CSU	83	90	85
Perceived working-class leanings			
SPD	75	75	86
Both or other parties	24	20	10
CDU/CSU	1	6	4
Perceived farmer leanings			
SPD	4	9	7
Both or other parties	39	22	26
CDU/CSU	57	69	67
Perceived middle-class leanings			
SPD	14	18	20
Both or other parties	53	35	35
CDU/CSU	33	48	45

a. 1957 figures are recalculated from tables in the DIVO report on the election, *Untersuchung der Wählerschaft und Wahlentscheidung,* app. B, pp. 60–62.

1969, despite Godesberg and the depolarizing 1969 election, an even higher percentage (86) of the public linked the working class to the SPD. Similarly, the electorate's views of the partisan leanings of most farmers have remained fairly distinct and constant.

Most important in this context, however, is the electorate's view of the middle class. The SPD was consciously appealing to the middle class, and its share of the two-party vote within this social stratum increased dramatically from 24 percent in 1957 to 47 percent in 1969. Yet the electorate saw only the slightest growth in the SPD leanings of the middle class over the same period. The middle class was difficult to place in 1957, probably because of its support for the FDP—53 percent of the sample would not link that class primarily to either the SPD or the CDU/CSU. However, by 1961 almost half of the public identified the CDU/CSU leanings of the middle class, and there was little change by 1969. Even if attention is restricted to only middle-class respondents, whose voting decisions should be most affected by perceptions of "normal" middle-class behavior, the trend differs only marginally.[17]

If one accepts Shively's argument that class voting is based on two requirements—a link between the electorate and class conflict, and a link between class conflict and the parties—then these data have helped to isolate the source of the decline in class voting. They show convincingly that the contemporary German voter positions major social groups within a partisan framework. Indeed, Franz Pappi notes that the workers and the old middle class—traditionally the major protagonists of the class cleavage—apparently continue to fulfill Shively's requirements, and our data generally support this view.[18] These two social strata are more heavily oriented toward the economic and security concerns underlying the class conflict: the bourgeoisie is clearly aligned with the CDU/CSU and the proletariat with the SPD. Only when one explicitly incorporates the *new* middle class into the analytic framework does a middle-class tendency toward the SPD appear.[19] Although the SPD has not been able to shed its working-class image and adopt a middle-class image, the Godesberg program and other policies have achieved the objective in another manner.

Through moderated economic policies the SPD has been able to decrease the salience of traditional class and economic conflicts for the German electorate. When both parties began to hold basically similiar positions on economic matters, the choice between the parties on these issues became less crucial for the voters. The increasing affluence of the postwar era has also weakened the link between the voter and the class structure, making economic issues even less important. In the place of traditional Old Politics concerns, the electorate is placing increased emphasis on the issues of the New Politics. The SPD has been especially successful in attracting support from the new middle class, whose interest in New Politics issues was an initial stimulus for the SPD's policy changes. In sum, class voting has declined because the electorate is less concerned with class-based political conflict, even though traditional class cues can still be readily identified.

Issues, Values, and Electoral Change

The declining salience of class-based conflicts has allowed the SPD to shift political debate toward other issues where support is potentially greater. These changes can be examined within the Old Politics–New Politics framework discussed in chapter 6.

Both the SPD and CDU/CSU were built upon an Old Politics base after World War II, when economic and security issues were emphasized. These materialist values still hold priority among a clear plurality of the German population, but for a growing portion of the electorate political horizons are broadening to include a new set of issue concerns. The young, well-educated, and economically secure segments of society are gradually seeing their basic sustenance and safety needs fulfilled. Consequently, their attention is turning to postmaterial goals, or what are termed the issues of the New Politics, to personal freedom and self-expression, to quality of life rather than quantity of material goods. Since the 1960s the SPD (and FDP) leadership has increasingly relied on these New Politics issues to attract support, and these concerns often cut across class-based cleavage lines.[20]

What images have the parties projected with respect to Old Politics and New Politics concerns? Beginning in 1961 and continuing through 1972, respondents were asked whether the SPD or CDU/CSU would be more competent to deal with a wide range of political issues. A typical question read:

> Please disregard for a moment which party you personally favor; which of the two large parties do you think can best deal with the following problems, the SPD or the CDU/CSU?

Although the battery of political problems has changed over time, a common New Politics–Old Politics issue dimension has been identified for each election.[21] The overall competency of the CDU/CSU and of the SPD to deal with these problems has been computed separately for both types of issues.[22]

Between 1961 and 1972 the electorate raised its evaluation of the SPD's competency to deal with both Old Politics and New Politics issues (table 9.2). In 1961 the CDU/CSU held the advantage in both issue domains, although the SPD came closer to parity on Old Politics

Table 9.2. Popular perceptions of SPD and CDU/CSU issue competency (all issues), 1961–1972.[a]

Issue	July 1961	Sept. 1965	Nov. 1969	Sept. 1972	Change per annum[b]
Old Politics full issue index	+0.15	+0.13	−0.24	−0.10	0.031
New Politics full issue index	+.41	+.23	−.32	−.50	.088

a. Cell entries indicate the mean scores of the competency indexes averaged separately for Old Politics and New Politics issues. The individual issue items were scored: (−1) SPD, and (+1) CDU/CSU.

b. Calculated by regressing competency scores on the year of the study.

topics. The Social Democrats' championship of higher wages and social benefits aimed primarily at the working class had left an imprint on the entire electorate. In the next eleven years the per-annum change in perceptions of party competency on Old Politics issues moved rather slowly (0.031 per annum), so that by 1972 the SPD enjoyed only a modest advantage.[23] In contrast, New Politics issue competency shifted toward the SPD at almost triple that rate (0.088 per annum). By 1972 the SPD was not only seen as considerably more competent than the CDU/CSU, but the New Politics domain had become the Social Democrats' stronghold. Hans Klingemann similarly describes the longitudinal trends for a set of nine identical issues from datasets partially overlapping those used here.[24] With a few exceptions, his results fit the Old Politics–New Politics framework well. Klingemann's findings show little change in perceptions of competency for issues tapping Old Politics concerns but strong movement toward the Social Democrats on New Politics issues.

In addition to the full set of issues, competency can be studied at each timepoint for four core issues: price stability, old age security, support for education, and relations with the United States. Although four issues are not as firm a basis for generalization as the full set of issues, tracking these four over time does reveal the details of changing issue images, and provide longitudinally comparable measures of issue competency. Moreover, this subset of four issues spans a reasonable range of the Old Politics–New Politics continuum.[25] On the one hand, price stability and old age security tap the concern for individual economic security; on the other hand, support for education and relations with the United States reflect New Politics interests in intellectual enrichment and a broadening world view.

In 1961 the CDU/CSU was viewed as more competent to deal with

Table 9.3. Popular perceptions of SPD and CDU/CSU issue competency (core issues), 1961–1972.[a]

Issues	July 1961	Sept. 1965	Nov. 1969	Sept. 1972	Change per annum[b]
Price stability					
CDU/CSU	52%	51%	37%	52%	
SPD	48	49	63	48	0.4%
% of sample	(83)	(91)	(90)	(64)	
Old age security					
CDU/CSU	53	51	38	37	
SPD	47	49	62	63	1.6
% of sample	(84)	(92)	(91)	(62)	
Education					
CDU/CSU	72	51	36	35	
SPD	28	49	64	65	3.4
% of sample	(79)	(91)	(85)	(50)	
U.S. relations					
CDU/CSU	84	69	67	50	
SPD	16	31	33	50	2.7
% of sample ·	(83)	(91)	(90)	(51)	

a. Cell entries in parentheses are the percentages of the total sample that believed either the CDU/CSU or SPD to be most competent to deal with the specific issue. Percentages are based only on those respondents naming one of the two major parties as most competent.

b. Change in SPD competency is calculated by regressing its competency scores on the year of the study.

all four issues (table 9.3). Substantial differences existed, however, between partisan images on Old Politics and New Politics issues. For the two Old Politics issues of price stability and old age security, a bare majority of the electorate favored the Christian Democrats. The SPD's relative strength on these issues was typical of the paradox it faced. By constantly representing the interests of the workers in these matters the SPD drew high praise from its traditional working-class base, but the majority of the electorate—farmers, new middle class, and old middle class—supported the economic policies of the CDU/CSU.[26]

The SPD's image fared even worse in 1961 on the emerging New Politics issues. Nearly 75 percent of those choosing the more competent major party saw the CDU/CSU as having a better educational policy, and an overwhelming 84 percent favored the CDU/CSU handling of foreign relations with the United States. Even among Social Democratic supporters in 1961 a considerable minority recognized the CDU/CSU's lead in these areas.

But the Social Democrats' positions on the New Politics issues were changing as a result of the Bad Godesberg conference and other party actions. The SPD had just reversed its foreign policy stance, supporting closer ties with the Western Alliance.[27] It was giving special attention to new social policies, such as educational opportunities, which, according to the party's socialist ideology, had always been an important means of improving the status of the working class. Education was an exclusive *Land* responsibility under the Basic Law, and SPD-led state governments took the lead in experimenting with educational reforms and expanding educational opportunities. In addition, elements within the SPD had supported and nurtured the modest educational reforms presented in the *Saarbrückener Rahmenplan* in 1959, and in the 1960 *Bremer Plan* of the SPD-oriented Teachers Union.[28] In 1961, however, the SPD's capabilities were still seen as dismally poor.

The Social Democrats faced a difficult challenge in the early 1960s. They needed to improve their image on New Politics issues in order to retain the support of the working class, but they also had to drop the strident socialist tones that in the past had repelled potential middle-class supporters. With historical perspective such a long-term strategy now appears to have been well suited to help bring about the political changes of the following years.

As the German people gradually came to believe in the success of the Economic Miracle, they turned their attention to other social problems. One example was the educational crisis (*Bildungsnotstand*). In 1964 over 37,000 primary school teachers were needed but could not be found.[29] Growing public realization of the inadequacies of the educational system prompted public debate and the introduction of reforms aimed at expanding educational facilities, increasing the number of teachers, and restructuring the primary and secondary schools. Although educational policy was fragmented because it was a state responsibility, the SPD Land governments generally appeared to be more responsive to these changing needs. In 1964 the party proposed a set of educational reforms to produce more democratic as well as more efficient schools. This proposal was basically administrative, calling for a restructuring of Germany's strictly tiered and tracked educational systems. And the SPD-led state governments took the lead in implementing such reforms. The Land of Hesse had already adopted intermediate schools (grades 5 and 6), which all students attended (*Förderstufe*), and West Berlin experimented with the far-reaching introduction of several schools that were comprehensive through the tenth grade (*Gesamtschulen*). As a result, in 1965 the perceptions of SPD competency on educational matters increased nearly 20 percent and achieved virtual parity with those of the CDU (table 9.3).

Party images in the foreign policy domain were also changing. Public concern for international cooperation was gradually replacing the national security fears of the immediate postwar period. The more open and conciliatory Eastern policies of the Social Democrats and especially of Willy Brandt, then mayor of West Berlin, stood in sharp contrast to the CDU/CSU's inability to adapt to the changing world situation. Consequently, the SPD was able to improve its image substantially. Between 1961 and 1965 the gain was 15 percent. As the New Politics component of foreign policy grew, SPD competency in this domain also increased.

But while the SPD succeeded in changing its image with regard to New Politics issues, it and the CDU/CSU maintained fairly constant positions in the early 1960s regarding the Old Politics issues of individual economic security.[30] As chancellor, Ludwig Erhard maintained the same economic policies he had developed as minister of economics under Konrad Adenauer, and the Wirtschaftswunder continued. Similarly, the SPD still represented the interests of the working class, only in a more modest way. Thus, virtually no change occurred between 1961 and 1965 in party images concerning price stability and old age security. So far, at least, the SPD had maintained its position on traditional economic issues while making great strides on New Politics themes.

In 1966 the German economy suffered a modest recession, which tarnished the economic reputation of the Christian Democrats; and in order to retain the chancellorship they agreed to join with the SPD to form the Grand Coalition. After three difficult years the economy was surging again by the 1969 election. Several surveys conducted during the Grand Coalition show that the majority of the electorate saw Karl Schiller, the SPD minister of economics, as primarily responsible for the economic recovery.[31] The SPD's reputation rose as Schiller helped the party to strengthen its image on economic issues. In 1969 a majority of Germans saw the SPD as more competent than the CDU/CSU to deal with both price stability (63 percent) and old age security (62 percent). Even if it was to be temporary, this image of the party in relation to Old Politics issues overcame the deep-seated mistrust of SPD socialist experiments found among potential supporters within the middle class.

The SPD also remained active on New Politics issues. In May 1969 the SPD and CDU/CSU had passed a constitutional amendment that finally authorized the federal government to become involved in setting educational guidelines. The SPD *Fraktion* ("parliamentary party") in the Bundestag began to develop an educational reform package, while CDU/CSU members were noticeably less concerned with this issue. And SPD-led state governments also continued to experiment with and reform educational policies more than their CDU counterparts. By 1969 several SPD-governed Länder boasted a total of over ninety comprehensive schools, while CDU/CSU-led states had instituted only twelve.[32] Perceptions of issue competency for educational policy thus continued to move toward the SPD, with the Social Democrats actually outscoring the CDU/CSU by a 64 to 36 margin. In addition, although Brandt was most concerned with Ostpolitik, his tenure as foreign minister further helped to raise SPD competency in U.S. relations slightly above that perceived in 1965.

By the 1972 election, tensions between the domains of the Old and New Politics had become visible in the parties' issue images.[33] With inflation increasing the electorate saw the cost of the SPD's social programs as a threat to price stability, especially since Schiller had left the SPD to campaign with Erhard for the CDU/CSU against the Social Democrats' economic policies and expensive social programs. Indeed, the electorate reversed its 1969 position and once more viewed the Christian Democrats as more competent to deal with price stability. On old age security, however, there was little change between elections.

Issue competency in the New Politics arena continued to favor the SPD. Brandt's success with Ostpolitik (often against the CDU/CSU's violent objections), the support he gained from the Western Alliance, and his Nobel Peace Prize increased the chancellor's stature as a statesman. From 1969 to 1972, perceptions of SPD competency in dealing with the West increased 17 percent.[34] During the same years the SPD also made striking advances in domestic policies. It was the goal of the SDP-FDP coalition to modernize Germany, and Brandt saw himself in the role of *Kanzler der inneren Reformen* ("chancellor of domestic reforms"). Making education a capstone of the modernization process, the *Bundesregierung* ("federal government") increased educational expenditures considerably, and continued its commitment to reform. As party politics became less consensual, SPD-proposals often encountered strong CDU/CSU objections, such as those over the 1970 *Bildungsbericht* ("education report"), advocating further educational reforms. As a result, the competency images of the parties on educational issues remained relatively unchanged between 1969 and 1972. Overall, as the SPD increased its standing on New Politics issues it gained at the polls, even though it slipped slightly on Old Politics issues.[35]

The data for both the four core issues and the complete set of issues suggest that images of issue competency have contributed to the long-term trend of increasing SPD partisanship. For the German electorate as a whole the trend toward images of greater SPD competency for Old Politics issues is probably too weak to have stimulated much consistent change in partisan attachments. In spite of the slight trend toward the SPD, Old Politics images of the parties give the impression of long-term stability. For example, perceptions of SPD competency increased only 0.4 percent per annum for price stability and 1.6 percent for old age security.[36] Further, it is likely that these trends reflect the voting gains of the SPD, rather than a causal influence. When controls for voting choice were introduced, both CDU/CSU *and SPD* voters increasingly viewed the CDU/CSU as more competent to deal with these two issues.[37] More likely, the electorate's constant movement toward SPD partisanship has been due more to the party's leadership qualities and to the increasing importance given to New Politics values. These values are increasing among the electorate, and the strategies of the SPD leadership have facilitated or even encouraged their potential to produce partisan change. Since the 1961 election there has been a dramatic increase in perceptions of SPD competency for New Politics issues: the per-annum increase for improving the educational system averages 3.4 percent, while for relations with the United States the increase is 2.7 percent. The relative magnitude of these shifts is probably sufficient to stimulate cognitive dissonance and produce attitudinal change. And in contrast to Old Politics issues, this trend is not merely a spurious partisan effect but is displayed by both SPD and CDU/CSU voters.[38]

Conclusion

The data in this chapter provide strong evidence of the impact of changing party images on the fortunes of the SPD and CDU/CSU. The SPD, by developing a credible and progressive image, especially on New Politics issues, has benefited most from these changing images. But these changes cannot be simply extrapolated into the future: electoral trends are not so simplistic. It seems that in German politics the foreseeable future, as today, will be characterized by a mix of Old Politics and New Politics themes. The parties, therefore, must build electoral coalitions spanning both sets of issues. So far the SPD's strategies have more successfully responded to this challenge, maintaining a stable party image on Old Politics issues and improving the party's image on the New Politics. But party images reflect a complex mix of elite actions, events, and unintended consequences; and there is no assurance that the SDP will be able to continue the success of the past.

10

A Causal Analysis of the
Components of the Vote

T HE POSTWAR PERIOD has seen continual change in German partisan behavior. The marked and fairly steady decline in the importance of social cleavages for voting choice raised the question, "What, if anything, is replacing social characteristics as a guide to behavior?" One possible answer is that party identification or a similar political affiliation (like the *tendance* of French politics) is a new cue-giving influence.[1] Another answer could be that partisan images, especially issue images, are serving this purpose.[2]

A change in the basis of voting behavior to either partisanship or issue images can have major implications for the operation of a political system.

In the first place, this transformation can have important consequences for the nature of electoral stability in a political system. A system based on social cleavages is stable only with respect to the citizen's placement in the social structure; his choice of party depends on his view of the party that best represents his social position. Such an elector discriminates little between parties perceived as equally representative of his or her social position. Attachment is primarily to the social group, and hence to a *bloc* of parties that can be seen as representing this group.[3] An enduring commitment need not be made to any specific party. If social characteristics were to be replaced by issue orientations, voting would continue to be an instrumental act, but one based on issues rather than group interests: voters would support the party (or bloc of parties) best reflecting their own issue preferences. Again, however, this basis of partisan behavior does not imply continuous support of a single party.

Under both of these conditions—social cleavage and issue-based voting—there is political stability for voting blocs but not necessarily

249

for specific parties. Indeed, despite the discontinuities of Germany's political history a number of researchers have found surprising stability in the electoral support of socially defined voting blocs.[4] Parties have competed for popular support, but apparently voters have switched primarily among parties within one bloc. "Flash" parties may develop in such a system if they can convince their prospective clientele that they represent the interests of the social group better than the existing parties. Shively, for example, emphasizes the instrumental nature of cleavage-based partisanship in accounting for the lack of party stability in the waning years of the Weimar Republic as well as for the sudden rise of the National Socialist party.[5]

A high degree of party identification in a political system leads to opposite expectations. Attitudinal partisanship is not mediated through social groups. These political affiliations contain affective and psychological components that attach the elector directly to a specific party. Since the indirect linkage through social position or issues is replaced by a direct link between the individual and "his" party, attitudinal attachments produce greater individual voting stability and greater stability in the voting results for specific parties, and they limit the rise of new parties.[6]

In the second place, a shift in the bases of partisan behavior to either partisanship or political issues should affect the relationship between the mass public and political elites. Instrumental voting—voting related to group interests or issue interests—implies a goal-oriented electoral decision. To the extent that election outcomes make such goals explicit, political elites are obliged to respond to the public's policy preferences, or to face the electoral consequences. Obviously the public's issue preferences can be a significant influence on policy-making even when voting is primarily dependent on party identification. In partisanship-based systems, however, the affective element of party identification often blurs the evaluative content of the voting decision.[7] The weaker presence of an evaluative component means that elites are likely to have more political discretion and freedom of action in such a system; that is, voters elect candidates mainly because they are Social Democrats or Christian Democrats, without specific knowledge of the candidates' (or even the parties') stances on contemporary issues.

The Causal Model

A causal model of voting behavior cannot be an entirely correct or even sufficient explanation for the patterns of change in postwar Germany if it is based either on partisanship or on issue images alone. Both concepts must be used if their relative importance and interrelationship are to be uncovered. To do this, the influences of all three causal forces on the vote—social characteristics as well as partisanship and issue images—must be considered simultaneously and assigned a causal ordering.[8] Although the actual processes determining voting decisions are more complex and subtle than can be reflected in a simple model, the results to be expected from the interaction of these three forces can be made relatively clear.

All three forces have been integrated into the hypothesized causal model of German voting behavior illustrated in figure 10.1.[9] Social characteristics are placed at the beginning of the causal sequence. They not only shape both partisanship and issue images, but they also exert a direct influence on voting behavior. Both the party-identification hypothesis and the issue-images hypothesis would predict that the direct link between social characteristics and the vote (path C) has been weakening over time, and similarly, the ability of social characteristics to explain both partisan attitudes (path A) and issue images (path B) may also be declining.

As the importance of social characteristics diminishes, the party-identification hypothesis predicts more voters will base their voting decisions on psychological attachment to their preferred party, and consequently the direct link between partisanship and the vote will become stronger (path D). The partisanship measure used here is likely to contain a larger component of short-term affect than a "true" measure of party identification would, but that problem can be lessened by using this partisanship indicator in multivariate analyses across time. Thus, the impact of partisanship can be evaluated in relative terms: relative to itself over time, and relative to social characteristics and issue images. Assuming that the partisan indicator at each timepoint includes this *short-term* affect, the relative change in the path coefficients for partisanship over time can be attributed to changes in the underlying *long-term* component of this indicator.

Figure 10.1. Hypothesized causal model of German voting behavior.

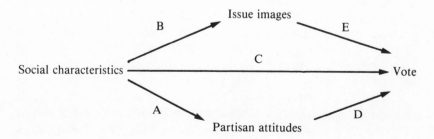

Hence, if the coefficient for path D increases over time, this can be taken as support for the party-identification hypothesis.

The issue-images hypothesis raises a different set of expectations. The independent influence of issue images can be most easily understood in terms of the Old Politics–New Politics dimension of the German political agenda.[10] On the one hand, issue images may reflect the continued attachment to Old Politics values by some voters, even though their social characteristics or partisanship would dictate different voting decisions. On the other hand, increasing New Politics values may give rise to other concerns that also influence behavior independently of partisanship or social characteristics. In either case, the path between issue images and vote (path E) should generally increase in importance if the issue-images hypothesis is an accurate description of political change in the Federal Republic.

This model as represented in figure 10.1 does not specify a causal relationship between partisanship and issue images. Both attitudes should be fairly stable and central elements of an individual's belief structure, but it is not clear which of the two attitudes would have a greater impact on the other. Issue images are influenced by attachments to a party, which would imply that the predominant causal flow is from partisanship to issue images. At the same time, however, issue images may work to redefine standing partisan commitments, implying that the causal flow runs at least partially in the opposite direction. In any event, the direction of this causal flow cannot be determined by means of the model in figure 10.1, whose purpose it is to assess the independent impact of partisanship and issue images on vote choice.[11] Thus, while the correlation between these two concepts will be presented, the linkage between them will not be incorporated into our causal analyses.

To measure the influence of the three causal forces on vote choice, the value of each path coefficient in the hypothetical model has been calculated for every election between 1961 and 1972 (figure 10.2).[12] Even though caution must be exercised in evaluating the validity of long-term processes in terms of this limited timespan, such a procedure should yield a fuller understanding of the changing bases of German voting behavior. Path coefficients, both unstandardized (presented above the line for each election) and standardized (presented below the line and enclosed in parentheses for each election) are shown in the figure because the causal paths are compared across variables and also across time.

In the 1961 election, the impact of social characteristics on voting is largely mediated by partisanship and issue images. Social characteristics have substantial influence in determining both partisan attitudes (b

Figure 10.2. Causal models of German voting behavior, 1961–1972. Unstandardized path coefficients (b in text) appear above the arrows; the standardized (B) coefficients appear below the arrows enclosed in parentheses. Listwise exclusion of missing data was used.

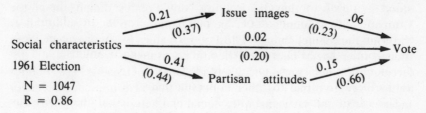

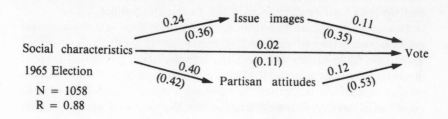

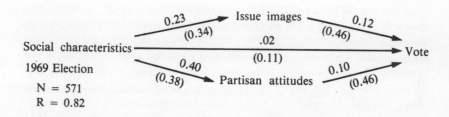

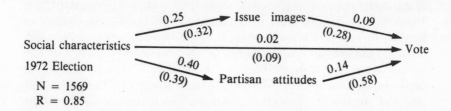

= 0.41, B = 0.44) and issue images (b = 0.21, B = 0.37), but they show only a moderate direct effect on vote choice (b = 0.02, B = 0.20). As for the two attitudinal variables, partisanship clearly outweighs the issue dimension in causal importance. This probably reflects, in part, the psychological proximity of the vote to the short-term affective component of the partisan indicator. In addition, it reaffirms the finding that party lines were still clearly drawn in 1961, when both the SPD and CDU/CSU campaigned intensely. Furthermore, the policy changes made by the SPD at Godesberg still had not had time to affect the party's popular image.

This causal pattern begins to change in 1965. Social characteristics still show only a weak direct impact on voting behavior, but the relative influence of partisan attitudes and issue images is changing. Affective partisan ties are weakening in the face of the changing content of German politics in the mid-sixties. In step with this new agenda, the path between issue images and vote has nearly doubled since 1961, while the partisanship-to-vote path has declined noticeably. Additional analyses have shown that the increasing strength of issue images reflects a growth in the causal influence of both Old Politics and New Politics items: the persistence of Old Politics values in the face of a changing environment, and the development of New Politics values independent of traditional social and partisan alignments.[13]

The most significant aspect of the pattern for the 1969 election is the extent to which issue images have continued to gain in relative importance, becoming about equal to partisanship in determining the vote. The actions of party elites probably facilitated this increase in the relevance of issue images. The "era of good feelings" surrounding the Grand Coalition minimized the psychological distance between the two major parties, thereby easing partisan conversions and lessening the direct impact of partisanship on vote choice. Moreover, the changing climate of opinion led the SPD to emphasize New Politics alternatives in its party program, typified by the 1969 slogan; "We Create the Modern Germany." The SPD's support for New Politics issues such as abortion on demand, educational reform, Ostpolitik, and quality-of-life concerns undoubtedly strengthened the impact of issue images on the vote—especially the New Politics component of these images.[14] Indeed, the separation of Old Politics from New Politics issues makes it clear that the overall increase in the causal influence of issues between 1965 and 1969 can be attributed entirely to the New Politics concerns.[15]

The span of these three elections (1961–1969) does not provide a basis for very confident conclusions, but the pattern does appear to support the hypothesis that advanced industrialism is changing the values and consequently the partisan behavior of the German public.

Because both social characteristics and partisanship decline in importance from 1961 to 1969, electoral changes probably cannot be traced primarily to either of these factors. Rather, these changes seem to be linked to the impact of issue images, which have become increasingly important to voting decisions during the period. Furthermore, New Politics issues, which tap the concerns of an advanced industrial society, have gained most in salience and causal influence.

It could be that issue images have only a short-term influence on voting behavior, but by 1969 the force of these images has become strong enough to suggest that they may be causing a more fundamental change in the nature of German political behavior. The data for 1972 should suggest the form this change may be taking.

In 1972 the direct causal link from social characteristics to vote reflects a weak relationship. More important is the reversal in the trends of the party-to-vote and issues-to-vote paths. For the first time, the causal link between issues and vote decreases, while the path from partisan attitudes to vote increases. Issues are a weaker predictor and partisanship is a stronger predictor than in 1965.

This rise in the importance of partisanship could be attributed to the reassertion of partisan differences after the 1969 election when the Grand Coalition ended and the CDU/CSU went into opposition. But in addition the 1972 election was unique. Voters displayed an intensely affective reaction to the person of Chancellor Brandt, which may appear in the affective measure of partisanship. Furthermore, the CDU/CSU's attempt to oust the SPD/FDP coalition through a "constructive vote of no confidence" led the forces of both major parties to close ranks during the campaign. The 1972 results might, therefore, be explained by specific short-term factors.

The trouble with this idiosyncratic explanation of the 1972 election, however, is that the dramatic shift in the voting patterns of social groups that had occurred in 1969 was also present in 1972, as if issue images were still highly important. For example, the overall level of class voting in 1972 was still far below the pre-1969 level, the new middle class was still giving more support to the SPD, and class voting was still declining among the young. In short, there is a seeming paradox. The weight of partisanship increased in 1972, but the overall evidence indicates that partisanship was not producing the same social alignments and voting patterns as it had in the past. Rather, issue images were influential in 1972, although the causal model would suggest their decline. How can this paradox be resolved?

As Germany has moved toward the postindustrial era, the impact of sociostructural influences on voting behavior has declined. In this situation, the key question to be asked is not "What is replacing social cues?'' but "Why are social cues declining?'' The answer suggested by the data is that the rise of the New Politics–Old Politics dimension, which runs counter to previous cleavage ties, is at least partially responsible. And as new issues and values develop, the tension between issue images and social characteristics mounts, weakening the impact of social cleavages on voting behavior.

Issue images may well provide a vehicle for changing the more fundamental partisan attachments.[16] Ronald Inglehart suggests that the Old Politics–New Politics dimension may eventually become integrated into partisan attitudes and the party systems of Western Europe.[17] Indeed, the reversed trends in the 1972 issue and partisanship paths shown in figure 10.2 might suggest that the tension existing in 1969 between issue images and partisanship led to partisan conversion after that election. In addition to the evidence available from the causal model, two pieces of "side information" add weight to this conversion hypothesis. First, issue images became more independent of partisanship between 1965 and 1969 before rising again in 1972.[18] Second, panel data indicate far less stability of partisanship and voting intentions in 1969 than in 1972; in 1969 partisanship was in a state of flux.[19] Taken together, these facts suggest that at least some of the issue component was "absorbed" into more general partisan attitudes between the 1969 and 1972 elections.

It is not clear whether the German party system's response to New Politics concerns or its efforts to provide a partisan outlet for these accumulating forces of change is typical or atypical.[20] The rate of electoral change may have been accelerated because of specifically German conditions. This, of course, has been the primary reason for focusing on Germany as a test case. Nevertheless, after a period of increasing concern with New Politics issues, some segments of the electorate may have developed or adjusted their partisanship to fit this value dimension. Hence partisan attitudes gained a new importance in 1972.

It is difficult, if not impossible, to make a direct test of the conversion hypothesis without long-term panel data. This would require the estimation of the reciprocal causal paths between issues and partisanship, but this reciprocal relationship cannot be estimated with the available data. The conversion hypothesis is therefore an enticing idea that cannot be either empirically confirmed or denied.

It is possible, however, to develop an indirect test of the hypothesis by using the available data. If younger Germans, who are more interested in New Politics issues than the older people, are developing their partisan loyalties on the basis of these concerns, that may partially explain the persistence of partisan patterns associated with the New

Politics even after the weakening of issue images in 1972. For the young, partisanship may strongly overlap with New Politics orientations, serving to some extent as a surrogate measure of value priorities.[21]

When the issue indicator is divided into its two component parts—Old Politics and New Politics—generational differences in the bases of partisanship can be examined. In table 10.1 the partial correlations between partisanship and the two issue domains have been broken down for two cohorts: the young (Federal Republic) and the old (Third Reich, Weimar, and Wilhelmine). As the table shows, the German electorate is primarily oriented toward Old Politics (or materialist) concerns. In all four election years the Old Politics issues are correlated more highly with partisanship for both generations. There are, however, generally consistent differences in the weight given to the two domains by young and old cohorts. In 1961 the partial correlation for Old Politics issues with partisanship is 0.59 for the older cohort and 0.52 (slightly weaker) for the young. For the New Politics index in the same year the opposite pattern emerges: a slightly stronger correlation for the young (0.36) than for the old (0.26). In 1965 the differences between the generations narrow. The partisan loyalties of the young are more closely related to Old Politics issues than are those of the old cohort. With the 1969 election, however, the young place increasing emphasis on New Politics issues. And in 1972 the pattern becomes clearer: the gap between the Old Politics correlations for the young (0.50) and for the old (0.59) is substantial; and New Politics issues are more closely related to partisanship for the young than for the old (0.31 versus 0.22).

These data suggest that when evaluating the two major parties younger Germans place somewhat more emphasis on New Politics

Table 10.1. Partial correlations of issue competency and partisanship, 1961–1972.[a]

Issue by generation	July 1961	Sept. 1965	Nov. 1969	Sept. 1972
Old Politics issues				
Young	0.52	0.55	0.48	0.50
Old	.59	.51	.48	.59
New Politics issues				
Young	.36	.33	.34	.31
Old	.26	.33	.31	.22

a. Cell entries are the partial correlations between each index of issue competency and partisanship, controlling for the other issue competency index.

issues than do older cohorts. Therefore the partisan attachments of the young are more likely to include both New Politics and Old Politics interests. In this way the partisanship of the young—and presumably of other change-oriented groups such as the new middle class—is helping to perpetuate the impact of the New Politics.[22]

Conclusion

The trends examined in this chapter represent the converging effects of many familiar causal factors: elite actions, economic prosperity, generational change, and general environmental change. Although it is possible that a reversal of these causal forces may alter electoral trends, and although restraint must be exercised in basing long-term hypotheses on relatively short-term data, these empirical findings suggest a pattern of political change that may explain recent German electoral history.

Clearly, sociostructural influences on voting behavior are declining as the postindustrial era approaches. What will replace these cues as a guide for voting behavior? Shively and others suggest that party identification may serve as an immediate replacement, but this view focuses on the consequences of declining social influences without giving equal attention to the causes of the decline.[23] The evidence of this chapter and of other research suggests that an emerging Old Politics–New Politics issue dimension is a major factor in weakening the influence of social characteristics. Hence it must be that these issue images (and values) are replacing the old sociostructural cues.

Party identification, on the other hand, might be a long-term consequence of declining cleavage-based voting. After a period of strong issue-based voting at least some segments of the electorate should develop direct psychological ties to a party resulting from their issue preferences; then attitudinal partisanship would increase. In this light, the Old Politics–New Politics issue dimension can be viewed as an intermediate step between a system based on social cleavages and one based on attitudinal partisanship—at least for the cleavage-oriented systems of Western Europe. Thus, the development of party attachments in these systems may partially be a function of Old Politics–New Politics value change and the responsiveness of elites and the party system to this emerging dimension of politics.

Part Four

Epilogue

11

The 1976 Election

THE LONGITUDINAL NATURE of the research undertaken for this book has presented a unique picture of postwar West Germany. It has provided a clearer, sounder view of the fundamental sources and characteristics of social and political behavior than could have been gained by analyzing a single election campaign or the actions of specific political leaders.

This longitudinal methodology has led the analysis into many areas, but it has consistently underscored a common theme: change. Such a theme could have been predicted because the changes in postwar German society and politics have been so dramatic. And the consistency of several basic social and political trends has made these changes all the more visible. From 1945 until the final timepoint of the analysis, 1972, a generally steady rate of economic growth accompanied the *Wirtschaftswunder*. In the foreign policy arena a steady increase in understanding between Germany and its neighbors occurred: first there was reconciliation with the West; then, with the gradual thaw in the Cold War, came increased contact with the East, leading to the fruition of *Ostpolitik* in 1972. In addition, the acceptance of the political norms and institutions of the Federal Republic steadily expanded to reach a high plateau of popular support; and political involvement constantly grew throughout the 1953–1972 timespan of the data. Even in partisan politics there has been a dramatic change, with a 3 percent gain for the SPD in each federal election, a phenomenon referred to as the "comrade trend."

It is not surprising, then, that this book has stressed the theme of basic political change, or that it has turned to long-term theories to explain these trends. The broad theoretical approach has made it possible to reduce a voluminous mass of data to manageable proportions. Moreover, the structure and coherence generated by such a perspective give, we believe, a realistic interpretation of the basic forces shaping German political behavior.

Most of the analyses and interpretations for this book were completed and committed to paper well before the 1976 federal election. Then in 1977 the Mannheim 1976 Election Study became available for analysis. At the least, the new election offered an opportunity to extend the timeseries of the preceding chapters by four years. But the new data arising from the 1976 election could also be used to fulfill an even more valuable purpose.

Because the earlier analyses had been based on data collected between 1953 and 1972, they were largely examples of ex post facto research: fitting data to theory (and adapting theory to data). From this process causal relationships were hypothesized that linked various political phenomena. However, after using the 1953–1972 data to develop these hypotheses, we could not draw on the same data to test the models. But the 1976 election offered a "natural experiment" in which prior theorizing could prove itself. This election is a particularly stringent test case because of the marked changes that occurred between 1972 and 1976 in many of the environmental factors that have been stressed throughout this book. For example, the affluence of the Wirtschaftswunder was drastically threatened by the Arab oil embargo and the worldwide recession that followed. The early enthusiasm accompanying Ostpolitik gave way to more reserved and cautious East-West exchanges. The growing terrorist activities of the Baader-Meinhof group resurrected fears about the internal stability of German democracy. Thus, the interelection period saw the apparent reversal of several of the trends previously identified as important for understanding German political behavior.

On the surface, the reversal of these trends might imply that the findings in this book are no longer valid. The emphasis, however, has been on the causal *relationships* between political phenomena, rather than on attempts to extrapolate trends into the future. These relationships should continue to exist, whether the independent variables are increasing or decreasing. Thus, if increasing affluence leads to one set of consequences, the impact of economic reversals (though different) should be just as predictable, assuming that the hypothesized causal relationship is accurate.

Even a brief look at the 1976 election reveals the impact of the changing trends on party and elite behavior.[1] The CDU/CSU responded to the altered environment by trying to recreate the public mood of the 1950s that had favored it at the polls. The SPD's campaign strategy was also affected by environmental change. The SPD lost support at the polls for the first time since 1953; the "comrade trend" had deserted the party.

Many analysts see the 1976 election as marking a return to the traditional political issues and cleavages of earlier years. It is true that environmental changes are likely to have some impact on mass and elite behavior, but other factors are also involved; and the evidence amassed in this book indicates a complex interaction between environmental factors and politics. Some effects are strong and direct, others are weak and indirect; some attitudes are immediately affected by the environment, others are affected only after a substantial timelag or not at all. The 1976 election therefore needs to be examined in detail. Which attitudes and behaviors actually changed, and which were relatively immune to environmental factors? The seeming reversal of trends between the 1972 and 1976 elections provides a valuable opportunity to put the findings of this book to a rigorous empirical test. This chapter, then, is both an epilogue focusing on the 1976 election and a reassessment of the conclusions derived from the 1953–1972 period of German electoral behavior.

Further Changes in the Political Environment

Clearly the 1976 election took place in an environment very different from that of the 1972 contest. The breadth and cumulative impact of the changes in social, economic, and political factors that occurred between elections increased the likelihood that political behavior would be affected. To set the stage for this examination of the 1976 election, the descriptions of the political environment already given for earlier years will be extended to cover the significant trends after 1972.

Economic Trends   Although economic matters are still of interest to the German public, intense economic concerns have been gradually fading as the affluence of the postwar economy has continued. Inflationary pressures brought on by the domestic reforms of the SPD attracted some attention in 1972, but by and large, economic concerns were overshadowed by the governing coalition's dramatic steps in Ostpolitik and its domestic reforms, as well as Willy Brandt's personal popularity and status. Furthermore, the question of the inflationary pressure of domestic programs soon became academic. In 1973 the Arab oil embargo precipitated a general economic crisis in virtually all industrialized nations, which outweighed, or at least compounded, the domestic difficulties of high inflation and slowing economic growth.

The subsequent deterioration of the German economy can be indicated by tracing some of the measures used to portray the Economic

Table 11.1. Economic trends, 1972–1976.

Measure	1972	1973	1974	1975	1976
GNP growth rate	3.6%	4.9%	3.5%	−2.5%	5.6%
Unemployed as percent of labor force	1.1	1.3	2.7	4.7	4.6
Annual rate of inflation (percent)	5.5	6.9	7.0	5.5	4.2

Source: OECD, *Main Economic Indicators* (Paris, monthly).

Miracle in chapter 4 (table 11.1). For example, GNP growth rates were above 3 percent in 1972 (as they had been in 1971), and they increased to almost 5 percent in 1973, following an election year stimulus. In the following year, however, the economy grew more slowly, and in 1975 the GNP actually shrank (−2.5 percent). In 1976 the election year stimulus was sufficient to return the economy to a strong growth rate (5.6 percent), but the 1974–1975 downturn caused renewed concern.

Like other Western industrial economies Germany was experiencing a new situation of "stagflation"—simultaneous stagnation and inflation—following the OPEC oil price increase. Inflation had already topped 5 percent in 1971, and it continued to climb, reaching 7 percent in 1974. A sharp rise in unemployment was an even clearer result of the oil price increase. The jobless rate reached almost 5 percent in 1975, and, perhaps more important psychologically, the number of unemployed broke the million barrier in the spring of that year. Although economic growth revived in time for the fall 1976 federal election and inflation abated somewhat, the Wirtschaftswunder had not returned. Instead of following the expectations expressed in the Phillips curve, in which inflation varies inversely with unemployment,[2] both indicators rose significantly above the levels to which the German public was accustomed.

Domestic Politics   The preoccupation with economic issues tended to overshadow most other domestic concerns during the 1972–1976 period. Nevertheless, the Social Democrats and Free Democrats continued to follow a course of domestic reforms. They aided women's rights by passing liberalized divorce and abortion laws. They continued working to extend the social security net. They attempted to expand access to education by eliminating university admission quotas. But public interest and support for these and other domestic reforms apparently waned after 1972.

This change may have reflected the uncertainty of the economic situation and the sense of insecurity caused by a marked increase in terrorist activities between 1972 and 1976.[3] Led by young educated members of the upper middle class, small extremist organizations such as the Baader-Meinhof group (*Rote Armee Fraktion*) attempted to generate popular support for establishing a Marxist state in West Germany. The methods employed in their urban guerrilla campaign had a noticeable impact on German politics and public life. Bombing, bank robberies, arson attacks, and kidnappings and murders of public figures created a feeling of political insecurity and instability. For example, in February 1975, Peter Lorenz, the CDU candidate for mayor of Berlin, was kidnapped; later in the same year a band of terrorists occupied the German embassy in Stockholm.

The government reacted by restricting certain civil liberties and increasing expenditures for security forces. This response was at least partially successful in curbing the activities of terrorist groups. It was, however, a response predicted (and hoped for) by the leftist groups, supporting their desire to destroy the optimistic climate of progressive reform that had characterized the early 1970s.[4] Once again the stability and security of Germany seemed in question. Rather than giving open support to further domestic reforms, therefore, German public opinion shifted in favor of stability and maintaining the status quo.[5]

Ostpolitik and Foreign Affairs   The Federal Republic's Ostpolitik represented an effort to break with past foreign policy and normalize relations with Eastern Europe. The achievement of these goals has continued since 1972 to motivate German foreign policy makers concerned with eastern affairs, but the pace of Ostpolitik has slowed considerably. A treaty with Czechoslovakia was ratified by parliament in 1974, and in 1976 supplementary treaties were signed with East Germany and Poland. But the constant and intense negotiations and the periodic dramatic breakthroughs that characterized the period between 1969 and 1971 have been generally absent since ratification of the 1972 treaties.[6]

The slowed pace of Ostpolitik has been accompanied by renewed (or continuing) opposition to these policies. Ostpolitik was accused of sacrificing German interests without gaining anything in return. Some Germans felt that several treaties contained thinly veiled reparation payments, and that the Federal Republic had renounced all claims to lands in the East. And yet, despite these concessions the expected normalization of East-West relations was not fully achieved. The East Germans pursued a policy of *Abgrenzung* ("demaraction"), which reduced the possibility of a complete rapprochement between the two

Germanies. Because other East European nations also adopted this policy, it retarded the development of a new peace in Europe (*Europäische Friedensordnung*). Furthermore, the Berlin problem still remained.

East-West interaction data document this deterioration of German relations with the East from 1972 until the 1976 election.[7] From the strongly cooperative tone evident in the early 1970s, international relations with Eastern Europe have regressed to a fluctuating pattern of conflictual and cooperative exchanges. Moreover, public opinion polls show that West Germans have become increasingly concerned about the threat of communism and less optimistic about the possibility of improved relations with the Soviet Union. Substantial proportions continue to want better relations with East Germany, but an increasing number insist that "tougher policies" must be used to accomplish this goal.[8]

The 1970s have also witnessed a change in Germany's influence in world politics. Since the German economy is highly dependent on international trade, it is not surprising that recent governments have been greatly concerned with the condition of the international marketplace. Efforts have been initiated to shape this environment in ways that are beneficial to German interests. The activities and "presence" of the Federal Republic on the international scene have increased significantly, and German activity has been characterized by a new assertiveness. As memories of the Nazi period have begun to fade and the economic potential of the Federal Republic has continued to increase, West Germany has become an increasingly outspoken advocate of certain policy options in international councils. In the European Community, for example, Germany has shown a greater reluctance to lend its resources to the continuing development of European unity without concessions from other members.[9] Even its relations with the United States have changed. The Federal Republic vigorously protested the shipment of American arms to Israel from German soil during the 1973 Middle East conflict; and it has criticized and disputed American policy initiatives, even on matters as sensitive as the "offset" payments that maintain U.S. troops in the Federal Republic.[10]

Since the mid-1970s, therefore, West Germany has become not only an economic giant but an increasingly important political actor as well. Relations with the East are not entirely harmonious, but some degree of détente has been achieved. Relations with the West remain strong, though West Germany is increasingly willing to introduce and pursue its own goals and interests in the formulation of international policy.

Political Elites   Party and government elites have stimulated, or at least reinforced, changes in mass attitudes and political behavior throughout the entire postwar period. Elite consensus on the institutions of the Federal Republic has strengthened the development of civic attitudes among the general public and helped encourage participation in the new political system. Similarly, the decline in class cleavages and the rise of New Politics concerns have been facilitated by party programs and, especially since 1969, by government policies.

Between 1972 and 1976, however, elite actions turned in a new direction. Economic issues returned to the elites' political agenda. The CDU/CSU opposition seized the initiative and pointed to unemployment, inflation, and retarded economic growth as evidence that the government (SPD-FDP) was unable to manage the economy. The opposition called upon Germans to evaluate the parties on the basis of their economic performance and to return the CDU to power—the party of the Economic Miracle. In contrast, the government sought to de-emphasize the economic difficulties. The shift in leadership in 1974 from Brandt to the "economic crisis manager," Helmut Schmidt, underscored the competency of the government and partially avoided the potential damage of the economic problems. Chancellor Schmidt and his party attempted to parry the CDU/CSU's criticisms by pointing to increased international dependency as the source of Germany's economic problems.

The CDU/CSU also challenged the general themes of progress and change that had characterized recent German politics. It no longer catered, even cautiously, to the themes of progress and reform. Instead, it sought to capitalize upon the resurgent fears of economic and social uncertainty, promising a return to the *heile Welt* ("intact world") of old German values. In a confidential speech to CSU party members in Sonthofen, Franz Josef Strauss welcomed the degree of societal insecurity and instability brought about by increased unemployment and terrorist activities as conditions favorable to a CDU/CSU resurgence. The speech was noteworthy only because it was the most open acknowledgment of a strategy designed to recreate the public mood of the 1950s and thereby to repeat the CDU/CSU successes of that era. The CDU/CSU slogans of the 1976 campaign, "Freedom instead of Socialism" and "Out of Love for Germany—CDU," sought to recapture the old antagonisms and to appeal to traditional patriotic sentiments.

These economic and political developments made it difficult for the SPD to continue its stress on social reform and progress. By attempting to deflect the economic issue and control terrorist activities, the SPD sought to redirect the political agenda. As a result, strategists felt that they could still adopt a forward-looking campaign slogan that appeared to continue the progressive and reform orientation of the 1969 and 1972 elections: "Keep Working for a Model Germany" (*Weiter arbeiten am*

Modell Deutschland).[11] But clearly the SPD's past enthusiastic support for the New Politics was replaced by guarded moderation in the 1976 campaign.

Perceptions of the Political Agenda   All of these influences—economic trends, domestic politics, Ostpolitik and foreign affairs, and political elites—defined a new setting for the 1976 election. Moreover, just as these influences had stimulated patterns of change in earlier years, they now *seemed* to be working to moderate or reverse these trends. It is fair to ask, therefore, whether the impact of these environmental changes was sufficient to seriously affect the trends and relationships described in this book.

One piece of evidence concerns the public's perception of the political agenda, that is, the most important problem facing the country at the time. Following the 1973 oil embargo and price increase, the public reacted immediately and sharply to the developing economic crisis, as table 11.2 indicates. In 1972 only 38 percent of the population mentioned economic matters like employment or inflation as being among the three most pressing problems, while in 1974 the figure is 69 percent, and in the 1976 election year, 73 percent. Thus, the overall picture of Germany between 1972 and 1976 is clearly one of a society in which

Table 11.2. Public perception of the political agenda, 1972–1976.[a]

Theme	1972	1973[b]	1974	1975	1976
Economic problems[c]	38%	62%	69%	85%	73%
Energy	—[d]	—[d]	16	—[d]	—[d]
Social policies and domestic issues	24	18	13	14	21
Peace or détente	28	20	4	5	3
Berlin	1	1	—[d]	—[d]	—[d]
Reunification	1	1	—[d]	—[d]	1

Source: Elisabeth Noelle-Neumann, ed., *Jahrbücher der Öffentlichen Meinung* (Allensbach: Institut für Demoskopie, 1951–1976).

a. "Don't know" and other responses are excluded from the table but included in the calculation of percentages. No other issues were mentioned by more than 10 percent in any of the above surveys. Percentages total to more than 100 percent because multiple responses were possible.

b. The 1973 data are based on an average of two surveys conducted in this year. In addition, the question asked about the most important *questions* facing the Federal Republic, rather than the most important question.

c. In the 1975 and 1976 surveys, economic problems include energy problems.

d. Less than 1 percent response.

economic troubles have resurfaced and once again acquired prominence.[12]

Not surprisingly, energy problems had a dramatic impact upon the
public. Before 1973 only isolated mentions were made in this area, but
in early 1974, 16 percent rate the energy crisis as the most important
problem. The impact of the energy shortage appears very transient,
however, because the issue is hardly mentioned again in 1975 or 1976.[13]
This underscores the interpretation that the oil embargo was perceived
as only a precipitating factor of the subsequent recession, not as a
problem in itself. Indeed, public concern with the economic situation
preceded the energy crisis, for the percentage expressing economic
worries almost doubles between 1972 and the spring of 1973.

The dramatic rise and high level of economic concerns appear to
document a reversal in the agenda of German politics. Yet, when the
trend for domestic and reform issues (social policies) is also considered, the picture becomes more ambiguous. In the short run, there is
a sharp reduction in reform interest as first inflation and then the
energy emergency take precedence on the public agenda. By 1976,
however, the salience of domestic reforms returns to almost the 1972
level.

The public's preoccupation with economics and social reforms in
1976 is almost sufficient to remove foreign policy (peace or détente)
from the political agenda. After appearing as a very salient issue in the
1972 contest, foreign policy drops between 1974 and 1976 to the lowest
level of importance in the quarter-century for which data are available.
Continuing debates on Ostpolitik and the Federal Republic's new
world role apparently do not hold the public's interest.[14]

The short-run political agenda—that is, "the most important question in Germany *today*" (italics added)—will always be quite sensitive
to events and conditions (chapter 6). However, this is only one aspect
of the political changes described in this book. Many other postwar
developments reflect more fundamental, long-term processes. Once
underway, these trends may be more difficult to reverse, and even the
events of the 1970s may not have been dramatic enough to achieve this.
For example, while economic concerns are likely to respond to the
immediate economic environment, other political changes are tied to
the restructuring of the labor force and to absolute levels of affluence,
which are less affected by economic changes. Similarly, deeply rooted
and therefore more stable orientations, such as the basic value priorities explored in chapter 6, might be relatively impervious to short-term
changes in the environment. Therefore the impact of the changing
environment of the 1970s on other aspects of German politics and
political behavior deserves examination.

Political Orientations

The political culture of the Federal Republic has changed considerably since 1945 and even since 1959, when it was examined empirically by Gabriel Almond and Sidney Verba.[15] Germans can no longer be characterized as quiescent subjects who are neither involved in politics nor politically efficacious. The analyses in this book show that the postwar regime has inspired widespread support among the general public and that this support has become at least partially diffuse. These findings, which were based mostly on longitudinal analyses, document a real transformation in the orientations of Germans toward politics and the political system, rather than a merely momentary or temporary effect.

However, the period between 1972 and 1976 did see considerable change in the political environment of the Federal Republic. The economic crisis brought on by the oil embargo and the terrorist activities of extremist groups raised the possibility that the public might revert to those nonsupportive and nondemocratic attitudes that had lain more or less dormant during the stable period of the preceding two decades. But though these disturbing events were important, they did not severely challenge the viability of the political system. And, assuming that political support has become more diffuse, they should have had only a limited impact on the basic political orientations of the German public. An analysis of these attitudes, therefore, should provide a clear test of prior findings.

Satisfaction with the political system was more or less universal in 1972 (table 11.3). Only about 5 percent of the population voiced any serious objection to the existing regime. By 1976 the generalized support for the system has changed only marginally, and over 90 percent still remain "very" or "somewhat" satisfied. The proportion of the total population that is "not satisfied" with democracy in Germany increases to 9 percent, but this seems a very minor shift in public opinion in view of the magnitude of the events that occurred in this time period. Positive evaluations of government performance also decline somewhat between 1972 and 1976, while negative evaluations increase from 19 to 25 percent. While only a weak relationship between system performance and system evaluation was uncovered by the analysis presented in chapter 1, these data show the dynamic aspects of that relationship. Again, though, the decline in confidence seems small when compared with the magnitude of the changes that were taking place in the political environment.

Because feelings of political efficacy are even more independent of government performance than is political satisfaction (see chapter 1), changes in the 1972–1976 environment should have affected efficacy

Table 11.3. Political satisfaction, 1972 and 1976.

Satisfaction with	Sept.–Oct. 1972[a]	June 1976
Political system (regime)		
Very satisfied	22%	22%
Somewhat satisfied	73	69
Not satisfied	5	9
Total	100	100
(N)	(1506)	(2057)
Government in Bonn (authorities)		
Satisfied	72	66
Undecided	9	9
Not satisfied	19	25
Total	100	100
(N)	(2003)	(2046)

a. The data on regime satisfaction are based on the October timepoint, while those for government satisfaction come from the September survey.

even less than they did system evaluations. Three of the four political efficacy questions asked in the 1972 survey were also included in the 1976 poll. These data show that efficacy levels indeed remained fairly constant over the four years (table 11.4). None of the three items displays a statistically significant change from 1972 to 1976. Thus, although the political environment can obviously influence feelings of political efficacy,[16] recent changes in Germany either have not been of sufficient intensity or of the right nature to alter these feelings.

The changing environment may have prompted minor declines in system evaluations; nevertheless, these declines did not lead to anti-system activities like those that occurred during the 1966–1967 recession. At that time, the economic downturn stimulated the growth of the neo-Nazi National Democratic party (NPD), but neither the radical

Table 11.4. Feelings of political efficacy, 1972 and 1976.[a]

Type of feeling	Oct. 1972	June 1976
Officials don't care what people like me think	47%	45%
People like me have no say in government	40	39
Politics is too complex for people like me to understand	39	39

a. Entries are the percentages of respondents giving efficacious replies, that is, disagreeing with the efficacy items.

right nor the left was able to make significant electoral gains during the 1976 campaign. Basic support for the present regime thus appears only slightly dependent on performance: system norms have become largely diffuse, rather than specific.

This interpretation receives substantiation from an extensive cross-national study of European youth conducted in 1977.[17] Only 12 percent of German youth reported that they had "a lot to find fault with" in the current regime form. This contrasts with the 28 percent of French youngsters and the 36 percent of British youth who expressed similar criticisms. Although the form of the survey question is not strictly comparable to those used in the 1972 and 1976 election studies, it suggests that considerable support for the present German system is found among the population in general and the youth in particular, especially when viewed in comparative perspective.

Even more telling evidence comes from a separate survey of German youth conducted in 1976, which repeats a question about national pride asked by Almond and Verba in 1959.[18] Heavy stress has been placed on Almond and Verba's finding that Germans took greater pride in the economic system than in the political system.[19] In 1976 German youth still had high regard for the country's economic achievements, but by then the political system had become the most important source of national pride (table 11.5). An impressive 43 percent of younger Germans expressed pride in the democratic institutions and political freedoms of the Federal Republic, compared with only 6 percent of the equivalent age group in the Almond and Verba survey. Thus after three decades of experience with the Federal Republic, German youth apparently saw the political system of the Federal Republic as an achievement to be proud of.

These generational findings are significant for two reasons. First, current youth represent the future of the country, and as the "successor generation" their views will influence the course of German politics. Second, young people are generally more likely than older citizens to be affected by significant changes in the environment. Hence, these findings suggest that diffuse attachments to the political system, which at least temporarily resist the effects of deterioration in the environment, have been successfully socialized in postwar Germany.

In sum, whether the focus is on general satisfaction with the existing political system or inculcation of requisite regime norms, the German political system seemed fairly secure in 1976. Significant changes in the environment had not underminded the pervasive support found in 1972 and earlier. At this point, therefore, one can be somewhat more confident in rejecting the notion that Germans are "fair weather" democrats ready to revert to authoritarian forms if faced with severe economic or political crisis.[20]

Table 11.5. Sources of national pride, 1959 and 1976.[a]

Source of pride	1959	1976
Government, political institutions,		
democratic freedoms	6%	43%
Economic system	41	40
Characteristics of people	34	15
Social legislation	5	8
Foreign policy	4	5
Cultural achievements	16	3
Other specific		13
Other general	34[b]	16
None	3	7
Don't know	10	7
Not applicable	—[c]	2
Total	153[d]	168[d]
(N)	(196)	(1598)

Sources: For 1959, Almond and Verba, *Civic Culture;* for 1976, U.S. International Communications Agency, "German Youth Study, 1976" (Washington, D.C.).

a. Citizens aged 30 or below.

b. "Other specific" and "Other general" were combined in the Almond and Verba study.

c. Not used in the Almond and Verba study.

d. Percentages are greater than 100 because of multiple response.

Political Involvement

Another basic element of German political behavior is the average voter's involvement and interest in politics. In sharp contrast to earlier characterizations of Germans as passive and quiescent, by 1972 over half of the electorate were expressing an interest in politics and discussing politics daily during the campaign. Moreover, turnout in the 1972 election reached the record level of 91 percent (table 11.6).

From the perspective of the 1976 election some analysts have suggested that political involvement was exceptionally high in 1972.[21] The 1972 election was a heated contest stimulated by the debate over Ostpolitik and the CDU/CSU's attempted *konstruktives Misstrauensvotum* ("constructive vote of no confidence"). Furthermore, the dynamic personality of Willy Brandt heightened interest in the campaign. By contrast, it has been argued, the 1976 campaign lacked intensity and therefore could not have stimulated so much public interest.

Clearly, political involvement cannot be expected to continue climbing as steadily as it did between 1953 and 1972. The environmental factors that prompted this increase have stabilized, and consequently

Table 11.6. Participation in politics, 1972 and 1976.

Type of participation	Dec. 1972	Nov. 1976
Voted in the federal election[a]	91%	91%
Discussed politics during campaign[b]	84	90
Interested in politics	56	55
Showed support for party	30	36
Attended meeting	13	20

a. Turnout figures are from the official voting results.

b. The 1976 entry for political discussion is drawn from a relatively comparable question in the June 1976 ZUMABUS (an omnibus study conducted by the Zentrum für Umfragen, Methoden und Analysen (ZUMA), Mannheim).

political involvement should begin to level off. Rising educational levels and further generational turnover should result in a slow long-term increase in participation. But at the same time, participation rates can be expected to fluctuate between elections in response to the short-term effects of campaigns.

Yet, Max Kaase describes a dramatic decline in political discussion for 1976 that is far larger than was anticipated.[22] If valid, this finding, which could suggest that political involvement in Germany is not yet deeply ingrained in the political culture, would conflict with the conclusions drawn in chapter 2. It appears, however, that Kaase's findings are an artifact of question wording.[23]

In fact, the overall pattern of the data for 1976 describes a constant or slightly increasing level of political participation as compared with 1972. Exactly comparable measures of political interest show no significant change between the two elections (table 11.6). The political discussion question was reworded in the 1976 survey, but the one comparable response category—"never discuss politics"—drops from 16 percent in 1972 to only 10 percent in 1976. Moreover, the 1976 figure comes from an early point in the election when campaign activity and interest were just starting to increase.[24] Thus, a completely comparable indicator should register even higher levels of political discussion in 1976. Several other forms of political participation also show increases over these four years. For example, while only 13 percent of the public had attended a campaign meeting in 1972, 20 percent had done so in 1976. As for turnout in state and federal elections, that was essentially the same in both electoral periods. And in 1976 German voters were more willing to publicly display their party preferences. The CDU/CSU and its supporters adopted the open campaign methods of their SPD and FDP counterparts, and partisans of all persuasions were willing to stand up for their political beliefs.

Perhaps the most dramatic evidence of rising participation levels has been the growth of citizen initiatives in the past several years.[25] More and more, Germans have begun to organize at both the local and national level in order to articulate political demands, protest policies, and influence political decisions. These movements may imply some popular dissatisfaction with contemporary German political parties, but there is little doubt that the increase in citizen initiatives signifies an expanding awareness of the role a citizen can play in a popular democracy as well as an expanding repertoire of political action.

Analyses of participation in the 1976 campaign indicate that the correlates of political involvement continue the pre-1976 causal patterns. For example, a substantial difference still exists between the participation rates of individuals of upper and lower status. Hence, there is little evidence of a decline in the "participation gap," which was discussed in the conclusion to chapter 2. Moreover, the tendency of younger Germans to be more involved in politics remains quite visible in the 1976 data. The frequency of political discussion increases monotonically from the Wilhelmine to the Federal Republic generations.[26] However, the 1976 data may also suggest the emergence of a life-cycle pattern of political participation. Among the youngest Federal Republic cohort the age pattern reverses; participation is lower than for other postwar cohorts. This suggests that future German cohorts may begin to display the "normal" life-cycle pattern of increasing political involvement with age that is common to other stable democracies.

Finally, the media continue to be major sources of political information in postwar Germany. For example, over 75 percent of the 1976 respondents reported watching at least part of the marathon debate between Schmidt, Genscher, Kohl, and Strauss that was held shortly before the election, and almost 60 percent indicated that they watched at least one of the special campaign programs presented earlier in the campaign. These findings are quite similar to those for the 1972 campaign when approximately 85 percent reported they watched at least one of the three debates among the party leaders.

The debates provide a good example of the media's importance in conveying political information and influencing voter behavior. Kendall Baker and Helmut Norpoth find evidence of information gain even among highly interested viewers of the first 1972 debate, and they report that results from both 1972 and 1976 demonstrate that viewers of the debates and special campaign programs tended to change their votes in a fashion quite different from nonviewers.[27] Elisabeth Noelle-Neumann comes to a similar conclusion.[28] She demonstrates that regular viewers of German news broadcasts tend to change their views about the likely winner of the election.

In conclusion, all the indicators give substantial evidence that popular involvement in politics was as strong in 1976 as it was in 1972. Germans continued to seek political information from the media, discuss politics with others, and engage in a wide variety of political activities. Therefore, popular attitudes about the role of the individual in the political process do not appear to have been significantly reversed by the environmental changes that occurred between 1972 and 1976.

Partisan Politics

The most obvious indicator of change in 1976 was the election itself. The campaign signaled a very different contest from that of 1972. The Christian Democrats took the offensive on many issues of both domestic and foreign policy, and in Old Politics as well as New Politics domains. From the opposition bench they criticized the SPD's management of government, and the products of seven years of SPD-FDP leadership. The Social Democrats' attempts to deflect or rebut these criticisms met with only partial success. A series of Land election victories signaled the new electoral strength of the CDU/CSU. As the election approached, the possibility of a CDU/CSU victory was very real.[29] On election day the Christian Democrats gained nearly 4 percent more of the vote than in 1972, once again becoming the largest single party. Polls also showed the CDU/CSU scoring broad gains in issue competence across virtually all policy domains.[30] The CDU/CSU won the electoral battle, but not the electoral war, for the SPD-FDP coalition managed to hold on to power with an eight-seat majority in the Bundestag.

There are several possible ways to explain the 1976 election results. Explanations could focus on the effects of issues, candidates, and other short-term factors. These influences were undoubtedly important in deciding the election outcome. Often, however, the reason why particular issues become important, or why specific images of candidates or parties evolve is left unexplained by this short-term focus. Instead, the specific events of a campaign need to be examined in the broader context of long-term electoral trends.

One long-term explanation for the changes in party fortunes in 1976 posits a resurgence of Old Politics concerns centering on the economy, domestic order, and internal security. In this connection, the narrow win of the anti-Social Democratic coalition in Sweden in 1976 encouraged CDU/CSU hopes, because the condition of Sweden seemed to presage Germany's future under continued SPD leadership. Both the SPD and the CDU/CSU reacted to the apparent shift to Old Politics interests in their campaign slogans, strategies, party statements, and in the overall tenor of the campaign. Was the 1976 election, then, a regression to the traditional politics and cleavages of an earlier period—a characterization that would challenge the conclusions already reached in this book?

The analysis argues against the likelihood of a strong resurgence of the Old Politics. Old Politics–New Politics orientations, which are deeply rooted in the individual, should be relatively unaffected by short-term factors because of their origin in the formative experiences of youth and long-term social forces.[31] The decline of the Old Politics class cleavage was tied to fundamental changes in the nature of German society and the occupational structure—factors that remained relatively constant during the 1972–1976 period.[32] Therefore, although the issues and party images of the 1976 campaign may have aided the electoral fortunes of the Christian Democrats, it is unlikely that this single election could have seriously altered the characteristics of contemporary partisan politics.

The 1976 election provides an opportunity to test this theorizing. The distribution of value priorities over time can serve as a starting point. If the values of the German public echo only current elite themes and the immediate social, political, and economic environment, then we should find considerable change in the distribution of value priorities over the preceding decade. In 1969, for example, interest in the New Politics should have been relatively strong as both the SPD and FDP appealed to the public's desire for change and modernity. "Democratization" was also a topic of the 1969 campaign, and the first voter initiatives reflected the participatory inclination of the New Politics. The themes of the 1972 election should have further strengthened commitments to the New Politics. But, if environmental factors effect instantaneous change in value orientations, the political changes of the 1972–1976 period outlined earlier in this chapter should have all but erased the New Politics.

Ronald Inglehart has developed a battery of questions to assess materialist and postmaterialist value orientations.[33] Responses to these questions can serve as an acceptable measure of the conceptually broader Old Politics–New Politics dimension.[34] Three national surveys (1970, 1973, 1976), each conducted within a year of the preceding federal election, measure the distribution of value types over time (table 11.7).[35] These data indicate that only a small minority of the German mass public has turned its attention fully to the New Politics.[36] This is not surprising; the transition from the Old to the New Politics should take several generations, and in historical perspective the conditions fostering the New Politics have existed in Germany only for a

Table 11.7. Distribution of value priorities, 1970–1976.

Value type	1970	1973	1976
Old Politics	46.6%	42.1%	41.5%
Mixed priorities	43.7	49.5	47.4
New Politics	10.7	8.4	11.1
Sample mean[a]	1.66	1.67	1.70
(N)	(1865)	(1953)	(891)

Source: European Community Studies (Ann Arbor, ICPSR Study nos. 7260, 7330, 7551).

a. Mean scores are based on the following coding: (1) Old Politics, (2) mixed, (3) New Politics.

relatively short time.[37] But more important, instead of registering a sharp decline between 1970 and 1976 in the number of people holding New Politics values, the data actually describe a slight increase in the size of this group.[38] Conversely, the pure Old Politics group is slowly but steadily declining in size; since 1970 less than half of the population have focused exclusively on Old Politics concerns.

These results would be of less interest if values were not related to partisan politics. However, not only have New Politics values persisted from 1970 to 1976, but this value dimension has become increasingly relevant to voting choices. The SPD proportion of the two-party vote distributed among the three value types is displayed in table 11.8. In each of the three years the SPD percentage declines monotonically from New Politics supporters to Old Politics supporters. Furthermore, the gap in SPD votes between the two extreme groups widens, and the gamma correlation between these measures also increases

Table 11.8. SPD voting preferences by value priorities, 1970–1976.[a]

Value type	1970	1973	1976
Old Politics	50.9%	46.0%	37.5%
Mixed priorities	58.5	60.9	47.9
New Politics	73.2	70.5	80.0
Gamma	0.22	0.31	0.38
(N)	(1361)	(1171)	(675)

Source: European Community Studies (Ann Arbor, ICPSR Study nos. 7260, 7330, 7551).

a. Cell entries are the percentages preferring the SPD out of the two-party vote intention.

substantially from 1970 to 1976. The higher correlations in 1976 may be one consequence of the CDU/CSU's campaign, which stressed Old Politics themes. Only when the parties are polarized on the New Politics–Old Politics dimension can these orientations realize their potential for guiding voting decisions.[39] By offering clearer choices in 1976, the CDU/CSU gained the votes of Old Politics supporters, who should have voted for that party's conservative policies. At the same time, the Old Politics appeals of the CDU/CSU pushed New Politics voters slightly more toward the SPD. Thus, the changing influence of value priorities on the vote is a major factor in explaining the CDU/CSU gains in 1976. Nevertheless, the increased importance of value priorities for voting choices did little to alter the distribution of value priorities.

Clearly, then, the environmental changes of 1972–1976 have not erased New Politics concerns from the German political landscape. Indeed, these concerns have a persisting, perhaps increasing, relevance to German partisan politics. But because they represent a separate dimension of political cleavage, this finding cannot fully answer the question whether the CDU/CSU gains in 1976 meant a sharpening of the traditional cleavages of the Old Politics. The preceding analyses would *suggest* that this was not the case, but there are ways to answer the question more directly.

In analyses paralleling those performed in chapter 4, the impact of economic forces on party popularity was estimated to determine whether these forces had grown in importance after dropping to low levels during the 1960s. Monthly public opinion surveys measured the parties' strengths among the electorate; the independent variables used were the economic indicators of level of unemployment, changes in unemployment rate, and inflation rate.

The estimates of economic influences on party support for the 1973–1976 period are presented in table 11.9. The overall effects, as represented by the R^2 column, indicate that economic factors had greater impact upon the popularity of the CDU/CSU than on that of the SPD ($R^2 = 0.36$ versus $R^2 = 0.21$). Thus, the CDU/CSU's attempt to link its support to the performance of the economy evidently had some success. One notable aspect of these results is that party popularity appears to be more dependent on unemployment levels than on the inflation rate—at least as long as price increases remain at "only" 5 percent per annum. This view contradicts newspaper editorials and the conventional wisdom of popular discourse in Germany, but it is supported by other empirical research.[40] However, if these results are compared with those presented in chapter 4, the overall impact of economic forces in the 1973–1976 period is not substantially different

Table 11.9. Impact of economics on party popularity, 1973–1976.[a]

| Dependent variable | Constant | Independent variables | | | | R^2 | DW | Rho |
		Level of unemployment	Change in unemployment rate	Inflation rate $(t - 4)$				
SPD	43.76[b]	-0.46	-2.40	-0.13		0.21	1.77	0.75
CDU/CSU	48.99[b]	0.06	2.27	-0.52		0.36	1.78	0.61

a. The N is 48 monthly data points. All models are AR1. For further technical details about the entries in this table, see chapter 4, note 73.
b. Significant at $p < 0.05$.

from that of the 1960s and early 1970s. By 1976, economic factors were far from regaining the dominant position they had held in the 1950s, and the reversal in economic conditions between 1972 and 1976 apparently had not halted the trend away from the economic determination of partisan politics.

An even more crucial test of the impact of the Old Politics involves actual voting decisions. Citizens probably give their voting decisions more careful consideration than they do their replies to party preference questions between elections. And election results carry more weight for the political system than any public opinion poll.

A steady decline in the impact of several class-related (and hence economically based) attributes upon German voting decisions has been documented. This decline was seen as a consequence of the receding political role of economics, and of a simultaneous turn of German politics toward other matters. However, the renewed attention given to inflation and unemployment since 1973 may have strengthened group-related economic self-interest, leading to substantially higher levels of class voting in 1976 than in 1972.

Although the CDU/CSU gained votes in 1976, its gains did not come primarily from any one social stratum (table 11.10). Instead, the Christian Democrats' gains are about equal among working-class and middle-class voters, and the Alford index displays little change compared to the 1972 results (1976-16 points, 1972-17 points).[41] The electorate did not respond to the 1976 campaign and political environment in class

Table 11.10. Class voting, 1972 and 1976.

Class	Sept. 1972	June 1976
Percentage voting for SPD		
Working class	70%	58%
Middle class	53	42
New	57	47
Old	38	23
Alford indexes of class voting[a]		
Worker/Middle class	17%	16%
Worker/New middle	13	11
Worker/Old middle	32	35
New middle/Old middle	19	24

a. The Alford indexes represent the simple difference in SPD vote between two groups.

terms any more than it did in 1972, despite the attempts of the CDU/ CSU to resurrect economic and class antagonisms.

Previous chapters have placed special emphasis on the role of the new middle class in explaining the decline in class voting. Free of the traditional ties in the conflict between bourgeoisie and proletariat, this class is available for political mobilization; its members are also concerned with New Politics issues and committed to New Politics values. By appealing to these interests the SPD has been able to entice the new middle class to cross class lines. The CDU, on the other hand, has continued to approach this stratum by appealing to traditional middle-class values, and consequently it has consistently lost support from this group.

The resurgence of Old Politics themes in the 1976 election and the concomitant decline in the salience of New Politics issues might have been expected to upset this pattern among the SPD's electorate. However, roughly half of the new middle class continued to support the SPD in 1976 (table 11.10). In fact, as the Alford indexes show, the new middle class was still more closely aligned with the working class (11-point difference) than with the old middle class (24-point difference). Although all three social classes gave relatively more support to the CDU/CSU in 1976 than in 1972, the new middle class registered the smallest increase of the three. The old middle class and the workers— the two groups most concerned with Old Politics themes—responded more to the Old Politics appeals of the CDU/CSU.

The decline in the importance of class voting is not limited to the occupational dimension of social status. Other measures, such as income and education, show a parallel decline in importance.[42] Indeed, the combined impact of all three social-status indicators on vote choice displays a further drop between 1972 (R = 0.26) and 1976 (R = 0.20). Thus, since 1969 German politics appears to have entered a new electoral era in which the traditionally sharp middle class–working class cleavage has been blurred by the emergence of the new middle class. The commitment of the new middle class to New Politics values is likely to continue this gradual conversion in the social bases of German partisanship.

Religious differences represent the second major social cleavage in German politics. While New Politics concerns should weaken the class alignment, they do not necessarily lead to a similar decline in the importance of the religious cleavage. This is true because the lines of the religious cleavage run parallel to the alignments of the New Politics, and the class cleavage cuts across this dimension.[43] New Politics supporters are disproportionately Protestants and nonchurchgoers, but these groups are already more likely to support the left. Conversely,

Catholics and churchgoers adhere to more traditional values and life styles, but they already support the conservative parties.

Thus, the causal importance of religion should be relatively unaffected by the ebb and flow of New Politics concerns. In fact, there was remarkable persistence in the importance of the religious cleavage between 1953 and 1972, despite attempts by the SPD to de-emphasize religious conflicts. This pattern also carried over to the 1976 election.[44] A gap of 24 percent separated Protestant and Catholic support of the SPD—identical to that in 1972. The causal impact of church attendance displays considerable consistency over time.

These two major dimensions of social cleavage, class and religion, whose influence still follows the trends described earlier in this book—were combined with two additional social cleavages—rural-urban and regional—in order to examine the total impact of social cleavages on German voting behavior (table 11.11). The combined impact of these four dimensions declines slightly from the 1972 election (R = 0.38) to the 1976 contest (R = 0.36).[45] Furthermore, none of the predictors displays a significant increase in independent effects (beta) over the same timespan.

The general impression that the 1976 election maintained the basic electoral pattern of 1972 can be further confirmed by examining the causal model presented in chapter 10 with data from the 1976 survey.[46] This model has two crucial elements. The first is the measure of general partisanship. Partisanship showed a modest shift toward the CDU/CSU, so that in 1976 CDU/CSU and SPD supporters were near parity.[47] More important, the tests of partisanship replicated from chapter 8 show that it continued to perform the cue-giving functions—polarization, participation, and constraint—that indicate the further growth of attitudinal partisanship among the German electorate.[48] The second crucial element of this model is the index of issue images. The

Table 11.11. Social structure and voting intentions, 1972 and 1976.[a]

Social structure	Sept. 1972	June 1976
Religion	0.26	0.27
Occupation	.25	.20
Rural-urban	.13	.10
Region	.08	.09
R	.38	.36
(N)	(1608)	(1531)

a. Cell entries are MCA beta coefficients.

Figure 11.1. Causal models of German voting behavior, 1972 and 1976. Entries above the line are unstandardized partial regression coefficients, while those below the line and in parentheses are standardized partial regression coefficients.

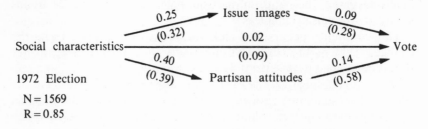

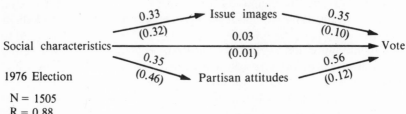

1976 data on issue images indicate that the electorate's evaluations of the Christian Democrats also improved in terms of issue competency.[49]

The causal model for 1976 shows a striking similarity to the 1972 model (figure 11.1). The influence of social characteristics on vote continues the long-term decline traced throughout this book (B = 0.03). There is a slight increase in the impact of issue images in 1976, which primarily reflects a growth in the causal influence of Old Politics issues.[50] As already mentioned, the CDU/CSU's stress on Old Politics themes in 1976 was an important force in the marginal electoral change between the two elections. Overall, however, the coefficients for issue images and for partisanship in 1976 closely parallel those of 1972.

Conclusion

The data in this chapter have painted a consistent pattern. Although several aspects of the social, political, and economic environments appeared to reverse earlier trends and some political elites consciously exploited this *Tendenzwende* (trend reversal), the nature of German political behavior in 1976 generally reflected the basic characteristics of preceding elections. Political involvement remained at high levels, or even increased. System support endured despite the challenges it faced. The political agenda continued to reflect a mix of Old Politics and New Politics issues. And even though the comrade trend was finally reversed, the nature of partisan behavior continued the trends uncovered in earlier chapters.

This continuity occurs, we feel, for two basic reasons. First, the changes of the mid-to-late 1970s apparently were not sufficient to alter trends developed over several decades. Indeed, with even a few years of historical perspective, the events that appeared earthshaking at the time have lessened in significance. Moreover, several of the political trends discussed in this volume are tied to long-term changes in such things as the occupational structure, social norms, and institutional frameworks; and the changes of the 1970s have not existed long enough or been of the type to influence these long-term sources of political change.

Second, our emphasis has been on causal relationships that translate environmental forces into political change. These causal relationships largely persisted in 1976, although with different inputs they sometimes led to different results. For example, while the *vote totals* for the 1976 election resemble 1969 and earlier elections more than the 1972 contest, the *causal pattern* of partisan behavior continued relatively unchanged. The same conclusion applies to the correlates of political involvement and issue orientations.

The continuity of the past does not, however, justify a simple extrapolation of these trends into the future. We cannot anticipate the direction short-term and long-term sources of political change will take, even if their consequences could be predicted from past causal patterns. Critical events or elections may even restructure causal processes.

It is likely, however, that the dramatic economic, social, and political changes of the postwar period are over. Neither a *Wirtschaftswunder* nor the dramatic political changes it stimulated are likely to be seen again. Similarly, the tremendous generational variation among Germans is steadily being replaced by a citizenry raised exclusively during the Federal Republic. The lack of intense and reinforcing sources of change suggests that we can expect a different pattern of political change in the future. Political involvement, for example, should level off after its skyrocketing growth in the 1950s and 1960s. Further changes will more likely be smaller and tied to the stimuli of specific election campaigns and gradual long-term increases brought about by population turnover and the expansion of education, communications, and New Politics values. Similarly, long-term changes in the occupational structure and income distribution and reactions to short-term fluctuations in the economy will probably condition the electoral impact of economics. But even if the overall pace of change slackens or temporarily reverses, it will continue.

12

West German Politics
in Transition

IN THIS BOOK, we have been primarily concerned with the discovery and explanation of patterns of political change. Germany has been a fertile ground for this endeavor because the postwar period has witnessed the transformation of the Federal Republic simultaneously to a modern, a democratic, and an advanced industrial society. The purpose of this chapter is to extend the basic ideas and conclusions developed earlier in order to throw light on the future direction of politics in West Germany and the processes of political change in other industrial societies.

A New Crisis of Legitimacy?

One of the most dramatic changes affecting the West German electorate has been the transition from a subject political culture to a truly "Civic Culture."[1] Democratic and participatory norms have become widespread, and system support is well developed and generalized. Throughout the 1970s, the German population continued to express almost universal satisfaction with the democratic system.[2] German democracy is apparently better rooted today than at any previous time in history.

Just as Germany has "caught up" with the more established democracies in terms of the civic culture model, however, another interesting development has occurred. A general decline in civic attitudes has been observed in many Western democracies. Public confidence in political elites has been shaken in North America and Western Europe, and in some countries basic system support may already have begun to erode.[3] There is evidence of these tensions in West Germany as well. In 1979 Kurt Sontheimer entitled a series of essays on contemporary

287

Germany *Die verunsicherte Republik* ("The Insecure Republic"), implying that the Federal Republic has perhaps been made unsafe but certainly has been made unsure of itself.[4] Although a closer look at public satisfaction with the political system reveals that the severe criticism is concentrated within a small group, this minority includes some potential and future elites, such as students and intellectuals. Thus, the elements most critical of German society in the late 1970s are found among the same groups, the young and the well educated, that spearheaded the growth of democratic norms during the preceding three decades. This fact enhances the importance of the criticism, just as the support of the young, educated generations was considered crucial to the success of the postwar democratic Federal Republic.

The wave of radical German terrorism and the popular and state reactions to these events have recently stimulated increased concern for civil liberties both in Germany and among foreign observers. Measures like the *Radikalenerlass* (which prohibits civil service employment for radicals) and the *Kontaktsperregesetz* have evoked perceptions of repression among many young people and intellectuals.[5] Even if only a few individuals are directly affected by these measures, the perception that civil liberties and free speech are threatened may itself act to stifle political discussion and discourage political activity. The government thus faces a dilemma. Antiterrorist measures, designed to calm the worries of large parts of the population, in turn alarm a smaller group of vocal and important critics. To relax these safeguards in order to assuage the disaffected, however, might raise general public concern for law and order, and perhaps encourage the call for more authoritarian responses.[6]

In part, then, the tensions that have surfaced in the Federal Republic have distinctively German roots. But at the same time the German experience parallels developments in other Western democracies. External pressures on the industrial world, like the rising cost and growing shortage of energy, have increased the "load" placed on government.[7] Unsuccessful and unpopular government policies have reduced political support, and popular demands and protests have challenged representative institutions. These developments have led to concern about a "legitimacy crisis" in advanced industrial societies and to questions about the "governability" of the modern state. Both concerns culminate in the prospect of a "crisis of democracy."[8] The similarities among the crises in the various Western democracies suggest that some common factors lie behind this pattern. One explanation for it focuses on the transition to an advanced industrial society and on the value changes accompanying that transition.

In many ways, it has become obvious that the citizens of Western industrial societies are now concerned with more than basic economic questions. Quality-of-life issues are an increasingly salient component of the public agenda. For instance, environmentalists are deeply concerned about the consequences of efforts to achieve energy self-sufficiency. Tax revolts—while often backed by tangible economic interests—express opposition to big government. The call for increasing citizen input and self-determination in reaction to perceived over-bureaucratization is echoed by groups interested in education, urban politics and planning, and many other aspects of society. In the United States and Western Europe, more people are turning to alternative life-styles instead of suffering the economic and bureaucratic demands of modern life. For an increasing proportion of the population, economic needs and interests are no longer the sole—or in some cases even the primary—motivation for behavior.

As popular attitudes and values have changed, so, too, has the substance of political debate. The questions that occupy the minds of political decision-makers today differ in nature from those that concerned them twenty or twenty-five years ago. Environmental issues, the dangers of nuclear energy, women's rights, educational quality (as opposed to educational opportunities) are questions that have only recently become the foci of political debate in Germany, the United States, and other advanced industrial societies. As earlier chapters have shown, the emergence of these issues is at least partially due to a slow process of value change among the public.

As conditions of affluence and (relative) external security have reduced the urgency of material needs and security concerns, small but growing portions of the mass public in Western societies have placed priority on "nonmaterial" values, such as self-actualization and a sense of belonging. In politics, these new values have led to a New Politics, in which the emphasis has shifted from economic issues and security (or law and order) issues to participation, self-determination, and the pursuit of minority rights, and from the raising of the standard of living to the improvement of the quality of life.

Of course, such processes can be reversed, but that is not likely to happen as a result of short-term economic difficulties. More drastic declines in economic conditions may be required to alter existing values, or to prevent further value changes. The groups most likely to exhibit or to develop New Politics values are fairly well insulated against the consequences of economic hard times. Moreover, because they stress nonmaterial goals, they may be more willing to forego marginal material gains if forced to choose between the two. In any case, if the new values possess any stability at all, the consequences of economic reverses will not be felt immediately in the population distribution of political values; rather, the effects will be lagged because the impact will be strongest among the youngest cohorts who are just forming these values. It is therefore not so surprising as it might seem that the balance of values has continued to shift throughout the 1970s; the noneconomic political issues of the New Politics are consequently bound to become more important, at least in the long run, both for the mass public and for political elites in Germany and in other advanced industrial societies.[9]

New Politics issues are significant in our context because they may contribute to the malaise now affecting Western democracies. In the past, governments have been able to "buy" support with economic success. The majority of the publics in Western societies continue to demand more and better services from the social welfare state, and many governments continue to believe in economic solutions for all problems. New Politics issues are difficult to negotiate on those terms, and attempts at economically reasoned solutions may appear to be designed to buy off principles. New Politics issues tend to polarize the electorate because they focus on values, and it is more difficult to compromise on values when they are in conflict.[10] If governments attempt to follow centrist policies, as catch-all parties normally do in the case of traditional economic issues, such policies may alienate more citizens than they satisfy, and they may cause opposition and cynicism at both political extremes.[11] In part, then, the present "crisis" may be unavoidable because of the nature of New Politics issues.

Moreover, the new values emphasize open access to participation and decision-making, as well as an increasingly active role for the citizen. Citizens want to be directly involved in reaching decisions; they are not content merely to participate in the selection of individuals and groups who will make political decisions. In many Western societies, new, more direct modes of participation are already apparent. In West Germany, for example, *Bürgerinitiativen* ("citizen initiatives") are increasingly demanding access to all levels of the political system. In fact, the citizen initiatives claim to have twice as many members as the political parties do. Germans are also resorting more often to unconventional forms of political behavior, such as demonstrations, in order to articulate political demands. These "elite-challenging" modes of participation have been attributed to the changing values and skills of Western publics that have accompanied increases in affluence and education.[12] Therefore, further increases in this kind of political activity are likely if education levels continue to rise and New Politics concerns continue to spread.

The interaction between the policy dissatisfaction caused by the New Politics and the new elite-challenging forms of political participation may be a major factor in the "legitimacy crisis" of Western societies. Not only are citizens dissatisfied, but they are also more willing to express their dissatisfaction and to demand solutions. Thus, as has been suggested throughout this book, the transition to an advanced industrial society will not lead to an end of ideological conflict and public dissatisfaction in Germany or in other Western democracies.[13] The short-run forecast may, in fact, be quite the opposite. Having just developed a consensus on democratic norms, Germany may soon experience the kind of legitimacy crisis, with the consequent declines in system support and civic attitudes, that has already surfaced in the older Western democracies.

The long-term consequences of this extension of the repertory of political action are much less clear.[14] While unconventional forms of direct participation can be taken as expressions of the legitimacy crisis, they may at the same time be part of the solution to the problem of governability. Disaffection with the delivery of goods and services by the government bureaucracy stems in part from the technocratic nature of the decision-making process. Increasing public participation may not only satisfy the demand for better access to political decisions, but it may also improve the decisions themselves as concerned citizens contribute information on public preferences as well as their accumulated expertise.

Political Parties and the New Politics

Value change will not only affect the relationship between citizens and government; it will also affect the political parties. The research on which this book is based indicates that the rise of New Politics concerns has weakened the traditional social bases of German politics. And indeed, throughout Europe the impact of class and economics has declined during the postwar period.[15] One result of this process is that the voter must find new cues for guiding political behavior. The German data imply that attitudinal partisanship has increased over the long term as social cleavages have decreased in importance.[16] Thus, although European researchers have recently doubted the relevance of party identification in the European context, the decline of social cleavages may force a reassessment of this conclusion.[17]

But again, just as Germany appears to be "catching up" with the pattern of political behavior in the established democracies, this pattern is changing. In the United States and Britain the number of party identifiers has decreased over the past decade. Furthermore, a broader debate is under way on the declining role of parties in general.[18] And several aspects of the changes outlined here call into question the importance and the role of political parties. Individuals who want to participate directly in the making of decisions may be less likely to rely exclusively on parties as input structures. Supporters of New Politics issues often organize ad hoc single-issue groups and use other vehicles to press their demands instead of having to compromise their commitments in order to win the endorsement of party organizations that have been designed to aggregate and mediate diverging interests.

Moreover, parties are probably badly equipped to handle the issues of principle that partly constitute the New Politics. The difficulty Western parties have experienced in reaching decisions on the use of nuclear energy is just one example of the divisive force of such issues. One strategy followed by the parties has been to shy away from taking a clear stand. This option avoids immediate party splits, but the parties give up the virtual monopoly they have enjoyed and valued in forming and aggregating public preferences.

Although parties may become less important in the political realm through the loss of this monopoly, they are unlikely to lose their role entirely. The Old Politics will continue to be conducted largely through parties; but even New Politics advocates—at least for the time being—express commitments to political parties that are as strong as those of other groups. Rather than choosing between parties and direct forms of political action, they are likely to use sometimes one and sometimes the other, depending on the issue they are supporting. It may be painful for party leaders to give up their complete control over access to political decisions and decision-makers, but allowing for a mix of direct and representative forms of democracy may save the parties from destructive internal contradictions and conflicts. While saving the parties, however, this extension of political conflict to the decision-making organs (parliaments or cabinets) could make it more difficult for those institutions to reach decisions.[19]

In addition to redefining or reducing the role of political parties, the advent of advanced industrial politics could also stimulate realignments or even breakups of the party systems in Germany and other Western democracies. The major dimension of political and partisan conflict in the Old Politics of Germany is captured by the familiar labels "left" and "right." Most of the contentious positions in economic, social, and welfare policy, as well as general views of the extent of the state's role in society, are located on this dimension. Since the turn of the twentieth century the cleavage between left and right has been predominant in European politics, and it is not surprising that the major parties also define their positions in those terms.[20] The overwhelming majority of the electorate are not only able to position themselves and the parties on the left-right dimension, but they have an active understanding of the concept.[21]

The battle lines of industrial society led naturally to class-based parties. Consequently, social background variables reflecting this division can generally explain a substantial amount of the variation in individual voting behavior. The bourgeoisie and most of the farmers are aligned with the right, the proletariat with the left. But the new middle class is separate from the bourgeoisie. It is located between that class and the workers on the traditional dimension of political conflict, and its members, salaried white-collar employees and civil servants lack the clear class characteristics of the older groups.

The potential of New Politics issues for disrupting familiar political alignments arises because these values (like the new middle class) lack a clear place in the old order.[22] They cannot be easily located in the left-right framework of the Old Politics because they imply different political goals rather than merely new positions on the old issues. In principle, then, the major dimensions of conflict in advanced industrial politics may be quite different from those in industrial politics.[23]

New Politics value priorities may generate political realignment because their distribution among the social groups does not follow the industrial class cleavage. Members of the new middle class deemphasize the economic goals of the Old Politics and stress New Politics issues. In contrast, the old middle class and the farmers are conservative in regard to both the New and the Old Politics. The workers, however, shift from a leftist, change-oriented stance on the Old Politics problems of economic distribution and welfare policy to a conservative position on the questions of the New Politics. Although the workers and the old middle class take opposite sides in the class-based Old Politics conflicts, they jointly resist the growing role of the new values in shaping societal and political decisions.[24]

Thus, the transition to an advanced industrial society in the West could produce a political realignment of social groups. The bourgeois-proletariat cleavage can be expected to weaken (as the German data indicate), and class differences in voting behavior should narrow further as the transition progresses. Ultimately, the Alford indexes of class voting may actually be reversed as the majority of the middle class, that is, the new middle class, supports the party identified as the left on the New Politics, while the working class increases its support for the more conservative party.

Obviously, contemporary Western politics cannot yet be characterized as a New Politics system. Most voters are still primarily concerned with the economic and security issues of the Old Politics. But in recent years the advanced industrial societies have begun to experience this transition process.[25]

The party systems of Europe and North America have responded to this situation in different ways. To some extent, smaller parties like the

PSU in France and (at least partially) the FDP in Germany have altered their positions to represent a New Politics perspective.[26] It can even be argued that in the United States in 1972 the New Politics supporters temporarily captured control of the Democratic party.[27] Where the old parties have refused or been unable to incorporate New Politics goals, new parties have been formed to specifically cater to New Politics voters. Such parties include the "Democrats '66" in the Netherlands and, more important, the recent ecologist ("green") parties in France, Germany, and elsewhere. However, a permanent realignment of entire party systems is unlikely in the near future because New Politics voters constitute only a small, albeit important and vocal, minority of the electorates.

In Germany, however, the process of value change seems to have affected the larger parties more than in most other Western politics. The advent of the New Politics was accelerated by the political strategies of the SPD, which successfully emphasized many of the new priorities in order to increase its appeal to the new middle class. At the same time, the SPD's lead in incorporating (or exploiting) New Politics themes resulted in an association of the New and the Old Politics dimensions. Increasingly, New Politics supporters place themselves on the left in Old Politics terms, although many of them come from socioeconomic backgrounds that would traditionally predispose them to right or centrist positions.[28] As a result, voters with New Politics concerns have largely chosen to support the SPD. Indeed, these groups have become more and more visible within the old working-class party; they represent a growing percentage of the SPD vote and membership, and they are disproportionately active, vocal, and politically resourceful. The party, however, must also represent the materialist interests of its traditional base, the workers. During election campaigns, the Social Democrats have succeeded until now in bridging (or covering up) this value gap. Through segmented and well-aimed appeals they have mobilized their traditional working-class support and at the same time have won new voters from among the new middle class. Nevertheless, within the party organization the tensions between the Old and New Politics have resulted in factional strife. These intraparty battles are often fought over which goals should receive priority in Social Democratic policies: whether maintenance of the natural environment or the generation of more energy to sustain economic growth.[29]

The steady growth of the "new left," "green lists," and Bürgerinitiativen suggests that the potential of the Old Politics–New Politics value conflicts in Germany is far from spent. The founding of a national green party in 1980 is a direct consequence of disappointing experiences with the SPD. As economic difficulties and citizens' fears have moved the governing SPD to emphasize economic growth and security, SPD elites have appeared to be pursuing Old Politics themes once again, driving recently acquired young SPD supporters to the new alternatives. But these groups remain crucial to SPD electoral victories, and they have gained sufficient ground in the party ranks to ensure a continuing struggle there.

The CDU/CSU has not felt the Old Politics–New Politics tensions to the same extent as the SPD. As the majority party until the late 1960s, the Christian Democrats only had to keep their old voters, not to win new ones. Furthermore, the traditional CDU supporters occupy positions on the political right in terms of both the Old and the New Politics. Indeed, the CDU's appeal to some groups, like the Catholic workers, has always been as much on the basis of traditional values as on economic principles. In the short run the CDU/CSU might even gain from conflicts over New Politics issues. As the new values engage larger portions of the electorate and find organizational foci, they are more likely to arouse opposition on their own terms. Thus, the CDU's grounding in conservative moral values may serve to focus opposition against direct political action, women's rights, or educational reforms by promoting the more deferential representative democratic styles, the virtues of home and family, and the traditional educational values.[30] The nucleus of resistance to the themes of the New Politics may indeed be religious values. This would help explain why, in the face of declining religiosity, the traditional, preindustrial religious cleavage continues to manifest itself in politics and voting behavior in Germany and other advanced industrial societies.[31] In order to "use" such a strategy to wean conservative workers away from the SPD, the CDU would have to relax its rightist (Old Politics) emphasis on the economic interests of the middle class. Consequently, the conflict between Old and New Politics could eventually gain in importance for the CDU/CSU as well.

If the transition to the New Politics continues—and so far the indications are that it will, in spite of economic setbacks—the resulting tensions will present increasingly difficult problems for the major political parties in all advanced industrial democracies. In trying to bridge the Old and New Politics, a party opens itself to challenges from both directions. And although these value dimensions will not lead to immediate realignment, they will channel future political developments in advanced industrial societies, and act to constrain the broad-range and long-term direction of elite behavior.

Throughout this book the themes of change have been stressed in the transition of German politics from an authoritarian to a democratic society, from a war-ravaged economy to an affluent, advanced industrial society, from a fragmented and socially polarized party system to a system of broadly based catch-all parties. This transition process is ongoing. The instability and uncertainty of the immediate postwar period is over, but the politics of the future is likely to be as volatile as the politics of the past. Political conflicts, however, are less likely to stress economic growth, security, or the existence of basic democratic norms; instead, they will evolve around the development of public policies that will satisfy the demands of citizens living in an increasingly advanced industrial society.

Appendixes

Notes

Index

Appendix A

The Database

THE RESEARCH IN THIS VOLUME is based upon an exceptionally rich timeseries of ten surveys of German political behavior conducted in the following election years: 1953, 1961 (three surveys), 1965 (two), 1969 (two), 1972, and 1976. These data are valuable for three reasons. First, the timeperiod they cover is unique, providing an opportunity to study political change, especially the impact of economic forces and the development of democratic norms, in a Western democratic society. Second, the themes adopted by the principal investigators, including party identification, issue beliefs, and value priorities, are of major interest to political scientists. And third, the continuity of indicators—especially since the 1961 surveys—facilitates longitudinal research.

The dataseries starts with a survey made prior to the 1953 *Bundestagswahl,* or election, that includes questions on several political topics. The next three surveys were conducted by researchers at the University of Cologne as part of an elaborate sociological and political study of the election of 1961. This 1961 study played a major role in determining the content and future direction of research on German political behavior.[1] Many themes from the 1961 surveys were replicated by the two surveys of 1965, one of which was also conducted by the Cologne researchers. The two 1969 surveys saw a further extension of this series, and both of them were directed by members of the 1961 research team.

The 1972 and 1976 surveys, the most complex of the series, are three-wave panel studies; they continued the influence of the Cologne school, which by then had been transplanted to Mannheim. These surveys with their combined assets provide an invaluable storehouse of data that go far beyond the topics explored in this volume.

299

These data have been made available to researchers as the result of a joint archival project of the Inter-university Consortium for Political and Social Research (ICPSR; Michigan), the Zentralarchiv für empirische Sozialforschung (ZA; Cologne), and the Zentrum für Umfragen, Methoden, und Analysen (ZUMA; Mannheim). The Conference Group on German Politics contributed to the translation costs of the project.

During 1974 the data and documentation for the first nine surveys were collected in Cologne, and the bulk of the data processing was completed. The three authors of this volume all contributed to this effort. The data and documentation were distributed to Consortium and Zentralarchiv members in 1975. The 1976 election study was subsequently added to this collection, and it is hoped that future German election studies will be added to the series. The data are available to researchers from either of the two archives:

The Inter-university Consortium for Political and Social Research
P.O. Box 1248
Ann Arbor, Michigan 48106

The Zentralarchiv für empirische Sozialforschung
5 Cologne 41
Bachemer Strasse 40
Federal Republic of Germany

Sampling Design

German survey research has been characterized by a relatively high degree of sampling precision since early in the timeseries. This development has been facilitated by the availability of accurate and detailed information on small areal sampling units and by the complete enumeration of the German population in central community registries of inhabitants (*Einwohnermeldekartei*). Based upon this information, each study has used some form of stratified, three-stage, probability sampling procedure. First, the sampling points were selected; then households were chosen within each sampling point; and finally an individual was selected within each household.

In the first stage, a complete listing of all communities (*Gemeinden*) in the Federal Republic was stratified according to state (*Bundesland*) and population in the most recent census. Sampling points, or communities, were then chosen within each stratum with a probability of selection proportionate to population size.

Within each of these communities, clusters of households were systematically drawn from the central registry of inhabitants to form the second sampling stage. The registry serves as the basis for the electoral register, tax rolls, passport registration, and other government records; and federal law requires all persons to maintain this registration in their community of residence. Thus, the registry provides a fairly accurate enumeration of the inhabitants of a community organized by their household of residence. Because there are inevitable inaccuracies in the registry, a sample of households was drawn rather than a sample of individuals. This allowed for a more precise re-enumeration of the sample households at the next sampling stage.

A slightly different procedure was used in three of the ten surveys (September 1969, 1972, and 1976). The sampling points at the first stage were electoral districts (*Wahlbezirke*) rather than communities. In the second sampling stage a list of households was enumerated in each district, and from this list a sample of households was drawn.

The third sampling stage was the same for all the surveys. Interviewers enumerated all eligible persons living in the sample households according to a fixed order. A single respondent was then selected from each household list by using a random numbers table, without the possibility of substitution.

The sampling universe of all of these studies therefore consists of the adult German population living in private households. This excludes persons living in group quarters, the institutional populations, and those with no place of residence. The basic descriptive information for each survey is presented in table A.1: The ICPSR/ZA study number, sample universe, dates of fieldwork, and sample size.

Response Rates

Those conducting national sample surveys must always resign themselves to less than perfect response rates. For a variety of reasons some intended respondents are never contacted, and others are never interviewed. The response rate for each survey for which this information is available is presented in table A.2[2] To lessen nonresponse each of the surveys required multiple callbacks by the interviewer. Relatively short fieldwork periods placed some constraints on the amount of additional effort possible; but these response rates appear quite respectable in comparison with those of other national surveys of the German population.

Three of the studies consist of panel surveys, in which an attempt was made to reinterview respondents after an initial interview. The panels faced not only the challenge of first recruiting respondents but also the difficulty of maintaining these initial recruits. The extent and source of panel mortality are given in table A.3. Although all three

Table A.1. German electoral surveys, 1953–1976.

ICPSR/ZA study no.	Population	Dates of fieldwork	Number in sample
	1953		
7104/ 145	Citizens aged 18–79	July–Aug. 1953	3246
	1961		
7099/ 055	Citizens aged 16 and over, including Berlin	July 7–Aug. 12, 1961	1679
7100/ 056	Citizens aged 16 and over, including Berlin	Sept. 4–Sept. 16, 1961	1633
7101/ 057	Citizens aged 16 and over, including Berlin	Nov. 14–Dec. 16, 1961	1715
	1965		
7103/ 556	Citizens aged 21 and over	Sept. 1–Sept. 14, 1965	1411
7105/ 314	Citizens aged 21 and over	Oct. 2–Oct. 23, 1965	1305
	1969		
7098/ 426, 427	Citizens aged 21 and over	Sept. 5–Sept. 22, 1969 / Oct. 14–Nov. 9, 1969	1158 / 763
7108/ 525	Citizens aged 21 and over, including Berlin	Aug. 8–Sept. 9, 1969 / Aug. 28–Sept. 28, 1969	1006 / 939
	1972		
7102/ 635, 636, 637	Citizens aged 18 and over[a]	Sept. 23–Oct. 11, 1972 / Oct. 20–Nov. 6, 1972 / Dec. 9–Dec. 30, 1972	2052 / 1603 / 1222
	1976		
7513/ 823, 824, 825	Citizens aged 18 and over	May 19–June 23, 1976 / Aug. 5–Sept. 18, 1976 / Oct. 26–Nov. 22, 1976	2076 / 1529 / 1196

a. In 1970 the voting age had been lowered from 21 to 18.

panels are relatively short-term, the loss of initial respondents is fairly substantial. Such extensive panel mortality appears to be the norm in German survey research, probably reflecting the basic reluctance of the German population to be interviewed rather than a lack of effort on the researchers' part.[3]

Sample Representativeness

The fundamental question concerning response rates is not the degree of nonresponse but the bias that may result from it. If the persons who

Table A.2. Survey response rates, 1953–1976.[a]

Interview information	1953	1961			1969		1972	1976
	7104	7099	7100	7101	7098	7108	7102	7513
Number of sampling points	152	—	—	—	173	275	520	265
Total addresses	4000	2350	2371	2562	1551	1512	3030	3047
Incorrect address		52	43	53	28	—	17	68
Premises empty or no eligible respondent	128[b]	45	33	50	22	66	141	75
Total attempted interviews	3872	2253	2295	2459	1501	1446	2872	2904
No one home	234[c]	137	221	209	81	68	135	327
Respondent unavailable		144	87	10	51	37	225	54
Refused sampling information	332[d]	59	55	84	26	52	78	273
Respondent refused		128	166	233	122	175	268	127
Respondent ill	45	80	100	95	18	65	96	37
Other reason	15	22	33	26	45	72	18	10
Completed interviews	3246	1683	1633	1802	1158	977	2052	2076
Response rate	83.8	74.7	71.1	73.2	77.1	67.5	71.4	71.5

a. Information on the 1965 surveys is not available.
b. Combined with "Incorrect address" in 1953.
c. Combined with "No one home" in 1953.
d. Combined with "Refused sampling information" in 1953.

Table A.3. Reinterview rates for panel surveys, 1969–1976.

Interview information	1969 Second wave	1972 Second wave	1972 Third wave	1976 Second wave	1976 Third wave
Sample from previous wave	1158	2052	1603	2076	1529
No contact, or address empty, or respondent died	—	74	89	51	11
Other reason	—	—	8	12	7
Total attempted interviews	1158	1978	1506	2013	1511
No one home	55	51	54	225	75
Respondent unavailable	83	107	83	77	17
Refused sampling information	5	3	4	27	24
Respondent refused	83	167	101	108	127
Respondent ill	15	30	30	16	30
Wrong respondent interviewed	98	—	—	—	—
Other reason	53	17	12	31	42
Completed interviews	766	1603	1222	1529	1196
Response rate	66.1%	81.0%	81.1%	76.0%	79.2%

Table A.4. Sample and population comparisons with respect to age and sex, 1953–1976.

	1953		1961			1965	1969	1972	1976
Statistics	7104	7099	7100	7101	7103	7105	7098	7102	7513
chi-square	69.5	17.2	41.4	27.4	52.9	58.9	39.1	13.7	30.8
phi-square	0.021	0.012	0.030	0.019	0.037	0.045	0.033	0.006	0.017

are not interviewed differ from those who are, and if they constitute a substantial part of the whole, the data from the interviewed sample will not be representative of the entire electorate.

Information derived from electoral statistics can provide a check for possible bias from nonresponse and sampling error. The electoral statistics contain accurate data on the age and sex distribution of the adult population in the Federal Republic, which can be compared with the sample distributions.

For each sample the age-by-sex distribution was tabulated by using four age groups: 25–29, 30–44, 45–59, and 60 and over.[4] The comparable distributions for the population were used to estimate the eight-cell frequencies for each sample. Expected and observed cell frequencies were then compared statistically (table A.4).

The chi square statistics obtained by this procedure show that significant age-by-sex differences exist in each sample. (In an eight-cell table a chi-square greater than 11.34 is significant at the 0.01 level.) The specific pattern of these differences varies from study to study, but generally males and the youngest and oldest cohorts are underrepresented. In all likelihood these differences are largely unavoidable, arising from the greater mobility of youth, the unavailability of many employed males, and the greater resistance and unavailability of the elderly. In addition, some portion of the difference may arise because of the inequivalencies between the universe of the central registries and the universe of the sampling frames.

The value of chi square is, however, highly dependent on sample size. With large surveys many differences may be statistically, but not substantively, significant. Therefore, phi-square statistics which measure the magnitude of sample differences adjusted by sample sizes, were computed for each study (table A.4). Although samples differ statistically from the expected population values, the phi-squares are relatively small. Consequently, the analyses of this volume are based upon the unweighted data files.

In addition to these demographic comparisons, the five postelection surveys in the series (1961, 1965, 1969, 1972, 1976) can be used to assess representativeness in terms of two political variables: election turnout and vote division. Several investigators have shown that substantial unsystematic (but also systematic) measurement errors must be considered when dealing with these variables.[5] Thus sample discrepancies cannot be attributed solely to nonresponse and sampling error. This makes it all the more important, however, to assess the pattern of error for these two political variables.

The first two columns of table A.5 compare the turnout rates of the 1961–1976 surveys to the official turnout statistics. The data indicate a

Table A.5. Voting results and sample estimates, 1961–1976.

Date	Turnout		SPD % of second ballot	
	Sample[a]	Actual	Sample[a]	Actual
Nov. 1961	86.5%	87.7%	35.0%	36.2%
Oct. 1965	93.5	86.8	38.1	39.3
Oct. 1969	94.0	86.7	45.4	42.7
Dec. 1972	97.2	91.1	54.1	45.8
Oct. 1976	97.9	90.7	43.3	42.6

a. Sample estimates do not include refusals and no replies in the calculation of percentages.

slight inflation in reported turnout, especially in the later surveys. But voter validation studies in the United States suggest that this overre-porting is within reasonable bounds.[6]

The last two columns in table A.5 present the SPD share of the vote in each sample and in the official election returns. Here the error is normally quite small and within the range of sampling error. The one noticeable deviation is the overreporting of SPD voting in 1972, a phenomenon probably tied to the climate of opinion during the election.[7] Overall, these sampling checks suggest that the surveys adequately represent the characteristics and behaviors of the German electorate.

In discussing sample representativeness special attention should be devoted to the three panel studies. A single cross-section survey may incur bias from the differential recruitment of initial respondents. Panels face not only this challenge but also the possible biases resulting from the differential losses of these initial recruits. To check for such bias, the representativeness of surviving panel members was checked against the full sample.

The procedure used in checking for mortality bias was to compare the first-wave frequency distribution of a variable for the full sample with the distribution for respondents reinterviewed in later waves. These data show little evidence of systematic bias resulting from panel mortality (table A.6). In nearly all instances the first-wave distribution for the full sample is quite similar to the first-wave distribution of respondents who also provided a second or third interview. For exam-ple, 39.9 percent of those reinterviewed in the second wave of the 1969 panel had expressed a voting preference for the CDU/CSU in the first-wave interview. This figure is very close to the 37.8 percent of the total first-wave respondents who favored the CDU/CSU. In general terms, then, panel mortality has very little effect on the representative-ness of panel waves.

Table A.6. Panel mortality and panel bias, 1969–1976.

Response	1969		1972			1976		
	First-wave responses, full sample	First-wave responses, second wave	First-wave responses, full sample	First-wave responses, second wave	First-wave responses, third wave	First-wave responses, full sample	First-wave responses, second wave	First-wave responses, third wave
Economic satisfaction	82.4%	83.0%	61.1%	61.3%	62.4%	57.5%	58.2%	59.1%
High interest in politics	16.7	15.9	45.4	45.6	46.7	48.0	48.6	49.7
Voted in last election	89.3	90.2	86.6	87.0	87.8	87.8	89.3	90.1
CDU/CSU voters	37.8	39.9	32.5	32.5	31.7	38.0	39.0	39.7
High education	6.4	5.9	8.9	8.2	7.7	13.4	11.8	10.2
Male	46.3	45.6	42.6	41.9	42.9	49.9	49.6	48.8
(N)	(1158)	(766)	(2052)	(1603)	(1222)	(2076)	(1529)	(1196)

Constructed Measures

THE PURPOSE OF THIS APPENDIX is to describe the major constructed indices and recoded variables used throughout the volume. In many instances various scaling procedures were explored before a final decision was made. These explorations were guided by several criteria. The primary concern was that constructed measures should be reliable and valid indicators of the underlying concept. Both of these properties were tested by internal and external checks on the data. In addition, the longitudinal research design stressed cross-temporal comparability as a major requirement of the indicators. In practical terms this meant that otherwise acceptable indicators from a single timepoint were passed over in favor of measures that were available over time. Finally, wherever possible, cross-nationally comparable indicators were developed so that these findings could be tied into a larger body of behavioral research. In several instances comparability was maximized because the German surveys adopted questions from the Michigan election study series.

This appendix documents only the variables drawn from the ten German surveys archived by the ICPSR, ZA, and ZUMA (see appendix A); other data analyzed in this volume are not discussed here but are documented where they are used. Documentation is based upon the datasets distributed by the ICPSR and ZA. Question wording, responses, and frequency distributions are presented when they are needed to explain the construction of variables. Additional details on question wording, the original German language questionnaires, and code categories are available from the ICPSR and ZA codebooks for these surveys. Frequency distributions in this appendix refer to the unweighted samples. Distributions for the three 1961 surveys exclude respondents from Berlin in order to maximize comparability with the other surveys.

Social Characteristics

Generation   The classification of generations is based upon the historical period during which the respondent reached the age of fifteen (fourteen years during the Third Reich because of its more intensive socialization efforts). It is presumed that at this age the respondents were maximally influenced by the events and forces of their environment.

Until 1969 the surveys generally record age in groups of five-year intervals, which makes the coding of generations somewhat imprecise. Since 1969 the respondent's exact age has been recorded in each survey. The resulting generational units are defined by the year of birth in each study as follows:

Generation	1953	1961	1965	1969–1976
Wilhelmine (1918 and earlier)	–1908	–1901	–1905	–1903
Weimar (1919–1932)	1909–1923	1902–1916	1906–1915	1904–1917
Third Reich (1933–1945)	1924–1928	1917–1931	1916–1930	1918–1931
Early FRG (1946–1955)	1929–1935	1932–1940	1931–1940	1932–1940
Late FRG (1956–1965)	—	—	1941–1944	1941–
Later FRG (1966 on)	—	—	—	1951–

The resulting percentage distributions of generation in these surveys are as follows: (in this and succeeding tabulations, the surveys for 1961, 1965, and 1969 appear in chronological order: for 1961—7099, 7100, 7101; 1965—7103, 7105; and 1969—7098, 7108).

	1953	1961	1961	1961	1965	1965	1969	1969	1972	1976
Wilhelmine	44.9%	20.9%	20.8%	21.3%	20.1%	20.2%	15.3%	16.3%	13.3%	6.9%
Weimar	31.8	30.6	32.1	31.6	28.1	20.8	25.5	25.0	25.3	20.1
Third Reich	11.0	29.4	29.9	30.5	23.6	31.6	23.7	26.0	24.5	20.9
Early FRG	12.2	19.1	17.1	16.6	20.7	20.6	22.3	19.9	17.7	19.2
Late FRG	—	—	—	—	7.5	6.8	13.2	12.8	19.3	20.7
Later FRG	—	—	—	—	—	—	—	—	—	12.2

Class or Occupation   Social class is based on the occupation of the head of the household. When the respondent was unemployed or retired, former occupation was used where available. Detailed, and closely comparable, occupation codes in each survey have been re-coded into four broad occupation groups for analysis:

Old Middle Class   Free professions, self-employed, owner of a busi-
                    ness
New Middle Class   Salaried employees, clerical workers, civil ser-
                    vants
Workers   Skilled, semiskilled, and unskilled blue-collar
                    workers
Farmers   Farm owners and farm workers

This variable is distributed as follows:

	1953	1961	1961	1961	1965	1965	1969	1969	1972	1976
Old middle	15.2%	11.1%	12.5%	12.5%	12.0%	10.4%	10.2%	10.2%	11.0%	9.8%
New middle	24.1	23.8	22.4	25.4	29.9	31.1	28.1	35.0	34.1	42.5
Workers	45.4	45.8	44.8	41.6	43.1	36.3	40.4	45.6	38.9	33.3
Farmers	13.8	10.1	9.1	10.4	6.1	4.8	5.4	4.2	4.2	3.2
Other;										
missing data	1.2	8.9	11.2	10.0	8.6	17.3	15.7	5.0	11.6	11.2

Education   In all surveys since 1961 the education of the respondent is collapsed into categories: (1) *Volksschule* or less; (2) *Volksschule* plus some vocational training (*Berufsschule*) or some secondary schooling; (3) *Mittlere Reife*; and (4) higher specialized or technical school, *Abitur*, or university training. In the 1953 survey vocational training was not coded separately; consequently these cases are included in category (1). The percentage distribution of this variable across samples is as follows:

	1953	1961	1961	1961	1965	1965	1969	1969	1972	1976
Volksschule	62.6%	45.9%	49.1%	49.0%	39.8%	36.7%	37.2%	35.8%	33.5%	22.4%
Volksschule plus	23.3	45.0	41.0	40.8	43.0	48.1	48.9	31.5	48.1	46.4
Mittlere Reife	8.7	4.4	5.2	5.3	9.9	6.5	7.5	24.9	8.6	19.8
Abitur	4.9	4.7	4.7	4.9	7.3	8.7	6.4	4.9	8.9	10.4
Other;										
missing data	0.3	—	—	—	—	—	—	2.9	0.6	1.1

Income   The income variable is based upon the total family income (in 1965, the income of the head of the household). To adjust for rising affluence and inflation, the raw income variable in each survey has been collapsed into approximate quartiles using the following cutting points (expressed in DM per month):

Quartile	1953	1961	1965	1969	1972	1976
Lowest	−150	−400	−600	−800	−800	−1200
Second	150–249	400–599	600–799	800–999	800–1199	1200–1999
Third	250–399	600–899	800–999	1000–1249	1200–1999	2000–2499
Highest	400–	900–	1000–	1250–	2000–	2500–

This collapsed income measure has the following percentage distributions:

	1953	1961	1961	1961	1965	1965	1969	1969	1972	1976
Lowest	19.2%	16.2%	16.2%	17.7%	24.8%	24.4%	24.6%	28.4%	18.8%	22.1%
Second	22.3	28.9	27.6	25.2	29.6	28.2	23.1	20.2	25.9	30.9
Third	31.2	28.7	28.6	28.4	11.4	17.9	20.2	14.1	35.6	14.8
Highest	21.8	19.2	19.3	20.8	26.2	18.6	30.1	34.0	17.3	19.8
Other; missing data	5.2	6.7	8.3	7.8	7.7	10.9	1.7	3.3	2.1	12.5

Frequency of Church Attendance   This question is asked in varying formats across the series of surveys. For analysis purposes the variable is recoded into three broad categories based upon the following scheme:

Category	1953	1965–1969	1972–1976
Frequently	Frequently	At least weekly	Almost every Sunday
Occasionally	Occasionally	Monthly or several times a year	Now and then or once a year
Never	Never	Annually or less	Less than annually

The percentage distributions of this recoded variable are as follows:

	1953	1965	1965	1969	1969	1972	1976
Frequently	38.1%	32.4%	28.6%	27.3%	22.8%	25.3%	22.4%
Occasionally	49.4	36.0	37.7	36.9	41.7	38.4	39.2
Never	12.7	30.7	33.6	35.4	34.7	35.4	32.1
Other; missing data	—	0.4	—	0.3	0.6	0.7	0.3

Region   Because of the small sample number in several states (*Bundesländer*), the individual states are normally combined into four larger regions:

North	Schleswig-Holstein, Bremen, Hamburg, Lower Saxony
Central	Northrhine-Westphalia
Rhine	Rhineland-Palatinate, Saar, Hesse
South	Baden-Württemberg, Bavaria

The regional distribution of each study is as follows:

	1953	1961	1961	1961	1965	1965	1969	1969	1972	1976
North	22.3%	22.0%	22.1%	20.6%	20.3%	19.8%	20.6%	21.7%	20.5%	22.3%
Central	29.0	28.7	30.5	28.9	30.3	31.3	27.2	28.6	29.8	30.3
Rhine	14.6	18.0	16.7	17.7	18.1	17.2	17.4	18.7	17.3	14.4
South	34.1	31.3	30.6	32.8	31.2	31.6	34.7	30.9	32.5	33.0

Rural or Urban Residence   Based on the population of their place of residence, respondents have been grouped into one of four broad categories: (1) under 2,000 inhabitants (rural); (2) 2,000–19,999; (3) 20,000–99,999; and (4) 100,000 or more inhabitants (urban). The distributions of this variable are as follows:

	1953	1961	1961	1961	1965	1965	1969	1969	1972	1976
Under 2,000 (rural)	33.6%	23.6%	23.9%	26.0%	21.8%	23.8%	23.1%	21.4%	21.2%	16.5%
2,000–19,999	29.9	32.0	32.1	32.9	27.7	29.2	32.0	30.9	27.8	31.0
20,000–99,999	11.2	14.7	14.4	15.4	16.8	16.0	17.6	16.6	16.6	17.8
100,000 or more (urban)	25.4	29.7	29.6	25.7	33.7	31.0	27.4	31.1	34.4	34.6

Social Characteristics Summary Index   This index is derived from MCA analyses predicting two-party vote on the basis of: occupation, income, education, religion, region, and rural or urban residence. The scores on the index are the predicted values from the MCA analyses.

Political Discussion

Nearly every survey includes a slightly different question measuring the frequency of political discussion:

1953 "Do you ever discuss politics?"
1961, 1965 "How is it, do you discuss political affairs with other people?"
1969   "And when did you last talk about politics?"
1972   "Were the parties, the politicians, and the election discussed in your family (with your friends and acquaintances) prior to the election?" (Two separate questions concerning discussions about political subjects with one's family and friends.)

Because the response categories differ between questions; the variable was recoded into a generally comparable three-point scale. Both 1972 questions were combined into a single measure using the respondent's highest rating from either question. The 1976 data in chapter 11 are based on still another question from the 1976 ZUMABUS, which is omitted here. (The ZUMABUS is an omnibus study conducted by the

Zentrum für Umfragen, Methoden and Analysen (ZUMA), Mannheim, in May-June 1976. It is based on a representative sample of Germans over the age of 18, with an N of 2,036.) The categories of the recoded variables are:

Category	1953	1961, 1965	1969	1972
Frequently	Frequently	Almost daily	Today	Frequently
Occasionally	Occasionally	Weekly or occasionally	Weekly or occasionally	Occasionally
Never	Rarely or never	Never	Long time or never	Rarely or never

The distributions of political discussion are presented in chapters 2 and 11.

Political Agenda

Several issue-interest indices have been constructed from the issue-salience questions available in the 1961, 1969, and 1972 surveys. Table B.1 presents the list of issues in each survey, ranked by issue salience.

Old Politics–New Politics Issue Orientations A measure of Old Politics–New Politics issues orientations was constructed from the issue-salience questions described above. Old Politics and New Politics issues were distinguished by their opposite polarity on the second dimension of a principal components analysis. Separate analyses were based on the full set of issues in each survey and the subset of four longitudinally comparable issues: price stability, old age security, support for education, and relations with the United States.

The least-squares (regression) method was used to compute component scores from the factor-score matrix for the full issue set and again for the four core issues. Both resulting indices have standardized values. That is, these indices have a mean of zero and a standard deviation of one. Listwise deletion of missing data was used in extracting the principal components and computing the component scores.

Foreign Policy Issues Indices There are two foreign policy issue indices: issue salience and cooperative-conflictual orientations. These two foreign policy issue dimensions were defined by principal components analyses (chapter 5). All issues in each study loaded positively on the first component, representing issue salience. Cooperative and conflictual issues were distinguished by their opposite polarity on the second dimension.

Table B.1. Salience ratings for issues, 1961–1972.[a]

July 1961		Nov. 1969		Sept. 1972	
Price stability	(8.72)	Price stability	(8.94)	Price stability	(3.82)
Old-age security	(8.46)	Old-Age security	(8.51)	Law and order	(3.60)
Reunify Germany	(8.40)	Honesty in public life	(8.21)	Old-Age security	(3.59)
Security from Russian attack	(7.89)	Reduce taxes	(7.57)	Protection against terrorist attacks	(3.56)
Improved economy	(7.69)	Security from Russian attack	(7.31)	Health insurance	(3.55)
Honesty in public life	(7.61)	Improve educational facilities	(7.18)	Just taxes	(3.45)
Reduce taxes	(7.51)	Reunify Germany	(7.14)	Environmental protection	(3.35)
				Extend educational facilities	(3.21)
Relations with U.S.	(7.11)	Relations with U.S.	(6.95)	Relations with West	(3.14)
Relations with USSR	(6.53)	Relations with USSR	(6.35)	Relations with East	(3.08)
Housing construction	(6.49)	Codetermination	(5.75)	Better housing	(2.94)
European unity	(6.48)	Abolish church tax	(4.94)	Military security	(2.85)
Improved schools	(5.89)	Lower voting age	(3.98)	Agricultural representation	(2.69)
Nuclear questions	(5.37)	Reduce draft	(3.95)	Abortion on demand	(2.68)
Shortening hours	(4.98)	Recognize GDR	(3.91)	Relations with China	(2.58)
Aid underdeveloped countries	(4.41)	Redefine states	(3.54)	Gastarbeiter rights	(2.24)

a. Issues are ranked by their average issue salience. In 1961 and 1969, salience was measured on a scale running from 1 (least important) to 11 (most important). In 1972 a different instrument was used, running from 1 (completely unimportant) to 4 (very important). Issue salience responses were usually given by over 90% of each sample, varying slightly from issue to issue.

A least-squares (regression) method was used to compute component scores from the factor-score matrix. Both resulting indices have standardized values. That is, these issue indices have a mean of zero and a standard deviation of one. Listwise deletion of missing data was used in extracting the principal components and computing component scores.

Partisan Attitudes

Partisanship   Since 1961 a series of scalometers, or feeling measures, has been available to construct a comparable indicator for all of the subsequent surveys. See chapter 8 at note 25 for a discussion of the scalometers.

The direction of partisanship was determined from the scores the respondent gave to the SPD, CDU/CSU, or FDP. Respondents preferring the FDP were given missing-data scores and deleted from the analysis of partisanship. Otherwise, respondents were coded as SPD or CDU/CSU partisans depending on which party received the higher score; or they were coded as nonpartisans if both major parties received the same evaluation. The strength component of partisanship was determined by the absolute value of the scalometer for the preferred party. Scores of +5 define strong partisans, +4 a weak partisan, and +3 and below a partisan leaner. The distribution of partisan types is given in chapters 8 and 11.

Old Politics Issue Competence   This measure is based upon the perceived competence of the major parties in dealing with two Old Politics issues: old age security and price stability. Each issue is trichotomized into: (1) SPD more competent; (2) mixed responses (neither, both, don't know, FDP, and so on); and (3) CDU/CSU more competent. The two issues were combined to form a single three-point scale based on the coding procedure illustrated in Figure B.1.

The percentage distribution of this scale in each survey is as follows:

	1961	*1965*	*1969*	*1972*
SPD	32.3%	35.9%	51.0%	38.5%
Mixed	30.8	25.9	21.8	29.8
CDU/CSU	36.9	38.1	27.2	31.6

New Politics Issue Competence   New Politics issue competence is based upon two issues: support for education and relations with the

Figure B.1. Coding procedure for Old Politics issue competence.

Issue B \ Issue A	SPD	Mixed	CDU/CSU
SPD	SPD	SPD	Mixed
Mixed	SPD	Mixed	CDU/CSU
CDU/CSU	Mixed	CDU/CSU	CDU/CSU

United States. The indicator construction procedure was identical to that followed for Old Politics issue competence. The percentage distributions are as follows:

	1961	*1965*	*1969*	*1972*
SPD	10.2%	23.0%	26.9%	34.6%
Mixed	30.4	35.8	41.5	39.9
CDU/CSU	59.4	41.2	31.6	25.5

Overall Issue Competence This measure is based upon a combination of the Old Politics and New Politics subindices described above. The three-point scales were added in order to give equal weight to both issue domains. This variable has the following distribution in each survey:

	1961	*1965*	*1969*	*1972*
SPD	8.4%	17.8%	24.5%	26.8%
—	10.2	16.6	21.5	16.0
—	32.3	21.2	21.5	25.5
—	17.3	16.2	13.3	13.0
CDU/CSU	31.8	28.2	19.0	19.8

Notes

Introduction

1. S. M. Lipset, *Political Man* (Garden City: Doubleday, 1960); Charles Tilly, ed., *The Formations of National States in Western Europe* (Princeton: Princeton University Press, 1975); S. M. Lipset and Stein Rokkan, eds., *Party Systems and Voter Alignments* (New York: Free Press, 1967).

2. Daniel Bell, *The Coming of Post-Industrial Society* (New York: Basic Books, 1973); Zbigniew Brzezinski, *Between Two Ages* (New York: Viking, 1970); Ronald Inglehart, *The Silent Revolution* (Princeton: Princeton University Press, 1977); Seymour M. Lipset, "The Changing Class Structure and Contemporary European Politics," *Daedalus,* 93 (Winter 1964), 271–303; Robert Lane, "The Politics of Consensus in an Age of Affluence," *American Political Science Review,* 59 (December 1965), 874–895.

3. Franz Urban Pappi, "Sozialstruktur und Politische Konflikte in der Bundesrepublik" (Habilitationsschrift, Cologne, 1976); Inglehart, *Silent Revolution,* chap. 1.

4. Alvin Toffler, *Future Shock* (New York: Random House, 1970).

5. Norman Nie, G. Bingham Powell, and Kenneth Prewitt, "Social Structure and Political Participation," *American Political Science Review,* 63 (June and September 1969), 361–378 and 808–832; Karl Deutsch, "Social Mobilization and Political Development," *American Political Science Review* 55 (September 1961), 493–515.

6. Lipset and Rokkan, *Party Systems,* chap. 1; Inglehart, *Silent Revolution,* chaps. 7, 8.

7. Bell, *Post-industrial Society;* Ronald Inglehart and Samuel Barnes, "Affluence, Individual Values and Social Change," in Burkhard Strumpel, ed., *Subjective Elements of Well-being* (Paris; OECD, 1974), 153–184; Ronald Inglehart, "Socioeconomic Change and Human Value Priorities," in Samuel Barnes and Max Kaase et al., *Political Action* (Beverly Hills: Sage Publications, 1979), 305–342.

8. Inglehart, *Silent Revolution;* Kai Hildebrandt and Russell Dalton, "The New Politics," in Max Kaase and Klaus von Beyme, eds., *German*

317

Political Studies: Elections and Parties (London: Sage Publications, 1978), 69–96; Warren Miller and Teresa Levitin, *Leadership and Change* (Cambridge: Winthrop, 1976); Lane, "Politics of Consensus."

9. Readers interested in placing this book in the wider context of longitudinal studies of political behavior are advised to consult: David Butler and Donald Stokes, *Political Change in Britain* (New York: St. Martin's, 1974); Norman Nie, Sidney Verba, and John Petrocik, *The Changing American Voter* (Cambridge: Harvard University Press, 1976).

10. There are a number of good histories of Germany. Two have proved particularly useful in the development of the following brief historical sketch: Hajo Holborn, *A History of Modern Germany, 1840–1945* (New York: Knopf, 1970); and Kurt Reinhardt, *Germany: 2000 Years* (New York: Ungar, 1961). In addition the historical discussions in the following standard texts provide a useful introduction to German politics: Arnold Heidenheimer and Donald Kommers, *The Governments of Germany* (New York: Crowell, 1975); Lewis Edinger, *Politics in West Germany* (Boston: Little, Brown, 1977); David Conradt, *The German Polity* (New York: Longman, 1978); and John Herz, *The Government of Germany* (New York: Harcourt, Brace and Jovanovich, 1972). Finally, Ralf Dahrendorf's interpretation of German history is valuable in integrating the historical events: *Society and Democracy in Germany* (New York: Doubleday, 1967). A particularly stimulating interpretation of the importance of the sequencing of historical and social changes is Barrington Moore, *Social Origins of Dictatorship and Democracy* (Boston: Beacon Press, 1967).

11. Dahrendorf, *Society and Democracy,* p. 61.

12. Several institutional factors also contributed to this consensus. First, the 5 percent clause set an electoral hurdle for participation in the Bundestag that minor extremist parties had difficulty in surmounting. Second, based on provisions in the Basic Law concerning support for democratic principles, the Constitutional Court outlawed the SRP (neo-Nazi Socialist Reich Party) in 1952, and the KPD (Communist Party of Germany) in 1956.

13. Douglas Chalmers, *The Social Democratic Party of Germany* (New Haven: Yale University Press, 1964); Lewis Edinger and Douglas Chalmers, "Overture or Swan Song," *Antioch Review,* 20 (1960), 163–175.

14. There has been some reappearance of extremist parties in recent years: the neo-Nazi NPD (National Democratic Party of Germany) in 1966–1969, and the DKP (German Communist Party) since 1972. However, neither of these parties has passed the 5 percent hurdle and won Bundestag representation.

15. On the 1969 election see the special issue of *Comparative Politics,* 2 (July 1970).

16. See Heidenheimer and Kommers, *Governments of Germany,* p. 44; and Edinger, *Politics in West Germany,* p. 43. For a more detailed examination of economic trends, see chapter 4.

17. Heidenheimer and Kommers, *Governments of Germany,* chap. 2; Edinger, *Politics in West Germany,* chap. 3.

18. Statistisches Bundesamt, *Statistisches Jahrbuch der Bundesrepublik Deutschland, 1979* (Wiesbaden, 1980).

19. Edinger, *Politics in West Germany*, p. 47. See also Statistisches Bundesamt, *Statistisches Jahrbuch* for 1978 figures.

20. Bell, *Post-industrial Society*; Brzezinski, *Between Two Ages*.

21. Hildebrandt and Dalton, "New Politics"; Inglehart, *Silent Revolution*.

22. Quoted in T. Allen Lambert, "Generations and Change," *Youth and Society*, 4 (September 1972), 23.

23. Karl Mannheim, "The Problem of Generations," in his *Essays on the Sociology of Knowledge* (New York: Oxford University Press, 1952), 276–332.

24. On political socialization research see Stanley Renshon, ed., *The Handbook of Political Socialization* (New York: Macmillan, 1977); Kenneth Dawson et al., *Political Socialization* (Boston: Little, Brown, 1977); Robert Weissberg, *Political Learning, Political Choice and Democratic Citizenship* (Englewood Cliffs: Prentice Hall, 1974). For discussions of early learning experiences see, among others: David Easton and Jack Dennis, *Children in the Political System* (New York: McGraw Hill, 1969); Robert Hess and Judith Torney, *The Development of Political Attitudes in Children* (Chicago: Aldine, 1967); Fred Greenstein, *Children and Politics* (New Haven: Yale University Press, 1965); M. Kent Jennings, "The Variable Nature of Generational Conflict: Some Examples from West Germany," *Comparative Political Studies*, 9 (July 1976), 171–188.

25. Kendall Baker, "Generational Differences in the Role of Party Identification in German Political Behavior," *American Journal of Political Science*, 22 (February 1978), 106–129.

26. For example, M. Kent Jennings and Richard Niemi, *The Political Character of Adolescence* (Princeton: Princeton University Press, 1974); Joseph Adelson and Robert O'Neil, "The Growth of Political Ideas in Adolescence," *Journal of Personality and Social Psychology*, 4 (1966), 295–306. For discussion of generational cutting points in the German context that are similar to the one used here see Derek Urwin, "Germany: Continuity and Change in Electoral Politics," in Richard Rose, ed., *Electoral Behavior* (New York: Free Press, 1974), pp. 109–170; M. Rainer Lepsius, "Wahlverhalten, Parteien und politische Spannungen," *Politische Vierteljahresschrift* 14 (June 1973), 295–314; Philip Converse, "Of Time and Partisan Stability," *Comparative Political Studies*, 2 (July 1969), 139–171.

27. For empirical evidence on the actual attitudes of German political elites see: Samuel Eldersveld, Ronald Inglehart, and Robert Putnam, eds., *Elite Political Culture* (forthcoming); Jeff Fishel, "On the Transformation of Ideology in European Political Systems," *Comparative Political Studies*, 4 (January 1972), 406–437; Karl Deutsch and Lewis Edinger, *Germany Rejoins the Powers* (Stanford: Stanford University Press, 1959); Karl Deutsch et al., *France, Germany and the Western Alliance* (New York: Scribner, 1967); Rudolf Wildenmann, *Eliten in der Bundesrepublik* (Unpublished volume of tables, Mannheim, 1968; Ursula Hoffmann-Lange, et al. *Konsens und Konflikt zwischen Führungsgruppen in der Bundesrepublik Deutschland* (Frankfurt: Peter Lang, 1980).

28. Erwin Scheuch, "The Cross-cultural Use of Sample Surveys," in Stein Rokkan, ed., *Comparative Research across Cultures and Nations* (Paris:

Mouton, 1968); also see Stein Rokkan et al., *Comparative Survey Analysis* (New York: McKay, 1970); Robert Holt and John. Turner, eds., *The Methodology of Comparative Research* (New York: Free Press, 1970).

29. Peter Merkl, "Trends in German Political Science," *American Political Science Review*, 71 (September 1977), 1097–1108.

30. Gabriel Almond and Sidney Verba, *The Civic Culture* (Princeton: Princeton University Press, 1963). For excellent summaries of more recent evidence see David Conradt, "Changing German Political Culture," in Gabriel Almond and Sidney Verba, eds., *The Civic Culture Revisited* (Boston: Little, Brown, 1980), 212–272; and Martin and Sylvia Greiffenhagen, *Ein Schwieriges Vaterland* (Munich: Paul List, 1979).

1. Legitimizing a System

1. Walter Stahl, ed., *Education for Democracy in West Germany* (New York: Frederick Praeger, 1961); Walter Stahl, ed., *The Politics of Postwar Germany* (New York: Frederick Praeger, 1963); Harold Zink, *The United States in Germany, 1944–1955* (Princeton: Van Nostrand, 1957).

2. Anna Merrit and Richard Merritt, *Public Opinion in Occupied Germany* (Urbana: University of Illinois Press, 1970); Richard Merritt and Anna Merritt, *Public Opinion in Semi-Sovereign Germany* (Urbana: University of Illinois Press, forthcoming).

3. Gabriel Almond and Sidney Verba, *The Civic Culture* (Princeton: Princeton University Press, 1963); see also Lewis Edinger, *Politics in West Germany*, 2d ed. (Boston: Little, Brown, 1977); Ralf Dahrendorf, *Society and Democracy in Germany* (Garden City: Doubleday, 1967); Sidney Verba, "Germany: The Remaking of Political Culture," in Lucian Pye and Sidney Verba, eds., *Political Culture and Political Development* (Princeton: Princeton University Press, 1965).

4. Steven Warnecke, "The Future of Right Extremism in West Germany," *Comparative Politics*, 2 (July 1970), 646.

5. Kurt Sontheimer, *The Government and Politics of West Germany* (New York: Frederick Praeger, 1972), p. 65.

6. Almond and Verba, *Civic Culture*; Pye and Verba, *Political Culture*.

7. Almond and Verba, *Civic Culture*, p. 101.

8. David Conradt, "Changing German Political Culture," in Gabriel Almond and Sidney Verba, eds., *The Civic Culture Revisited* (Boston: Little, Brown, 1980), 212–272. Conradt's chapter is also an excellent synthesis of other recent research on German political culture. Another extensive compilation of material on German political culture is Martin and Sylvia Greiffenhagen, *Ein Schwieriges Vaterland* (Munich: Paul List, 1979).

9. David Easton, *A Systems Analysis of Political Life* (New York: John Wiley, 1965).

10. Ibid. It should be noted, however, that recent research raises doubts about the possibility of distinguishing empirically between these objects. See Edward Muller and Thomas Jukam, "On the Meaning of Political Support," *American Political Science Review*, 71 (December 1977), 1561–1595.

11. Conradt, "Changing German Political Culture," p. 222.

12. See G. R. Boynton and Gerhard Loewenberg, "The Development of Public Support for Parliament in Germany, 1951–1959," *British Journal of Political Science,* 3 (April 1973), 169–189; G. R. Boynton and Gerhard Loewenberg, "The Decay of Support for the Monarchy and the Hitler Regime in the Federal Republic of Germany," *British Journal of Political Science,* 4 (October 1974), 453–488; David Conradt, "West Germany: A Remade Political Culture?" *Comparative Politics,* 7 (July 1974), 222–238; David Conradt and Dwight Lambert, "Party System, Social Structure and Competitive Politics in West Germany," *Comparative Politics,* 7 (October 1974), 61–86; Bradley Richardson, "Democratic Attitudes in the Federal Republic of Germany" (Manuscript, Ohio State University).

13. For discussions of the changing German party system, see Edinger, *Politics,* and David Conradt, *The German Polity* (New York: Longman, 1978).

14. For statistics on these and other economic matters, see Arno Poller, *Zahlenspiegel zur Politik, 74* (Stuttgart: Bonn Aktuell, 1974); and chapter 4 of this study.

15. For discussion of political satisfaction, see Russell Dalton, "The Quality of Life and Political Satisfaction," (Ph.D. diss., University of Michigan, 1978); Ronald Inglehart, "Political Dissatisfaction and Mass Support of Social Change in Advanced Industrial Societies," *Comparative Political Studies,* 9 (October 1977), 455–472; and Angus Campbell et al., *The Quality of American Life* (New York: Russell Sage, 1976).

16. Inglehart, "Political Dissatisfaction."

17. Almond and Verba, *Civic Culture;* Norman Nie, G. Bingham Powell, and Kenneth Prewitt, "Social Structure and Political Participation" *American Political Science Review,* 63 (June and September 1969), 361–378 and 808–832; Philip Converse, "Change in the American Electorate," in Angus Campbell and Philip Converse, eds., *The Human Meaning of Social Change* (New York: Russell Sage, 1972); Angus Campbell et al., *The American Voter* (New York: John Wiley, 1961), esp. pp. 515–519; and Angus Campbell, Gerald Gurin, and Warren Miller, *The Voter Decides* (Evanston: Row, Peterson, 1954).

18. Almond and Verba, *Civic Culture.*

19. Nie, Powell, and Prewitt, "Social Structure."

20. Almond and Verba, *Civic Culture,* p. 481.

21. George Balch, "Multiple Indicators in Survey Research: The Concept 'Sense of Political Efficacy,' " *Political Methodology,* 1 (Spring 1974), 4.

22. Converse, "American Electorate."

23. Conradt has demonstrated an increase in another set of democratic norms by noting that belief in the responsiveness of popularly elected leaders increased significantly between 1951 and 1970. He reports similar increases in support for a multiparty system and freedom of expression, and concludes that "basic agreement" or "consensus" on these democratic rules of the game has been achieved in the Federal Republic. See Conradt, "West Germany."

24. Samuel Barnes and Max Kaase et al., *Political Action* (Beverly Hills: Sage Publications, 1979); this finding might also imply that the notion that the act of voting satisfies the citizen's obligation remains quite pervasive.

25. Ronald Inglehart and Jacques-René Rabier, *The 1973 European Communities Study* (Ann Arbor: Interuniversity Consortium for Political and Social Research [ICPSR], 1977); see also Max Kaase and Alan Marsh, Political Action: A Theoretical Perspective," in Barnes and Kaase et al., *Political Action,* pp. 27–56.

26. Converse, "American Electorate." Admittedly, American feelings of political efficacy have suffered a marked decline in the past decade or so as German feelings of efficacy have increased. Still, few observers of American politics consider the republic threatened by the present levels of political efficacy.

27. Almond and Verba, *Civic Culture*; Adam Przeworski and Jacob Teune, *The Logic of Comparative Social Inquiry* (New York: John Wiley, 1970).

28. See Kurt Becker, "The Development of Domestic Politics," in Stahl, ed., *Postwar Germany,* 35–63.

29. See Karl Bracher, *The German Dictatorship* (New York: Frederick Praeger, 1970); Karl Jaspers, *Wohin treibt die Bundesrepublik* (Munich: Piper, 1966); Almond and Verba, *Civic Culture;* and Warnecke, "Right Extremism."

30. Boynton and Loewenberg, "Public Support"; and Conradt, "West Germany."

31. Converse, "American Electorate."

32. Seymour Martin Lipset, *Political Man* (Garden City: Doubleday, 1960).

33. Robert Lane, *Political Life* (New York: Free Press, 1959). Findings by Klingemann and Pappi suggest that this general situation may lead higher-status individuals to display greater support for the prevailing political system, whether it is democratic or authoritarian. See Hans Klingemann and Franz Urban Pappi, *Politischer Radikalismus* (Munich and Vienna: Oldenbourg Verlag, 1972).

34. Max Kaase, "Demokratische Einstellungen in der Bundesrepublik Deutschland," in Rudolf Wildenmann, ed., *Sozialwissenschaftliches Jahrbuch für Politik* (Munich: Guenter Olzog, 1971); Max Kaase, "Determinants of Political Mobilization for Students and Non-academic Youth" (Paper presented at the International Sociological Association World Congress, Varna, Bulgaria, 1970).

35. Kendall Baker, "Political Alienation and the German Youth," *Comparative Political Studies,* 3 (July 1970), 117–130; Kendall Baker, "Political Participation, Political Efficacy and Socialization in Germany," *Comparative Politics,* 6 (October 1973), 73–98.

36. M. Kent Jennings, "The Variable Nature of Generational Conflict: Some Examples from West Germany," *Comparative Political Studies,* 9 (July 1976), 171–188; M. Kent Jennings and Rolf Jansen, "Die Jugendlichen in der Bundesrepublik," *Politische Vierteljahresschrift,* 17 (September 1976), 317–343.

37. Past research has often inferred the importance of these potential causal factors without explicitly and empirically testing the relationships. For example, Almond and Verba never directly correlate indicators of system and

output satisfaction in order to verify that output orientation is an important source of the German public's support for their system. Other research has separately examined one or a few predictors, but without simultaneously assessing either the full range of potentially relevant sources of system support and civic norms, or the independent impact of each source. Since many of the causal factors are interrelated, a partial test leaves unclear what the true weight of each factor would have been if all relevant predictors had been considered. Finally, past research has provided little guidance on how—and indeed, if—the attitudinal sources vary across the three levels of political orientations discussed in this chapter: support for the authorities, support for the regime, and the sense of political efficacy. It is particularly important that the last omission be corrected because the source of political support and political efficacy defines the significance of these opinions for the political system. Since only the 1972 study contained all of the necessary variables, this analysis is confined to this timepoint.

38. See chapter 8 and appendix B for details on the construction of this scale and the properties of German partisanship.

39. See appendix B for the construction of this measure.

40. In these analyses, the political efficacy items were converted into a simple additive index. This decision was based on related factor analyses, which yielded essentially one-dimensional solutions not only in 1972 but also in 1969. The numbers (1) and (2) after dates indicate factors 1 and 2.

	1969(1)	1969(2)	1972(1)	1972(2)
Politics complex	0.66	0.56	0.68	0.49
No say	.77	− 0.03	.79	.04
Voting	.66	− .63	.64	− .72
Officials	.61	.10	.70	.13
Eigenvalue	1.98	.73	1.99	.77

41. Normally, we have avoided comparisons between causal effects based on standardized statistics because of several problems that are noted in the literature. But in this case the different scaling of dependent variables necessitated the use of standardized measures.

42. See chapter 5 for a discussion of foreign policy in German politics.

43. To underline this point, it should be noted that the standard set of predictors is significantly more successful in predicting satisfaction with the authorities $(R = 0.75)$ and political efficacy $(R = 0.40)$ than in predicting support for the regime $(R = 0.31)$.

44. Cf. Converse, "American Electorate."

45. Nevertheless, though age is an important predictor of efficacy in 1972, over-time data presented in the next chapter indicate that generational differences in political efficacy have actually declined.

46. One further bit of evidence that other factors are involved is the increase in political efficacy with education, income, and generations over time. For example, 19 percent of those with an *Abitur* felt voting was the only way they could influence the government in 1959, whereas by 1972 these feelings of efficacy had appeared among 48 percent of this group. Further support for this

hypothesis is drawn from Converse's discussion of decreasing efficacy in the American context, which argues many of these same points in reverse; that is, the confusion and uncertainties of American politics in the sixties, rather than dissatisfaction with policy outputs, led to the decline in efficacy. See Converse, "American Electorate."

2. The Involved Electorate

1. Sidney Verba and Norman Nie, *Participation in America* (New York: Harper and Row, 1972), p. 1.

2. Gabriel Almond and Sidney Verba, *The Civic Culture* (Princeton: Princeton University Press, 1963); Lewis Edinger, *Politics in West Germany* (Boston: Little, Brown, 1977); Kurt Sontheimer, *The Government and Politics of West Germany* (New York: Frederick Praeger, 1972).

3. Verba and Nie, *Participation in America,* chaps. 3, 4; Sidney Verba, Norman Nie, and Jae-on Kim, "The Modes of Democratic Participation," *Comparative Politics Series,* Sage Professional Paper no. 01–013 (Beverly Hills: Sage Publications, 1971); Sidney Verba et al., "The Modes of Participation," *Comparative Political Studies,* 6 (July 1973), 235–250.

4. Sidney Verba, Norman Nie, and Jae-on Kim, *Participation and Political Equality* (Cambridge: Cambridge University Press, 1978).

5. Ibid.

6. Ibid.

7. Discussing politics with other people was also a crucial element in Almond and Verba's original characterization of German political culture as nonparticipatory. Therefore, tracing the growth of political discussion over time can determine if this vital aspect of the German political culture has indeed changed. See Almond and Verba, *Civic Culture.*

8. For the construction of this measure and the question wording, see appendix B.

9. Almond and Verba, *Civic Culture,* p. 115.

10. Thomas Ellwein et al., *Politische Beteiligung in der Bundesrepublik Deutschland* (Goettingen: Schwarz, 1975); Heinz Crossmann, ed., *Bürgerinitiativen: Schritte zur Veraenderung* (Frankfurt: Fischer, 1971); Hanspeter Knirsch and Friedhelm Nickolmann, *Die Chance der Bürgerinitiativen* (Wuppertal: Hammer, 1976).

11. The 1972 measure combines two separate items asked in a format somewhat different from that used in other years. The 1972 items do not focus solely on the involvement of the respondent, but ask instead about the frequency of discussion in the respondent's environment. To some extent this may contribute to the increase in political involvement between 1969 and 1972, except that other strictly comparable indicators (e.g., political interest) also show an increase. See appendix B for details on indicator construction in 1972.

12. Max Kaase, "Die Bundestagswahl 1972: Probleme und Analysen," *Politische Vierteljahresschrift,* 14 (June 1973), 145–190; David Conradt and Dwight Lambert, "Party System, Social Structure and Competitive Politics in

Germany: An Ecological Analysis of the 1972 Election," *Comparative Politics* 7 (October 1974), 61–86.

13. The following tabulation shows the percentage of citizens discussing politics in the eight member nations of the European Community. Data were drawn from Ronald Inglehart and Jacques-René Rabier, *The 1973 European Communities Study* (Ann Arbor: ICPSR, 1977).

Germ.	France	Belg.	Neths.	Italy	Den.	Eire	Brit.
81	54	45	60	59	74	63	65

14. Elisabeth Noelle and Erich Peter Neumann, eds., *Jahrbuch der Öffentlichen Meinung 1965–1967* (Allensbach: Verlag für Demoskopie, 1967), p. 213, reprinted in David Conradt, *The German Polity* (New York: Longman, 1978), p. 57.

15. Verba and Nie, *Participation in America,* chap. 8.

16. Norman Nie, G. Bingham Powell, and Kenneth Prewitt, "Social Structure and Political Participation," *American Political Science Review,* 63 (June and September 1969), 361–378, 808–832.

17. See chapter 3 for a discussion of the growth of political information sources over time.

18. Nie, Powell, and Prewitt, "Social Structure"; Karl Deutsch, "Social Mobilization and Political Development," *American Political Science Review,* 55 (September 1961), 493–514; Daniel Lerner, *The Passing of Traditional Society* (Glencoe: Free Press, 1958); Donald McCrone and Charles Cnudde, "Toward a Communications Theory of Democratic Political Development: A Causal Model," *American Political Science Review,* 61 (March 1967), 72–79.

19. Nie, Powell, and Prewitt, "Social Structure,"; Almond and Verba, *Civic Culture*; Verba and Nie, *Participation in America.*

20. See appendix B for the construction and coding of these two items.

21. Frank Andrews, James Morgan, and John Sonquist, *Multiple Classification Analysis* (Ann Arbor: Institute for Social Research, 1967).

22. See appendix B for the construction and coding of this variable.

23. The reversal of several trends in relationships apparent in the 1972 data may reflect the different focus of the question, which asked about the frequency of discussion within the respondent's environment rather than explicitly asking if the respondent was involved. This slightly different focus may have weakened the correlation between individual attributes and involvement.

24. Nie, Powell, and Prewitt, "Social Structure," p. 813; Hans Klingemann and William Wright, "Levels of Conceptualization in the American and the German Mass Public" (Paper presented at the Workshop on Political Cognition, University of Georgia, May 1974).

25. For example, see Neal Cutler, "Toward a Generational Conceptualization of Political Socialization," in David Schwartz and Sandra Schwartz, eds., *New Directions in Political Socialization* (New York: Free Press, 1975), 254–288; M. Kent Jennings, "The Variable Nature of Generational Conflict: Some Examples from West Germany," *Comparative Political Studies,* 9 (July 1976), 171–188; M. Kent Jennings and Rolf Jansen, "Die

Jugendlichen in der Bundesrepublik," *Politische Vierteljahresschrift*, 17 (September 1976), 317–343; Ronald Inglehart, *The Silent Revolution* (Princeton: Princeton University Press, 1977).

26. David Easton and Jack Dennis, *Children in the Political System* (New York: McGraw Hill, 1969); Robert Weissberg, *Political Learning, Political Choice, and Democratic Citizenship* (Englewood Cliffs: Prentice Hall, 1974).

27. Richard Niemi, "Political Socialization," in Jeanne Knutson, ed., *Handbook of Political Psychology* (San Francisco: Jossey Bass, 1973), p. 118.

28. M. Kent Jennings and Richard G. Niemi, *The Political Character of Adolescence* (Princeton: Princeton University Press, 1974), p. 283.

29. Ibid.; chap. 10; Weissberg, *Political Learning*.

30. Verba and Nie, *Participation in America*, chap. 9; Norman Nie, Sidney Verba, and Jae-on Kim, "Political Participation and the Life Cycle," *Comparative Politics*, 6 (April 1974), 319–340; Norval Glenn, "Aging, Disengagement and Opinionation," *Public Opinion Quarterly*, 33 (Spring 1969), 17–33.

31. See appendix B for a description of the construction and coding of these generational units. A conceptual discussion of the importance of generations in the German context is provided in the introductory chapter.

32. Verba and Nie, *Participation in America*, chap. 9; Nie, Verba, and Kim, "Political Participation"; Glenn, "Aging."

33. The per-annum growth coefficient is the slope of a regression line obtained by regressing a cohort's political discussion score (mean) on the year of the survey. This procedure uses data from each timepoint to obtain a weighted estimate of long-term change.

34. Edinger, *Politics*, pp. 29–30.

35. The following tabulation presents the beta coefficients from this MCA analysis:

	1953	1959	1961	1965	1969	1972
Education	0.21	0.29	0.23	0.26	0.27	0.18
Income	.14	.09	.10	.12	.12	.14
Occupation	.05	—	.09	.08	.11	.06
Generation	.08	.04	.10	.05	.09	.16
R	.29	.30	.33	.36	.41	.37
(N)	(3225)	(941)	(1406)	(1278)	(1142)	(1190)

36. Giuseppe DiPalma, *Apathy and Participation* (New York: Free Press, 1970), p. 48.

37. Nie, Powell and Prewitt, "Social Structure."

38. The wording of the various questions is as follows:

1953: "There are matters on which one is not satisfied with the government. If you and your acquaintances did not like something, what could you do against that—possibly not right away, but maybe in the long run?" (Coded "could do something" or "nothing.")

1959: "People like me don't have any say about what the government does." (Coded "disagree" or "agree.")

1965: "Do you think that it is worthwhile for the individual to concern himself with politics and thus to influence political decisions, or is it your opinion that it is not worthwhile for the individual to concern himself with politics since he cannot influence decisions?" (Coded "can influence" or "cannot.")

1972: "People like me don't have any say about what the government does." (Coded "disagree" or "agree.")

39. Other factors that might influence participation levels are largely institutional sources (e.g., group membership, elite activity), and have not been increasing systematically over time in Germany. For a conceptual discussion of the different nature of these explanatory variables, see Verba, Nie, and Kim, *Participation.*

40. Nie, Powell, and Prewitt, "Social Structure," p. 826.

41. The single social-status measure in these analyses was obtained by regressing political discussion against income and education, and then saving the predicted scores as the composite index.

42. Because of the different scaling of the political norms variable, standardized statistics are used in the figure. For a discussion of standardized statistics, see Ronald Schoenberg, "Strategies for Meaningful Comparison," *Sociological Methodology, 1972* (San Francisco: Jossey Bass, 1972), 1–35; and Hubert Blalock, "Causal Inferences, Closed Populations and Measures of Association," *American Political Science Review,* 61 (March 1967), 130–136.

43. Again, the 1972 pattern may reflect the different phrasing of our political-discussion measure, as note 23 explains.

44. The product of both paths provides the following estimates of the indirect social status effects: 1953 = 0.08; 1959 = 0.06; 1965 = 0.03; 1972 = 0.03.

45. These results are not a function of the linear regression model; similar results have been obtained from nonlinear MCA analyses.

46. Noelle-Neumann, ed., *Jahrbuch;* David Conradt, "Changing German Political Culture," in Gabriel Almond and Sidney Verba, eds., *The Civic Culture Revisited* (Boston: Little, Brown, 1980), pp. 212–272; Samuel Barnes and Max Kaase et al., *Political Action* (Beverly Hills: Sage Publications, 1979).

47. P. J. Tichenor, et al., "Mass Media Flow and Differential Growth in Knowledge," *Public Opinion Quarterly,* 34 (Summer 1970), 159–170; Philip Converse, "Public Opinion and Voting Behavior," in Fred Greenstein and Nelson Polsby, eds., *Handbook of Political Science,* IV (Reading: Addison-Wesley, 1975); Philip Converse, "The Nature of Belief Systems in Mass Publics," in David Apter, ed., *Ideology and Discontent* (Glencoe: Free Press, 1964), 206–261.

48. Verba and Nie, *Participation in America,* chaps. 15–20; Susan Hansen, "Participation, Political Structure, and Concurrence," *American Political Science Review,* 69 (December 1975), 1181–1199.

49. Verba and Nie, *Participation in America,* pp. 256–259.

50. Max Kaase and Alan Marsh, "Political Action Repertory," in Barnes and Kaase et al., *Political Action,* p. 146.

51. DiPalma, *Apathy and Participation,* chap. 12.

52. Alvin Toffler, *Future Shock* (New York: Random House, 1970).

53. Barnes and Kaase et al., *Political Action;* Max Kaase, "Bedingun-

gen unkonventionellen politischen Verhaltens in der Bundesrepublik Deutsch-land," *Politische Vierteljahresschrift,* special issue 7 (1976), 184–200.

3. Source of Political Information

1. See Gabriel Almond and Sidney Verba, *The Civic Culture* (Princeton: Princeton University Press, 1963).

2. Throughout this chapter we shall regard obtaining information from media as a passive form of gathering political information and obtaining information from interpersonal interaction as an active process.

3. See Bernard Berelson et al., *Voting* (Chicago: University of Chicago Press, 1954); Joseph Trenaman and Denis McQuail, *Television and the Political Image* (London: Methuen, 1961); Jay Blumler and Denis McQuail, *Television in Politics* (Chicago: University of Chicago Press, 1969); Thomas Patterson and Robert McClure, *Political Advertising: Voter Reactions to Televised Political Commercials* (Princeton: Citizen's Research Foundation, 1973); Steven Chaffee, ed., *Political Communication* (Beverly Hills: Sage Publications, 1975); Sidney Kraus and Dennis Davis, *The Effects of Mass Communication on Political Behavior* (University Park: Pennsylvania State University Press, 1976); Thomas Patterson and Robert McClure, *The Unseeing Eye* (New York: G. P. Putnam's Sons, 1976); Donald Shaw and Maxwell McCombs, *The Emergence of American Political Issues* (St. Paul: West, 1977); Steven Chaffee et al., "Mass Communication in Political Socialization," in Stanley Renshon, ed., *Handbook of Political Socialization* (New York: Free Press, 1977), 223–258; and Jay Blumler et al., "A Three-Nation Analysis of Voters' Attitudes of Election Communication," *European Journal of Political Research,* 6 (1978), 127–156.

4. John Robinson, "Mass Communication and Information Diffusion," in F. G. Kline and P. J. Tichenor, eds., *Current Perspectives in Mass Communication Research* (Beverly Hills: Sage Publications, 1972), p. 74.

5. See P. J. Tichenor et al., "Mass Media Flow and Differential Growth in Knowledge," *Public Opinion Quarterly,* 34, (1970), 159–170.

6. Robinson, "Mass Communication."

7. See Maxwell McCombs, "Mass Communication in Political Campaigns: Information, Gratification and Persuasion," in Kline and Tichenor, eds., *Current Perspectives,* pp. 169–194; Douglas Fuchs and Jock Lyle, "Mass Media Portrayal: Sex and Violence," ibid., pp. 235–264; Leo Bogart, "Warning: The Surgeon General Has Determined That TV Violence Is Moderately Dangerous to Your Child's Mental Health," *Public Opinion Quarterly,* 36 (Winter 1972), 491–571; Michael Robinson, "Public Affairs Television and the Growth of Political Malaise: The Case of the Selling of the Pentagon," *American Political Science Review,* 70 (June 1976), 409–432; Arthur Miller et al., "Type-Set Politics: Impact of Newspapers on Public Confidence," *American Political Science Review,* 73 (March 1979), 67–84; and Michael Robinson, "Prime Time Chic: Between Newsbreaks and Commercials, the Values are L.A. Liberal," *Public Opinion,* 2 (March–May 1979), 42–48.

8. Robinson, "Mass Communication," p. 74.

9. See Walter Weiss, "Effects of Mass Media of Communication," in Gardner Lindzey and E. Aronson, eds., *Handbook of Social Psychology* (Reading: Addison-Wesley, 1969), pp. 77–195.

10. See Steven Chaffee, "The Interpersonal Context of Mass Communication," in Kline and Tichenor, eds., *Current Perspectives,* 95–120. As examples of news items, Chaffee cites Viet Nam, campus demonstrations, and population growth; consumer topics include such things as birth control and fashion.

11. McCombs, "Mass Communication," p. 176.

12. In all years, at least the following interpersonal and media sources were listed: friends, people you work with, and acquaintances; family and relatives; people interested in politics; radio; television; and daily newspapers.

13. There is no doubt that a substantial amount of political information is available in German newspapers and on television. In a comparative study conducted in 1964, for example, Alphons Silbermann found that political information accounted for approximately 45 percent of the total informational programming on German television. This proportion was over twice as large as that devoted to any other kind of information. Moreover, the two German networks ranked first and fourth in presentations of political information among the nine European stations examined. In the case of newspapers, a study conducted in January and February 1965 revealed that coverage of politics varied rather extensively by type of circulation. In national newspapers like *Die Welt,* approximately 38 percent of the coverage was devoted to politics; in regional newspapers like the Kölner *Stadt Anzeiger,* the proportion was about 25 percent; and in local newspapers like the Hellweger *Anzeiger,* only about 15 percent of the total coverage dealt with political questions. For weekly newspapers, coverage of politics is quite similar to that of the national newspapers. In 1963–64, for example, 32.5 percent of *Rheinischen Merkurs* total coverage, excluding advertisements, concerned politics; in the same years, *Die Zeit* devoted 31.7 percent of its coverage, excluding advertisements, to politics. See Alphons Silbermann, *Bildschirm und Wirklichkeit* (Berlin, 1966); DIVO-Institut für Wirtschaftsforschung, Sozialforschung und angewandte Mathematik and INFRATEST, "Politische Information in Fernsehen und Tageszeitung: Ein Vergleich der Angebotssituation beider Medien," in *Rundfunkanstalten und Tageszeitungen: Eine Materialsammlung* (Frankfurt: Arbeitsgemeinschaft der öffentlich-rechtlichen Rundfunkanstalten der Bundesrepublik Deutschland [ARD], 1966), pp. 64–89; Rolf Zoll and Eike Hennig, *Massenmedien und Meinungsbildung* (Munich: Juventa Verlag, 1970), chap. 4: and *Public Opinion* (Bonn: Press and Information Office, 1971).

14. For discussions of the impact of television on German politics, see Elisabeth Noelle-Neumann, *Oeffentlichkeit als Bedrohung* (Freiburg: Karl Alber Verlag, 1977); Elisabeth Noelle-Neumann, "The Dual Climate of Opinion: The Influence of Television in the 1976 West German Federal Election," in Max Kaase and Klaus von Beyme, eds., *Elections and Parties* (Beverly Hills: Sage Publications, 1978), 137–170; Elisabeth Noelle-Neumann, "Return to the Concept of Powerful Mass Media," in H. Eguchi and K. Sata, eds.,

Studies of Broadcasting (Tokyo: Radio and Culture Research Institute, 1973); and Elisabeth Noelle-Neumann, "Voting Behavior in the Television Age: A Socio-psychological Interpretation of the 1972 Federal Election" (Manuscript, Institut für Demoskopie, 1972).

15. See Jürgen Huether, *Sozialisation durch Massenmedien* (Opladen: Westdeutscher Verlag, 1975).

16. See Arno Poller, *Zahlenspiegel zur Politik, 74* (Stuttgart: Bonn Aktuell, 1974).

17. See Huether, *Sozialisation.*

18. See Neil Hollander, "Adolescents and the War: The Sources of Socialization," *Journalism Quarterly,* 48 (Autumn 1971), 472–479; Fuchs and Lyle, "Mass Media Portrayal'; Bogart, "Warning"; Patterson and McClure, *Unseeing Eye;* Robinson, "Public Affairs Television"; and Miller et al., "Type-Set Politics."

19. Walter Weiss, "Mass Media and Social Change," in Bert T. King and Elliott McGinnies, eds., *Attitudes, Conflict and Social Change* (New York: Academic Press, 1972), p. 141.

20. Chaffee, "Interpersonal Context," p. 108.

21. See Lee Becker et al., "The Development of Political Cognitions," in Chaffee, ed., *Political Communication,* pp. 21–64.

22. It was not possible to evaluate, longitudinally, how tolerant respondents were of diverse opinions encountered in interpersonal discussions. However, two questions from the 1969 postelection survey suggest that such tolerance has been growing in Germany in the postwar period, especially among heavy users of interpersonal sources. One question asked respondents to rank six interpersonal sources of information in terms of whose opinions were most important on political matters, while the other asked them to rank the same sources in terms of the extent to which they agreed with these sources on political questions. The responses showed that heavy users, unlike light users, value the opinions of co-workers and friends more than those of relatives (spouse, father, and siblings). But they certainly do not always agree with the political attitudes of these individuals. In short, heavy users of interpersonal sources seem to want to interact with people they do not always agree with.

23. See, for example, Robert Lane, *Political Life* (New York: Free Press, 1959).

24. See Lester Milbrath and M. L. Goel, *Political Participation* (Chicago: Rand McNally, 1977).

25. For general discussions of the impact of television on politics, see Kurt Lang and Gladys Lang, *Politics and Television* (Chicago: Quadrangle Books, 1968); Herbert Asher, *Presidential Elections and American Politics* (Homewood: Dorsey Press, 1976), pp. 222–243: Kraus and Davis, *Mass Communication*; Patterson and McClure, *Unseeing Eye*; and Anne Rawley Saldich, *Electronic Democracy* (New York: Frederick Praeger, 1979).

26. Political interest and political discussion, though related, are not identical. They correlate at 0.61 in 1969.

4. Politics and the Economic Environment

1. This figure is based on the index of German wholesale prices: the index (1913 = 100) was 278,500 in January 1923 and reached 72,600 billion in November 1923. The figures are presented in Karl Hardach, *Wirtschaftsgeschichte Deutschlands im 20. Jahrhundert* (Göttingen: Vandenhoeck and Ruprecht, 1976), p. 27. See also the *Statistischen Jahrbücher für das Deutsche Reich* (Berlin: Statistisches Reichsamt), for 1923 and 1924–25. Since the runaway inflation made statistical accounting difficult, this figure should be seen as illustrative; the point can also be made by citing 50 billion marks as the price for a single newspaper late in 1923.

2. The Nazi's success in reducing unemployment was achieved mainly through "make work" projects and later through the military buildup. See Hardach, *Wirtschaftsgeschichte*; and Werner Kaltefleiter, *Wirtschaft und Politik in Deutschland* (Cologne: Westdeutscher Verlag, 1968).

3. See, for example, Kaltefleiter, *Wirtschaft*, p. 120; Sidney Verba, "Germany: The Re-making of a Political Culture," in Lucian Pye and Sidney Verba, eds., *Political Culture and Political Development* (Princeton: Princeton University Press, 1965); Kurt Sontheimer, *The Government and Politics of West Germany* (New York: Praeger, 1973), pp. 40–53; G. R. Boynton and Gerhard Loewenberg, "Economic Sources of Rising Support for the Regime in Postwar Germany: An Interpretation of a Mathematical Model" (Paper delivered at the Conference on Alienation and System Support, Iowa City, 1975), and by the same authors, "The Development of Public Support for Parliament in Germany, 1951–1959," *British Journal of Political Science*, 3 (April 1973), 169–189.

4. Hardach, *Wirtschaftsgeschichte*, p. 116. For this section we have also drawn on Kaltefleiter, *Wirtschaft*; and Süphan Andic and Jindrich Veverka, "The Growth of Government Expenditure in Germany since the Unification," in *Finanzarchiv*, 23 (1964), 169–278.

5. For the original plan presented to President Roosevelt, see Henry Morgenthau, *Germany Is Our Problem* (New York: Harper, 1945). See also John H. Backer, *Priming the German Economy: American Occupation Policies, 1945–1948* (Durham: North Carolina University Press, 1971).

6. Hardach, *Wirtschaftsgeschichte*, p. 120.

7. See Ossip K. Flechtheim, *Dokumente zur Parteipolitischen Entwicklung in Deutschland seit 1945* (Berlin: Wendler, 1963), III.

8. The quotation is from the "Ahlener Wirtschaftsprogramm" of 1947; see Flechtheim, *Dokumente*, II (our translation).

9. See most of the textbooks on German politics, e.g.: Sontheimer, *Government;* Arnold J. Heidenheimer and Donald Kommers, *The Governments of Germany* (New York: Crowell, 1975).

10. Kaltefleiter, *Wirtschaft*, p. 103 (our translation).

11. Hardach, *Wirtschaftsgeschichte;* and Kaltefleiter, *Wirtschaft*.

12. The figures are based on the Statistisches Bundesamt, *Bevölkerung und Wirtschaft, 1872–1972* (Stuttgart: Kohlhammer, 1972). The comparison

with constructed prewar equivalents for the territory of the present Federal Republic is based on Andic and Veverka, "Government Expenditure."

13. For a long time, West Germany had the third largest Gross National Product in the world, but by 1970 Japan with its own version of an economic miracle surpassed the German economy.

14. The comparisons are based on data in U.S. Department of State, *The Planetary Product in 1974*, Special Report 22 (Washington, D.C.: Department of State, 1975).

15. Bundesministerium für Wirtschaft, *Leistung in Zahlen '75* (Bonn, 1976). The dollar equivalents are based on the current exchange rates for each timepoint.

16. Elisabeth Noelle-Neumann, ed., *Jahrbuch der öffentlichen Meinung, 1968–1973* (Allensbach: Verlag für Demoskopie, 1976). See also Presse- und Informationsamt der Bundesregierung, *Gesellschaftliche Daten 1977* (Bonn, 1978), p. 197.

17. Heidenheimer and Kommers, *Governments of Germany*, pp. 49–53; there are, however, groups of people who do not share equally in the wealth, such as guest workers and the old.

18. Noelle-Neumann and Neumann, eds., *Jahrbücher*; Presse- und Informationsamt, *Gesellschaftliche Daten*, p. 199.

19. The amount of leisure time available to Germans has increased dramatically during the postwar years. However, changes in the work ethic have occurred slowly: even among the youngest workers in 1973 less than a third responded that they would be happy without work; among those sixty years old and older, only 12 percent agreed. See Peter Kmieciak, *Wertstrukturen und Wertwandel in der Bundesrepublik Deutschland* (Berlin, 1976), tables IV-5 and V-3A.

20. Bundesministerium für Wirtschaft, *Leistung*, p. 58; Statistisches Bundesamt, *Bevölkerung*. In addition, housing was upgraded considerably: in 1955, only 11% of all new housing units were built with central heating, and one unit in 7 had neither a shower nor a bath. By 1970, 97% of all new housing units had central heating, and only one new unit in 200 had neither bath nor shower facilities.

21. Statistisches Bundesamt, *Bevölkerung*.

22. See Arnold J. Heidenheimer et al., *Comparative Public Policy*, (New York: St. Martin's, 1975).

23. In simple terms, the GINI Index is based on the deviation of the actually observed distribution of wealth, or any other commodity—the Lorenz curve—over the first, second, . . . tenth decile of the population, from the ideal (equal) distribution, where each tenth of the population would "own" a tenth of the wealth, or other desirable good. The larger the GINI Index, the more unequal the distribution. The comparisons between Germany and the other OECD societies are based on Shail Jain, *Size-Distributions of Incomes: A Compilation of Data* (Washington, D.C.: World Bank, 1975). All cross-national comparisons of economic indicators present potential pitfalls, and this is particularly true for politically sensitive areas, such as income and wealth distributions.

24. See Horst Claus Recktenwald, "Gerechte Einkommens- und Vermögensverteilung," in Richard Löwenthal and Hans Peter Schwarz, eds., *Die Zweite Republik* (Stuttgart: Seewald, 1974), p. 767. The caveat in the previous note applies equally to over-time comparisons, even within the same country.

25. Urs Jaeggi, *Macht und Herrschaft in der Bundesrepublik* (Frankfurt: Fischer, 1969), p. 43.

26. See the various SPD election platforms of the 1950s; Heino Kaack, *Geschichte und Struktur des deutschen Parteiensystems* (Opladen: Westdeutscher Verlag, 1971).

27. Godesberger Programm of the SPD, cited from Flechtheim, *Dokumente* (our translation).

28. The SPD's adoption of the Godesberg program did not occur without internal opposition; however, the opposing voices remained largely silent for much of the 1960s. Only with the recession of 1966–67, and especially in the wake of the student unrest of the sixties and seventies, did the discussion over the desirability of capitalism and the free market economy revive in the SPD. The term capitalism was rarely used in political discussions between 1959 and the mid-1960s, but since then it has become increasingly common in theoretical and programmatic debates in the SPD.

29. The agricultural contribution to the Gross Domestic Product declined from 10.2% to 2.9% between 1950 and 1972; in contrast, the share of the industrial sector increased from 49.6% to 52.1% and that of the tertiary (service) sector from 30.6% to 33.2% during the same timespan. See Bundesministerium für Wirtschaft, *Leistung*.

30. See Daniel Bell, *The Coming of Post-industrial Society* (New York: Basic Books, 1976); Zbigniew Brzezinski, *Between Two Ages* (New York: Viking, 1970); Ronald Inglehart, *The Silent Revolution* (Princeton: Princeton University Press, 1977); J. K. Galbraith, *The New Industrial State* (Boston: Houghton Mifflin, 1967). However, this development is not limited to the Western democracies: many similar points have been made in M. Djilas, *The New Class* (London: Thames, 1957).

31. It will be demonstrated in chapter 6 that a new set of political values is indeed found more often among the new middle class.

32. A very careful study of social mobility and its political effects is contained in David Butler and Donald Stokes, *Political Change in Britain* (New York: St. Martin's, 1969), chap. 5.

33. A good, simple exposition of this relationship is provided in Samuel A. Morley, *The Economics of Inflation* (Hinsdale, Ill: Dryden, 1977).

34. After the currency reform of June 1948, there was an initial steep increase in unemployment, as many workers who had nominally held jobs (with little work or pay involved) in order to qualify for food rations were laid off. See Hardach, *Wirtschaftsgeschichte*, p. 119.

35. Kaltefleiter, *Wirtschaft*, pp. 124–130; Hardach, *Wirtschaftsgeschichte*, p. 119.

36. The correlation between the yearly rates of unemployment and the number of foreign workers is −0.66, and the brief peak in unemployment during the 1966–67 recession (to 2.1%) is mirrored by a dramatic but equally

brief valley in the number of guest workers (-1.2%, or 300,000 workers). See also Andrei S. Markovits and Samantha Kazarinov, "Class Conflict, Capitalism and Social Democracy," *Comparative Politics* 10 (April 1978), 373–387.

37. Cf. OECD, *Main Economic Indicators: Historical Statistics, 1960–1975* (Paris, 1976). Note, however, that unemployment statistics are often not strictly comparable between countries.

38. The original exposition of the Phillips curve is contained as an empirical description in A. W. Phillips, "The Relation between Unemployment and the Rate of Change of Money Wage Rates in the United Kingdom, 1862–1957," *Economica*, 25 (November 1958), 283–299. Our own calculations confirm the negative relationship between unemployment and price stability during the postwar years 1952–1972 in Germany, with a Pearson's r of -0.63. The relationship might be even stronger if the model took into account the curvilinear nature of the relationship. As a result of more recent economic developments, economists have begun to doubt the trade-off nature of this relationship; for details, see Edmund S. Phelps et al., eds., *Microeconomic Foundations of Employment and Inflation Theory* (New York: Norton, 1970).

39. See Douglas A. Hibbs, "Political Parties and Macroeconomic Policy," *American Political Science Review*, 71 (December 1977), 1467–1487.

40. Ibid. See also Ronald G. Bodkin et al., *Price Stability and High Employment: The Options for Canadian Economic Policy* (Ottawa: Economic Council of Canada, 1967); and David Smyth, "Unemployment and Inflation: Across-Country Analyses of the Phillips-Curve," *American Economic Review*, 61 (June, 1971), 426–429, as well as OECD, *Main Economic Indicators*.

41. Max Kaase, "Party Identification and Voting Behavior in the West-German Election of 1969," in Ian Budge, Ivor Crewe, and Donald Farlie, eds., *Party Identification and Beyond* (New York: John Wiley, 1976), pp. 92–93; and Max Kaase, "Determinanten des Wahlverhaltens bei der Bundestagswahl 1969," *Politische Vierteljahresschrift*, 11 (March 1970), 46–110.

42. See Otto Quandt, *Die Anfänger der Bismarckschen Sozialgesetzgebung* (Berlin: Ebering, 1938); and Horst Peters, *Die Geschichte der Sozialversicherung* (Bad Godesberg: Asgard, 1959).

43. Dieter Claessens, Arno Klönne, and Armin Tschoepe, *Sozialkunde der Bundesrepublik Deutschland* (Dusseldorf: Diederichs, 1968), pp. 307–308.

44. *Revenue Statistics of OECD Member Countries, 1965–1971* (Paris: OECD, 1973).

45. See George Katona et al., *Aspirations and Affluence* (New York: McGraw Hill, 1971), pp. 46–59 and 173; Burkhart Strümpel, *Die Krise des Wohlstandes* (Stuttgart: Kohlhammer, 1977). However, such observations are hardly new; in the early eighteenth century Gottfried W. Leibniz noted similar tendencies among his fellow Germans in "Ermahnung an die Teutsche", reprinted in *Wissenschaftliche Beihefte zur Zeitschrift des Allgemeinen Deutschen Sprachvereins*, 29 (1908), pp. 292–312. (This historical note was provided by Susan Wendt-Hildebrandt.)

46. Kaltefleiter, *Wirtschaft*, p. 109.

47. Noelle-Neumann and Neumann, eds., *Jahrbücher*.

48. Germans were also becoming less pessimistic about their future: in

1957, 30% expected to be worse off in the future, but in 1970 that figure had dropped to 18%; see Noelle-Neumann and Neumann, eds., *Jahrbuch, 1968–1973*, p. 357. Moreover, in 1969 (after the 1966–67 recession) even among the one-half of the German population that reported a decrease in economic status in the past five years, only 15% were dissatisfied with their standard of living.

49. Still, in comparison with other Europeans the Germans continue to rank low in self-assessed life satisfaction. See Ronald Inglehart, "Political Dissatisfaction and Mass Support for Social Change in Advanced Industrial Societies," *Comparative Political Studies*, 10 (October 1977), 455–472.

50. Chapter 6 will provide a more comprehensive view, including both foreign policy and nonmaterial domestic issues.

51. These data were collected from various *Jahrbücher*.

52. While such figures are therefore conservative measurements of the public agenda in that they do not immediately reflect new issues, the inclusion or exclusion of code categories by polling agencies is itself an indicator of public concerns.

53. For more detailed breakdowns, see the various *Jahrbücher*.

54. Among the many useful treatments are Angus Campbell et al., *The American Voter* (New York: Wiley, 1960), chap. 14; Butler and Stokes *Political Change*, chap. 18; Edward R. Tufte, *Political Control of the Economy* (Princeton: Princeton University Press, 1978); Kaltefleiter, *Wirtschaft*; Jon Pammet et al., *The 1974 Federal Election: A Preliminary Report*, Carleton Occasional Paper No 4 (Ottawa, 1975); Harold Clarke et al., *Political Choice in Canada* (Toronto: McGraw-Hill Ryerson, 1979), chap. 8; Dieter Roth, "Ökonomische Variablen und Wahlverhalten," *Politische Vierteljahresschrift*, 14 (June 1973), 257–274; Gisela Schnepf and Wolfgang Tschirner, "Wirtschaftserwartungen im Zeitverlauf," in *Transfer 2: Wahlforschung: Sonden im politischen Markt* (Opladen: Westdeutscher Verlag, 1976), pp. 57–67.

55. Ursula Feist and Klaus Liepelt, "Machtwechsel in Raten: Das Parteiensystem auf dem Weg zur Mitte," in *Transfer 2: Wahlforschung: Sonden im politischen Markt* (Opladen: Westdeutscher Verlag, 1976), pp. 38–39.

56. See the literature cited in note 54 above.

57. Dieter Roth, "Ökonomische Situation und Wahlverhalten: Das Beispiel Arbeitslosigkeit," *Politische Vierteljahresschrift*, 18 (November 1977), 537–550.

58. Roth, "Ökonomische Situation"; Roth, "Ökonomische Variablen"; Harmut Garding, "Ostpolitik und Arbeitsplätze: Issues 1972 und 1976," in Dieter Oberndörfer, ed., *Wählerverhalten in der Bundesrepublik Deutschland* (Berlin: Duncker & Humblot, 1978), pp. 327–390; Helmut Jung, "Ökonomische Einstellungen und das Wahlverhalten auf dem Hintergrund sozialstruktureller Variablen: Ein Zeitvergleich zwischen 1973 und 1976," in Oberndörfer, *Wählerverhalten*, pp. 391–464.

59. Parallel findings and arguments in the area of job satisfaction are presented in Frederick Herzberg, *Work and the Nature of Man* (New York: New American Library, 1973), esp. pp. 90–94.

60. For similar conclusions about the United States, see Campbell et al., *American Voter*, p. 401.

61. Recently the ability of governments to achieve economic success has come into question, and this has led to academic examinations of the "governability" of advanced industrial societies.

62. Campbell et al., *American Voter,* chap. 14.

63. See Roth, "Ökonomische Variablen."

64. The data contain measurements at two and sometimes three time-points for three separate sets of economic evaluations: judgments about the Federal Republic's past and present performance, expectations about the country's future, and expectations for the respondent's own future. Our conclusions are based on measures of association between the economic variables and present vote choice, calculated separately for stable voters and vote switchers. This distinction is based on the respondent's reported voting behavior in the present and the most recent election. The tables that support this analysis are not presented because they would be too cumbersome, even if only the measures of association were reported.

65. Gerald H. Kramer, "Short-Term Fluctuations in U.S. Voting Behavior, 1896–1964," *American Political Science Review,* 65 (March 1971), 131–143. Kramer's article touched off a lively discussion: see George J. Stigler, "Economic Conditions and National Elections," *American Economic Review,* 63 (March 1973), 160–167, and the comments by Paul W. McCracken and A. M. Okun, ibid. See also Francisco Arcelus and Allan H. Meltzer, "The Effect of Aggregate Economic Variables on Congressional Elections," *American Political Science Review,* 69 (December 1975), 1232–39 and 1266–69, and the additional contributions by Howard S. Bloom and H. D. Price, and by Saul Goodman and Gerald H. Kramer, ibid.

66. See C. A. E. Goodhart and R. J. Bhansali, "Political Economy," in *Political Studies,* 18 (1970), 43–106; Bruno S. Frey and Hermann Garbers, "Der Einfluss wirtschaftlicher Variabler auf die Popularität der Regierung-eine empirische Analyse," in *Jahrbücher für Nationalökonomie und Statistik* (1972); Butler and Stokes, *Political Change,* chap. 18; Gebhard Kirchgässner, "Ökonometrische Untersuchungen des Einflusses der Wirtschaftslage auf die Popularität der Parteien," *Schweizerische Zeitschrift für Volkswirtschaft und Statistik,* 110 (1974), 409–445.

67. Butler and Stokes, *Political Change,* chap. 14; Gebhard Kirchgässner, "Wirtschaftslage und Wählerverhalten," *Politische Vierteljahresschrift,* 18 (November 1977), 510–536. Since regularly spaced and uninterrupted electoral series over long time spans are not very frequent in Europe, most European studies have utilized monthly polling data on party popularity as the dependent variable rather than actual election returns.

68. Kirchgässner, "Wirtschaftslage," p. 512.

69. Some recent research has attempted to do so for the United States: John E. Mueller, *War, Presidents and Public Opinion* (New York: John Wiley, 1973); Samuel Kernell, "Explaining Presidential Popularity," *American Political Science Review,* 72 (June 1978), 506–522.

70. The "delayed" beginning (by two months) of the second period does not appreciably affect the results of the analysis. Note that all other breaks between time periods occur simultaneously with changes in the partisan com-

position of the government, when each party (our dependent variable) is thrust into its new role of government or opposition.

71. Our attempt to predict the level of economic concerns (see figure 4.8) between 1952 and 1972 showed that inflation and changes in the unemployment rate together accounted for 71% of the variance in the frequency with which economic problems were mentioned.

72. The data have been made available by Helmut Norpoth and the Zentralarchiv für empirische Sozialforschung, University of Cologne. The dependent variable, party popularity, is generally available in monthly survey measurements, but where necessary, missing timepoints have been linearly interpolated. The inflation values were lagged four months in these analyses.

73. Most timeseries data violate the regression assumption of uncorrelated error terms because the disturbances are serially correlated (autocorrelation). To avoid the problems of using Ordinary Least Squares under these conditions, the processes underlying the data (all are first-order autoregressive models—AR1—except one, which is AR2) were initially identified before the parameters shown in table 4.3 were estimated accounting for the form of the process. As the values of the Durban-Watson D statistic indicate, the procedure succeeds in eliminating autocorrelation. The estimated rho values are included in the table. For an overview of the problems of timeseries analyses, see Douglas Hibbs, "Problems of Statistical Estimation and Causal Inference in Dynamic Time Series Models," in Herbert Costner, ed., *Sociological Methodology 1973/74* (San Francisco: Jossey Bass, 1974), pp. 252–308. On autoregressive models, see G. E. P. Box and G. M. Jenkins, *Time Series Analysis* (San Francisco: Holden Day, 1970). The program used for the estimation was *SHAZAM,* by Kenneth J. White and Malcolm Craig, as implemented at the University of Michigan. We are grateful to Bill Domke for his help in setting up and interpreting these analyses.

5. Politics and the International Environment

1. For discussions of events analysis, see Charles McClelland, "Interactional Interaction Analysis: Basic Research and Some Practical Applications," Technical Report no. 2, *World Events Interaction Survey* (Department of International Relations, University of Southern California, 1968); Charles McClelland and Gary Hogart, "Conflict Patterns in the Interactions among Nations," in James Rosenau, ed., *International Politics and Foreign Policy* (New York: Free Press, 1969), pp. 711–723; Walter F. Corson, "Conflict and Cooperation in East-West Crises: Measurement and Prediction" (Paper presented at the Events Data Measurement Conference, East Lansing, April 1970); Philip Burgess and Raymond Lawton, *Indicators of International Behavior: An Assessment of Events Data Research* (Beverly Hills: Sage Publications, 1972); Edward Azar et al., *International Events Interaction Analysis: Some Research Considerations* (Beverly Hills: Sage Publications, 1972); and Sophia Peterson, "Events Data Studies, 1961–1972," in Patrick McGowan, ed., *Sage International Yearbook of Foreign Policies Studies,* III (Beverly Hills: Sage Publications, 1972).

2. One study is the dataset compiled by Walter Corson (cited in note 1). Two types of events were drawn from this study: those involving interactions between NATO and Warsaw Pact nations, with Germany or Berlin as a focal point; and those involving direct interactions between West Germany and the Eastern bloc. The other study is the *World Events Interaction Survey* (WEIS), from which all events were drawn that involved direct interaction between the Federal Republic (and West Berlin) and the Warsaw Pact nations (and East Berlin) for the period between 1966 and the last quarter of 1972. The total number of events has been aggregated by three-month periods to provide a more stable reading of the foreign policy climate. Consequently, the analysis covers 112 periods or timepoints from the first quarter of 1945 to the end of 1972.

3. Since data were combined from two different sources with slightly dissimilar methodologies, this differencing method also compensates for such factors as the total volume of events and the media sources used in the two studies. It is therefore unlikely that the gradual improvement in East-West interactions is an artifact of the different data sources.

4. Many thorough accounts of postwar West German foreign policy have been written. Those that we have found particularly useful include: Wolfram Hanrieder, *The Stable Crisis* (New York: Harper and Row, 1970); Peter Merkl, *German Foreign Policies, West and East* (Santa Barbara: ABC-CLIO Press, 1974); Karl Kaiser, *German Foreign Policy* (London: Oxford University Press, 1968); Lawrence Whetten, *Germany's Ostpolitik* (London: Oxford University Press, 1971); *Germany and Eastern Europe since 1945,* Keesing's Research Report, no. 8 (New York: Charles Scribner's Sons, 1973); Richard Hiscocks, *The Adenauer Era* (Philadelphia: J. B. Lippincott, 1966); Joseph Joffe, "The Foreign Policy of the German Federal Republic," in Roy Macridis, ed., *Foreign Policy in World Politics,* 5th ed. (Englewood Cliffs: Prentice Hall, 1976), pp. 117–151; and Karl Deutsch et al., "Foreign Policy of the German Federal Republic," in Roy Macridis, ed., *Foreign Policy in World Politics,* 4th ed. (Englewood Cliffs: Prentice Hall, 1972), pp. 119–173.

5. Quoted in *Germany and Eastern Europe,* p. 2.

6. Anna J. Merritt and Richard Merritt, *Public Opinion in Occupied Germany* (Urbana: University of Illinois Press, 1970), pp. 103–106, 137–139.

7. See Alfred Grosser, *Germany in Our Time* (New York: Frederick Praeger, 1971), chap. 4.

8. Alfred Grosser, *Die Bundesrepublik Deutschland: Bilanz einer Entwicklung* (Tübingen, 1967), p. 12, as quoted and translated by Kaiser, *German Foreign Policy,* p. 13.

9. Kaiser, *German Foreign Policy,* p. 20.

10. Quoted in Joffe, "Foreign Policy," p. 122.

11. Quoted in Hiscocks, *The Adenauer Era,* p. 63.

12. Hanrieder, *Stable Crisis,* p. 48.

13. Richard Mayer, *The Community of Europe* (New York: Norton, 1962), p. 101.

14. This was a provision of the Bonn Conventions of 1952, which formed the basis of the Paris Agreements of 1954.

15. See Deutsch et al., "Foreign Policy," pp. 127, 133. Only 11 percent thought the Federal Republic should cooperate closely with Poland at this time.

16. Hanrieder, *Stable Crisis*, pp. 134–135, 143.

17. These two positions have been explained in the following terms: "The Gaullists believed that the globally oriented détente policy of the Kennedy Administration implied Washington's readiness to make deals with the Soviet Union over the heads of Europe and Germany; and that by contrast de Gaulle's foreign policy concept, precisely because it sought to maximize the leverage of Europe in a future multipolar world, held out much greater promise for the resolution of German foreign policy problems." Hanrieder, *Stable Crisis*, p. 164.

18. Deutsch et al., "Foreign Policy," pp. 127, 133, 135.

19. For discussions of the Godesberg program, see Douglas Chalmers, *The Social Democratic Party of Germany* (New Haven: Yale University Press, 1964); and Lewis Edinger and Douglas Chalmers, "Overture or Swan Song: German Social Democracy Prepares for A New Decade," *Antioch Review*, 20 (1960), 163–175.

20. Joffe, "Foreign Policy," p. 138.

21. The Hallstein Doctrine was the official recognition policy of the Federal Republic. According to it, West Germany would not extend diplomatic recognition to any country that also recognized the German Democratic Republic. *Alleinvertretung* referred to the Federal Republic's claim that it represented *all* Germans rather than just those living in the West; it claimed this right because of the absence of free elections in East Germany.

22. Joffe, "Foreign Policy," p. 139.

23. Kaiser, *German Foreign Policy*, pp. 76–80.

24. Samuel Barnes et. al., "The German Party System and the 1961 Federal Election," *American Political Science Review*, 56 (December 1962), 903.

25. Hanrieder, *Stable Crisis*, p. 106.

26. See Deutsch et al., "Foreign Policy," pp. 127, 133, 135.

27. See Kaiser, *German Foreign Policy*, p. 45; and Merkl, *German Foreign Policies*, p. 149.

28. For further discussion of this conference, see Kaiser, *German Foreign Policy*, p. 101.

29. Merkl, *German Foreign Policies*, p. 121.

30. Hanrieder, *Stable Crisis*, p. 115.

31. Ibid, p. 121.

32. Joffe, "Foreign Policy," p. 145.

33. Merkl, *German Foreign Policies*, pp. 134, 135.

34. Ibid., p. 167.

35. See Deutsch et al., "Foreign Policy," p. 136.

36. See Merkl, *German Foreign Policies*, p. 171.

37. Joffe, "Foreign Policy," p. 145.

38. In 1961, respondents were asked to evaluate fifteen foreign and domestic policy issues on an eleven-point scale of "importance to them per-

sonally." The list included seven foreign policy issues: nuclear questions; good relations with the USA; better relations with the Soviet Union; reunification of Germany; security from a Russian attack; European unity; and aid to underdeveloped countries. In 1969, the same procedure was used, but only five foreign policy issues were included in the list of important problems: recognition of the GDR; good relations with the USA; better relations with the Soviet Union; reunification of Germany; and security from a Russian attack. Since "recognition of the GDR" formed a separate dimension in the principal components analysis, it was not included in the index built for this section of the chapter. Finally, in 1972, respondents were asked to evaluate sixteen domestic and foreign problems on a four-point scale of importance. The foreign policy issues included: further improvement in relations with the East European states; not neglecting friendly relations with the West; good relations with the People's Republic of China; military security; and effective protection against terror attacks from radical foreign groups.

39. The groups to be analyzed were selected partially on theoretical bases and partially because they displayed significant variation across the foreign policy space.

40. Daniel Willick has found that West Germans are considerably more interested in international affairs than Englishmen, Frenchmen, Japanese, and Italians. Indeed, he reports that 27.1 percent of the West German population are "very interested in international affairs." See Daniel Willick, "Public Interest in International Affairs," *Social Science Quarterly*, 50 (September 1969). However, Merkl points out: "Since measurements of voter interest in foreign policy are most likely to occur at the time of elections [and] only the 1965 and 1972 elections were undisturbed by foreign policy crises . . . the claim of high West German attentiveness to foreign affairs may well have been exaggerated." Merkl, *German Foreign Policies*, p. 15. Moreover, Klingemann notes that domestic issues have a greater "personal relevance" for West Germans than foreign policy questions, a finding that is corroborated by the analyses presented in chapter 6. See Hans D. Klingemann, "Issue-Kompetenz und Wahlentscheidung," *Politische Vierteljahresschrift*, 14 (June 1973), 227–256.

41. In 1961, the question read as follows: "In your opinion what is more important at the moment: West Germany's relations with other nations, or the problems within West Germany—that is, foreign policy or domestic policy?" In 1969, an index was constructed from a question that asked respondents to indicate which one of five domestic and foreign policy problems interested them most.

42. See chapter 8 and appendix B for a description of this index. Weak and leaning partisans have been collapsed into one category for this analysis.

43. For discussions of generational differences in foreign policy attitudes, see Ronald Inglehart, "An End to European Integration?" *American Political Science Review*, 61 (March 1967), 91–105; Ronald Ingelhart, "Changing Value Priorities and European Integration," *Journal of Common Market Studies*, 10 (1971), 1–36; and Merkl, *German Foreign Policies*, esp. chap. 1. As the following tabulation demonstrates, young Germans were more impressed with Brandt's Ostpolitik in 1972 than were older Germans.

	Wilh.	Weim.	Third Reich	Early FRG	Late FRG
Agree with Ostpolitk	70.3%	80.6%	83.4%	88.0%	87.8%
(N)	(179)	(323)	(353)	(292)	(376)

44. There is a second, much smaller group of Germans that might be expected to occupy positions in the foreign policy space similar to those of expellees, namely, the refugees who have chosen to come from East Germany to the West. However, the surveys contain only between thirty and sixty refugees, and for 1961 this group cannot be isolated at all. They have not been located in the space because their position shifts considerably between 1969 and 1972 and also because their number is so small that it is not possible to determine whether such movement represents meaningful change or is due to sampling error.

45. A simple measure of whether the respondent was an expellee was not included in the 1961 survey.

6. Old Politics and New Politics

1. Peter Kmieciak, *Wertstrukturen und Wertwandel in der BRD* (Berlin: Kommission für wirtschaftlichen und sozialen Wandel, 1976); Daniel Bell, *The Coming of Post-industrial Society* (New York: Basic Books, 1973).

2. For a general discussion of agenda setting, see Lee Becker et al., "The Development of Political Cognitions," in Stephen Chaffee, ed., *Political Communication* (Beverly Hills: Sage Publications, 1975), pp. 21–64; and for research focused on the German context, see Lutz Erbring, "The Impact of Political Events on Mass Publics" (Ph.D. diss., University of Michigan, 1975).

3. Elisabeth Noelle-Neumann and Erich Neumann, eds., *The Germans: Public Opinion Polls, 1947–1966* (Allensbach: Verlag für Demoskopie, 1967); Elisabeth Noelle-Neumann and Erich Neumann, eds., *Jahrbuch der öffentlichen Meinung, 1968–1973* (Allensbach: Verlag für Demoskopie, 1973).

4. For 1961, two separate timepoints are available that graphically point out the effect the Berlin Wall had on German perceptions of the agenda:

	February	August
Economic problems	23%	5%
Berlin	4	37
Reunification	35	19
Peace, détente	18	24
Social policies	0	8

5. See Kai Hildebrandt and Russell Dalton, "The New Politics," in Klaus von Beyme and Max Kaase, eds., *German Political Studies: Elections and Parties* (Beverly Hills: Sage Publications, 1978), pp. 69–96.

6. Ronald Inglehart, *The Silent Revolution* (Princeton: Princeton University Press, 1977).

7. The phrase is from Bertolt Brecht, as quoted in Inglehart, *Silent Revolution*, p. 37.

8. Ibid.; Russell Dalton, "Was There a Revolution?" *Comparative Poli-*

tical Studies, 9 (January 1977), 459–474; Ronald Inglehart, "Value Priorities and Socioeconomic Change," in Samuel Barnes and Max Kaase et al., *Political Action* (Beverly Hills: Sage Publications, 1979), 305–342.

9. For example, see the dimensional analyses in Hildebrandt and Dalton, "New Politics."

10. Ibid.; Warren Miller and Teresa Levitin, *Leadership and Change,* 2d ed. (Cambridge: Winthrop, 1977), presents a similar discussion of New Politics in the American context.

11. Inglehart, *Silent Revolution.*

12. Arnold Heidenheimer and Donald Kommers, *The Governments of Germany,* 4th ed. (New York: Crowell, 1975), p. 119.

13. Elisabeth Noelle-Neumann, ed., "Die Stille Revolution," in *Jahrbuch für Demoskopie, 1976–77* (Vienna: Molden, 1977), pp. vii-xxxix.

14. Inglehart, "Value Priorities."

15. For an elaboration of principal components analysis, see T. W. Anderson, *An Introduction to Multivariate Statistical Analysis* (New York: John Wiley, 1958), chap. 11.

16. For a conceptual discussion of the tendency of the first dimension to form a general salience measure, see Herbert Weisberg, "Dimensionland: Excursion into Spaces," *American Journal of Political Science,* 18 (November 1974), 743–776.

17. The unrotated principal components results can be transformed with a varimax rotation to identify a separate Old Politics dimension and a New Politics dimension. While this is empirically possible, it is not theoretically desirable; instead, Old Politics and New Politics are conceived as opposite ends of a single dimension and not as two independent dimensions.

18. These results should be compared with the dimensional analyses of foreign policy issues in chapter 5; see also Hildebrandt and Dalton, "New Politics."

19. Two items were deleted from the 1969 analyses because it was feared that their explicit reference to the problems of the young might unfairly strengthen age differences in issue salience: reducing the military draft, and reducing the voting age. Prior analyses that included these two issues uncovered essentially the same patterns as those described in this chapter. See Kendall Baker, Russell Dalton, and Kai Hildebrandt, "The Residue of History" (Paper presented at the annual meeting of the Western Social Science Association, Denver, April 1975).

20. To some extent the issue of codetermination may tap both Old and New Politics concerns. Codetermination may be seen as a working-class tool for economic control and as an outlet for the alienation of the working class—thus closely tied to the class struggle. Indeed, this aspect of the issue probably was dominant in the early 1950s. But with increasing affluence, workers and even unions lost interest in the issue until the late 1960s, when it was raised again by union leadership and the SPD in the New Politics context of participation in making life decisions.

21. An additional issue dealing with national security, though available for each timepoint, was not included as a core issue because this definition of core issues will be used in chapter 9 to analyze issue competency—for which

national security is not available in each survey—and also because these four issues alone gave an equal balance between Old Politics and New Politics concerns.

22. Inglehart, *Silent Revolution,* chap. 12; Ronald Inglehart, "The New Europeans," *International Organization,* 24 (Winter 1970), 129–139.

23. To ensure the similarity of issue perceptions throughout the population, the principal components analyses of the full issue set were repeated separately for the new middle class and workers, and for young (Federal Republic) and old cohorts. The following Pearson correlations comparing the second-dimension issue loadings suggest that these groups share basically similar issue perceptions:

	1961	1969	1972
New middle class/Workers	0.86	0.78	0.85
Young/Old	.90	.87	.83

24. Inglehart, *Silent Revolution;* Hildebrandt and Dalton, "New Politics"; Inglehart, "Value Priorities"; Hans Klingemann, "Issue-Kompetenz und Wahlentscheidung," *Politische Vierteljahresschrift,* 14 (June, 1973), 227–256.

25. Ronald Inglehart, "The Silent Revolution in Europe," *American Political Science Review,* 65 (December 1971), 995.

26. Inglehart, *Silent Revolution,* chap. 2; Hildebrandt and Dalton, "New Politics"; Inglehart, "Value Priorities."

27. See chapter 11 for the distribution of Inglehart's value types across time.

28. Ronald Inglehart, "Elite Values in Seven Nations: A Preliminary Working Paper," mimeographed (Ann Arbor: Center for Political Studies, 1976).

29. To some extent the description of Maslow's model as a *need hierarchy* suggests that values are amenable to a dominance model of attitudes, as in Guttman scaling. A dominance model, however, does not appear consistent with the belief that postmaterialist values are replacing materialist concerns. A dominance model would instead suggest that postmaterialist values are added to previously existing materialist values without decreasing the importance of the latter. Clearly, Inglehart's work implies that a proximity model is more appropriate, although he has also experimented with the dominance model. Thus, the term hierarchy appears to be a normative judgment on the quality of materialist versus postmaterialist concerns, rather than a description of attitudinal structure.

30. For a discussion of this scoring procedure, see Anderson, *Multivariate Statistical Analysis.*

31. Principal components scores are always computed to have a mean equal to zero and a standard deviation equal to one. These standardized scores therefore do not allow for over-time comparisons of absolute population scores, nor in a strict sense for the longitudinal comparison of subpopulation scores. The primary emphasis of comparison should consequently be to the population norm at the timepoint, i.e., the mean score of zero.

32. For the salience ratings for the full set of issues in each study, see appendix B.

33. Klingemann, "Issue-Kompetenz."

34. Inglehart, *Silent Revolution* and "Value Priorities"; Dalton, "Was There a Revolution?"

35. Karl Mannheim, "The Problem of Generations," in Karl Mannheim, ed., *Essays in the Sociology of Knowledge* (New York: Oxford University Press, 1952).

36. Inglehart, *Silent Revolution* and "Value Priorities."

37. Thomas Herz, "Effekte beruflicher Mobilität," *Zeitschrift für Soziologie*, 5 (1976), 17–37; Gerhard Kleining, "Soziale Mobilität in der Bundesrepublik Deutschland, II," *Kölner Zeitschrift für Soziologie und Sozialpsychologie*, 27 (1975), 502–552; Walter Müller, *Familie, Schule, Beruf* (Opladen, Westdeutscher Verlag, 1975).

38. See chapter 4 for a fuller discussion of the distinction between the old middle class and the new middle class. This concept is also central to much of the recent work on postindustrial societies; see Inglehart, *Silent Revolution*; Bell, *Post-industrial Society*; S. M. Lipset, "The Changing Class Structure and Contemporary European Politics," *Daedalus*, 93 (1964), 271–303.

39. Franz Urban Pappi, "Sozialstruktur, gesellschaftliche Wertorientierungen und Wahlabsicht," *Politische Vierteljahresschrift*, 18 (November 1977), 195–229.

40. Hildebrandt and Dalton, "New Politics"; Inglehart, *Silent Revolution*.

41. For a contrasting view, see Pappi, "Sozialstruktur, gesellschaftliche Wertorientierungen."

42. Müller, *Familie*.

43. Alan Marsh, "The 'Silent Revolution,' Value Priorities and the Quality of Life in Britain," *American Political Science Review*, 69 (March 1975), 21–30.

44. Paul Abramson, *Generational Change in American Politics* (Lexington: Lexington Books, 1975).

45. Klaus Allerbeck and Leopold Rosenmayr, eds., *Aufstand der Jugend?* (Munich: Juventa, 1971); Max Kaase, "Demokratische Einstellungen in der Bundesrepublik Deutschland," in Rudolf Wildenmann, ed., *Sozialwissenschaftliches Jahrbuch für Politik* (Munich: Guenter-Olzog, 1971), pp. 119–326; Edward Muller, "Behavioral Correlates of Political Support," *American Political Science Review*, 71 (June 1977), 454–467.

46. Dalton, "Was There A Revolution?"; Sidney Milkis and Thomas Baldino, "Life Cycle or Value Change" (Paper presented at the annual meeting of the Midwest Political Science Association, Chicago, 1978).

47. Ronald Inglehart, "Generational Change in Europe," in Mattei Dogan and Richard Rose, eds., *European Politics* (Boston: Little, Brown, 1971), 120–129.

48. Ronald Inglehart, "Political Dissatisfaction and Mass Support of Social Change in Advanced Industrial Societies," *Comparative Political Studies*, 10 (October 1977), 455–472; Barnes and Kaase, eds., *Political Action*.

49. Rudolf Brun, ed., *Der Grüne Protest* (Frankfurt: Fischer, 1978); Dietlef Murphy et al., *Protest: Grüne, Bunte und Steuerrebellen* (Reinbek:

Rowohlt, 1979); Herbert Gruhl, *Ein Planet wird geplündert* (Frankfurt: Fischer, 1978). More general aspects of value change are discussed in Helmut Klages and Peter Kmieciak, eds., *Wertwandel und gesellschaftlicher Wandel* (Frankfurt: Campus, 1979).

50. Inglehart, *Silent Revolution*; Lipset, "Changing Class Structure"; Otto Kirchheimer, "Germany: The Vanishing Opposition," in Robert Dahl, ed., *Political Oppositions in Western Democracies* (New Haven: Yale University Press, 1966), pp. 237–259.

7. Transition in the Social Bases of German Partisanship

1. Ralf Dahrendorf, *Society and Democracy in Germany* (Garden City: Doubleday, 1967), chap. 4; Lewis Edinger, *Politics in Germany* (Boston: Little, Brown, 1968), pp. 26–34; Gerhard Loewenberg, "The Remaking of the German Party System," *Polity*, 1 (1968), 86–113.

2. Klaus Liepelt, "The Infrastructure of Party Support in Austria and West Germany," in Mattei Dogan and Richard Rose, eds., *European Politics: A Reader* (Boston: Little, Brown, 1971); Morris Janowitz and David Segal, "Social Cleavage and Party Affiliation: Germany, Great Britain and the United States," *American Journal of Sociology*, 72 (May 1967), 601–618; Juan Linz, "Cleavage and Consensus in West German Politics: The Early Fifties," in S. M. Lipset and Stein Rokkan, eds., *Party Systems and Voter Alignments* (New York: Free Press, 1967); Derek Urwin, "Germany: Continuity and Change in Electoral Politics," in Richard Rose, ed., *Electoral Behavior: A Comparative Handbook* (New York: Free Press, 1974); Franz Urban Pappi, "Parteiensystem und Sozialstruktur in der Bundesrepublik," *Politische Vierteljahresschrift*, 14 (June 1973), 191–214.

3. Paul Abramson, "Social Class and Political Change in Western Europe," *Comparative Political Studies*, 4 (July 1971), 131–156.

4. Lipset and Rokkan, *Party Systems*.

5. Ronald Inglehart, *The Silent Revolution* (Princeton: Princeton University Press, 1977); Kai Hildebrandt and Russell Dalton, "The New Politics," in Max Kaase and Klaus Von Beyme, eds., *German Political Studies: Elections and Parties*, III (London: Sage Publications, 1979), 69–98.

6. Geoffrey Pridham, *Christian Democracy in Western Europe* (New York: St. Martin's, 1977). For a parallel discussion of the SPD's changing image, see Douglas Chalmers, *The Social Democratic Party of Germany* (New Haven: Yale University Press, 1964).

7. Lipset and Rokkan, *Party Systems*.

8. Cf. Angus Campbell et al., *The American Voter* (New York: John Wiley, 1961); David Butler and Donald Stokes, *Political Change in Britain* (New York: St. Martin's, 1969).

9. Robert Alford, *Party and Society* (Chicago: Rand McNally, 1963). Arend Lijphart, "Class Voting and Religious Voting in European Democracies," University of Strathclyde, Survey Research Centre, Occasional Paper no. 8, contains the following class voting indices: Great Britain (1959), 37%; Italy (1959), 19%; Germany (1959), 28%; The Netherlands (1956), 26%; Bel-

gium (1956), 25%; France (1956), 15%; Sweden (1955), 53%; Norway (1957), 46%.

10. The two major parties in Germany, the SPD and CDU/CSU, have dominated electoral politics in the Federal Republic. Since 1953 the only other party to capture more than 5 percent of the votes in national elections has been the FDP. Furthermore, replication of the analyses presented here using the SPD share of the *three*-party vote produces substantially similar findings. These analyses, therefore, are restricted to the two major parties, and FDP voters and the supporters of other parties have been excluded.

11. For a discussion of the international environment at the time, see chapter 5, or Karl Deutsch and Lewis Edinger, *Germany Rejoins the Powers* (Stanford: Stanford University Press, 1959). For the theoretical relationship between foreign policy and class voting, see Campbell et al., *American Voter*.

12. The 1957 data are from an Allensbach study of the adult population conducted in June 1957. We would like to thank Professor Bradley Richardson, Ohio State University, for making these data available to us. Where comparisons are possible, the data yield results very similar to those published in the DIVO report of the 1957 election: DIVO, *Untersuchung der Wählerschaft und Wahlentscheidung* (Frankfurt am Main: DIVO, 1957).

13. In 1949 the Berlin blockade influenced the election; in 1953 the Berlin uprising and Bundestag vote on the EDC were considered major foreign policy stimuli.

14. Edinger, *Politics in Germany*, pp. 259–260.

15. Erwin K. Scheuch and Rudolf Wildenmann, eds., *Zur Soziologie der Wahl* (Cologne and Opladen: Westdeutscher Verlag, 1965). (This work was published as special issue no. 9 of the *Kölner Zeitschrift für Soziologie und Sozialpsychologie*.)

16. David Conradt, *The West German Party System: An Ecological Analysis of Social Structure and Voting Behavior, 1961–1969*, Sage Professional Papers in Comparative Politics (Beverly Hills: Sage, 1972); Hans Klingemann and Franz Pappi, "The 1969 Bundestag Election in the Federal Republic of Germany," *Comparative Politics*, 2 (July 1970), 523–548.

17. Frederick Engelmann, "Perceptions of the Great Coalition in West Germany, 1966–1969," *Canadian Journal of Political Science*, 5 (March 1972), 28–54; Max Kaase, "Determinants of Voting Behavior in the West German Election of 1969," in Ian Budge, Ivor Crewe, and Dennis Farlie, eds., *Party Identification and Beyond* (New York: John Wiley, 1976), pp. 81–102.

18. Max Kaase has noted that working-class respondents substantially overreported their support for the SPD in surveys of the 1972 election. The effect of this misreporting is to artificially raise the class voting index in survey analyses. A completely accurate measure of class voting in 1972 would therefore be lower than the value obtained from these data. See Kaase, "Die Bundestagswahl, 1972: Probleme und Analysen," *Politische Vierteljahresschrift*, 14 (June 1973), 145–190.

19. See appendix B for details on the construction of these social-status measures.

20. John Goldthorpe et al., *The Affluent Worker: Political Attitudes and Behavior* (Cambridge: University Press, 1968).

21. One example of the narrowing of differences within the working class is the decline in voting differences as a function of union membership. In 1953 union members' support of the SPD was 23 percent above that of nonunion members of the working class. This gap increased slightly in 1965, but by 1972 the difference between union and nonunion workers had declined to only 13 percent.

	1953	1957	1965	1972
Union	76%	76%	77%	80%
Nonunion	53	53	50	67
Difference	23	23	27	13

22. Daniel Bell, *The Coming of Post-Industrial Society* (New York: Basic Books, 1973).

23. See Chapter 4.

24. Dahrendorf, *Society and Democracy;* Inglehart, *Silent Revolution*; Hildebrandt and Dalton, "New Politics"; S. M. Lipset, "The Changing Class Structure and Contemporary European Politics," *Daedalus*, 93 (Winter 1964), 271–303.

25. Thus, as Franz Pappi has also noted, the cleavage between the traditional bourgeoisie and proletariat has not weakened. Franz Pappi, "Sozialstruktur, gesellschaftliche Wertorientierungen und Wahlabsicht," *Politische Vierteljahresschrift*, 18 (November 1977), 195–229. This constancy should not, however, obscure the fact that the traditional cleavage is being overshadowed by the growth of the new middle class, which will soon outnumber the combined size of the traditional bourgeoisie and proletariat. See also chapter 6.

26. To estimate the effects of compositional change the class voting figures for 1969 (or any year) can be adjusted to reflect the relative size of the old and new middle class in the 1953 sample. In other words, the level of class voting can be estimated as if the composition of the middle class had not changed since 1953. The following tabulation shows that this adjustment raises the class voting index after 1953, but that even the adjusted indices generally decline. Some other source of change is therefore influencing class voting.

	1953	1957	1961	1965	1969	1972
Unadjusted	30	37	28	26	12	17
Adjusted	30	37	29	29	16	20

27. See Inglehart, *Silent Revolution*; Hildebrandt and Dalton, "New Politics." For a parallel study of American politics, see Warren Miller and Teresa Levitin, *Leadership and Change* (Cambridge, Mass.: Winthrop, 1976).

28. Inglehart, *Silent Revolution*; Russell Dalton, "Was There a Revolution?" *Comparative Political Studies*, 9 (January 1977), 459–474.

29. See appendix B for definition of the generational units. Stratifying vote by class and then again by generation can result in relatively small cell frequencies, and consequently sampling error might obscure generational patterns. To minimize the effects of sampling error, we combined two or more studies, where possible, at each timepoint. The 1953 timepoint uses the two half-samples that were asked either voting intentions or party preferences for a pooled N of 3246. Other 1953 analyses in the chapter utilize only the voting half-sample. For 1961 we combined two preelection studies and one postelec-

tion study for an N of 5027. The 1965 timepoint merges one preelection and one postelection survey, N = 2716. For 1969 one preelection and one postelection study (made available by Barbara Farah, University of Michigan) were combined for an N of 4977. The 1972 results are based on a single preelection study with an N of 2052. The 1957 study was not used in these generational analyses because of the small usable sample size, and because the wider age categories in that study were not equatable to our generational breakdown. The following tabulation gives the cell frequencies for the class voting trends in figures 7.3–7.7.

	1953	1961	1965	1969	1972
Wilhelmine					
Middle class	434	188	94	55	65
Working class	447	263	116	49	61
Weimar					
Middle class	400	333	246	293	170
Working class	362	450	245	202	154
Third Reich					
Middle class	95	336	222	482	180
Working class	110	466	239	423	186
Early FRG					
Middle class	—	192	188	359	140
Working class	—	302	222	396	139
Late FRG					
Middle class	—	—	60	248	156
Working class	—	—	75	222	129

30. The generational declines in class voting are also not solely or predominantly the result of compositional change in the character of the middle class between generations. Replication of the analyses in figures 7.3–7.7 separately for old and new middle classes found patterns of change similar to those just presented; however, change was again most noticeable within the new middle class.

31. E. Schmidt-Volkmar, *Der Kulturkampf in Deutschland, 1871–1890* (Göttingen: Musterschmidt, 1964); E. Blankenburg, *Kirchliche Bindung und Wahlverhalten* (Olten and Freiburg: Walter-Verlag, 1967).

32. Although religious cleavages have been important in Germany historically, the bi-religious appeal of the CDU/CSU has substantially changed the nature of this cleavage in contemporary politics. In this sense, Pappi notes that Germany has not frozen around the same religious cleavage that was present at the beginning of the century. See Franz Pappi, "Parteiensystem."

33. Gerhard Schmidtchen, *Zwischen Kirche und Gessellschaft* (Freiburg: Harder Verlag, 1972); Blankenburg, *Kirchliche Bindung*; Pappi, "Parteiensystem."

34. The 1953 and 1957 studies measured frequency of church attendance in subjective terms: frequently, occasionally, or never. The later studies used objective criteria: weekly, monthly, yearly or more often, or never. Because Catholics normally attend church regularly, they might tend to equate frequent church attendance with weekly attendance, whereas the different norms of Protestants might lead them to describe monthly attendance as frequent. These

different perceptions as to what frequent attendance means may be one source of the different relationship between the early and later years of Protestants.

35. For another perspective on the impact of religion, see Kendall Baker, "The Acquisition of Partisanship in Germany," *American Journal of Political Science,* 18 (August 1974), 569–582.

36. Inglehart, *Silent Revolution.*

37. The state variable was not available in our version of the 1957 survey. The eta coefficients for the remaining elections are based on the ten category variable.

38. Franz Urban Pappi, *Wahlverhalten und Politische Kultur: Eine soziologische Analyse der Politischen Kultur in Deutschland unter besonderer Berücksichtigung von Stadt-Land Unterschieden* (Meisenheim am Glan: Verlag Anton Hain, 1970).

39. For an examination of the empirical and theoretical bases of the "cross-pressures" assumption, see Linz, "Cleavage and Consensus"; Bernard Berelson et al., *Voting* (Chicago: University of Chicago Press, 1954).

40. Franz Pappi has already begun filling in some of these details. See Pappi, "Parteiensystem"; Franz Urban Pappi, "Sozialstruktur und Politische Konflikte in der Bundesrepublik" (Habilitationsschrift, Cologne, 1976).

41. The following tabulation presents the class voting index separately for Protestants and Catholics and the religious voting index separately for middle-class and working-class respondents. Although the longitudinal trends are parallel, they are not identical. The data show a uniform tendency for Protestants to have a class voting index approximately five points higher than that for Catholics. Perhaps the greater unifying force of their subculture joins Catholics together across class lines slightly more often than Protestants. In a similar manner one can consider how variation in the religious alignment cuts across the class dimension. Members of the working class display a level of religious voting generally five points greater than that of the middle class. The explanation probably lies in two directions. First, the middle class is more secularized in Germany, so that religion is a less salient guide to behavior. Second, the Catholic church's competition with the SPD has focused on the affiliations of the Catholic working class, and it is likely that the greater religious involvement of the working class (especially working-class women) has served to polarize this social stratum.

Yet while both indices display some evidence of an interaction effect between religion and class, the total impact of these interaction effects is relatively slight. As the last row of the tabulation shows, in no year was the interaction effect significant at the 0.10 level.

	1953	1957	1961	1965	1969	1972
Class voting indices						
Protestants	35	35	25	30	15	21
Catholics	27	41	23	24	13	16
Religious voting indices						
Middle class	20	6	26	20	29	22
Working class	28	20	36	26	31	27
Significance of interaction (p)	0.24	0.32	0.14	0.36	0.87	0.32

42. Because of the small Ns in several of the states, region was collapsed into four larger regions with somewhat distinct cultural heritages: (1) Bremen, Hamburg, Schleswig-Holstein, Lower Saxony; (2) North Rhine–Westphalia; (3) Rhineland-Palatinate, Saarland, Hesse; (4) Baden-Württemberg, Bavaria.

43. Berelson et al., *Voting*.

44. Lipset and Rokkan, *Party Systems;* Philip Converse, "Some Priority Variables in Comparative Research," in Richard Rose, ed., *Electoral Behavior* (New York: Free Press, 1974), 727–746.

45. Butler and Stokes, *Political Change,* chap. 16; W. Phillips Shively, "Voting Stability and the Nature of Party Attachments in the Weimar Republic," *American Political Science Review,* 66 (December 1972), 1203–1225; also see chapter 9 of this book.

46. Changes by party elites have also facilitated the rise of the New Politics and will be examined further in later chapters. Elite and mass behavior have thus gone hand in hand in promoting change in the social bases of German politics. Hence, future developments will depend on both of these components.

8. Partisanship and Political Behavior

1. This has been the emphasis of many studies of German voting behavior. See Juan Linz, "Cleavage and Consensus in West German Politics: The Early Fifties," in S. M. Lipset and Stein Rokkan, eds., *Party Systems and Voter Alignments* (New York: Free Press, 1967); Derek Urwin, "Germany: Continuity and Change in Electoral Politics," in Richard Rose, ed., *Electoral Behavior: A Comparative Handbook* (New York: Free Press, 1974); Franz Urban Pappi, "Parteiensystem und Sozialstruktur in der Bundesrepublik," *Politische Vierteljahresschrift,* 14 (June 1973), 191–213; Klaus Liepelt and Alexander Mitscherlich, *Thesen zur Wählerfluktuation* (Frankfurt: Europäische Verlagsanstalt, 1968); Franz Urban Pappi and Edward Laumann, "Gesellschaftliche Wertorientierungen und politisches Verhalten," *Zeitschrift für Soziologie,* 3 (April 1974), 157–188.

2. David Butler and Donald Stokes, *Political Change in Britain* (New York: St. Martin's, 1969), chap. 4.

3. Giovanni Sartori, "The Sociology of Parties: A critical Review," in Otto Stammer, ed., *Party Systems, Party Organizations, and the Politics of the New Masses* (Berlin: Free University, 1968), p. 1–26.

4. See, for example, the various articles by the "Michigan group" that build upon the idea of a "normal vote"; these have been collected as chapters 1–7 in Angus Campbell, Philip Converse, Warren Miller, and Donald Stokes, *Elections and the Political Order* (New York: John Wiley, 1966).

5. Butler and Stokes, *Political Change,* pp. 41–42.

6. Jan Thomassen, "Party Identification as a Cross-National Concept: Its Meaning in the Netherlands," in Ian Budge, Ivor Crewe, and Dennis Farlie, eds., *Party Identification and Beyond* (New York: John Wiley, 1976), chap. 4.

7. Werner Zohlnhöfer, "Parteienidentifizierung in der Bundesrepublik und in den Vereinigten Staaten," in Erwin Scheuch and Rudolf Wildenmann, eds.,

Zur Soziologie der Wahl (Cologne: Westdeutscher Verlag, 1965), pp. 126–168; however, Zohlnhöfer's inference that comparability of the concept and the measures of party identification follows from the comparable levels of partisanship in the two countries cannot be accepted.

8. Max Kaase, "Party Identification and Voting Behavior in the West German Election of 1969," in Budge et al., eds., *Party Identification*, chap. 5; Günther Radtke, "Gibt es in der Bundesrepublik eine Parteienidentifikation?" *Verfassung und Verfassungswirklichkeit*, 6 (1972), 68–91.

9. Kaase, "Party Identification."

10. Manfred Berger, "Parteiidentifikation in der Bundesrepublik," *Politische Vierteljahresschrift*, 14 (May 1973), 215–225.

11. Uwe Schleth and Erich Weede, "Causal Models on West German Voting Behavior," in Rudolf Wildenmann, ed., *Sozialwissenschaftliches Jahrbuch*, II (Munich and Vienna: Olzog Verlag, 1971), 73–97. The American causal model of party identification is presented in Arthur Goldberg, "Discerning a Causal Pattern among Data on Voting Behavior," *American Political Science Review*, 60 (December 1966), 913–922. As Schleth and Weede themselves note (p. 79), the party identification variable they use contains 63% nonpartisans; hence, the negative result of their replication is not surprising. In addition, they adhere very strictly to the American model, allowing for no direct impact of social background variables on vote. We believe that German political reality requires a more differentiated treatment. For analyses based on a similar argument, see Kendall L. Baker, "Generational Differences in the Role of Party Identification in German Political Behavior," *American Journal of Political Science*, 22 (February 1978), 106–129.

12. Franz Urban Pappi, "Parteiensystem"; also Pappi, "Sozialstruktur und Politische Konflikte in der Bundesrepublik" (Habilitationsschrift, Cologne, 1976), pp. 48–85.

13. Butler and Stokes, *Political Change*, p. 43.

14. For a similar functional argument involving the system as a variable, see Peter Gluchowski, "Parteiidentifikation im politischen System der Bundesrepublik Deutschland: Zum Problem der empirischen Überprüfung eines Konzepts unter variierten Systembedingungen," in Dieter Oberndörfer, ed., *Wählerverhalten in der Bundesrepublik Deutschland* (Berlin: Duncker und Humblot, 1978), pp. 265–323. Although recognizing these difficulties, Gluchowski considers partisanship nevertheless a useful concept for the analysis of German politics.

15. W. Phillips Shively, "Voting Stability and the Nature of Party Attachments in the Weimar Republic," *American Political Science Review*, 66 (December 1972), 1222.

16. Ibid.

17. See Otto Kirchheimer, "The Transformation of the Western European Party Systems," in Joseph LaPalombara and Myron Weiner, eds., *Political Parties and Political Development* (Princeton: Princeton University Press, 1966), pp. 177–200 and Kirchheimer, "Germany: The Vanishing Opposition," in Robert Dahl, ed., *Political Opposition in Western Democracies* (New Haven: Yale University Press, 1966), pp. 237–259.

18. Baker, "Generational Differences"; Paul Abramson, "Social Class

and Political Change in Western Europe," *Comparative Political Studies,* 4 (July 1971), 131–156; and chapter 7 of this book.

19. See Angus Campbell, Philip Converse, Warren Miller, and Donald Stokes, *The American Voter* (New York: John Wiley, 1960), chap. 7; Philip Converse, "Of Time and Partisan Stability," *Comparative Political Studies,* 2 (July 1969), 139–171.

20. See Jack Dennis and Donald McCrone, "Pre-Adult Development of Political Party Identification in Western Democracies," *Comparative Political Studies,* 3 (July 1970), 127. Based on samples of teenagers, Dennis and McCrone observe that the extent of partisanship for both Germany and Italy was higher than data from the overall population led them to expect. Like Baker ("Generational Differences"), they note the clear patterns of intergenerational transfer of partisan orientations, although the transfer was slightly weaker than observed in the United States.

21. Baker, "Generational Differences."

22. Miller emphasizes that the role of partisanship in the explanation of attitudes and of behavior other than voting has been largely neglected in European analyses; see Warren Miller, "The Cross-National Uses of Party Identification as a Stimulus to Political Inquiry," in Budge et al., eds., *Party Identification,* chap. 2. We have developed these ideas in Kendall L. Baker, Russell Dalton and Kai Hildebrandt, "Political Stability in Transition: Postwar Germany" (Paper presented at the annual meeting of the American Political Science Association, San Francisco, 1975). Both Manfred Berger, "Stabilität und Intensität von Parteineigung," *Politische Vierteljahresschrift,* 18 (November 1977), 501–509, and Jürgen Falter, "Einmal mehr: Lässt sich das Konzept der Parteiidentifikation auf deutsche Verhältnisse übertragen," in the same issue of *Politische Vierteljahresschrift,* pp. 476–500, end their discussions with a call for similar distinctions.

23. The German wording can be found in the original questionnaires, which are included in the ICPSR codebooks for these studies. A slightly different version of the 1972 question is used by the Konrad Adenauer Stiftung in its survey work.

24. Erwin Scheuch, "Die Sichtbarkeit politischer Einstellungen im alltäglichen Verhalten," in Scheuch and Wildenmann, *Zur Soziologie,* pp. 190, 191.

25. Respondents were handed a showcard containing the scalometer:

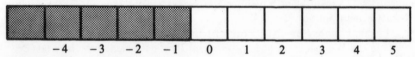

In 1972, CSU evaluations were substituted for CDU evaluations for Bavarian respondents.

26. Thus, in the analyses of partisanship two groups of respondents have been eliminated: the 4 percent (on average) who do not have scores on both SPD and CDU/CSU scalometers; and the 5 to 8 percent who prefer the FDP to both other parties (on the basis of their scalometer scores), and who should therefore be classified as FDP partisans. The exclusion of FDP partisans can be justified on substantive as well as conceptual and methodological grounds. The

position of the FDP in the party system is primarily defined by its role as a coalition partner. Its voters are much less likely to be convinced adherents of their party; rather, many vote for the FDP for instrumental, short-term reasons (see note 27). In addition, the focus of these analyses is primarily on the concept of partisanship and its changing nature in Germany, rather than on particular partisans. However, any measure of partisanship in a multiparty system lacks the convenient form of the American party identification variable, which combines the two dimensions of partisanship—direction and intensity— in the same scale. The simplicity and power that could be achieved by excluding followers of the small third party, the FDP, from the analysis justifies the distortion of German political reality.

27. In assessing how appropriate the scalometer evaluations are for creating an indicator of partisanship, it is useful to note that respondents' evaluations of their own parties were very stable, especially in the aggregate. The evaluations of the respective other (not preferred) parties, in contrast, were in the aggregate much less stable over time. Figure A, which plots the mean

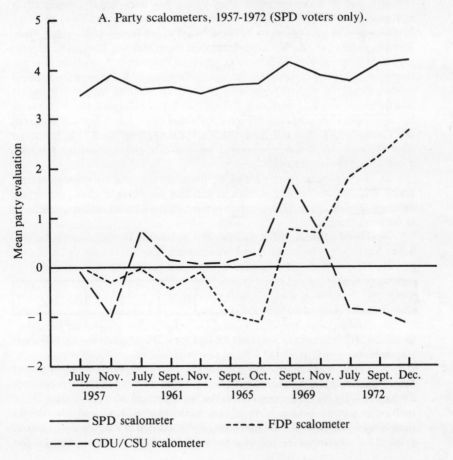

A. Party scalometers, 1957-1972 (SPD voters only).

B. Party scalometers, 1957-1972 (CDU/CSU voters only).

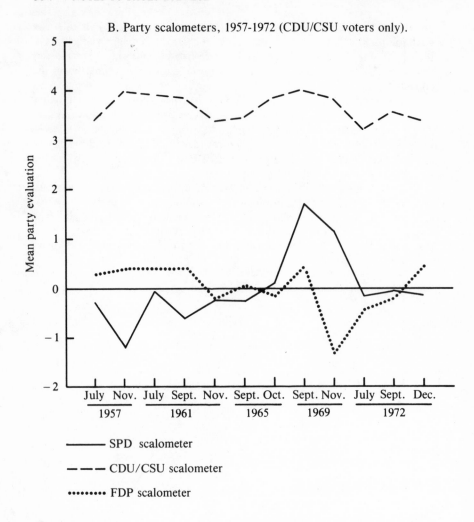

——— SPD scalometer

— — — CDU/CSU scalometer

•••••••• FDP scalometer

evaluation scores for SPD voters for 1957–1972, shows a wide over-time fluctuation in the way these voters evaluated the "other" parties; the mean evaluations of their own party are steadier as well as higher. (The values for 1957 were taken from DIVO, *Untersuchung der Wählerschaft und Wahlentscheidung, 1957* (Frankfurt, 1955).) CDU/CSU voters followed the same general pattern (see figure B). FDP voters, however, not only evaluated their own party much less consistently, but also did not rate their own party much above their respective coalition partners (CDU until 1965, SPD after 1969) (figure C).

28. This leaves open the possibility that individuals were classified as partisan leaners even though they evaluated "their" party negatively. Such cases were extremely infrequent, however. Although the terms used to describe the categories of the partisanship scale parallel the American terms, no

C. Party scalometers, 1957-1972 (FDP voters only).

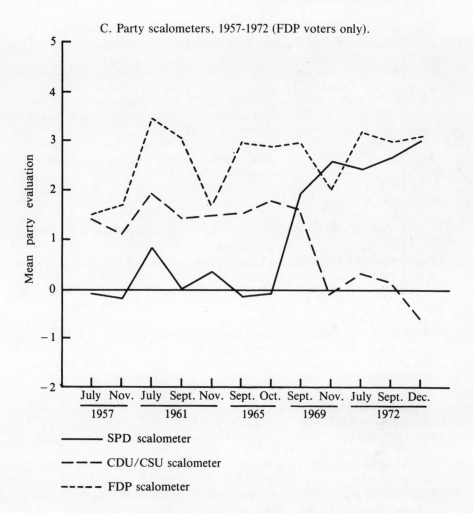

――――― SPD scalometer

――― CDU/CSU scalometer

― ― ― FDP scalometer

direct equivalence is suggested because this measure of partisanship is based on completely different questions.

29. Klaus Liepelt, "The Infrastructure of Party Support in Germany and Austria," in Mattei Dogan and Richard Rose, eds., *European Politics: A Reader* (Boston: Little, Brown, 1971), pp. 183–201.

30. Compare Almond and Verba's discussion of partisanship in Germany: Gabriel Almond and Sidney Verba, *The Civic Culture* (Boston: Little, Brown, 1963), chap. 4; and Scheuch, "Sichtbarkeit," pp. 190–191.

31. Only SPD and CDU partisans are included. The correlations for Berger's measure over the three panel waves are taken from Helmut Norpoth, "Party Identification in West Germany," *Comparative Political Studies,* 11 (April 1978), 36–61. Norpoth bases a very optimistic assessment of the possi-

bility of party identification in Germany on a sophisticated analysis of the 1972 panel data, but he does not deal with the question of longer-term change in the viability of partisanship.

In the text the stability of Berger's and our measures are compared over the three panel waves. The direct correlations between our and Berger's indicators are $tau_b = 0.668$ and gamma $= 0.772$. Cross-tabulations of the two measures show that the principal difference lies in the independent or nonpartisan categories. Of the respondents that are coded on both measures, 17 percent are classified as partisans on our measure but as Independents on Berger's, while the reverse is true for only 4.3 percent. Only 2.2 percent are coded in different partisan camps on the two measures.

Comparisons with Zohlnhöfer's party identification scale also indicate very similar relationships. The correlations for the 1961 study are $tau_b = 0.656$ and gamma $= 0.781$.

32. Our measure is probably only marginally less comparable than other partisanship questions across nations, but its base in the party scalometers makes the problem of comparability more obvious. The question of indicator equivalence is clearly not solved when a survey question is translated literally; for our context, see the discussions in David Conradt, "West Germany: A Remade Political Culture," *Comparative Political Studies*, 7 (July 1974), 222–238, and Kaase, "Party Identification." Besides the work by Butler and Stokes (for Great Britain) and Thomassen (for the Netherlands), see also Harold Clarke, Jane Jenson, Lawrence LeDuc, and Jon Pammett, *Political Choice in Canada* (Toronto: McGraw-Hill Ryerson, 1979), esp. chap. 5 and the literature cited there for further discussions of the application of the party identification concept in non-U.S. contexts.

33. This interpretation suggests that the Grand Coalition led to higher affect for the two major parties, at least among SPD and CDU/CSU supporters. Many contemporary German observers felt that three years of cooperation between the two large parties, without effective parliamentary opposition, would decrease affect for the political system and result in a tendency to vote for "anti-system" parties like the right wing NPD or the communist DKP. Engelmann, using elite surveys taken in 1968–1969, documented that members of parliament, party functionaries, and party members indeed held negative views of the Grand Coalition with respect to its effect on democracy. In contrast, mass surveys show a high acceptance of the Grand Coalition, as well as majorities wishing to continue it after the election. See Frederick Engelmann, "Perceptions of the Great Coalition in West Germany," *Canadian Journal of Political Science* 5 (1972), 28–54.

34. For a discussion of partisanship in relation to construct validation, see Jürgen Falter, "Zur Validierung theoretischer Konstrukte: Wissenschaftstheoretische Aspekte des Validierungskonzeptes," *Zeitschrift für Soziologie*, 7 (November 1977), 349–369; Falter, "Einmal mehr"; and Gluchowski, "Parteiidentifikation."

35. See Angus Campbell, Gerald Gurin, Warren Miller, *The Voter Decides* (Evanston: Paterson, 1954); an even earlier discussion is found in George Belknap and Angus Campbell, "Political Party Identification and Attitudes

towards Foreign Policy," *Public Opinion Quarterly,* 15 (1952), 601–623. A complete treatment of the concept, of course, is contained in Campbell et al., *American Voter.*

36. Of the respondents (voters only) whose partisanship changed between the preelection and postelection interviews, 64 percent in 1969 and 80 percent in 1972 voted for the party to which they switched. In both years, this process was particularly noticeable among CDU-leaners. Since the short-term forces largely favored the SPD in these elections, preelection CDU-leaners who decided to vote for the SPD transferred their partisanship to the SPD as well.

37. The vote variable is based on second (party) vote only and is coded: 1 = CDU/SCU; 2 = nonvoting, refused to state vote, or other party; 3 = SPD. The partisanship variable is the seven-point scale.

38. In *The American Voter,* Campbell and his colleagues argue that Independents who report always voting for the same party are possibly hidden partisans. The same argument will not be made for the people who are classified as nonpartisans here. Some of these nonpartisans probably vote on the basis of their socioeconomic or religious group membership, and can therefore very well exhibit stable voting behavior without having direct affective ties to a party.

39. See Lester Milbrath with M. L. Goel, *Political Participation* (Chicago: Rand McNally, 1977); Campbell et al., *American Voter;* M. Kent Jennings "Partisan Commitment and Electoral Behaviour in the Netherlands," *Acta Politica,* 7 (October 1972), 455–470; Ole Borre and Daniel Katz, "Party Identification and Its Motivational Base in a Multi-Party System: A Study of the Danish General Election of 1971," *Scandinavian Political Studies,* 8 (1973), 69–111.

40. For the United States, see Campbell et al., *American Voter,* chap. 19; Campbell et al., *Elections,* chap. 2. No similar analysis has been made for Germany.

41. Sidney Verba, Norman Nie, Jae-on Kim, *The Modes of Democratic Participation: A Cross-National Comparison* (Beverly Hills: Sage Publications, 1971); Verba and Nie, *Participation in America* (New York: Harper and Row, 1972); Verba, Nie, and Kim, *Participation and Political Equality* (Cambridge: University Press, 1978). For a systematic attempt to distinguish between conventional and unconventional forms of political activity, see Samuel Barnes and Max Kaase, *Political Action* (Beverly Hills: Sage Publications, 1979).

42. Analyses of earlier data suggest that a large proportion of those who refuse to indicate either their partisan vote or nonvoting are not very knowledgeable or interested in politics. Thus, it seems unlikely that refusals actually come from partisans who do not trust the democratic nature of the political system. For a different interpretation, see Almond and Verba, *Civic Culture,* p. 80.

43. The activities are, of course, not strictly comparable. Although the impression that the level of citizen involvement in campaigns and politics has increased cannot be rigorously tested with these data, it would conform to the other evidence of growing politicization presented in chapter 2. In this chapter,

however, the concern is not so much with absolute levels of participation as with the relationship between partisan attitudes and the level of campaign activity.

44. Scheuch, "Sichtbarkeit," pp. 200–205. For further discussion of this notion, see Kendall L. Baker, "The Acquisition of Partisanship in Germany," *American Journal of Political Science*, 18 (August 1974), 569–582.

45. Elisabeth Noelle-Neumann, "The Dual Climate of Opinion: The Influence of Television in the 1976 West German Federal Election," in Max Kaase and Klaus von Beyme, eds., *Elections and Parties: German Political Studies*, III (Beverly Hills: Sage Publications, 1978), pp. 137–170. Other discussions of the partisan imbalance include Max Kaase, "Die Bundestagswahl 1972: Probleme und Analysen," *Politische Vierteljahresschrift*, 14 (May 1973), 145–190; and Wolfgang Gibowski, "Der Effekt unterschiedlicher Plazierung der Wahlabsichten im Fragebogen," *Politische Vierteljahresschrift*, 14 (May 1973), 275–294.

46. The association between the measure of involvement (frequency of political discussion), which was used as a general indicator of politicization in chapter 2, and the strength of partisanship is quite weak in all elections. For 1961, 1965, and 1969—when exactly comparable measures of political discussion were used—tau_b averages 0.027. There is a persistent difference between nonpartisans and others, but little systematic variation between levels of party attachments.

47. Strictly speaking, such calculations require interval-level data. Although it is doubtful that respondents' reactions to the scalometer instrument fulfill this condition, party evaluation scales have been widely used to establish psychological distances between parties. See Berger, "Parteiidentifikation," and Borre and Katz, "Party Identification." *The American Voter* discussed psychological distances between the parties using different measures because the thermometer scales were not introduced into the SRC/CPS election studies until later. Nevertheless, the American data also show the relationship between the strength of partisanship and the absolute difference in the thermometer scores for the two parties.

48. Since the operationalization of our partisanship measure is based only on the scalometer evaluation of the respondent's preferred party, there is no threat of tautology when the evaluations of both parties are used. Although the conceptualization of partisanship used here focuses on the respondent's party only, the argument has been made in the United States that "hostility" toward the opposite party is a necessary part of party identification and that the predominant measure of party identification should be altered accordingly. See Michael A. Maggiotto and James Piereson, "Partisan Identification and Electoral Choice: The Hostility Hypothesis," *American Journal of Political Science*, 21 (November 1977), 745–768.

49. It is likely that the evaluations were influenced by a "government bonus," as CDU supporters saw larger distances between the parties until 1965, and SPD partisans saw more polarization thereafter. In comparison, our analyses with American election surveys show that not even in the 1972 election in the United States did strong partisans of either party locate the other party below the neutral point (50) on the feeling thermometers.

50. For example, see Hans Jochen Brauns et al., *SPD in der Krise* (Frankfurt: Fischer, 1976); and Wolf-Dieter Narr, ed., *Auf dem Weg zum Einparteienstaat* (Opladen: Westdeutscher Verlag, 1977).

51. Philip Converse, "The Nature of Belief Systems in Mass Publics," in David Apter, ed., *Ideology and Discontent* (Glencoe: Free Press, 1964); also Campbell et al., *American Voter,* chap. 6.

52. Thomassen, "Party Identification," p. 77.

53. Our cross-sectional data are not suitable for analyses of what Converse called the dynamic concept of constraint. Incongruence or dissonance between belief elements is likely to be solved by altering the less salient attitudes to "fit" the more central or salient ones. See Converse, "Belief Systems." Converse uses tau-gammas to determine constraint, while we use Pearson r's. For our data, the two measures differ in absolute levels but not in the order of the strength of the relationships.

54. An alternative approach is based on the analysis of levels of conceptualization; see Converse, "Belief Systems," as well as John Field and Ronald Anderson, "Ideology in the Public's Conceptualization of the 1964 Election," *Public Opinion Quarterly,* 33 (1969), 380–398; and Hans Dieter Klingemann's chapters in Barnes and Kaase, *Political Action.*

55. Converse, "Belief Systems," p. 207.

56. Converse, "Belief Systems"; also, Norman Nie with Kristi Anderson, "Mass Belief Systems Revisited," *Journal of Politics,* 36 (August 1974), 540–591; Norman Nie, Sidney Verba, and John Petrocik, *The Changing American Voter* (Cambridge: Harvard University Press, 1976). For an interesting analysis that combines the constraint approach based on correlations with the levels of conceptualization approach, see Hans Dieter Klingemann and William E. Wright, "Individual and Situational Determinants of Issue Constraint in the American Mass Public" (Manuscript, University of Mannheim, 1979).

57. Philip Converse, "Public Opinion and Voting Behavior," in Fred Greenstein and Nelson Polsby, eds., *Non-governmental Politics,* vol. IV of *Handbook of Political Science* (Reading: Addison-Wesley, 1975), p. 106.

58. See chapter 9 for a more detailed discussion of these questions.

59. Additional analysis shows that the increasing constraint is mostly due to the growing intercorrelations between two different kinds of issues: those that are more closely related to traditional cleavages and thus more salient (old age security; price stability); and those that are less salient and fit less clearly into the traditional cleavage structure (education; relations with the United States). In other words, *all* issues are increasingly drawn into the context of partisanship.

60. Note that the discussed increase in constraints is weakest (in fact, almost nonexistent) among nonpartisans: precisely the group among whom the hypothesized source of constraints (parties) would not be operating.

61. Campbell et al., *American Voter,* chap. 7; Norpoth, "Party Identification"; Butler and Stokes, *Political Change,* chap. 3; Jennings, "Partisan Commitment"; Borre and Katz, "Party Identification."

62. Campbell et al., *American Voter,* chap. 7; Philip Converse, *The Dynamics of Party Support* (Beverly Hills: Sage Publications, 1976), and the exten-

sive literature about the life-cycle vs. generational explanations cited by Converse.

63. Converse, "Time and Partisan Stability"; Converse, *Dynamics*.

64. Pappi, "Parteiensystem"; Pappi, "Sozialstruktur."

65. For voting returns that demonstrate continuity over the past seven decades, see Karl W. Deutsch, "The German Federal Republic," in R. C. Macridis and R. E. Ward, eds., *Modern Political Systems: Europe* (Englewood Cliffs: Prentice-Hall, 1968), p. 363.

66. This strength measure "folds" the original seven-point partisanship scale at the nonpartisan midpoint. Converse collapsed the five-nation data to form a three-point gradation of partisanship—nonpartisans, leaners, supporters-members—in order to arrive at cross-nationally comparable measures. See Converse, "Time and Partisan Stability."

67. First, the adjustment for different historical turnout rates was accomplished by discounting I_p according to how much the average turnout for a period (empire, Weimar) fell below the average turnout for the Federal Republic. Second, to account for age-related turnout differences, an average turnout rate for each age group was calculated using all postwar surveys, and I_p was discounted by this age turnout rate. Third, the resistance factor, a function of the lag a cohort experienced between reaching the age of twenty-one and actually becoming eligible to vote, was used to reduce I_p for women during the Wilhelmine empire and for all cohorts during the Third Reich. See also Converse, "Time and Partisan Stability," pp. 152–155.

68. See, for example, M. Kent Jennings and Richard Niemi, *The Political Character of Adolescence* (Princeton: Princeton University Press, 1974); Baker, "The Acquisition of Partisanship"; Russell J. Dalton, "Reassessing Parental Socialization," *American Political Science Review*, 74 (July, 1980); Barnes and Kaase et al., *Political Action*, chaps. 15, 16.

69. The effectiveness of transmitting partisanship declines as an exponential function of the duration of the disruption of democratic politics. See Converse, "Time and Partisan Stability," p. 158.

70. This is noted in passing, ibid., p. 155.

71. The Ns for the five-year cohorts range from 75 to 842 and average 289. The result of this cumulation procedure is also that the effects of a single election on the measurement of partisanship would be minimized.

72. Norpoth, "Party Identification," p. 55; Pappi, "Sozialstruktur," pp. 68–73.

73. See Converse, "Time and Partisan Stability," p. 169 and note 17.

74. Pappi, "Sozialstruktur," pp. 68–73. Moreover, Pappi is critical of Converse for assuming in his model that the effects of the Third Reich can be largely limited to the 1933–1945 period.

75. Hence, the results from single-nation replications have to be interpreted independently of and differently from Converse's findings. This point is missed by William Vanderbok, "Cohorts, Aggregation Problems and Cross-level Theorizing: The Case of Partisan Stability," *Western Political Quarterly*, 30 (March 1977), 104–111 (esp. 110).

76. See also the results in Barnes and Kaase et al., *Political Action*, chaps. 15, 16.

77. See the detailed analyses in Richard Niemi, *How Family Members Perceive Each Other* (New Haven: Yale University Press, 1974).

78. Philip Converse and George Dupeux, "Politicization of the Electorate in France and the United States," in Campbell et al., *Elections*, chap. 14.

9. Partisan Images and Electoral Change

1. Philip Converse, "Of Time and Partisan Stability," *Comparative Political Studies*, 2 (July 1969), 139–171; Jack Dennis and Donald McCrone, "Preadult Development of Political Party Identification of Western Democracies," *Comparative Political Studies*, 3 (July 1970), 115–136.

2. For a discussion of the electoral impact of candidates see Helmut Norpoth, "Kanzlerkandidaten," *Politische Vierteljahresschrift*, 18 (November 1977), 551–572; Hans Klingemann and Charles Taylor, "Partisanship, Candidates and Issues: Attitudinal Components of the Vote in West German Federal Elections," in Max Kaase and Klaus von Beyme, eds., *German Political Studies: Elections and Parties* (London: Sage Publications, 1978), pp. 97–136.

3. Donald Matthews and James Prothro, *Negroes and the New Southern Politics* (New York: Harcourt, Brace and World, 1966).

4. Ibid., p. 378. See also Richard Trilling, *Party Images and Electoral Behavior* (New York: John Wiley, 1976).

5. Charles Sellers, "The Equilibrium Cycle in Two-Party Politics," *Public Opinion Quarterly*, 29 (1965), 16–38.

6. David Butler and Donald Stokes, *Political Change in Britain* (New York: St. Martin's, 1969), p. 360.

7. Trilling, *Party Images*; Franz Urban Pappi, "Sozialstruktur und Politische Konflikte in der Bundesrepublik" (Habilitationsschrift, Cologne, 1976).

8. Otto Kirchheimer, "Germany: The Vanishing Opposition," in Robert Dahl, ed., *Political Opposition in Western Democracies* (New Haven: Yale University Press, 1966), pp. 237–259.

9. It should be noted, however, that some Germans considered the Social Democrats' opposition to the Third Reich unpatriotic. During the 1961 campaign, for example, Adenauer gained considerable political credit by intimating that his opponent, Willy Brandt, had been "unpatriotic" when escaping the clutches of the Gestapo in 1933 and emigrating to Norway.

10. Kirchheimer, "Germany"; Otto Kirchheimer, "The Transformation of the Western European Party System," in Joseph LaPalombara and Myron Weiner, eds., *Political Parties and Political Development* (Princeton: Princeton University Press, 1966), pp. 177–200.

11. These scales follow the basic "semantic differential" techniques developed by Charles Osgood and his colleagues: C. E. Osgood, G. J. Suci, and P. H. Tannenbaum, *The Measurement of Meaning* (Urbana: University of Illinois Press, 1957). Also see Butler and Stokes, *Political Change*, chap. 16.

12. Konrad-Adenauer-Stiftung, *1972 German Election Panel Study*, no. 7110 (Ann Arbor, ICPSR).

13. Butler and Stokes, *Political Change*, chap. 16.

14. W. Phillips Shively, "Voting Stability and the Nature of Party Attach-

ments in the Weimar Republic," *American Political Science Review*, 66 (December 1972), 1203–25.

15. A typical question reads: "I will now name some groups and institutions. Would you please tell me for each individual group whether this group, in your opinion, generally leans more toward the CDU/CSU, the SPD, or leans equally toward both parties?" In 1969 the questions also referred to the FDP. To maximize comparability, FDP responses were collapsed into the middle category of "both parties." The 1957 data have been recomputed from tables presented in DIVO, *Untersuchung der Wählerschaft und Wahlentscheidung, 1957* (Frankfurt: DIVO, 1957).

Also see Pappi, *Sozialstruktur*.

16. Perceptions of Protestant leanings in 1957 and 1961:

	1957	1961
SPD leaning	16%	24%
Both or other	68	52
CDU leaning	16	23

17. Perceptions of middle-class leanings by respondents from middle-class families produced the following trends:

	1961	1969
SPD leaning	16%	22%
Both or other	39	33
CDU leaning	45	44

18. Franz Urban Pappi, "Sozialstruktur und Wahlentscheidung bei Bundestagswahlen aus kommunalpolitischer Perspektive," in *Kommunales Wahlverhalten*, Series Studien zur Kommunalpolitik, vol. IV (Bonn: Konrad-Adenauer-Stiftung, n.d.) pp. 1–57; and Pappi, "Sozialstruktur"; Pappi, "Sozialstruktur, gesellschaftliche Wertorientierungen und Wahlabsicht," *Politische Vierteljahresschrift*, 18 (November 1977), 195–229.

19. The partisan tendencies of the *Mittelstand* are presented in table 9.1. In 1969 a separate question measured perceptions of the salaried employees (*Angestellte*), and their responses show closer agreement with the SPD (43 percent SPD, 15 percent mixed, and 41 percent CDU/CSU).

20. See chapter 7; also, Kai Hildebrandt and Russell J. Dalton, "The New Politics," in Kaase and Beyme, eds., *German Political Studies*, pp. 69–96.

21. See Chapter 6 above; for an alternative interpretation of these same issues, see Hans Klingemann, "Issue-Kompetenz und Wahlentscheidung," *Politische Vierteljahresschrift*, 14 (June 1973), 227–256.

22. The issues included in the analysis were scored: (-1) SPD, and $(+1)$ CDU/CSU; other replies were treated as missing data. Mean scores were computed for those respondents having valid data for at least half of the issues constituting an index. See appendix B for a list of the issues.

23. The per-annum change statistic is the slope of a regression line obtained by regressing competency scores on the year of the election. This procedure attempts to weight scores from all four timepoints to obtain the best estimate of change over time.

24. Klingemann, "Issue-Kompetenz"; Klingemann and Taylor, "Partisanship."

25. See chapter 6.

26. Indeed, in 1957 a majority of the electorate apparently viewed the SPD as most competent to deal with both issues: DIVO, *Untersuchung,* app. B, pp. 44–45. Without direct access to these data it is difficult to interpret this result. One explanation apparently supported by the DIVO analyses is that the SPD was more successful in attracting the total support of its traditional clientele in 1957 on Old Politics issues, while committed CDU/CSU partisans split their competency opinions between the two major parties or did not differentiate between them. Thus, the Godesberg program may have rapidly eroded the SPD's traditional strongholds on Old Politics issues after 1959, and it took time for the party to build an improved image on other dimensions.

27. The SPD had improved its image on the issue of U.S. relations by 8 percent since 1957: DIVO, *Untersuchung,* app. B, p. 49.

28. Saul Robinson and J. Caspar Kuhlmann, "Two Decades of Nonreform in West German Education," *Comparative Education Review,* 11 (October 1967), 311–330; Arnold Heidenheimer et al., "Secondary School Reform," in Heidenheimer et al., *Comparative Public Policy* (New York: St. Martin's, 1975), pp. 44–68.

29. Lewis Edinger, *Politics in Germany* (Boston: Little, Brown, 1968), p. 50.

30. In the Godesberg program the SPD revised its policies concerning the structure of the economic system, for instance, the socialization of industry. However, the basic goals of the party—to protect the workers and the little man—remained relatively unchanged. Only the means were altered.

31. Frederick Engelmann, "Perceptions of the Great Coalition in West Germany, 1966–1969," *Canadian Journal of Political Science,* 1 (March 1972), 28–54; Max Kaase, "Determinants of Voting Behavior in the West German Election of 1969," in Ian Budge, Ivor Crewe, and Dennis Farlie, eds., *Party Identification and Beyond* (New York: John Wiley, 1976), pp. 81–102.

32. Heidenheimer et al., "Secondary School Reform," p. 60.

33. The 1972 issue-competency data, which were collected in a slightly different format from that used for earlier timepoints, include only those who felt the issue was important. The findings in this chapter were compared with data collected in 1972 by Hans Klingemann (using a question exactly comparable to one asked in earlier years), and they show even more support for our hypotheses. See Klingemann and Taylor, "Partisanship," p. 131. Klingemann's data indicate the following perceptions of CDU/CSU and SPD issue competency:

	Prices	Old age	Education	USA
CDU/CSU	55%	43%	32%	56%
SPD	45	57	68	44
Percent of sample	69	77	69	72

34. Klingemann and Taylor present over-time data showing an equivalent increase in perceptions of SPD competency to deal with Soviet relations ("Partisanship," p. 131):

	1961	1965	1969	1972
CDU/CSU	44%	49%	20%	15%
SPD	56	51	80	85
Percent of sample	70	78	91	75

35. An excellent and detailed discussion of the SPD-FDP reform policies, albeit from a critical perspective, is presented by Manfred Schmidt, "Die 'Politik der Inneren Reformen' in der Bundesrepublik Deutschland 1969–1976," *Politische Vierteljahresschrift,* 19 (June 1978), 201–253.

36. The per-annum change statistic is explained in note 23.

37. The two Old Politics issues were combined into a single measure using the coding scheme described in appendix B. The same procedure was used in constructing a New Politics issue measure. The trends for both of these indexes for 1961–1972 are graphed below for SPD and CDU/CSU voters:

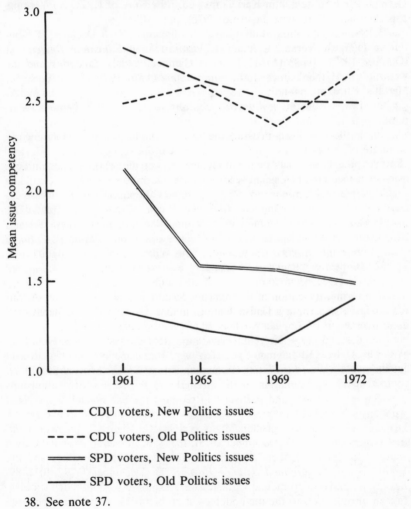

— — CDU voters, New Politics issues

- - - - CDU voters, Old Politics issues

═══ SPD voters, New Politics issues

——— SPD voters, Old Politics issues

38. See note 37.

10. A Causal Analysis of the Components of the Vote

1. W. Phillips Shively, "Voting Stability and the Nature of Party Attachments in the Weimar Republic," *American Political Science Review*, 66 (December 1972), 1203–25; W. Phillips Shively, "The Development of Party Identification among Adults," *American Political Science Review*, 73 (December 1979), 1039–54; and chapter 8.

2. Donald Matthews and James Prothro, *Negroes and the New Southern Politics* (New York: Harcourt, Brace and World, 1966); Richard Trilling, *Party Images and Electoral Behavior* (New York: John Wiley, 1976); and chapter 9.

3. Shively, "Voting Stability."

4. Gerhard Loewenberg, "The Remaking of the German Party System," *Polity*, 1 (1968), 86–113; Gerhard Loewenberg, "The Development of the German Party System," in Karl Cerny, ed., *Germany at the Polls* (Washington: American Enterprise Institute, 1978), pp. 1–28.

5. Shively, "Voting Stability."

6. Philip Converse, "Of Time and Partisan Stability," *Comparative Political Studies*, 2 (1968) 139–171; Angus Campbell et al., *Elections and the Political Order* (New York: John Wiley, 1966), chaps. 2–4, 7, and 10.

7. Angus Campbell et al., *The American Voter* (New York: John Wiley, 1960); Norman Nie, Sidney Verba, and John Petrocik, *The Changing American Voter* (Cambridge: Harvard University Press, 1976); Ian Budge, Ivor Crewe, and Dennis Farlie, eds., *Party Identification and Beyond* (New York: John Wiley, 1976).

8. The one obvious factor not included in this model is candidate image. However, because of Germany's parliamentary form of government, candidate image exerts only a minor influence on voting decisions. For over-time analyses see: Hans Klingemann and Charles Taylor, "Partisanship, Candidates and Issues: Attitudinal Components of the Vote in West German Federal Elections," in Max Kaase and Klaus von Beyme, eds., *German Political Studies: Elections and Parties* (London: Sage Publications, 1978), pp. 97–136; Helmut Norpoth, "Kanzlerkandidaten," *Politische Vierteljahresschrift*, 18 (November 1977), 551–572.

9. For an application of a similar model to the United States see Arthur Goldberg, "Discerning a Causal Pattern among Data on Voting Behavior," *American Political Science Review*, 60 (December 1966), 913–922.

10. See chapter 9; Kai Hildebrandt and Russell Dalton, "The New Politics," in Kaase and Beyme, eds., *German Political Studies*, 69–96; Ronald Inglehart, *The Silent Revolution* (Princeton: Princeton University Press, 1977).

11. Separate estimation of the strengths of the reciprocal relationships between issue images and partisanship requires the use of multiwave panel data or instrumental variables. See Gregory Markus and Philip Converse, "A Dynamic Simultaneous Equation Model of Electoral Choice," *American Political Science Review*, 73 (December 1979), 1055–70; Benjamin Page and Calvin Jones, "Reciprocal Effects of Policy Preferences, Party Loyalties and the Vote," *American Political Science Review*, 73 (December 1979), 1071–89. Several potential instrumental variables were explored without much success. For an introduction to the methodological problems of reciprocal effects see

Otis Dudley Duncan, *Introduction to Structural Equation Models* (New York: Academic Press, 1975), chap. 5–7.

12. The measurement of the components of this causal model were drawn from analyses in the preceding chapters. The indicator of partisan attitudes is the seven-point index developed in chapter 8. Issue images are measured by an additive index of perceived party competency for the set of four core issues: two related to the Old Politics (price stability and old age security); and the other two related to the New Politics (support for education and relations with the United States). This issue competency measure is used because it taps the direct relevance of valence issues to the party system; it is not intended to serve as an undifferentiated test of issue voting. Including a larger set of issues and weighting competency by issue salience would increase the total predictive power of the issues, but the content of the indicator is of more importance here than maximizing its correlation with the vote. The social characteristics indicator combines all four dimensions of traditional cleavage politics—social status, religion, region, and rural-urban residence—into a self-weighted composite measure of cleavage influences. This measure was obtained by saving the predicted values from an MCA analysis of social characteristics on vote. For further information on the construction and coding of these indicators, see appendix B.

13. The following tabulation presents the results of regressing the vote on social characteristics, partisanship, Old Politics issue images, and New Politics issue images. Entries are standardized regression coefficients.

	1961	*1965*	*1969*	*1972*
Social characteristics	0.116	0.107	0.105	0.087
Partisanship	.652	.515	.452	.566
Old Politics issues	.157	.302	.282	.222
New Politics issues	.051	.092	.130	.090

For additional discussion of these results see Kendall Baker et al., "Political Stability in Transition" (Paper presented at the APSA annual meeting, San Francisco, 1975).

14. Hildebrandt and Dalton, "New Politics."

15. See note 13.

16. Matthews and Prothro, *Negroes*; Trilling, *Party Images*.

17. Inglehart, *Silent Revolution*.

18. The Pearson correlation between issue images and partisanship is as follows: 1961 = 0.66, 1965 = 0.72, 1969 = 0.67, 1972 = 0.73.

19. The one-month correlations for election panels in 1969 and 1972 are as follows:

	1st vote	*2d vote*	*Partisanship*
1969	0.74	0.73	0.63
1972	.86	.89	.81

20. Cameron argues that the Federal Republic is unique in this respect: David Cameron, "Postindustrial Change and Secular Realignments" (Ph.D. diss., University of Michigan, 1976).

21. For another perspective on generational differences in German partisanship see Kendall Baker, "Generational Differences in the Role of Party Identification in German Political Behavior," *American Journal of Political Science*, 22 (February 1978), 106-129.

22. In statistical terms there is a large pool of shared variance between the New Politics issue images of the young and their partisan attachments.

23. Shively, "Voting Stability."

11. The 1976 Election

1. For analyses of the 1976 election see: Max Kaase and Klaus von Beyme, eds., *German Political Studies: Elections and Parties* (London: Sage Publications, 1978); Karl Cerny, ed., *Germany at the Polls* (Washington, D.C.: American Enterprise Institute, 1978); Max Kaase, ed., *Wahlsoziologie heute*, Special issue of *Politische Vierteljahresschrift*, 18 (November 1977).

2. For a discussion of the Phillips curve theory, see chapter 4.

3. Michael Stohl, *The Politics of Terrorism* (New York: Marcel Decker, 1978); Julian Becker, *Hitler's Children: The Story of the Baader-Meinhof Terrorist Gang* (New York: Lippincott, 1977).

4. Kendall Baker, "Terrorism, Post-material Values, and German Politics" (Paper presented at the Conference on German Terrorism, Notre Dame University, March 1979).

5. Ronald Inglehart, "Political Dissatisfaction and Mass Support for Social Change in Advanced Industrial Societies," *Comparative Political Studies*, 10 (October 1977), 455-472.

6. Roger Tilford, *The Ostpolitik and Political Change in Germany* (Lexington: D. C. Heath, 1975); Roger Morgan, *West Germany's Foreign Policy Agenda*, Washington Papers, vol. 6, no. 54 (Beverly Hills: Sage Publications, 1978); David Conradt, *The German Polity* (New York: Longman, 1977).

7. These analyses were based on the *World Events Interaction Study* data (Ann Arbor: ICPSR). The methods of the analysis are presented in chapter 5.

8. Werner Kaltefleiter, "Germans: Friendlier but Apprehensive," *Public Opinion*, 2 (March-May 1979), 10-12.

9. Morgan, *West Germany's Agenda*.

10. Tilford, *Ostpolitik*.

11. Although this holds for the SPD's general campaign slogan, three of the four topical SPD campaign posters stressed either security or stability in 1976.

12. These data are drawn from Elisabeth Noelle-Neumann and Erich Neumann, *Jahrbuch der öffentlichen Meinung*, 1968-1973 and 1974-1976 (Allensbach and Bonn: Institut für Demoskopie), and from a personal communication from the Institut für Demoskopie.

13. More precisely, in 1975 and 1976, mentions of the energy crisis were not frequent enough to justify a separate code. Mentions of the problem were grouped under the general heading of economics.

14. The 1976 findings are actually closer to the normally low levels of foreign policy interest found in other Western democracies: Richard Merritt

and Donald Puchala, eds., *Western European Perspectives on International Affairs* (New York: Praeger, 1968).

15. Gabriel Almond and Sidney Verba, *The Civic Culture* (Princeton: Princeton University Press, 1963).

16. A clear example of the possible impact of the environment is the decade-long decline of political efficacy in the United States. See Philip Converse, "Change in the American Electorate," in Angus Campbell and Philip Converse, eds., *The Human Meaning of Social Change* (New York: Russell Sage, 1972), pp. 263–337.

17. Viggo Blücher, *Jugend in Europa* (Jugendwerk der Deutschen Shell, 1977).

18. U.S. International Communications Agency, "German Youth Study, 1976." For similar data on the general public, see David Conradt, "Changing German Political Culture," in Gabriel Almond and Sidney Verba, eds., *The Civic Culture Revisited* (Boston: Little, Brown, 1980), p. 230.

19. Almond and Verba, *Civic Culture,* chap. 3.

20. See also Conradt, "Changing German Political Culture"; and Martin Greiffenhagen and Sylvia Greiffenhagen, *Ein Schwieriges Vaterland* (Munich: List, 1979).

21. Max Kaase, "Public Opinion Research in the Federal Republic of Germany," in Cerny, ed., *Germany,* pp. 195–225.

22. Ibid.

23. The 1976 question has a narrow time-line focus (*in letzter Zeit*), which limited positive responses about discussing politics. In contrast, the 1972 question is broadly worded (*in der Zeit vor der Wahl*), and thus people were more likely to say they discussed politics.

24. For example, political interest shows steady growth during the 1976 campaign: in June, 47 percent of the respondents were interested in politics; in September, it was 50 percent; and in November, it was 55 percent.

25. Thomas Ellwein et al., *Politische Beteiligung in der Bundesrepublik Deutschland* (Goettingen: Schwarz, 1975); Heinz Grossman, ed., *Bürgerinitiativen: Schritte zur Veränderung* (Frankfurt: Fischer, 1971); Hanspeter Knirsch and Friedhelm Nickolmann, *Die Chance der Bürgerinitiativen* (Wuppertal: Hammer, 1976); Peter Cornelius Meyer-Tasch, *Die Bürgerinitiativbewegung* (Reinbek: Rowohlt, 1976).

26. The following mean scores on political discussion were taken from the 1976 ZUMABUS. The question format was similar to the one used in 1969, and responses have been recoded to: (1) never, (2) frequently, (3) daily.

Generation	Wilh.	Weim.	Third Reich	Early FRG	Late FRG	Later FRG
Mean score	1.94	2.14	2.22	2.26	2.31	2.23

27. Kendall Baker and Helmut Norpoth, "Candidates on Television" (Paper presented at the annual meeting of the Midwest Political Science Association, Chicago, 1979); see also Helmut Norpoth and Kendall Baker, "Mass Media Use and Electoral Choice in West Germany, 1961–1976," *Comparative Politics* 13 (October 1980).

28. Elisabeth Noelle-Neumann, "The Dual Climate of Opinion," in

Kaase and Beyme, eds., *German Political Studies: Elections and Parties*, pp. 137–170.

29. Most polls showed the CDU/CSU leading the SPD from the early part of the 1976 campaign. See results cited in Kaase, "Public Opinion Research," and Noelle-Neumann, "Dual Climate of Opinion."

30. Hans D. Klingemann and Charles Lewis Taylor, "Partisanship, Candidates and Issues," in Kaase and Beyme, eds., *German Political Studies: Elections and Parties*, pp. 97–133.

31. Ronald Inglehart, *The Silent Revolution* (Princeton: Princeton University Press, 1976); Russell Dalton, "Was There a Revolution?" *Comparative Political Studies*, 9 (January 1977), 459–473.

32. In fact, the structural shifts toward the service sector and white-collar employment continued, making a return to traditional class politics less likely.

33. Inglehart, *Silent Revolution*. Inglehart terms "post-materialists" those respondents who believe that out of four political goals presented to them, "maintaining freedom of speech" and "increasing participation in important political decisions" are the two most important social goals. Those who stress "fighting rising prices" and "maintaining order in the nation" above the other two goals are considered to have "materialist" value preferences.

34. Kai Hildebrandt and Russell Dalton, "The New Politics," in Kaase and Beyme, eds., *German Political Studies: Elections and Parties*, pp. 69–96. In addition, a principal components analysis of issues in the 1976 survey continues to identify the Old Politics–New Politics dimension of issue salience discussed in chapter 6.

35. These Eurobarometer surveys were conducted by the Commission of the European Communities under the direction of Jacques-René Rabier and Ronald Inglehart. Additional information on these studies (ICPSR Study nos. 7260, 7330, 7551) can be obtained from the Inter-university Consortium for Political and Social Research, University of Michigan.

36. Even if only between 8 and 11 percent of the population hold New Politics values, these presently small numbers should not be discounted. Empirical data have shown that New Politics concerns are disproportionately represented among political elites and those active in politics. See Ronald Inglehart, Robert Putnam, and Samuel Eldersveld, eds., *Elite Political Culture* (forthcoming); Hildebrandt and Dalton, "New Politics," p. 94, n. 28.

37. Inglehart, *Silent Revolution*; Dalton, "Was There a Revolution?"

38. This slight increase might represent the effects of population turnover. Between 1970 and 1976 older citizens oriented toward Old Politics were dying, and they were replaced in the electorate by young New Politics voters. See Hildebrandt and Dalton, "New Politics."

39. For a discussion of the requirements of issue voting see the symposium in the *American Political Science Review*, 66 (June 1972), pp. 415–470.

40. Dieter Roth, "Ökonomische Situation und Wahlverhalten," *Politische Vierteljahresschrift*, 18 (November 1977), 537–550; Gebhard Kirchgässner, "Wirtschaftslage und Wahlverhalten," *Politische Vierteljahresschrift*, 18 (November 1977), 510–536.

41. The Alford index measures the difference between the percentages of

two social classes voting for the SPD. Robert Alford, *Party and Society* (Chicago: Rand McNally, 1963).

42. The following tabulation presents the MCA results of these analyses (entries are MCA beta coefficients):

	1972	1976
Occupation	0.25	0.21
Income	.06	.03
Education	.06	.05
R	.26	.20

43. Inglehart, *Silent Revolution*. The following data from 1976 are typical of the relationships between religion (Catholic, Protestant, none), frequency of church attendance (frequent, occasional, never), and value priorities:

	Catholic	Protestant	None	Frequent	Occasional	Never
New Politics	7.6%	8.6%	29.8%	6.3%	7.7%	19.5%
Mixed values	48.8	46.1	51.9	43.9	49.2	48.4
Old Politics	43.6	45.3	18.3	49.7	43.1	31.9

44. The following tabulation presents the relationships between religious denomination, church attendance, and the SPD percentage of the two-party voting intentions:

	1972	1976
Denomination		
Protestant	69%	59%
Catholic	45	35
Difference	24	24
Church attendance		
Never	74	72
Occasional	61	45
Regular	28	20
Difference	46	52

45. See the discussion associated with table 7.6 and appendix B for the coding of the four predictor variables.

46. The causal model is based on the 1976 ZUMABUS study conducted by the Zentrum für Umfragen, Methoden und Analysen, Mannheim.

47. The following tabulation gives the distribution of the seven-point partisanship index in 1972 and 1976 (S = strong, W = weak, L = leaning):

	SPD(S)	SPD(W)	SPD(L)	NON-P	CDU(L)	CDU(W)	CDU(S)	Total
1972	19.7%	16.3%	17.0%	10.9%	16.2%	10.7%	9.2%	100.0%
1976	14.8	14.4	17.8	6.6	16.3	14.5	15.7	100.0

48. Several aspects of these findings deserve mention. First, perceptions of party polarization are still a function of the strength of party ties. In addition, although most commentators considered the 1976 campaign to be less acrimonious than the 1972 contest, polarization increased to the largest difference (4.20) since these perceptions were first measured (table 8.6). The apparent effect of the CDU/CSU's strident rhetoric, campaign themes, and attempts to reverse the "Spiral of Silence" was to increase polarization significantly for

CDU/CSU partisans, while it decreased slightly for Social Democrats. Second, campaign activity still varied according to the strength of partianship. But again, the CDU/CSU's campaign disproportionately increased the activity of its supporters, and reduced the imbalance in campaign activity among the major parties that was noted in 1972 (table 8.5). See INFAS, *Transfer 2: Wahlforschung: Sonden in politischen Markt* (Opladen: Westdeutscher Verlag, 1977), pp. 256–259. Finally, partisanship continued to increase its influence on attitudinal constraint, suggesting a further development of attitudinal partisanship. The following tabulation extends the data of figure 9.2. The first column under each heading refers to 1972 and the second to 1976.

	Core Issues		All Issues		Candidates	
Strong	0.70	0.74	0.58	0.71	−0.68	−0.48
Weak	.52	.62	.47	.58	− .50	− .39
Leaning	.54	.53	.48	.52	− .41	− .09
Nonpartisans	.21	.22	.30	.22	.20	0.57

49. Klingemann and Taylor, "Partisanship."

50. The following tabulation presents the results of regressing the vote on social characteristics, partisanship, Old Politics issue images, and New Politics issue images. Entries are standardized regression coefficients.

	1972	1976
Social characteristics	0.087	0.028
Partisanship	.566	.533
Old Politics	.222	.318
New Politics	.090	.076

12. West German Politics in Transition

1. Gabriel Almond and Sidney Verba, *The Civic Culture* (Princeton: Princeton University Press, 1963).

2. Ronald Inglehart, "Political Dissatisfaction and Mass Support for Social Change in Advanced Industrial Societies," *Comparative Political Studies,* 10 (October 1977), 455–472.

3. Arthur Miller, "Political Issues and Trust in Government," *American Political Science Review,* 68 (September 1974), 951–972; Philip Converse, "Change in the American Electorate," in Angus Campbell and Philip Converse, eds., *The Human Meaning of Social Change* (New York: Russell Sage, 1972); Alan Marsh, *Protest and Political Consciousness* (Beverly Hills: Sage Publications, 1976); Samuel Barnes and Max Kaase et al., *Political Action* (Beverly Hills: Sage Publications, 1979).

4. Kurt Sontheimer, *Die verunsicherte Republik* (Munich: Piper, 1979).

5. See Richard Löwenthal, "Why German Stability Is So Insecure," *Encounter* 39 (December 1978), 31–37; Jane Kramer, "A Reporter in Europe," *New Yorker,* March 20, 1978, pp. 44–87; Jonathan Carr, "West Germany: A Survey," *The Economist,* February 20, 1977; and Richard L. Merritt, "The Terrorist Threat to Civil Liberties in West Germany," *The American Spectator,* 11 (April 1978), 17–19.

6. See Kendall L. Baker, "Terrorism, Postmaterial Values and German Politics" (Paper presented at the Conference on German Terrorism, Notre Dame University, March 1979).

7. Barnes and Kaase, *Political Action*.

8. M. J. Crozier, S. P. Huntington, and J. Watamike, *The Crisis of Democracy: Report on the Governability of Democracies to the Trilateral Commission* (New York: New York University Press, 1975); Juergen Habermas, *Legitimationsprobleme im Spätkapitalismus* (Frankfurt, 1973); Claus Offe, *Strukturprobleme des kapitalistischen Staates* (Frankfurt, 1972); Wilhelm Hennis, Peter Graf Kielmansegg, Ulrich Matz, eds., *Regierbarkeit: Studien zu ihrer Problematisierung,* vols. I and II (Stuttgart: Klett-Cotta, 1977, 1978).

9. Helmut Klages and Peter Kmieciak, eds., *Wertwandel und gesellschaftlicher Wandel* (Frankfurt: Campus, 1979). The following tabulation updates the distribution of political values presented in chapter 11.

	1973	1976	1977	1978	1979	1980
Materialists	42.1	41.5	41.0	37.2	36.8	37.9
Mixed priorities	49.5	47.4	52.1	51.8	51.7	48.4
Postmaterialists	8.5	11.1	6.9	10.9	11.5	13.7
Mean	1.67	1.70	1.66	1.74	1.75	1.8
(N)	(1953)	(891)	(893)	(944)	(948)	(2903)

10. Ronald Inglehart, *The Silent Revolution* (Princeton: Princeton University Press, 1977), pp. 370–373.

11. Miller, "Political Issues and Trust."

12. Barnes and Kaase, *Political Action*.

13. Here we deal only with Germany and the Western democracies, but it is interesting to speculate whether such value change may also, albeit with some time lag, occur in Eastern Europe, and whether East European systems and their ideology will be any better equipped to deal with such changes and their political implications.

14. Barnes and Kaase use this notion to point out that new forms of participation are often (although not exclusively) used by citizens who also employ the traditional means of participation to press demands.

15. Philip Converse and Roy Pierce, "Basic Cleavages in French Politics and the Disorders of May and June 1968" (Paper presented at the International Sociological Conference, Varna, Bulgaria, 1970); Mark Franklin and Anthony Mugham, "The Decline of Class Voting in Britain," *American Political Science Review,* 72 (June 1978), 523–534; Everett Ladd with Charles Hadley, *Transformations of the American Party System* (New York: Norton, 1975).

16. This is consistent with the position taken by W. Phillips Shively, "Voting Stability and the Nature of Party Attachments in the Weimar Republic," *American Political Science Review,* 66 (December 1972), 1203–25.

17. Ian Budge, Ivor Crewe, and Dennis Farlie, eds., *Party Identification and Beyond* (New York: John Wiley, 1976); see also, with a different emphasis, Peter Gluchowski, "Parteiidentifikation im politischen System der Bundesrepublik Deutschland," in Dieter Oberndoerfer, ed., *Wählerverhalten in der Bundesrepublik Deutschland* (Berlin: Duncker und Humblot, 1978).

18. Philip Converse, *The Dynamics of Party Support* (Beverly Hills: Sage Publications, 1976); Budge, Crewe, and Farlie, eds., *Party Identification;* Walter Dean Burnham, *Critical Elections and the Mainsprings of American Politics* (New York: Norton, 1970).

19. This "solution" to the problem of the parties does not even address the issue of the legitimization of direct action groups, which often represent concerned minorities with which the majority would not agree.

20. S. M. Lipset and Stein Rokkan, *Party Systems and Voter Alignments* (New York: Free Press, 1967); Richard Rose and Derek Urwin, "Social Cohesion, Political Parties, and Strains in Regimes," *Comparative Political Studies,* 2 (April 1969), 7–67.

21. See Barnes and Kaase, *Political Action,* pp. 229–232. In Germany, over 90 percent of the public can place themselves on a left-right continuum, and over 80 percent can fill the terms with some meaning, although not all of these fulfill the requirements of "ideological" understanding.

22. The realignment potential of the New Politics has been discussed in Inglehart, *Silent Revolution*; Kai Hildebrandt and Russell Dalton, "The New Politics," in Max Kaase and Klaus von Beyme, *Elections and Parties* (Beverly Hills: Sage Publications, 1978), pp. 69–96; Scott Flanagan, "Value Change and Partisan Change in Japan," *Comparative Politics,* 11 (April 1979), 253–278; Scott Flanagan, "Value Cleavages, Economic Cleavages, and the Japanese Voter," *American Journal of Political Science* (in press).

23. The correlation between Inglehart's value-priorities measure and the respondent's self-placement on a left-right scale is only moderate. Over the last few years, this relationship has been increasing slowly as the New Politics has been drawn into party conflicts. The following German correlations between these two "dimensions" for five years in the 1970s are consistently much lower than those in France, but usually higher than the British correlations, which hover only slightly above 0.

	1973	1976	1977	1978	1979
Correlations	.16	.24	.14	.16	.24

24. Miller and Levitin have labeled the coalition of workers and old middle class the "Silent Minority": Warren Miller and Teresa Levitin, *Leadership and Change* (Cambridge, Mass.: Winthrop, 1976). There is evidence that a realignment has occurred at least temporarily in France and Germany: Inglehart, *Silent Revolution*; Hildebrandt and Dalton, "New Politics."

25. See Suzanne Berger, "Politics and Anti-politics in Western Europe in the 1970s," *Daedalus,* 108 (Winter 1979), 27–50.

26. Charles Hauss and David Rayside, "New Political Parties in Western Democracies," in Louis Meisel and Joseph Cooper, eds., *Political Parties: Development and Decay* (Beverly Hills: Sage Publications, 1978).

27. Miller and Levitin, *Leadership and Change*.

28. The reverse of this statement, namely, that the left respondents are also following the New Politics, is not true to the same extent, because among those who position themselves on the left the New Politics respondents constitute a minority.

29. Kai Hildebrandt and Ferdinand Mueller, "The Ideological Conflicts of the Social Democratic Party" (Paper prepared for the Annual Meeting of the Conference Group on German Politics, Washington, D.C., 1977.

30. At the same time, groups within the CDU, such as the *Sozialausschüsse* ("Social Committees," leaning toward labor unions), are resurrecting the themes of Social Catholicism, emphasizing a "New Social Question," to compete with the SPD for New Politics voters; see Manfred Grosser and Wolfgang W. Veiders, *Die Neue Soziale Frage* (Melle: Knoth, 1979).

31. Franz Urban Pappi shows that religiously based value positions have increased their power to differentiate voting behavior, even though church attendance has declined over the last twenty-five years. Pappi, "Sozialstruktur, gesellschaftlicher Wertorientierungen und Wahlabsicht," *Politische Vierteljahresschrift,* 18 (November 1977), 195–229.

Appendix A. The Database

1. Peter Merkl, "Trends in German Political Science," *American Political Science Review,* 71 (September 1977), 1097–1108.

2. Over several years of usage four cases were lost from the data file for the July 1961 survey, and eighty-seven cases were lost for the November 1961 survey. The present N for each study is as follows: July 1961, N = 1679; November 1961, N = 1715. In addition, the data for thirty-eight Berlin residents interviewed for the September 1969 study are not included in that dataset: therefore the final N of that survey is 939.

3. For other panel results see Günter Radtke, "Gibt es in der Bundesrepublik eine Parteiidentifikation?" in Ferdinand Hermens and Werner Kaltefleiter, eds., *Verfassung und Verfassungswirklichkeit,* Jahrbuch, 1972 (Cologne: Carl Heymanns, 1972); Dieter Oberndoerfer, ed., *Wählerverhalten in der Bundesrepublik Deutschland* (Berlin: Duncker und Humblot, 1978).

4. Four age groups were selected because they are compatible with the codes used in all ten surveys.

5. Wolfgang Gibowski, "Der Effekt unterschiedlicher Plazierung der Wahlabsichten in Fragebogen," *Politische Vierteljahresschrift,* 14 (June 1973), 275–294; Max Kaase, "Die Bundestagswahl 1972: Probleme und Analysen," *Politische Vierteljahresschrift,* 14 (June 1973), 145–190.

6. Aage Clausen, "Response Validity: Vote Report," *Public Opinion Quarterly,* 32 (1968), 588–606; Michael Traugott and John Katosh, "Response Validity in Surveys of Voting Behavior," *Public Opinion Quarterly,* 43 (1979), 359–377.

7. Elisabeth Noelle-Neumann, "The Dual Climate of Opinion," in Max Kaase and Klaus von Beyme, eds., *German Political Studies: Elections and Parties* (London: Sage Publications, 1978), pp. 137–170.

Index